The Civic Conversations of Thucydides and Plato

The Civic Conversations of Thucydides and Plato

Classical Political Philosophy and the Limits of Democracy

GERALD M. MARA

Published by
State University of New York Press, Albany

© 2008 State University of New York

All rights reserved

Printed in the United States of America

No part of this book may be used or reproduced in any manner whatsoever without written permission. No part of this book may be stored in a retrieval system or transmitted in any form or by any means including electronic, electrostatic, magnetic tape, mechanical, photocopying, recording, or otherwise without the prior permission in writing of the publisher.

For information, contact State University of New York Press, Albany, NY
www.sunypress.edu

Production by Eileen Meehan
Marketing by Anne M. Valentine

Library of Congress Cataloging-in-Publication Data

Mara, Gerald M.
  The civic conversations of Thucydides and Plato : classical political philosophy and the limits of democracy / Gerald M. Mara
        p. cm.
  Includes bibliographical references and index.
  ISBN 978-0-7914-7499-0 (hardcover : alk. paper)
  ISBN 978-0-7914-7500-3 (paperback : alk. paper)
  1. Political science—Philosophy. 2. Democracy. I. Title.

JA71.M6415 2008
321.8—dc22   2007035625

10 9 8 7 6 5 4 3 2 1

For Joy, once again

Contents

Acknowledgments		ix
Chapter 1	Political Space and Political Purpose in Contemporary Democratic Theory	1
Chapter 2	The Borders of Rational Choice	31
Chapter 3	Deliberating Democracy	87
Chapter 4	Culture's Justice	143
Chapter 5	Proximate Others	197
Chapter 6	Conclusion: Extending the Limits of Democracy	227
Notes		261
References		301
Index		315

Acknowledgments

This book has been in preparation for several years, and many colleagues have provided helpful and challenging comments. Inevitably, I will omit names that I should mention. I am particularly indebted to Jill Frank, who read a significant portion of the manuscript. The final effort is immeasurably better thanks to her generosity and intelligence. Several other colleagues read all or part of individual chapters. Particular thanks should be extended to Harley Balzer, Bruce Douglass, Thomas Kerch, John Lombardini, Stephen Salkever, George Shambaugh, Rachel Templer, and Mark Warren. Though I do not know their names, I am also enormously grateful for the careful critical readings and comments of the two anonymous scholars who reviewed the manuscript for SUNY Press. Generosity in response does not always mean agreement in substance, of course, and I look forward to the continued conversations that will undoubtedly follow. My broader conversations on Thucydides involving Mary Dietz, Douglas Durham, Peter Euben, and Arlene Saxonhouse were of more value for me than they probably realize. The same could be said for what I learned about the Platonic dialogues from Susan Bickford, Cheryl Hall, Barbara Koziak, Elizabeth Markovits, and Sara Monoson. An earlier version of an argument on political trust, spanning parts of chapters 2 and 3, was presented at the Annual Meeting of the American Political Science Association in 1998, and a portion of the conclusion was presented at the Association's Annual Meeting of 2004. I am grateful to the panels' participants, including Richard Dagger, Suzanne Dovi, Albert Dzur, Jill Frank, Maria Murray Reimann, Stephen Salkever, and Christina Tarnapolski, for their constructively critical responses. I continue to be thankful and appreciative of so many fine colleagues at Georgetown, many of whom contributed to the thinking that went into this project. These include George Carey, Patrick Deneen, Bruce Douglass, Leona Fisher, Alfonso Gomez-Lobo, James Lamiell, David Lightfoot, Joshua Mitchell, Henry Richardson, James Schall, Alexander Sens, Nancy Sherman, and Mark Warren. Valuable suggestions on sources came from James O'Donnell, Douglas Reed, and Alan Tansman. A large number of current and former students have been exposed to many of the interpretations offered here. Their patient and critical responses were invaluable. I profited particularly from the comments of Richard Avramenko, Avi Craimer, Mihaela Czobor-Lupp, Christian Golden, Jordan Goldstein, Farah Godrej, Thomas Kerch, Jonathan Monten, James Olsen, James Poulos, Daniel Quattrone, Felicia Rosu, Maureen Steinbruner, Rachel Templer, and Ashley Thomas.

Translations of passages from the Platonic dialogues are largely my own, though I have been guided by the English versions in the Loeb series. Additionally, for translations of passages in the *Republic*, I have consulted Bloom (1968), for the *Charmides*, West and West (1986) and for *Gorgias*, Zeyl (1987). My central resources for Thucydides are the translations of Lattimore (1998) and Smith (1962–1988), though I have made a number of changes when they seemed appropriate.

Some portions of this book have appeared in earlier versions in professional journals. Elements of chapters 2 and 3 were organized into "Thucydides and Plato on Democracy and Trust," *Journal of Politics* 63, no. 3 (August 2001). A very early version of part of chapter 3 appeared as "Cries, Eloquence and Judgment: Interpreting Political Voice in Democratic Regimes," *Polity* 26, no. 2 (1993). A shorter version of chapter 5 was published as "Democratic Self-Criticism and the Other in Classical Political Theory," *Journal of Politics* 65, no. 3 (August 2003). I am grateful for permission to use portions of this material here.

I am very grateful to Michael Rinella, SUNY's acquisitions editor, for his encouragement and professionalism and to Eileen Meehan, Amanda Lanne and the rest of the SUNY staff for their support through the review and production processes. At Georgetown, Edeanna Johnson and Richard Pike provided absolutely invaluable support that made the production process much easier.

1

Political Space and Political Purpose in Contemporary Democratic Theory

Political Theory as Democratic Theory

While the enthusiasm surrounding democratization movements of the late 1980s has given way to more cautious appreciations of the complexities and imperfections of democratic transformations,[1] it is undeniable that these events have reaffirmed confidence in the power and justice of democratic ideas and institutions. As recent events have clearly shown, the apparent triumph of democracy does not mean that political crises and crimes will cease. But it does imply that the most legitimate way to cope with such dilemmas is through the collective actions of democratic societies, often in cooperation with one another.[2] Within the more confined realm of political theory, the effects of democratization have been even more decisive. It is now virtually axiomatic that constructive theorizations about politics must take their bearings from an acceptance of the priorities and principles of democratic theory.[3] Whatever departs from these premises is either relegated to the history of political thought or dismissed as antidemocratic.[4] Consequently, successful democratization seems to have had opposing effects on political practices and political theories. Together with the global influences of consumer capitalism and communication technologies, democratic institutions seem capable of effecting political changes scarcely imagined twenty years ago. Yet the ways we theorize these possibilities are shrinking as contemporary democratic political theory, for all of its variety, becomes more hegemonic.

What if this relationship is the reverse of what is needed for the success of democratic regimes? The first broad thesis of this book is that the power and justice of democratic institutions are in need of continued reexamination. This does not mean that democracy, particularly liberal social democracy, must be subjected to searches for oppression and cruelty festering beneath its appearance of welfare and civility. However, powerful and attractive political institutions are always in need of critical revisiting, never more so than when prideful confidence is intensified by experiences of stress. This book's second broad thesis is that one of the most valuable resources for this scrutiny can be found in a body of thought that democratic theorists often regard with suspicion: classical political philosophy, and, more specifically, the works of Thucydides and Plato.

In what follows I will try to make this case by engaging the work of these thinkers with four significant forms of modern democratic theory: the rational choice perspective, deliberative democratic theory, the interpretation of democratic culture, and postmodernism. Though these perspectives differ significantly from one another, their common concern is to identify the proper structuring or functioning of democratic political space. Rational choice theory emphasizes how arrangements for the articulation and negotiation of interest claims allow formulations of and responses to public policy. Theories of deliberative democracy focus on institutions that enable citizens to reach rational understandings to guide collective action. The interpretation of democratic culture stresses the ways that the shared meanings of democracy shape and maintain its political practices. And postmodern democratic theory highlights the need for political energy as social forms are established, challenged, and revised. These perspectives differ on the most important functions, institutions, and practices of democracies. Yet they all in some respect reject political theory's undertaking critical examinations of the controversial questions with which democratic regimes must cope—namely, democratic purposes.

For most of those who write within these perspectives, silence about the character of democratic purposes is a good thing, for it defers substantive political decisions to the collective choices of citizens. Theory does not displace or tyrannize practice (Knight and Johnson 1997, 279; Habermas 1996, 489; Honig 1993, 2; Shapiro 2003, 65–66). Yet this reticence is accompanied by a number of significant costs. In spite of the concern to preserve maximal space for democratic politics, none of these positions is able successfully to remain agnostic about the content of political goals. To the degree that these frameworks implicitly endorse visions of democratic outcomes or purposes, they encounter serious conceptual and practical problems. By taking stands on questions that they say are inappropriate for theorizing, they court uncertainties about the stability or coherence of their own positions. And by failing to acknowledge their own controversial stands on the ends of politics, they threaten to displace rather than to support the political activities of democratic citizens.

I draw these approaches into conversation with Thucydides and Plato in order to expand the ways in which democratic theory and practice can be understood. Read both historically and theoretically, these authors are often viewed as two of democracy's enemies. When they address the limits of democracy, they are suspected of attacking democracy's shortcomings in the name of more hierarchical or aristocratic forms of governance.[5] I argue instead that they address the limits of democracy by extending the borders of what can legitimately be talked about within democratic political deliberations. Neither author believes that establishing democratic political institutions is a sufficient guarantee against mistaken or destructive political acts. And both suggest that the language of democratic political culture resists some intellectual sources whose presence is vital for democracy's well-being. However, these criticisms do not mean that democracy can or should be replaced with any alternative form of politics. Instead, I show the ways in which both authors broaden practical discourse, potentially making democratic politics more thoughtful and more just. While I devote significant attention to the interpretations of the texts as written, my principal goal is to offer reconstructed readings[6] of their works that argue for the value of a style or form of political thinking that is different from and a needed alternative to the major theoretical perspectives that are currently dominant.

In relying on these classical sources as corrections to more familiar positions, I am not urging the creation of a more-encompassing theoretical framework guided by classical concerns. My complaint about current forms of democratic theory is not that they are insufficiently architectonic, but that they provide inadequate resources for what Jill Frank characterizes as the work of democratic citizenship (2005, 15). At the most general level, my readings underscore the need to focus critically on the purposes of politics, and therefore of democracy, as controversial yet unavoidable questions for political theory. The principal outcome of this engagement is not new theory but a mode of political thinking capable of greater sensitivity to the need for self-criticism within democratic theory and practice, a style of political thought that serves as a resource for democratic citizens.

Before I try to develop these claims, I would like to say more about what it means to problematize democratic ideas and institutions, then to sketch why the examination of democratic purposes is difficult for most contemporary forms of democratic theory, and, finally, to indicate more fully why these two classical authors offer appropriate resources for such a task.

Democracy's Problematics

When I speak of problematization, I mean more than subjecting a familiar institution or practice to sustained theoretical scrutiny. In my terms, a social practice is problematized when it is shown that its advantages can be partially overridden or undermined for reasons that its supporters must take seriously.[7] Problematizing a practice does not mean rejecting its supporting arguments, such as by showing their origins in suspect political agendas or exposing their strategic functions as weapons in social conflicts. Critics would accept problematized practices as valuable and treat their justifying arguments with intellectual respect. Moreover, problematization looks toward adjustments that are themselves imperfect. No alternative practice in which all problematics would simply disappear is envisaged. This is not a recognition of the inevitable gaps between theory and practice, but an admission that all solutions include their own intrinsic imperfections. At the same time, to problematize is not simply to acknowledge the regrettable prices that are paid where there are no worlds without loss. Problematization envisages constructive changes, but recognizes that any reconstruction will nonetheless be subject to problematizations of its own. This is therefore a kind of immanent critique that is continuous with pragmatic deliberations about social and political arrangements.

If we were to identify the major accomplishments of recent forms of democratization, we would surely focus on the protection of individual freedom and the establishment of individual rights, the creation of institutions allowing appropriate popular involvement in public governance, and the expansion of opportunities for material well-being and economic progress.[8] As experiences with democratic and democratizing experiences proliferate, scholars, social commentators, and political activists are scrutinizing these guiding templates in ways that contribute to an important series of problematizations in the sense understood above.

Rights

Critical reflections on the phenomenon called globalization have led to the critical scrutiny of rights from at least two directions. First, since the liberal tradition grounds its political and social rights in more fundamental claims about human rights, limiting those rights to citizens of liberal communities seems indefensible. Uma Narayan's recent examination of the problems associated with modern citizenship further interrogates how criteria for membership in democratic societies should be constructed. Her immediate concern is that liberal states provide all of those who reside within them with access to the basic goods (education, health care, adequate housing, and so on) needed for a minimally decent life respectful of human dignity (1999, 64). Seyla Benhabib goes further in arguing for the extension of basic political rights, such as opportunities for expressing political voice, to those who are not fully citizens (Benhabib 2004, 3–4).

Second, liberalism's commitment to human rights sharpens dilemmas that arise when liberal societies encounter cultures or subcultures with antiliberal traditions. As liberal societies become more multicultural and globally connected, they cannot easily avoid encounters with abusive social conditions that cry out for remedy. These include domestic subcultures that subordinate women or restrict their children's access to education and health care and nonliberal societies whose institutions damage well-being even more outrageously, permanently suppressing the voices of religious or ethnic minorities, often through the use of extreme state or state-sanctioned violence. Proposed responses to such dilemmas range from John Rawls's (1999, 105–20) cautiously stated duty of assistance through Michael Walzer's respect for political self-determination (1977, 88–99) to the activism of Martha Nussbaum (1996, 21:5). All of these proposals raise difficulties. Generalized toleration for the integrity of nation-states and the respect for political self-determination can blind critics to even the most flagrant abuses (cf. Benhabib 2004, 10; Ignatieff 2001, 23–24). Yet a greater degree of activism runs the risk of lapsing into imperialism or hegemony, all the more so because such justifications can too easily be enlisted in the service of interests that are not at all high-minded (cf. Benhabib 2004, 10; Ignatieff 2001 23–24). The growing numbers of proposals for making the international political realm more democratic encounter equal theoretical and pragmatic concerns. It is difficult to see how democratizing international politics could occur without requiring significant shifts in a large number of political cultures' self-understandings.[9] The project of spreading democracy across the globe can also be used to justify political intrusions that may cause more ills than they cure.

Governance

Questions regarding the public governance of democracies have elicited significant disagreements about what this should mean and about the conditions needed to foster it. Political theories of democratic elitism that flourished in the early 1960s have given way to proposals that insist on widespread civic involvement if collective choices and actions are to be truly democratic (Barber 2003, 117–18; Habermas 1996, 366–73; and Warren 2001, 60–61). Yet the mechanisms and implications of structuring effective citizen involvement are by no means clear. Analyses that see democratic governance as simply emerging from the interactions of self-interested egoists have encountered significant criticisms from approaches that are more sociological and cultural in focus.[10] For such critics, democratic politics seems to require the deeper support of a democratic civil society (Putnam 1993, 152–62). Absent such traditions, democratic initiatives will be ineffective or dysfunctional. Yet this conclusion has been complicated by empirical and theoretical claims. First, these associative traditions often seem threatened by the very political efficiencies that they foster. Robert Putnam's recent work on American society suggests that many of the social outcomes that mark the presence of effective democracy (especially the delivery of services by responsive administrative agencies leading to more widespread economic progress) may also erode the civic associations that make long-term democratic governance possible (1995, 677–81; 2000, 247–76). Second, strong associations do not invariably contribute to liberal democratic health. Questions about this relationship arise particularly in response to those commentators who argue that strong subpolitical associations are needed to enhance the quality of life in a democratic society. If a decent democratic way of life involves and requires forms of virtue and character that are incompletely captured by the presence of personal freedom, a political sociology adequate to what William Galston calls "liberal purposes" must appreciate, for example, how religious institutions (Galston 1993, 6, 12–16; cf. Bellah et al., 1985, 28–30; S. Carter 1993, 15–17; Elshtain 2001, 45–47) affect what one does with one's freedom. Yet precisely because such associations strive to exert a strong influence on personal choice, enhancing their social roles would seem to violate liberalism's strong commitment to personal autonomy.[11]

Ways of Life

Classical liberal democracy's pride in enabling widespread economic well-being is complicated by criticisms that are both internal and external to the liberal paradigm. The vast opportunities for economic progress that liberal democratization has stimulated often create heavy social casualties, intensify pressures on the natural environment that is development's uneasy partner, and reinforce global inequalities. Earlier (1970s) claims of the so-called postmaterialists that such difficulties would be addressed as Western societies became more prosperous and secure are now being read more as scenarios of possibilities and ambiguities than as predictable outcomes.[12] Moreover, even those who concentrate on the government's capacity to assure conditions for the pursuit of economic well-being are encountering difficult questions about what this means. Amartya Sen's approach (Sen and Nussbaum 1993, 30–31; Sen 1999, 18–25; Sen 1999, 90–92) to comparative economic analysis shows the limitations of measuring economic health by levels of income without considering how income impacts the basic capabilities that are essential to a decent life. More generally, by treating development as including a certain kind of substantive freedom, Sen insists on attending to the purposes or goods supported by economic progress, making it clear that being economically secure is only one part of the quality of life.[13]

What is apparent within all of these concerns is a greater need for the critical examination of the purposes or goals of liberal democratic society within at least three broad areas. Extending from ambiguities concerning the proper scope and grounding of democratic rights is a need to focus more seriously on how categories constructed and articulated within democratic culture relate to a humanness that cuts across cultures. Extending from concerns about the fragile status of democratic governance is the broader need to examine not only how democracies can work better but also what the "better" working of democracies might mean. Extending from the problematic relationship between democratic institutions and the amassing of national wealth are more basic questions about the merits of the different forms of well-being that democratic communities foster or discourage.

None of these concerns displace or ignore the fact that democratic political institutions are mechanisms for creating and exercising power. Indeed, it is the ubiquity of power that makes serious examinations of liberal democratic purposes all the more essential. The gap between fellow citizens and outsiders may insulate applications of civic power toward outsiders from critical attention. To the extent that forms of civic association fail to encourage deeper considerations of public purposes or to enhance the strength of public institutions, collective actions may come to originate in suspect power bases or to function through mechanisms less susceptible to public scrutiny.[14] And the failure to examine the forms of well-being for which public power is exercised threatens to turn questions about the uses of power into purely strategic calculations whose purposes neither require nor allow the critical discourse of citizens.

Contemporary statements of the problematics of liberal democracy thus underscore the need for resources that can contribute to the examination of democratic purposes. However, currently available forms of democratic theory fall seriously short in their abilities to provide what is needed.

Theoretical Insights and Limitations

Current frameworks for theorizing democratic political life have advanced well beyond the liberal—communitarian debates of the 1970s and 1980s.[15] While these perspectives have not been disregarded, they have been revisited, deepened, and nuanced. What has resulted is a series of contemporary positions that enrich and provoke one another in theoretically interesting (and at times underappreciated) ways.

Though rational choice theory claims to be valid transhistorically and cross-culturally, it has particular conceptual affinities with classical liberalism. Its methodological individualism means that it analyzes political and social forms as outcomes of decisions made by interacting individuals concerned to further their self-defined interests (Downs 1957, 17; Chong 2000, 13). Within this psychological perspective, rationality refers to instrumental decisions aimed at outcomes that agents believe to be good; the designations "rational" or "irrational" do not apply to practical ends (Downs 1957, 6; cf. Hardin 1995, 46). Political institutions are therefore treated as mechanisms that organize interactions so that it is in the agents' interests to be bound by the outcomes (Hardin 1999, 26). While this description of politics is applied to all forms of political associations, including authoritarian regimes that punish defection and theocratic states that promise salvation as a reward for obedience, democratic political arrangements most fully allow individual preferences to be articulated and aggregated in ways that influence public policy (Downs 1957, 18, 23–24). It is in the citizens' interest to be bound by collective outcomes, because this reinforces processes that best enable future satisfactions (Dahl 1956, 75–76; Dahl 1956, 132–33; Shapiro 2003, 90). Insofar as rational choice theory implies a normative political orientation, it endorses institutions that most effectively enable the cooperation of self-interested individuals (Axelrod 1984, 124–41; Downs 1957, 197; Hardin 1995, 26–27; Putnam 1993, 180–81).

While deliberative democratic theory does not emerge out of disagreements with rational choice,[16] a number of its distinctive features can be highlighted by comparing the two positions. They have some shared commitments. Both assess political and social forms in terms of their contributions to the self-determined well-being of individuals, and both focus primarily on how institutions affect the ways interests are pursued. Furthermore, both try to explain why individuals will accept the political decisions of their community as binding. However, they have different views on how individuation occurs, particularly with respect to the construction of interests, and they differ over the scope and function of relevant institutions. This leads them to explain the binding character of political decisions in very different ways.

Some of these perspectives' differences are sociological and political, arising from deliberative democratic theory's agreement with portions of communitarianism's focus on the constitutive role of social memberships and the importance of civic agency (cf. Cohen and Arato 1992, 376–77, 396, 400).[17] Others are ethical, rooted in deliberative democracy's adoption of a Kantian, rather than a Lockeian, understanding of free rationality. Sociologically, deliberative institutions enable forms of communication extending beyond strategic calculation to include the discovery and creation of purposes through shared discourse. Democracy, therefore, does more than facilitate the expression and aggregation of individual preferences. It also allows citizens to cooperate for more associational purposes. Ethically, the Kantian influence demands that politics respect individual autonomy, principally by providing all affected individuals and groups with meaningful access to collective deliberation (Benhabib 2004, 131–32; Cohen and Arato 1992, 398; Habermas 1993, 50; Kymlicka 1995, 140–42; Young 1997, 402–3). Consequently, what binds individuals to deliberative democratic outcomes is not simply prudential concern to maintain a system offering the best opportunities for preference satisfaction, but also moral appreciation of deliberative democracy's basic fairness (Habermas 1996, 108; Richardson 2002, 84; Warren 2001, 91–93).

The perspective relying on the priorities of democratic culture expands deliberative democracy's attention to institutions beyond those that contribute directly or indirectly to communicative action. Though the idea of culture may seem vague, a useful model is found in the work of interpretive anthropologists such as Clifford Geertz. For Geertz, culture is the web or network of meanings that human beings spin for themselves (1973, 5), the interactions and expressions through which they cooperate to construct and reconstruct their lives. In focusing on democracy as a culture, social theory examines not only the ways in which democratic collective action is enabled, but also the processes through which the identities of democratic citizens and regimes are produced; it must therefore be attuned to the educative or semiotic as well as to the strategic or pragmatic aspects of political structures.

This cultural turn is skeptical about any sort of universalism. One of the most important moments in this turn was the transition from John Rawls's *A Theory of Justice* to his later work, *Political Liberalism*. In the first book, Rawls attempted to develop a theory of justice that was valid sub specie aeternitatus (1971, 587), relying on rational choices made by hypothetical individuals under stipulated conditions of uncertainty (1971, 136–42). *Political Liberalism* has the more modest goal of clarifying the principles of justice consistent with the constitutive tenets of a liberal democratic society, the most important of which is a recognition of the impossibility of any agreement about comprehensive human goods (Rawls 2005, 24–25). Any attempt to work from such a vantage point would violate the reasonable pluralism that is central to the liberal democratic way of life (2005, xxxvii, 97–98). While Locke's rights-bearing individual and Kant's autonomous agent have played important roles in the development of liberal democracy's self-understanding, they cannot serve as foundations for a universal argument in favor of democratic institutions. The proper task for theory, then, is to identify the political arrangements consistent with liberal democratic culture's continuity and flourishing (Rawls 2005, 223).

Like many of the democratic cultural theorists informed by Rawls, postmodern democratic theorists understand the self as a social or cultural construction. However, postmodernism sees the cultural claim going wrong by failing to recognize that all representations of culture are politicized and contestable. Informed by the general framework of Michel Foucault,[18] postmodern democratic theory replaces the focus on culture as the construction of shared meanings with a focus on politics as the assertion and contestation of competing identities and allegiances. Democracy is the form of politics most open to projects of identity formation and least susceptible to the establishment of permanent hegemonies. Figures such as Judith Butler, William Connolly, Bonnie Honig, and Chantal Mouffe thus describe a properly functioning democratic culture as a condition of agonistic pluralism, whose members practice innovative and unsettling experiments in living bound only by the most basic civilizational norms (Butler 1997a, 161–63; Connolly 1995, 180, 194; Honig 1993, 13–15; Honig 2001, 85–86; Mouffe 2000, 98–105).

Because these four perspectives engage the same broad set of political phenomena, they often intersect theoretically. Putnam uses a rational choice framework to explain the persistence of cultural environments that enhance or prevent effective democratic governance (1993, 177–81). Rawls sees liberal democratic culture as contextualizing the respect for autonomous individuals that lies at the core of deliberative democratic theory (2005, 98). While there is no reason to believe that these perspectives exhaust the ways in which contemporary social theory can investigate democratic political life, they do represent a number of the most influential current alternatives. They are persistent sources of mutual criticism; the clarified articulation of each is due in part to reciprocal provocations. One conclusion arising from these critical interactions is that each perspective focuses on a part of democratic political life and may therefore overtheorize its own particular area of concern. Yet, beyond this, they share a basic resistance to engaging in more substantive examinations of the goals or goods of democratic communities, precisely those sorts of questions raised but not answered by the problematizations considered earlier.

Though each of the perspectives outlined above explicitly confines itself to developing a view of democratic space, they all implicitly rely on unexamined endorsements of particular democratic purposes. One reason for the reluctance to engage deeper questions of purpose is that such a project seems to require judging the value of democratic institutions and culture in light of the general needs and potentials of human beings (cf. Taylor 1967, 54–55), and all of the contemporary perspectives are suspicious about political appeals to anything resembling a conception of human nature (Connolly 1995, 106; Geertz 2000, 51–55; Rawls 2005, 13; Habermas 1979, 201; Habermas 1993, 21; Benhabib 2004, 129–30). Yet since each of these frameworks nonetheless presumes the validity of a certain psychology, each rests on a functional equivalent to just such a view. By failing to acknowledge this dependence, each position limits its ability to argue for the human value of democratic practices in the face of determined opposition or to examine critically the justifications of the political spaces they endorse. Since goods provided by or dangers threatening to democratic societies are identified on the basis of a prior acceptance of democratic principles, each perspective is also limited in its ability to deal fully with the goods that democratic regimes make possible or the dangers that threaten those regimes' integrity. For example, while deliberative democratic theory can explain why trust is good for deliberative democracy, it is less equipped to show why a deliberative democracy that nourishes a healthy sense of trust is good. Because postmodern democratic theory insists that the problem of what has come to be called "the other" must be solved (see chapter 5) as a condition for healthy democratic politics, it ignores both threatening and salutary others whose presence is continuous with political life.

By confining their attention to characterizations of democratic space, these perspectives also deprive themselves of the resources needed to accomplish even their own purposes effectively. Though each focuses on institutions or processes through which democratic outcomes can be achieved, the refusal to comment independently on the substance of those outcomes constrains assessments and even descriptions of the processes. Some essential insights about the health or pathology of ways of doing things can only be provided by judgments about the quality of that which is predictably or characteristically done. To the extent that such judgments are excluded, understandings of what it means for democratic processes to function well are constrained, and the ability to determine the full range of institutional or cultural resources that would enable them to do so is diminished. If one reason why we should value deliberative democratic institutions is that they characteristically generate outcomes that are more egalitarian, more open to the potentially marginalized, or more respectful of the natural environment (cf. Habermas 1996, 355–56), we must also more fully identify the institutional and cultural forms that would make those substantive outcomes attractive to democratic citizens. If the contests within agonistic pluralism are to remain gentle (cf. Connolly 1993, 155–57), a sociology of postmodern democratic society must identify the social and cultural forms that civilize.

Finally, in limiting abilities to consider democratic purposes or projects in light of broader reflections on the characteristics of human beings, contemporary democratic theories disconnect themselves from the substantive concerns of democratic citizens. Our political deliberations, broadly construed, do not exclude critical reflection on democratic purposes and the ways in which these purposes intersect or clash with a range of other human goods. While many of these reflections may seem naive or culture-bound, they are valuable precisely because they refuse to limit themselves according to the more sophisticated languages of theory. This feature of American democratic political life was observed by Tocqueville in the nineteenth century (Tocqueville 1988, 441–42). The spirit of practical openness has been, if anything, intensified by a pluralization of democratic communities that may exert an influence opposite to what Rawls (2005, 38) expects, by broadening rather than narrowing forms of democratic political conversation (Sanjek 1998, 367–93). Democratic citizens do not regard one another simply as bargaining agents whose interests are formed prior to their interactions. Deliberative democratic procedures are considered in light of expected outcomes. The cultural bases of democracy are celebrated and challenged as well as interpreted. And attempts to construct individual and collective identities are regarded as proposed ways of life requiring critical examination, not simply as experiments in living demanding space.

From one vantage point, disconnection between the limited forms of contemporary democratic theory and the more expansive requirements of democratic practice is appropriately respectful of democracy, for any attempt to correct or constrain democratic processes and conversations in light of more rigorous and exact theoretical conclusions would rightly be seen as antidemocratic and even antipolitical (cf. Honig 1993, 2). Yet this theoretical silence also deprives democratic citizens of valuable resources that could assist them in grappling with substantive political dilemmas. It is not appropriate to try to meet this need by constructing a more elaborate conceptual resource that could more fully theorize democracy while remaining deferential to its political space. More valuable are resources that would pragmatically respect the goods of democracy while continuing to problematize them intellectually. We can find important resources of this kind in classical political theory, particularly in Thucydides and Plato.

The Persistence of Classical Political Theory

But why these two authors? Questions arise from several sources. The first is a more general suspicion about the value of classical political philosophy for democratic societies. This rests on at least three general grounds. First, there is the seemingly unbridgeable gap that separates the premodern society surrounding the classical writers from our own modern social forms (cf. Habermas 1996, 25–26; Warren 2001, 40; Benhabib 2004, 15–17). Second, classical political theory seems to lack the analytic tools supplied by modern social theory. Without access to these more sophisticated conceptual categories, classical political theory is unable to differentiate and interconnect the various social realms (Habermas 1996, 106–7). Finally, virtually every influential voice among the classical Greek political philosophers seems hostile to democratic politics and culture. This is partially a historical assessment, based on the political-cultural allegiances of most Greek writers on politics during the fifth and fourth centuries BCE (cf. Ober 1998, 5). Beyond historical judgments, this criticism is also generated by what is seen as a principled clash between the emphasis that many of the classical authors place on the development of the virtues and the democratic priorities of freedom and equality. Opposition to references to human virtue thus stems in part from a presumption that they presume essentialist assertions about a permanent human identity existing apart from empirical practices and historical change. (Cf. Habermas 1996, xli; Geertz 2000, 52–55). The language of virtue is also assailed because it seems to privilege hierarchies or elites. This is one basis for Rawls's rejecting what he calls "perfectionism" as a standard for social justice, a standard "directing society to arrange institutions and to define the duties and obligations of individuals so as to maximize the achievement of human excellence in art, science and culture" (1971, 325).

Beyond these general objections, there are particular concerns focusing on Thucydides and Plato. If the goal is to make a serious case for the contributions of classical political philosophy to thoughtful assessments of democratic political life, a more appropriate source is surely Aristotle. Despite Aristotle's unusual style of political discourse, he does develop theoretical concepts and employ them in the empirical analysis and pragmatic evaluation of political life.[19] Thus, the form of his analysis seems more compatible with contemporary democratic theory than either the philosophical dramas of Plato or the historical narrative of Thucydides. And while Aristotle is often acutely critical of democracy, he seems on the whole more open to democratic possibilities than either Plato or Thucydides is.[20] Plato's explicit presentations of preferred forms of governance, in the dialogues *Republic* and *Laws*, seem to award political control directly or indirectly to philosophers who rule on the basis of superior wisdom. Thucydides apparently compliments the Periclean paradigm under which what was in name a democracy was in fact under the rule of the *protos anēr* (the "foremost man," in Lattimore's translation) who controlled the citizens by means of hegemonic rhetoric (2.65.9–10).

These objections need to be taken seriously and continually borne in mind, but they are not conclusive. With respect to the generic rejection of classical political theory, it should first be observed that both the significance and the degree of distance between classical Greek culture and ours can be exaggerated.[21] Arguments that classical political thought is irrelevant to contemporary political discourse often seem to rely on the unexamined premise that these forms of thought are so embedded in their political cultural contexts that no attempt to employ them in broader conversations can be successful. Unless one bases this conclusion on a radical historicism asserted before the fact, it can only be supported by arguments that show how particular cultural and historical barriers prevent classical political theory from speaking to our political concerns. Moreover, as Bernard Yack has argued, empirical investigations of developed societies may identify premodern as well as modern aspects, just as historical investigations of ancient societies may discover institutions or practices quite compatible with ours (1997, 7).

Likewise, while there are striking differences between the categories of modern social theory and the political and cultural concepts employed by classical authors, they can be interactive as well as oppositional. Social theories focus by organizing conceptual fields, leading inevitably to both precision and incompleteness.[22] From this perspective, all social theories are partial views that draw our attention both toward and away from certain classes of phenomena, enabling certain questions while discouraging others. At one level, classical political theory can be read as providing a particular conceptual framework, focusing on distinctive aspects or functions of society. What informs the perspectives of Plato and Aristotle is how political and cultural forms contribute to human flourishing. While classical political theory may downplay aspects of society that modern social theory highlights, it also reminds us of the significance of outcomes that modern social theory may obscure.[23]

Finally, while classical political theory's treatment of democracy is generally critical, there are important differences and nuances, both historical and theoretical, within this literature. The antidemocratic criticisms leveled by the author known as the "old oligarch" or by Isocrates (cf. Ober 1998, chaps. 1 and 5) are not those of Thucydides, Plato, or Aristotle. Moreover, the critical contributions of these texts are also pragmatic acts within political contexts that are generally democratic. While the speeches or arguments of these authors often point to serious shortcomings in democratic politics and culture, the speech-acts themselves (the articulation of arguments in specific political contexts) can be read as more discursive and conciliatory. Practical criticisms of democratic practice, including those that point to attractive nondemocratic alternatives, may be offered to improve rather than to replace democratic forms of governance, problematizing rather than simply condemning democracy. When Socrates offers his vision of philosophic kingship as the only effective remedy for individual and civic evils in books 5 through 7 of the *Republic*, he does so within a discursive setting that is egalitarian and dialogic and a dramatic context that reminds the readers of the destructiveness of antidemocratic rule.[24] Therefore, the same books also include Socrates' attempt to reconcile a skeptical, if not hostile, young aristocrat with democratic practices (cf. *Republic* 499e). Thucydides' endorsement of the regime known as the Five Thousand, a moderate blending of the few and the many, as the best government in his time (8.97.2–3) is not simply antidemocratic, for it implies preservation of significant aspects of the rule of the many.[25] Perhaps the most striking implication of this praise is not that Thucydides prefers a mixed regime over radical versions of democracy or oligarchy, but that he prefers this blend to the rule of Pericles, to the arrangement that was "democratic only in name."

These historical complications are reinforced by more nuanced assessments of the classics' attention to virtue. The charge that conceptions of human virtue must depend on intangible and ahistorical essences seems wrong in light of the many forms of practical philosophy that rely on visions of excellent human activities that are identified and defended in more empirical and revisable ways. Indeed, visions of human excellence inform most of democratic political theory's founding texts.[26] While philosophical conceptions of human virtue can be used to justify social hierarchies, this move seems unnecessary, perhaps even indefensible, from the point of view of the classical writers themselves. We can acknowledge that potential candidates for life choices are of unequal merit, while also maintaining that the human beings making those choices possess generally equal capabilities for making them.[27] This broad equality of capabilities is more plausible once we recognize that frameworks for evaluating life choices can be general and provisional rather than specified and dogmatic. From this perspective, taking human virtue seriously is compatible with egalitarian and individualized descriptions of human capabilities.[28] Finally, even if human beings are in some respects unequal in moral capabilities, there is no reason to think that such inequalities are reflected in conventional social or political hierarchies. Significant portions of both Aristotle's *Ethics* and *Politics* and Plato's dialogues aggressively challenge this association.[29]

Theories and Texts

If we acknowledge that classical political philosophy is not so disconnected from contemporary democratic theory as to be useless or pernicious, there are particular advantages to considering the contributions of Thucydides and Plato. While Aristotle theorizes ethics and politics more systematically, texts that are more literary in character have their own advantages. They are better situated as cultural resources for conversations about the things that matter to individuals and communities.[30] While both authors write within specific cultural circumstances and address particular historical concerns—such as Pericles' responsibility for the Peloponnesian War or the justice of Athens's execution of Socrates—each also engages questions about human and political purposes that are broader and deeper than those occupying their immediate audiences. The focus of many of these questions concerns the institutions and purposes of democracy.

Yet there is considerable uncertainty about how these texts respond to human and political complexity and, therefore, about the real depth of their literary character. Modern disciplinary classifications of Plato as philosopher and Thucydides as historian imply that their work is only literary on the surface, masking more rigorous or finalizing projects. While Sacvan Bercovitch sees literature resisting what he calls the cognitive imperialism of disciplinary frameworks, he situates Plato among the imperialists. Bercovitch says, "Once we set disciplines loose on culture, they tend *sui generis* toward absolutes, closure and solutions.... They are incurable cognitive imperialists..." (1998, 75). The proper antidote to these fruitful but dangerous disciplinary abstractions is literature, which insists on giving "those abstractions...a specific textual habitation and a name" (1998, 74). Yet even though Plato's insights are communicated almost exclusively in dramatic form (cf. *Second Letter* 314c; *Seventh Letter* 342e–343a), their substance parallels the systematic philosophic statements of Descartes or Marx. Bercovitch thus sees through the dialogue form to discover a monologic content (1998, 75).

That Thucydides establishes his own form of cognitive imperialism has been argued in the recent work of Gregory Crane. Crane argues that Thucydides' literary style is constructed to convince the reader of the validity of a universalizing theory that sees through the rich world of social practices to reveal the foundational reality of power moves (1996, 72), ending with the acknowledgment of Thucydides' perspective as supplying "the last word" (1996, 50, 56; see also Wohl 2002, 70). While Plato's literary form is absorbed by a systematic and dogmatic philosophical content, Thucydides' is undermined by a reductionist social theory aiming at nearly mathematical precision (Crane 1996, xiii).

We should resist seeing the literary features of the Platonic and Thucydidean texts as cosmetic. Bercovitch's reading of Plato arbitrarily dismisses the dialogue form as attractive but misleading packaging. Yet this claim succeeds only by ignoring the real complications that the dramatic character of these works creates for attempts to interpret them as didactic monologues. The *Gorgias* is emblematic. Socrates' efforts to argue against the political ethos of competitive self-aggrandizement are met continuously with objections and resistances that he is never able to overcome (cf. 513c). The text itself inscribes a monologue represented as a dialogue (505e ff.), revealing in dramatic and comedic fashion the deficiencies of a mode of speaking that is only conversational on the surface. Though the dialogue contains an unusual number of long, uninterrupted, and vehement Socratic speeches, it ends with Socrates' extreme skepticism about what has been said. Referring to his concluding myth of the afterlife, but extending his reservations to the entire conversation, he concludes, "This myth may seem to you to be the saying of old women and [you may therefore] despise it; and there would be no wonder at our contempt if with all our searching we could somewhere find something better and truer than this.... But among all of our speeches, though all have been refuted, one speech (*logos*) stands, that doing injustice is to be avoided more than having injustice done to one, that more than anything a man should take care not to seem good but to be so, in private as well as in public" (527a–b). This conclusion is dialogic, resting not on dogmatic affirmation, but on the failure to discover a more suitable alternative in question and answer.

Bercovitch's perspective also reinforces the disciplinary hegemonies he challenges, for he implies that the same work cannot theorize with explanatory power while also questioning the certainty or closure that theory seems to provide (cf. Bercovitch 1998, 74). In different ways, both Plato and Thucydides bring these disparate intellectual functions together. Perhaps the most striking example of this in the Platonic corpus occurs in book 7 of the *Republic*. Socrates has completed his account of the educational program that will prepare prospective philosopher-kings for the science of dialectic, the intellection that enables its practitioners to give an account of the basic premises of the highest and most comprehensive kind of knowledge. He is then asked by his young interlocutor Glaucon to give a full account "of the character of dialectic's power ... and, then, of the forms into which it is divided; and then of its ways. These, as it seems likely, would lead at last toward that place which is for one who comes to it a resting place from the road ... and an end of his journey." Socrates' response to this insistence is telling: "You will no longer be able to follow.... [Y]ou would no longer be seeing an image of the things we are saying, but the truth itself, as that appears to me" (533a). Even the foundational grounding of wisdom is expressible only as a point of view. The radical separation of knowledge from opinion that has justified Socrates' distinction between the real philosophers and those trapped in the cave of illusions is now called seriously into question. Referring to another philosophical framework, Bercovitch observes, "Philosophy says 'I think, therefore I am.' Literature says 'That's what you think'" (Bercovitch 1998, 73). Within dialogues that are not at all monologic, the Platonic Socrates is both conclusive and provisional in a way that insists on their mutuality.

Likewise, while he is right that Thucydides' form of writing is integrally linked to his intellectual purposes, Crane's characterizations are too reductive. An alternative way of reading Thucydides' narrative is as a text that acknowledges the impossibility of "render[ing] *erga* perfectly into language" (Crane 1996, 72) and therefore as one that complicates rather than resolves the most vexing political questions. Thucydides, the universalizing theorist, seems to find his clearest voice in assessing the causes of the hideous civil *stasis* in Corcyra (3.82). Spurred by love of gain and honor, humans are incorrigibly violent and competitive. This position is systematized and extended by de Romilly (1963, 322–39), Crane (1996, 8), and Jonathan Price (2001, 11–19) into a universal Thucydidean explanation of political disorder. Crane finds the same impulse within many of the speeches of Thucydides' characters (Crane 1996, 8, 74). Yet in a provocative speech given earlier in book 3 we find less authority than ambiguity. Supporting a moderate response toward the rebellious city of Mytilene, the Athenian citizen Diodotus considers the psychological basis of crime—or error. Driven by greed and irrational hopes, humans continually overreach. Like the most monologic and imperialist theorist, Diodotus offers a series of lawlike statements revealing depressing human necessities that cannot be addressed through education. Yet his own attempt to persuade the Athenian assembly to behave moderately even as the passions of fear and anger urge otherwise presupposes the sort of educability that his explicit claims deny.[31] Diodotus does not act as if his statements about human motivation were universally and necessarily true. The same sort of undermining of universal pronouncements may be found in the pragmatics of Thucydides' narrative as a whole, which attempts to educate even as it reveals the extent and depth of human passion.

The literary character of their texts does more than complicate familiar classifications of Thucydides as historian[32] and Plato as philosopher; it also points to the complex ways in which these authors can intersect with the modern forms of democratic theory outlined earlier. From one perspective, Plato and Thucydides can be read as offering their own theoretical conclusions about political institutions and cultures. At the most general level, Plato argues that political forms should be assessed according to how well they contribute to the citizens' practice of the virtues (cf. *Gorgias* 504d–e, 517b–c). Thucydides' complex treatment of regimes suggests that they arise from coordinated exercises of power, yet conduct themselves in ways that contribute to destabilization and vulnerability. Too simply put, while Plato theorizes politics in a way that points to enhanced political possibilities, Thucydides draws our attention to the disruption that lies at the core of all political identities. However, both authors resist the tendencies toward the cognitive imperialism that characterizes theorization by showing the limitations of their own dominant templates. For Socrates, the teachability of the virtues is fundamentally problematic (*Protagoras* 361a–c). For Thucydides, some forms of culture enable thoughtful challenges to the power that they presuppose and reflect. In suggesting the provisionality of their own frameworks, both writers practice a conversational rather than a deductive form of political thought.[33]

Yet even if we read the texts of Thucydides and Plato among those that Bercovitch identifies as literary, why should we read them as resources for democrats? In setting a time horizon that is "forever," Thucydides suggests that his narrative is a cultural resource for those who can resist the urges of advantage or passion and ascend to a height that is more synoptic and penetrating.[34] Plato implies that the dialogues should be understood in the same way when he writes in the *Phaedrus* that "a serious (*spoudē*) speech ... uses the dialectical art to plant and sow in an appropriate soul knowing words, that can help themselves and the one who planted them, [words] that are not fruitless, but yield seeds from which there spring up other words in other souls" (276e–77a). From this perspective the appropriate audiences for both authors can be seen as indefinite and self-selecting. For some commentators, this self-selection works against contributions that the texts might make to democratic political discourse. Philosophers as different as Hobbes and Nietzsche have noted that Thucydides' narrative needs extraordinarily careful examination and resolutely applied curiosity. Plato acknowledges that his own beliefs are carefully masked within the speeches of a Socrates "made young and fair" (*Second Letter* 314c). These statements have led some to see both authors constructing texts that can be read at two very different levels: the popular or conventional and the sophisticated or philosophic. In commenting on the need to invest "much meditation" in the interpretation of Thucydides, Hobbes recalls that "Marcellinus saith he was obscure on purpose; that the common people might not understand him. And not unlikely: for a wise man should so write, (though in words understood by all men), that wise men only should be able to commend him."[35] Leo Strauss connects Socratic irony to a seemingly elitist response to the varying capacities of human beings. "If irony is essentially related to the fact that there is a natural order of rank among men, it follows that irony consists in speaking differently to different kinds of people" (1964, 51).[36] To the extent that a recognition of a natural order among human beings informs the writings of Thucydides and Plato, we must question the value of these texts for democratic citizens. Perhaps their democratic sympathies are only detectable by misreadings (cf. Ober 1998, 157); a truly democratic scrutiny of both authors would reinforce the conclusion that they are among democracy's harshest critics.[37]

However, such characterizations of both texts and audiences are artificially bipolar. Plato's and Thucydides' works are capable of multiple readings, and while individuals' abilities to read them well surely vary, such variations are continuous as well. From this perspective, good readings of these texts do not require extraordinary gifts as much as a reasonable sensitivity to "the characters of men's humors and manners" and a committed diligence to go beyond what is communicated by "the first speaking." Thus understood, these textual subtleties and audience variations are compatible with a democratic culture that includes a number of sensitive readers.[38]

The Intersection of Philosophy and History

A second reason to consider the contributions of Thucydides and Plato together as cultural resources is that both recognize that political theory is always articulated within pragmatic and contentious political contexts. Power may be justified, accepted, or contested; irrationality may be excused, diagnosed, or condemned. However, the presence of both power and irrationality must be acknowledged. Reading Plato and Thucydides as acknowledging similar harsh realities challenges the conclusions of a number of commentators who see this focus as precisely what separates them (de Romilly 1963, 362, 365; Edmunds 1975, 169, 209; Crane 1996, 257–58; Crane 1998, 8, 325). Nietzsche's remarks are almost paradigmatic. "Thucydides, the great sum, the last revelation of that strong, severe, hard factuality (*starken, strengen, harten, Thatsächlichkeit*) which was instinctive with the ancient Hellenes. It is courage before reality that at the last distinguishes natures like Thucydides and Plato. Plato is a coward before reality, consequently, he flees into the ideal; Thucydides has himself in control (*in der Gewalt*), consequently he also keeps control of things" (Nietzsche 1954, 558).

This polarization is too extreme. Virtually all of the conversations represented in the Platonic dialogues are politically contextualized. This does not mean simply that Plato's responses to political events (such as the execution of Socrates) condition the content of the dialogues. Political reality is, rather, inscribed within the texture of the dialogues to the degree that separations between texts and contexts blur. Much of this inscribed reality includes the events of the Peloponnesian War. The *Protagoras* occurs the year before the war begins. The *Charmides* represents a conversation involving Socrates with Critias and Charmides, two of the eventual leaders of the group of tyrants known as the Thirty, just after the battle of Potideia, one of the engagements marking the beginning of the war. The dramatically extended time horizon of the *Gorgias* tracks nearly the entire course of the conflict.[39] The dialogues anticipate (*Charmides*) or recall (*Apology*) the subversion of the democracy by the Thirty and image the power of the restored *dēmos* (*Meno*). Most of all, there is the disturbing and bizarre trial and execution of Socrates, an event that extends well beyond the dialogues *Euthyphro, Apology, Crito,* and *Phaedo*. The indictment and impending trial contextualize other conversations (*Theaetetus, Sophist, Statesman*); Socrates' death is the subject of both threats (*Gorgias*) and memories (*Theaetetus*). Even dialogues whose themes seem pointedly disconnected from politics are dramatized in ways that reinscribe politicality. In the *Cratylus*, Socrates precedes what seems to be a whimsical examination into the right use of names with a reference (396d) to an earlier conversation with Euthyphro, whom he questions about piety on the day of his indictment. The intricate and critical investigation into the theory of ideas that is recalled in the *Parmenides* begins by mentioning young Socrates' previous conversation with a young man named Aristoteles, "later one of the Thirty" (127d).

These political inscriptions are much more than contextualizations; they provide keys for the interpretation of the dialogues' content.[40] The discussion about names in the *Cratylus* confronts the question of how investigation of the nature of things relates to shared cultural meanings (384c–d). The deeper impact of that question is underscored by Socrates' impending indictment for threatening the city's culture by disbelieving in its gods and corrupting its youth. The extended conversation in the *Charmides* about *sōphrosynē*, a word often translated as "moderation," takes on a very different and much more threatening meaning in light of Critias's and Charmides' later political activities.[41] The *Republic* occurs in the Piraeus, the site of the democracy's resistance to the Thirty, in the presence of some of the tyranny's victims (Polemarchus, Niceratus) and resisters (Lysias). Socrates' principal interlocutors are Plato's brothers, Glaucon and Adeimantus—whose political allegiances are, at the very least, unsettled. Glaucon, who at times sounds a bit like his uncle Critias, provokes Socrates' introduction of philosopher-kings by asking how the city in speech can be made real (473c–e). When we read Socrates' account of philosophic kingship with an appreciation of this pragmatic context, we may conclude that a flight into the ideal is the last thing that Plato has in mind when he introduces the notion of the ideas. The dialogue ends with Socrates telling Glaucon a myth that recommends the choice of a nonpolitical but very human life. At a dramatically later time, Adeimantus and a silent Glaucon arrange the retelling of the conversation that makes up the *Parmenides*, and their presence suggests that one of the dialogue's themes is the relation of a very elevated form of philosophy to politics.[42]

Just as Plato inscribes his dramas with political disruptions, Thucydides' narrative of the greatest of these disruptions inscribes efforts to understand or to control the order of political events through the exercise of a pragmatic agency informed by what is presented as rational calculation or judgment.[43] In his own methodological statements, Thucydides distinguishes the speeches (*logoi*) he represents from the deeds (*erga*) he narrates. He notes that he has been as accurate as possible with respect to the *erga*, "neither crediting what I learned from the chance reporter nor what seemed to me [to be credible], but [writing only] after examining what I was involved with myself and what I learned from others" (1.22). With respect to the speeches, "recalling precisely what was said was difficult"; consequently, he represents what "seemed to me each would have said [as] especially required (*ta deonta malist eipein*) on the occasion, [yet] maintaining as much closeness as possible to the general sense (*gnōmēs*) of what was truly said." (1.22). Ober builds on this distinction to suggest that Thucydides privileges *erga* over *logoi* in the narrative as a whole, for speeches can wildly distort or tragically misunderstand the factual truth (1998, 57; cf. Edmunds 1975, 151). This is said to be connected with Thucydides' critical assessment of democracy, since the democratic assembly is structurally vulnerable to misleading and manipulative speeches that distort reality with devastating consequences for civic life (Ober 1998, 119–20; cf. Balot 2001, 161).

Ober is right to see the thematic treatments of *logos* and *ergon* as one of Thucydides' fundamental concerns. Whether Thucydides privileges *erga* over *logoi* and what this relationship implies for Thucydides' assessment of democracy are questions whose answers are less clear. Thucydides himself suggests that the criteria for distinguishing between these two areas of human practice are not as definite as his preliminary methodological statement suggests. He considers the entire war as an *ergon* (1.22). and the narrative that represents it is a *logos*.[44] The repertoire of narrated speeches is also varied; the text offers a large number of indirect discourses as well as direct statements. While drawing distinctions between these two narrative presentations seems arbitrary in many cases, Thucydides' use of them appears to be deliberate. The only direct speech in book 8—at 8.53—quotes a planned statement prior to its actual delivery; the effect of that statement, which argues for the necessity of replacing the democracy with a form of oligarchy, is to eliminate or constrain future speeches. As stated, "In our deliberations [we must] take less heed of the [form of the] regime and more of safety."[45] Some of the indirect speeches are noted mainly for their role in achieving pragmatic results, such as Alciabiades' speech that dissuades the democrats on Samos from attacking an Athens become more oligarchic (8.86).[46] Others are important because of the ways their claims are developed or justified, as in the competing heraldic statements on the relationship between piety and force positioned within the narrative of the failed Athenian attack on Delium (4.97–99). Though the direct speeches are highlighted as statements and thus are distinguished particularly from things done, they must also be read as doings in the form of speech-acts.[47] Some of these speech-acts' meanings or influence are conferred substantially by their institutional contexts. Like all funeral speeches, Pericles' is a political-cultural event with its own rhetorical expectations and cultural traditions. Others should also be interpreted as *erga* because of their pragmatic consequences, such as, Diodotus's rhetorical rescue of the Mytilene democrats (3.41–49) or the Melians' defiance of the Athenians (5.84–116).[48] But still others—the hopeless defense of the defeated Plataeans (3.53–59) or the platitudes of Nicias during the retreat from Syracuse (7.77)—are empty words.

One reason to reject sharp distinctions between *logoi* and *erga* within the narrative is Thucydides' own admission (noted by Ober 1998, 59–60; cf. Saxonhouse 2004, 64–65; Saxonhouse 2006, 148–51) that much of his knowledge of the war's *erga* originated in reports of others, vulnerable to mistakes and biases. This does more than raise a methodological problem with which Thucydides the historian must somehow cope. It is an acknowledgment that no facts can ever speak for themselves. Yet if this is true, how should we interpret those occasions (particularly 1.1 and 1.23) on which Thucydides seems to say precisely that they can? The very facts or deeds (*erga*) of the war are said to provide sufficient testimony of its importance.

We should note, however, that in the two places where Thucydides suggests that the facts speak for themselves, the facts "say" significantly different things. In the first, Thucydides explains his decision to write about the war by noting his belief that it would be "great and more worthy of being spoken about than any previous war." Emphases on power and sweep follow. "For this was the greatest motion (*kinēsis . . . megistē*) that had come to be among the Greeks and even [among] portions of the barbarians, indeed one may speak of [the involvement of] most of humanity" (*pleiston anthrōpōn*) (1.1.2). Here, the war is worthy of being spoken about because of its spectacular appearance; *logos* truly seems to follow *ergon*. Yet this focus on the war's appearance is itself dependent upon the application of particular criteria of worth: size, greatness, motion, and energy, all of which represent the standards of valorization that one would expect from an Athens characterized by the Corinthians in book 1 (1.70–71) as a regime dedicated to daring and disruptive motion. Pericles appeals to these same evaluative standards in the funeral speech, where the appearance of greatness itself requires no embellishment in language. "With great display and asserting power that has not gone unwitnessed, we will be the wonder of both those now living and those who follow, needing no Homer to praise us nor any other whose phrases might please for the moment, but whose claims the truth of [our] deeds (*ergōn . . . hē alētheia*) will destroy" (2.41). This statement extends to Pericles' broader characterization of Athens as a city focused on deeds, not words. It uses its wealth and other resources "for critically timed action (*ergou . . . kairō*) rather than boastful speech" (2.40). Yet these claims cannot be validated by a simple perception of Athens' power; they depend upon Pericles' *logos* persuading the audience about appropriate criteria of judgment, including the implication that a philosophy practiced without softness (*aneu malakias*) is superior to gentler or soberer cultural forms that may offer alternatives to or critiques of power.

In using size and energy as criteria for assessing the importance of the war, Thucydides seems to accept these broadly Periclean standards of evaluation.[49] Yet those standards are challenged by the second way in which the facts demonstrate the war's significance. At 1.23, the facts involve not only the war's extended scope and duration, "but also such sufferings as came to afflict Hellas unlike those [experienced] in any like [length of] time. For never had there been so many cities seized and abandoned, some by barbarians and others by the Hellenes warring against each other (and some even changed population after they were overpowered), nor were there so many human beings dislocated or slaughtered, both on account of the war itself and because of factional fighting." On this occasion the significance of the war is proven not simply by size and energy, but by the great sufferings caused by this massive and energetic motion. In pointing to the sufferings brought on by the war, Thucydides thus reintroduces perceptions and criteria that Pericles' *logos* has excluded. In neither case do the facts simply speak for or display themselves. They are constructed first by the Periclean affirmation of nobility and greatness and then by the more complex and problematizing *logos* of Thucydides.[50]

Since the facts speak only through *logoi* and since forms of *logoi* can signify and valorize facts in dramatically different ways, how should we interpret Thucydides' claim to represent the speeches "especially required in the given situation"? Thus understood, the narrated speeches can hardly be read simply as carefully researched transcriptions of statements made. Yet neither can we treat them as Thucydides' own version of what *he* would have said on these occasions. It seems more reasonable to interpret them as indicating what the speakers (individuals or regimes) would have said were they responding to the situations in a way that was consistent with their truest identities and most fundamental priorities. *Logos* in this case is a means of disclosing character, and these various *logoi* are therefore embedded in networks of desire and power, ambition and fear. To this extent, the narrated *logoi* taken together provide a set of political responses to the events of the war. By positioning them within the narrative as he does, Thucydides invites his readers to reflect on the strengths, vulnerabilities, and pathologies of these responses and the particular form of political agency they signify. By representing the speech required in each situation, Thucydides both defers to and challenges the *logoi* of his characters. Deference and challenge can be read as particular features of democratic speaking in which citizens are entitled to their say but none is taken to be the authority.[51]

This blending of deference and challenge thus connects Thucydides with democracy in positive as well as in critical ways. In refusing simply to adopt or repeat Periclean criteria of worthiness in his assessment of why the war was worthy of being spoken about, Thucydides acknowledges the multivocality of democratic speech that allows challenge. Periclean *logos* is very different. In the funeral speech, those who decline to play roles in Athens's public life are labeled not simply as "apragmonists," those who stay out of the way and mind their own business, but as useless (*ta achreia*) (2.40.2). In Pericles' last speech, the "apragmonists" become the targets; they are sharply distinguished from those "wishing to do something" (2.64.3–5). The politically inactive are not just those who decline involvement in political affairs, but those whose vision of Athens's good challenges the Periclean project of greatness and expansion. By characterizing dissenters in a way that excludes them from the public realm, Pericles' rhetoric attempts to silence these oppositional views. Periclean political speech is in this respect monologic, another reason why what was "in name" a democracy was in reality (*ergō*) the rule of the foremost man (2.65.9–10). In challenging the complete adequacy of the Periclean criteria of assigning worth, Thucydides acknowledges the importance of a *logos* that is more contestative and thus, in a way, more democratic.[52]

Thucydides' political posture thus seems closer to that of the citizen Diodotus, whose sole appearance in the narrative is his persuading the assembly to be lenient toward the Mytilene *dēmos*.[53] He prefaces his plea with a more general defense of speech as a guide to prudent action, made necessary by the violent attacks launched by his demagogic opponent, Cleon. The *logos* that Diodotus defends is not a monologic rhetoric but a more interactive form of speech made possible within an idealized democratic assembly. In the fuller treatments of these speeches, I will suggest that Diodotus also identifies democratic causes that prevent the assembly from functioning as needed. Consequently, his performance cannot altogether respect the priorities valorized in his speech. He can only achieve decent political outcomes by both respecting and subverting certain forms of democratic practice. By dissenting from both Pericleanism (democracy in name) and the actual practices of the assembly (democracy in fact), Diodotus's focused political *logos* parallels the extended human *logos* that is Thucydides' book. Just as Plato's *logos* does not attempt to overcome or transcend *erga*, Thucydides' recognition of the overwhelming power of political *erga* does not exclude possible contributions from a constructive *logos*. Thus, while major differences between Plato and Thucydides remain, neither builds an artificial case for rationality in abstraction from the influences of power, and neither consigns politics to the exclusive control of power with no prospective contributions from rationality as *logos*. These sensitivities to the nuances of culture and the continued presence of power result in works that address the broadest and deepest questions of politics not with abstract or distant theorizing but with contributions to the civic conversations that occur within these cultural and political contexts.

Political Theory and Political Thought

Thucydides' and Plato's texts can thus be read as intersecting resources for citizens focused on improving democratic practice. In one sense, their work insists on a greater need to recognize the limits of democracy by revealing the human damages that an immensely confident and powerful democratic society is capable of inflicting or by disclosing the valuable human possibilities that such a society neglects. Yet both writers also expand the limits of democracy by insisting that democratic civic discourse can benefit from engaging questions that it would normally find dissonant or threatening. While both writers suggest that political theory should do more than clear a space for politics, they also reject attempts to replace those politics with more directive forms of political theory as both undesirable and impossible. Instead, these texts imply that the best kind of democratic theory provides resources that enable democratic citizens to think more intensely and critically about the purposes and dilemmas informing their common life.

In the chapters that follow I suggest that these texts can play analogous roles within our political discourse. I try to make this case by placing Plato and Thucydides in critical conversations with the four contemporary forms of democratic theory introduced earlier.

Chapter 2 engages the classical perspective with rational choice theory, as articulated in both the positive social science of (for example) Robert Axelrod, William Riker, and Kenneth Waltz and the more empirically based work of Dennis Chong and Russell Hardin. I argue that rational choice theory's focus on strategic calculation and bargaining ignores the broader psychocultural and pragmatic concerns that border, by both defining and limiting, strategic rationality. Thucydides and Plato together provide fuller attention to these borders, Thucydides by revealing the compulsive origins of seemingly rational strategies, the Platonic Socrates by insisting that strategic calculations need to be examined in light of the broader purposes or life choices that surround them. Attention to these borders thus provides a vision of the relationship between politics and rationality that is fuller and more useful than the constrained view offered by rational choice theory.

In chapter 3, I engage the two classical authors with deliberative democracy, paying particular attention to the works of Jürgen Habermas, Mark Warren, and Iris Marion Young. While deliberative democratic theory represents a significant advance over the rational choice perspective, it is hamstrung by its exclusive focus on the procedures of democratic decisions. This focus limits the critical capacities of deliberative democratic theory in two ways. First, it cannot criticize outcomes determined in procedurally correct ways. Second, it cannot explain why the political-cultural practices that enable democratic deliberation are themselves social goods. I make this case by examining the ways in which classical political theory assesses the importance of trust and judgment in democratic deliberation.

In chapter 4, I focus on positions that rely on the meanings of democratic culture to provide sufficient resources for political practice. My principal conversation partners are the John Rawls of *Political Liberalism* and the interpretive anthropologists (most notably, Clifford Geetz), both of whom situate normative judgments within shared cultural meanings. I argue that while Thucydides and Plato also rely on such meanings for normative guidance, they defend this reliance on the basis of insights concerning the human condition. Privileging the value of democratic culture requires forms of inquiry and argument that extend beyond the languages and priorities of any particular political community. This attention to a broader range of human practices allows us to see possibilities and difficulties within democratic political culture that that culture itself obscures or ignores. From this perspective, democratic culture creates a condition for discourse that can be both a resource for and an object of rational criticism.

In chapter 5, I engage Thucydides and Plato with postmodern democratic theory, particularly as represented in the work of Judith Butler, William Connolly, Bonnie Honig, and Chantal Mouffe. I examine classical political theory's treatment of the nature and status of what postmodernism calls "the other," a constructed opposite whose alleged vices reveal the comparative virtues of those who control the terms of political and cultural discourse. I argue, controversially, that the various forms of postmodernism see a solution to the problem of the other as a necessary condition for the healthy practice of democratic politics. By contrast, Thucydides and Plato suggest, in dramatically different ways, that the problem of the other is coterminous with all forms of politics. On the basis of these readings, I suggest that democratic politics is preferable, not because it alone resolves the problem of the other, but because it is the sort of politics best equipped to cope with the vulnerabilities and opportunities that the other continually represents.

The conclusion returns to the problematizations of democratic practices that I have outlined here to suggest how these conversations can contribute to the health of a democratic regime by extending the limits of what can be seriously discussed within democratic political cultures. I call this an extension of conversational limits because many of these contributions insist on the value of questions and categories that democratic culture often treats as settled or suspect.

Stretching the limits of what can be talked about within democracies is central to the health of democratic political life, particularly when no political alternative better than democracy is envisaged. While the results of these contributions may challenge the validity or at least the completeness of modern democratic theory, the same cannot be said of the consequences for democratic practice. On the contrary, I show that the classical perspective enhances the resources available to citizens as they attempt to understand, criticize, and contribute to democratic collective action. In this respect, my return to Thucydides and Plato is intended not to displace politics by constructing still more political theory, but to enhance politics by encouraging more serious political thought.

2

The Borders of Rational Choice

Introduction: Rational Politics?

For both political theory and political science, questions about the relationship between politics and individual rationality are ongoing and vexing. Important voices within both fields give the choices and actions of rational individuals a central role in justifying or explaining political phenomena. Such projects are not without their critics, however, and the difficulties that such attempts encounter challenge the connection between politics and rationality. While these challenges remind us of the political importance of nonrational needs or emotions, they also eclipse the relationship between politics and rationality as a central problem, replacing the question with foci on culture or power. Here I offer readings of Thucydides and Plato that recognize the limitations of rational choice theory yet insist on the primary importance of examining how politics and rationality do and must intersect.

For social contract theorists, the choices of rational agents under specified conditions of stress, constraint, or uncertainty support normative conclusions concerning the purposes and limits of political institutions.[1] As social theory, rational choice offers a framework for explaining the structure and influence of social institutions and processes.[2] Its basic premise is that the emergence, continuation, or alteration of social forms can be traced to self-interested decisions of individuals (cf. Axelrod 1984, 6; Becker 1996, 1–2, 21–22; Chong 1996, 42–43; Chong 2000, 12; Hardin 1995, 4–5; Riker 1962, 12–16). The resulting social forms channel or constrain subsequent individual choices that in turn reinforce or alter contexts.

Rational choice theory seems particularly privileged within empirical social science for at least two reasons. First, it offers the possibility of discovering the causes and not merely the correlatives of a wide range of social events. For Jon Elster, no social investigation can be scientific without identifying causal mechanisms, and causality can only be determined by moving from a social to an individual level of analysis (Elster 1989, 13; cf. Chong 1996, 4; Chong 2000, 16–17). Since the individuation of interests occurs prior to social interactions (cf. Axelrod 1984, 3; Downs 1957, 83), rational pursuits of such interests are the fundamental causes of social configurations. So, Robert Putnam's exploration of the differences in democratic performance in northern and southern Italy uses a rational choice framework to explain persisting conditions of functionality in one region and failure in another (Putnam, 1993, chap. 6).

The second reason for rational choice's appeal is that it appears to respect the ethical neutrality that social science demands. Rational choice theory is concerned exclusively with the rationality of means, withholding comment on the quality of ends (Downs 1957, 5). It is but a short step to avoiding the use of the term "rationality" in the description of practical ends altogether.[3] Russell Hardin distinguishes between conceptions of self-interest, which can, at least in principle, be understood in objective ways, and rationality, which is confined to subjective beliefs or intentions. "You act rationally if you do what you believe serves your interest" (1995, 46; cf. Elster 1989, 24–25; Riker 1962, 18–19; Brams 1980, 20–21; Chong 2000, 14). Neither a mistaken belief about strategy nor an even deeper mistake about the character or value of goals condemns a choice as irrational. Consequently, rational choice theorists do not see themselves making controversial assumptions about ends (cf. Friedman 1996, 2). While James Buchanan and Gordon Tullock acknowledge that this framework assumes the motivation of economic man, they deny that this assumption introduces normative bias: "Reduced to its barest essentials, the economic assumption is simply that the representative or average individual, when confronted with real choice in exchange, will choose 'more' rather than 'less' " (1965, 18).[4]

Though originating in the relatively abstract world of microeconomics, rational choice theory is increasingly employed within investigations of a wide range of political phenomena. Its causal influence can be traced by reconstructing the self-interested motives underlying observed political behavior or by confirming its assessments and predictions through empirical tests.[5] This form of rational reconstruction has been used to explain a variety of social practices, ranging from the formation of political coalitions (Riker) through participation in movements for social change (Chong) to attachments to ethnic or religious communities that seem on the surface to overwhelm or eclipse individual interests (Hardin).

Rational choice theory is particularly influential within two fields of political inquiry. The first is the examination of liberal democratic institutions. Though the limited government associated with constitutional democracy is not the only form of politics that might be chosen by individuals inhabiting rational choice environments, there are strong conceptual affinities between the characteristics of these individuals and the priorities of democratic constitutionalism (cf. Buchanan and Tullock 1965, 306). Though rational behavior can occur in cultures of patronage (Putnam 1993, 177–79), tribal societies (Hardin 1995, 168–72), theocracies (Brams 1980, 36–37), and even tyrannies (Downs 1957, 11), liberal politics "enabling [the citizen] to play his part in selecting a government efficiently" (Downs 1957, 24) seems most compatible with the interests and motivations of those inhabiting rational choice models (cf. Riker 1980a, 433).

The second realm that draws particularly on the premises of rational choice theory is the so-called neorealist paradigm within international politics. This perspective explains the structure of international relations as a network arising out of the self-interested interactions of individual nation-states in the absence of common authority. While the parallel between individuals and nation-states may seem far-fetched, there is a closer resemblance between the nation-state and the firm (Waltz 1979, 94). Firms, like political parties in rational choice explanations of domestic politics, are assumed to pursue goals rendered as single, consistent preference orderings (Downs 1957, 25–26; Buchanan and Tullock 1965, 9; see also Friedman 1996, 2). Like Buchanan and Tullock's economic man, such states are presumed to want more rather than less within exchanges (Waltz 1979, 91). And like Downs's individuals, their interests are presumed to be constructed prior to their strategic interactions. These interests are either universal (such as survival) or preferentially stipulated within each political culture (Waltz 1979, 91–92).

In both of these applications, then, rational choice theory focuses on the ways in which political space emerges from and affects the strategic decisions of political agents. Within democratic theory, rational choice analyses explain how the processes (periodic elections) or institutions (party systems) of constitutional democracy enable or frustrate citizens' efficient pursuit of individual goods (Downs 1957, 23–24; Buchanan and Tullock 1965, 7). Within neorealist international-relations theory, political space is comprised of the structures that constrain state behavior, in the way market structures constrain the behavior of economic agents (Waltz 1979, 95–97). Both frameworks also presuppose that rational interactions within political spaces are ordered by an equilibrium that is analogous to the clearing of the market in classical microeconomics (Riker 1980a, 433).[6] In this context, an equilibrium designates a structural condition that is definite and stable enough to allow valid predictions about the behavior of relevant agents.[7] In democratic theory, equilibrium means the continued functioning of the rules of the game; it is rational for agents to limit the pursuit of interests within constitutional democracy as long as the benefits of playing by the rules outweigh the costs (Downs 1957, 10–11; Buchanan and Tullock 1965, 71–72, 78; Riker 1962, 30). For neo-realism, the relevant equilibrium is a balance of power reinforced by the self-help strategies of individual states (Waltz 1979, 118–19).

Thus understood, the rational choice perspective partially illuminates and partially obscures the phenomena it engages. Its most important illumination is its insistence on the need to examine how politics and rationality intersect. What obscures is its limited treatment of rationality.[8] This is not simply an objection that rational choice theory is inadequate as a guide for empirical research (cf. Green and Shapiro 1994, 5–7), but rather a concern about the constraints it imposes on the kinds of questions that can be asked about political processes. The rational choice framework cannot successfully confine itself to elaborating the conditions and consequences of a strategic rationality practiced by self-interested individuals without encountering what might be called the borders of rational choice, the nonstrategic human practices that make strategies what they are and the nonrational dimensions of human life that deploy and potentially distort strategic reason.

Most causal accounts within the rational choice paradigm assume that interests develop exogenously to the structures that surround and affect them. For Downs, strategies may change as a result of acquiring new information, but goals (or "tastes") remain constant (Downs 1957, 85). Robert Axelrod is even more explicit that interests precede and persist throughout interactions (1984, 3); his approach to the problem of cooperation "is to make some assumptions about individual motives and then deduce consequences for the behavior of the entire system" (1984, 6). Axelrod's research focuses on a computer tournament among a variety of decision rules determining when rational agents should cooperate or defect. He finds the most successful rule (named "tit for tat") to be that which begins with cooperation and follows with reciprocation (cooperating in response to cooperation and defecting in response to defection). The results suggest that institutional and cultural structures that foster realistic possibilities of cooperation are most conducive to securing the interests of rational egoists (1984, 125–26 ff.).

However, Axelrod's project shows that structures play roles in creating, not simply coordinating, interests. Axelrod's conception of an "absent central authority" envisages an institution needed to settle disputes between interest claims that already exist. Yet this conception of structure is too narrow, for it ignores the influence of standards and norms that become socialized as a result of interactions within particular institutional contexts.[9] Axelrod's initial example of an arrangement under which self-interested egoists are led to cooperate absent a central authority is the United States Senate (1984, 5–6). Yet while the Senate may lack a central authority in the sense indicated above, it is also characterized by what Donald Matthews (1973, 68) calls "folkways," practices with the functional status of norms that not only set boundaries around strategic alternatives, but also impart cues or templates for the conceptualization of interests. Axelrod's tournament results thus suggest that the formation of interests is not independent of the contestants' interactions. The most successful decision programs are those that presuppose and fit within a culture of cooperation (cf. Ross, 1993, 29). This mutual dependence between interests and structures is more complicated than the sequential development from interests to structures to constrained interests that is presumed by Axelrod and Waltz. If individual interests—and, indeed, the structure of rationality itself—cannot be characterized apart from systemic influences, then a causal analysis that deduces systemic consequences from individual strategies runs the risk of mistaking effects for causes or of artificially isolating as causal variables phenomena that cannot themselves be explained without reference to the structures that they putatively determine.

Then there is the claim to neutrality. Though the rational choice paradigm depends on a separation of rationality from self-interest (Hardin's terms), this distinction is in the end elusive. Conceptions of interest set limits on the range of available strategies, just as the examination of strategies elicits deeper scrutiny of interests. This means that rational choice theory cannot confine itself to reconstructing instrumentally rational processes of strategic thinking, but must also take a substantive and controversial stand on the rationality of interests or purposes. For example, Downs's mapping of the rational strategies available to citizens and political parties presumes that both are motivated exclusively by desires to achieve income, power, or status goods (1957, 27–28). "Since none of the opportunities of office can be obtained without being elected, the main goal of each party is the winning of elections. Thus . . . it treats policies as a means toward this end" (Downs 1957, 35; cf. Dahl 1956, 68–69; Riker 1962, 207–8). Yet if the point of winning elections is seen as the opportunity to implement definite public policies, then rational strategies for success would change as well. For example, policy prices that would have to be paid for some electoral successes might well seem too high. Axelrod's work likewise reveals the impossibility of disconnecting the rationality of means from an assessment of the substantive character of ends. The successful strategies in his computer tournament do not simply reflect the superiority of a particular decision rule but the preferability of a particular style or way of life characterized by cooperation, forgiveness, and the absence of envy (1984, 20).[10]

To the extent that the various forms of rational choice theory move beyond considerations of strategy to an examination of purposes, they also provide a normative, not simply a positive or descriptive, theory of rationality. Downs, Buchanan and Tullock, and Riker privilege their own sketches of rationally efficient egoists over the naive portraits of dedicated political leaders and public-spirited citizens painted by (usually unnamed) "traditional" political philosophers. And Axelrod's analytic conclusions about the most successful decision rules for interactive games turn quickly into norms praising the rationality of accommodation and mutuality (1984, 126). In all of these cases, the controversial question of the content of a substantively rational form of life is supposedly settled by a scientific deduction from positive premises. Yet in offering these normative visions, rational choice theory both overreaches and undercuts its commitment to positive science. It overreaches by providing a scientific validation of human purposes (Downs's pursuit of income, prestige, and power, Riker's desire to win) that it elsewhere treats as tastes or preferences.[11] Yet in shaping its account of strategic choice with a view to controversial claims about the good, rational choice theory also undercuts the scientific character of its analysis. At best, this form of positive science can reveal consistencies or inconsistencies between strategies and particular conceptions of the good (Weber 1949, 20–21). But it cannot privilege one model of strategic rationality over others, because such models inherit the controversial features of their framing conceptions of the good.[12]

Rational choice theory's difficulties in offering a causal and neutral account of rationality open the perspective to challenges that threaten not simply to revise or expand political theory's general concern with rationality, but also to obscure or distort it. Unconvincing conceptions of the social exogeny of interests invite accounts that focus much more on the constitutive influence of culture. According to this view, the shared meanings that hold societies or regimes together do not simply provide resources for or constraints upon the rational pursuit of self-interest. Culture also determines the content and the form of rationality itself.[13] For Clifford Geertz, thinking or rationality is a public or cultural phenomenon, because such processes always draw upon and reshape shared symbol systems (1973, 214–27).[14] From this perspective, Putnam does not go far enough in tracing the different social outcomes generated by rational decisions made in varying civic contexts. He needs also to recognize that interests and rationality mean different kinds of things within different cultural environments. In the northern region of Italy, social practices and traditions reinforce utilitarian or agent rationality where rational action is either efficient calculation of the costs and benefits of political involvement or effective expression of an individual voice that influences collective action. In the dysfunctional south, rationality means maintaining familial or patronage loyalties or performing tasks assigned by ascriptive roles and determined by historical patterns of dependency (1993, 177–81).[15]

Challenges to rational choice theory's neutrality invite suspicions that the perspective establishes a controlling vision of rational behavior that supports particular economic or political agendas. It advantages liberal capitalism to characterize behavior associated with its maintenance as rational. Assertions of the rationality of the balance of power foster the legitimacy of unequally distributed capabilities (cf. Waltz 1979, 97–99). From this perspective, the most important concern for social theory is neither rationality nor culture but power.[16] Simplistic versions of this thesis tend to see through intellectual categories to discover the power imbalances that such categories express and reinforce. More sophisticated variants, found, for example, in the work of Michel Foucault, construe power as a condition for all social identities and forms of knowledge (1979, 27–28). Yet, either way, the influence of rationality in the creation and criticism of social forms gives way to the analysis of power dynamics, an analysis that is itself conditioned by the analyst's position within relevant power configurations.

While these turns to culture and power raise legitimate concerns about the limitations of rational choice theory, both alternatives threaten to displace rationality both as a central concern of social theory and as a pragmatic civic question. Those who argue for the centrality of cultural interpretation face the question of how rationality might be distinguished from other forms of public activity, art, religion, production, or war. The diagnosticians of power confront the impossibility of providing a rational critique of power except as part of some other power move.[17] In both cases, rational choice theory's failure to recognize its borders threatens to obscure the distinctive ways in which rationality may engage culture and power.[18]

This consequence is particularly problematic for those endeavoring to connect political theory and the practices of citizens in democratic regimes. In limiting itself to analyzing the relationship between structures and strategies, rational choice theory intends to provide maximal space for the articulation and pursuit of individual or group interests. Yet if, as I have suggested, rational choice theory is hardly silent on the rational content of political purposes, it displaces one of the central activities of democratic citizens, substituting the derivations of positive science for the outcomes of political practice (Riker 1962, 5–6).[19] Once determinations of the content of rational politics have been settled, what remains is the selection of efficient strategies, a matter for technical expertise, appropriately reflected in Axelrod's choice of a computer tournament as a venue for testing cooperation strategies.[20] Yet critics who object to rational choice theory's marginalization of culture and power seem to move at least as far away from recognizing the importance of rational political action, absorbing rationality within the creation of cultural symbols or subordinating it to exercises of or resistances to power.

In the remainder of this chapter, I shall try to engage the priorities and problems of rational choice theory in light of the more complex treatment of rationality and politics that informs the work of Thucydides and Plato. For both, rationality is neither a powerful explanatory category nor a derivative cultural or political phenomenon, but a problem to be seriously investigated. According to my readings, both authors deny that assessments of the causes and consequences of strategic decisions can occur without examinations of the broader human drives and purposes that frame them. For Thucydides, the rational calculation of strategy is too often driven by compulsions or obsessions that remain unexamined. Thucydides emphasizes the overarching importance of examining those individual or cultural compulsions, even as he diagnoses why such examinations seem so daunting. The Platonic Socrates presses his interlocutors to recognize the need for examining the overall character or pattern of the ways of life that individual choices both presuppose and construct. The rationality or irrationality of ways of life reflexively influence the rationality or irrationality of the strategies that are devised to support them. Yet while Socrates focuses initially on the consequences of choosing rationally for the lives of individual moral agents, the dramatic contexts of the dialogues point to the sizable barriers that impede prospects for an examined life. Together, Thucydides and Plato can be read as underscoring both the importance of and the barriers against rationality in politics.

Imagination, Obsession, and Rationality in Thucydides

The Ambiguous and Contested Character of Rationality

For Thucydides, the calculative strategies devised by self-interested agents are included within the broader realm of *gnōmē*, translated as "thought" or "consideration" or "rationality."[21] What gives *gnōmē* its presence and influence within Thucydides' narrative is speech or *logos*, as in Pericles' statement of his abilities to discover and to articulate what is most conducive to the city's well-being (2.60.4–6). In distinguishing between facts or deeds (*erga*) and the speeches (*logoi*) that attempt to make sense of facts or to propose deeds (Thucydides 1.22.1–4), Thucydides thus suggests that attempts at rationality are distinctive within his narrative. As noted in chapter 1, however, no fact or deed comes to our attention without some *logos* that provides shape or focus, and all of the direct and indirect speeches contained within the narrative are also speech-acts and therefore, at some level, deeds. In focusing attention on the speeches, even as he blurs the lines between speeches and deeds, Thucydides suggests that the place of rationality in politics is a central yet problematic question.

In spite of its distinctiveness within human practice, *logos* is embedded in surrounding political and cultural forms and continually involved with power relations. Consequently, none of the speeches represented by Thucydides is allowed to stand as assessment or proposal without challenge. Many of these challenges occur within debates (*antilogoi*), but even unopposed orations (those of Pericles or Brasidas, for example) are set within the distinctive and often highly critical *logos* of Thucydides.

Thucydides' broad use of *logos* and, therefore, of *gnōmē* complicates a number of key elements of rational choice theory. First, it becomes difficult to contend that rationality can be inferred even from the most sophisticated observation of behavior.[22] This is not only because behavior is quite often irrational, but also because no behavior can become the focus of an observation without the prior contribution of some cohering *logos*. The oppositional character of many of the express *logoi*, to say nothing of their positioning within the surrounding explanatory and evaluative claims of Thucydides himself, suggests that no behavior can simply be reconstructed from a perspective whose rationality is not subject to challenge. Second, particularly within political contexts even purely strategic courses of action are not determined monologically. The rationality of (the *logos* behind) any choice is always open to contestation and in need of justification in light of competing *logoi*. Thus, coordination strategies involve more than simply determining how individual interests will be jointly pursued. Coordination also requires the more difficult task of coming to agreement about interests or the purposes of action. Pericles' eloquent affirmation of Athens's imperial identity (2.41.1–5) confronts recurring objections from the anti-imperialists in Athens (2.64.4–5) and the subject cities of the empire (1.143.5). This means that political interactions are not simply framed by a stable equilibrium; they can be disputes over what the relevant equilibrium might be. Finally, Thucydides' recognition of the multivocality of *logos* implies that rationality is a culturally constituted practice. The voices offering *logoi* in Thucydides' narrative are communities or regimes (the Corcyreans, the Corinthians, the Mytilenes, the Melians) as well as individuals. Yet precisely because the formation of a cultural *logos* is multivocal, characterized by challenge, it is misleading to compare such *logoi* to a firm's single, consistent preference orderings. Thucydides can narrate the *logoi* of individuals and regimes only by recognizing, not ignoring, their differences.

For critics, this broader understanding of *logos* might disadvantage efforts to employ rationality as an explanatory tool within social theory, for it seems to ignore the conceptual categories needed to distinguish rationality from pseudorationality or to differentiate among the various loci and functions of rational forms. Yet such criticisms would ignore how much Thucydides' characters acknowledge these distinctions in their own speeches. The Athenians on Melos contrast their rational proposals with the naive fantasies or desperate hopes of the Melians (5.113). Diodotus challenges Cleon's proposals for dealing with Mytilene because Cleon has failed to identify the right strategy for the appropriate end (3.47). Yet an awareness of the importance of these distinctions does not mean that political agents are able successfully to act on them. The rational Athenians' superiority to the irrational Melians is largely an Athenian construction rooted in a kind of pseudorationality. And Diodotus's appeal to ends that are seemingly obvious masks the degree to which political ends need critical scrutiny. Thus, distinguishing between rationality and pseudorationality (Downs 1957, 8–11) and between the strategic calculation of means and the purposive identification of ends (Hardin 1995, 46–47) are not components of an elaborate rational choice theory, but puzzles that complicate efforts to investigate the role of rationality in politics.

Contested Equilibria

The first of the *logoi* narrated by Thucydides are arranged within a debate before the Athenian assembly between representatives of the cities of Corcyra and Corinth. They have clashed over providing aid to the embattled city of Epidamnus, a colony of Corcyra, itself a colony of Corinth. Corcyra has defeated Corinth in a sea battle, but now fears retaliation should Corinth enlist its allies within the Peloponnesian coalition. Isolated, Corcyra seeks to ally with Athens. If Athens agrees, however, it would violate its treaty with the Peloponnesians. Eventually, Athens decides on a defensive alliance with Corcyra, a decision that fails to prevent open conflict between Athens and Corinth (1.44.1–3, 1.49.7). These hostilities lead Corinth to demand that the Peloponnesians wage war on Athens for breaking the treaty. Thucydides thus considers the Athenian response to Corcyra as one of the triggering causes of the war.[23]

Each of the two cities attempts to convince Athens that a certain course of action (accepting or rejecting the Corcyrean offer) is in Athens's rational interest. However, the speeches are not simply strategic, and the frame of reference is not set by a stable political equilibrium. Instead, each appeal originates in a cultural conception of the good that privileges a particular equilibrium. Because such conceptions are so ingrained within a regime's self-understanding, they often resist rational scrutiny and criticism. As such, they take on the character of compulsions or obsessions.

As many commentators (Strauss 1964, 174; Orwin 1994, 38; Price 2001, 82–83; Connor 1984, 34) have noted, the speech of the Corcyreans begins with *dikaion*, "it is just." In light of their actions throughout the *History*, the Corcyrean reference to justice is one of Thucydides' compelling ironies. Any pretense to justice on the part of Corcyra is hollow and cosmetic; the city is driven continuously by a grasping, highly combative form of interest.[24] Though their speech begins by commenting on Athens's just expectations for a defensible argument in favor of the alliance, the Corcyreans quickly move to the advantages that Athens can expect: strategic acquisitions useful within endless conflicts over gain and influence. The environment that Corcyra inhabits is one characterized by opportunities and threats within incessant contests between hostile competitors (1.35.4–5). In saying that the war with the Peloponnesians has already begun (1.33.3–4, 1.36.1–2) and in referring to potential naval campaigns against Sicily, the Corcyreans anticipate the time when Athens is fighting two major wars at once (7.27), engulfing virtually all of Greece. The equilibrium consistent with this conception of advantage is achieved when political entities who might otherwise be adversaries reach temporary accommodations that allow each to pursue political gains.[25] In this respect, Corcyra shows its time horizon to be an immediate future to which both Corcyra and Athens should look if they are rational.

Corinth's time horizon reverses Corcyra's, drawing upon a different political equilibrium. Whereas Corcyra promises future advantages, Corinth recalls past favors and promises. Athens is indebted to Corinth for assistance provided in time of need (1.41.1–3) and is obliged to her owing to the oaths sworn in concluding the treaty with the Peloponnesians (1.40.1–3). The political equilibrium implicit in this appeal is one of extended order and lawfulness, where gratitude and obligation create the conditions for stability. Thus, one of the festering causes of the hostility between Corinth and Corcyra is Corcyra's failure to treat Corinth with the respect that a founding city deserves (1.38.1–6). Consequently, while Corcyra's appeal makes repeated reference to advantage, Corinth's focuses on the expectations set by traditional conceptions of justice and piety (1.40.4–5; 42.1–2).

Each appeal encourages Athens to accept the vision of political equilibrium conducive to its own proposal. These equilibria are in fundamental opposition to one another, causing the two cities to see themselves and their relationship in incompatible ways. In insisting on deference, Corinth is, in the eyes of the Corcyreans, demanding servitude (1.34.1–2). In insisting on equality, Corcyra is, in the eyes of the Corinthians, violating its traditional duties (1.38.1–3). Thucydides' representation of the Corcyrean-Corinthian debate thus reinforces rational choice theory's contention that cooperation is impossible in the absence of a relevant equilibrium. Yet Thucydides suggests that political inquiry's task is not to discover a settled equilibrium enabling rational interaction, but to identify those factors that contribute to the construction of and conflict between competing equilibria and to critically assess the conceptions of equilibrium presumed by different political communities.

For both Corcyra and Corinth, preferred equilibria are tied to regime priorities and accompanying conceptions of political goods. Corinth's equilibrium is not simply a reverential acknowledgment of intersecting obligations in an ordered world. If the order that Corinth reveres were taken seriously, the city would have substantial power over regimes that might be materially superior (1.38.6). To this extent, Corinth's insistence on justice could be read as an appeal to advantage and, thus, as a validation of the Corcyrean equilibrium. Yet by characterizing advantage as the reward of ascriptive merit (the older over the younger, the sworn to over the swearing), Corinth challenges Corcyra's view of advantage as success in competitive engagements. Corinth begins its own speech with *anankaion*, "it is necessary" (1.37.1), because it is compelled to rebut Corcya's outrageous charges that Corinth is unjust (1.37.1–1.39.3).[26] Being just, in the way they see justice, is an essential part of who the Corinthians are.

After hearing both appeals, the Athenians agree to accept a limited, defensive alliance with Corcyra (1.44.1–3), a course of action that seems indecisive (Ober 1998, 78–79). Yet this decision is a consistent reflection of Pericles' policy of strengthening Athens's resources while continuing to provide the obsessively cautious Spartans with grounds for restraint (1.141–42). Thus, neither Corcyra's nor Corinth's political equilibrium is consistent with that of Athens. In part, the Athenians would reject the Corinthian equilibrium because it is transparently false. The Corinthians offer a self-serving version of past cooperation and ignore the obvious record of recent confrontation between the two regimes (1.105–6). Yet more fundamentally, the Corinthians' reliance on lawful order, where merit derives from status, is opposed by the Periclean political culture that values energy and daring and derives merit from achievement (1.77.1–9; 2.37.1–2.42.2). For these reasons, the Athenian and Corcyrean attachments to interest might seem more compatible. Yet Corcyrean equilibrium clearly suffers from devastating internal contradictions. In confronting Corinth, Corcyra counsels Athens to ignore the past and look only to the present and future benefits that the alliance would provide (1.33.1–4; 1.36.1–3). Yet the case is convincing only if the Athenians believe that Corcyra will remain grateful, that Corcyra's own future behavior will be the opposite of that which it urges upon Athens now. However, the clear implication of the Corcyrean argument is that there are no stable futures or revered pasts that cannot be undercut by more pressing considerations of advantage. In this respect, the Corcyrean rhetoric that their gratitude to the Athenians will persist in an "eternal remembrance" (*aieimnēstou*) (1.33.1) is another of Thucydides' ironies. Yet without stable futures there can be no prospects for cooperation in the present. The Corcyrean equilibrium is no equilibrium at all. Here Axelrod (1984, 127–29) seems perfectly positioned to diagnose the irrationality of the Corcyreans' proposals; they assume a shrunken time horizon, where the implications of the reality of future encounters are ignored owing to the immediate attractions of success. Corcyra will extend this pathology into its own politics. The horrible civil war (*stasis*) that engulfs their city is caused in part by contempt for any institutions limiting competitions for gain and honor (3.82).[27]

The Athenian vision of political equilibrium is, by contrast, clearly aware of a time horizon extending into the indefinite future. Unlike the Corcyreans, the Athenians anticipate ongoing political encounters. Yet unlike Axelrod's cooperative players, Athens is not deferential to the interests of others in expectation of continuously iterated games. What privileges Athens in its behavior (making the regime less "nice," in Axelrod's terms) is power, the sign of the city's being an "education to Greece" (2.41.1) and the source of a shining reputation that is truly capable of enduring in "eternal memory" (2.64.5–6). Though the Corcyrean time horizon is suicidally irrational, what would both rationalize and ennoble the dismissal of future punishments is power.

Athens's reliance on power is bluntly displayed in a speech that has several narrative and thematic connections with the speech of the Corcyreans. This is the presentation of the Athenian named Euphemus, given before representatives of the Sicilian city of Camarina as part of the massive Athenian invasion of Sicily (cf. 6.1.1). In support of Athens's campaign against Syracuse, Euphemus urges Camarina's aligning with Athens. He is opposed by the Syracusan Hermocrates. While the debate between Corcyra and Corinth is the first of Thucydides' "antilogies," the contest between Euphemus and Hermocrates is the last. In both cases, representatives of two cities argue over the rationality of an alliance before a third. Like the Corcyreans, Euphemus builds his case around considerations of interest that undercut initial bows to justice, whereas Hermocrates appeals, at least in part, to Camarina's and Syracuse's shared Doric heritage (6.77.1–2) and thus to the continuing influence of a certain kind of ethical order.

In his speech, Hermocrates says that Athens is hypocritical and untrustworthy. It has come to Sicily on the pretense of assisting Chalchideans in the allied city of Leontini, which is engaged in an ongoing quarrel with Syracuse; yet it has enslaved Chalchideans on the large island of Euboia, lying northeast of Attica (6.2.2). Euphemus responds by claiming that Athens's strategies are consistently predictable and therefore trustworthy. Paralleling the Corcyreans, Euphemus plainly acknowledges that Athens's actions are guided exclusively by its interests. It consistently suppresses Chalchideans in one place and supports them in another, because both projects support Athens's interests against the Peloponnesians (6.84.1–3).[28] Euphemus urges the Camarineans to see the compatibility of their interests with Athens's because both would profit from the diminution of Syracuse (6.85–86).

Though Euphemus and the Corcyreans are consistent in emphasizing the centrality of interest, they differ in their assessments of their respective cities' power positions. While the Corcyreans acknowledge vulnerability (1.32.1–3), Euphemus's account rests on an arrogant confidence in the magnitude and scope of Athens's power.[29] Because Athens is capable of bringing significant force to bear simultaneously at the eastern and western ends of Hellas, the very awareness of that power affects the behavior even of "very remote" cities, encouraging those hoping to gain through cooperation and cautioning those tempted to overreach (6.87.4–5). Given the differences between Athenian and Corcyrean power, the speech of Euphemus is, from one perspective, the more consistent and therefore the more rational of the two. From Euphemus' perspective, accommodation and restraint, Axelrod's niceties, would be irrational. The different consequences of the two regimes' power positions are reflected in Athens's treatment of Corcyra, which is used more or less as Athens's interests dictate. The *stasis* in Corcyra occurs in part because of Athens's manipulation of internal Corcyrean conflicts (3.70–82).

Yet, at a deeper level, Euphemus's position is seriously disordered. His attempt to persuade the Camarineans is a practical recognition of Athens's limited power to compel.[30] His goal is likewise undercut by what he says. In suggesting that Athens's behavior is exclusively interest-driven, Euphemus virtually confesses that it would abandon or move against Camarina should advantage require it. Predictability is different from trustworthiness; therefore, Camarina can trust Athens only as long as their interests can be predicted to coalesce. Moreover, Euphemus's continued references to Athens's power makes it obvious that any association with Camarina will be highly unequal (6.87.2). Euphemus boasts of Athens's ability to rule or to liberate as its interests demand (6.83.2-3), and he eventually compares Athens as a ruling city to a tyrannical man (6.85.1). However, since Athens pursues its interests through the use of force, its pressure is effectively neutralized by Hermocrates' reminding Camarina of the coercive power of closely situated Syracuse (6.80.4).[31] Camarina remains neutral, a decision that in the near term harms Athens more than Syracuse; and Camarina begins to support Syracuse when it becomes clear that Athens's power in Sicily is far less than what Euphemus's rhetoric presumed (7.33.1-2).

Euphemus's error is not simply a matter of poor strategy. It follows directly from claims about Athens's motivations and capacities or its general political identity. Seeking its own interest through the use of its great power, Athens's use of *logoi* both depends upon and is limited by its capacity to coerce. Euphemus's speech would be futile absent Athenian force (he thus rejects any reliance on "noble words" [6.83.2]), yet the naked factuality of that force also controls what he can say. He can claim that Athens is predictable, but he cannot plausibly persuade anyone that it is trustworthy.[32] The entrapment of strategy by identity or speech by power is reflected in his very language. Though he says that Athens (like a tyrant) is able to rule or to liberate as it pleases, its interests are also sources of compulsion (*anankē*). "We are compelled (*anankazesthai*) to many actions because we are on guard on many fronts..." (6.87.2).

Euphemus's reference to the compulsive character of power ties the concerns of his speech to Thucydides' fundamental explanation of the war's causes. On two occasions (1.23; 5.25), he notes that the Athenians and the Spartans were compelled (*anankasai*) to wage war. The precise character of these compulsions has been variously interpreted. Donald Kagan suggests that Thucydides unconvincingly attempts to trace the war to impersonal historical forces (Kagan, 1969, 372-73); Thucydides' own evidence shows the influence of "anger, fear, undue optimism, stubbornness, jealousy, bad judgment, and lack of foresight" (1969, 356), thus falsifying claims about the supposed inevitability of the war. I believe this interpretation is compromised by Kagan's reading of *anankē* as historical inevitability and by his broader claim that Thucydides works "on the edge" of philosophy by trying to uncover the influence of more impersonal forces on human practice (1969, 373). It may be valid to read Thucydides as a kind of philosopher, but wrong to define his philosophical project in these terms. And Thucydides may well agree that the war resulted from contingent instances of anger, fear, and so on, while still finding reasons to call these compulsions. Martin Ostwald thus sees Thucydides' most important use of *anankē* and its cognates as indicating that concatenations of specific circumstances constrain historical agents in ways that make certain responses unavoidable (1988, 31–32). In so doing, Ostwald offers but does not develop the observation that such inevitabilities vary with the individuals or populations involved (1988, 18–19), thus complicating assessments of what unavoidability means. Tim Rood suggests that what matters more than the circumstances themselves is how they are interpreted; consequently, Thucydides' references to necessity refer primarily to human perceptions (Rood 1998, 212). As valuable as this insight is, it should not obscure the fact that Thucydides' treatment of the necessary goes beyond identifying the forces that his characters interpret as compelling. Jacqueline de Romilly therefore seeks to discover a Thucydidean thesis on necessity by identifying psychological, political, and philosophical imperatives compelling the behavior of the powerful (de Romilly 1963, 336–37) in ways that rationality may systematize, but not oppose (1963, 357). Yet de Romilly's account of these influences treats the contentions of powerful individuals or subcultures as if they were Thucydides' conclusions. Clifford Orwin is more accurate when he characterizes the claim that "man is compelled to assert himself by a necessity of his nature" not as a Thucydidean but as an Athenian thesis (1994, 106), articulated originally by the Athenians at Sparta (1.72.3–1.73.2) who trace the Athenian empire to the compulsive urges of fear, honor, and interest. Orwin finds Thucydides himself far less willing to agree that all motives that prompt aggression are compulsory (1994, 141). Yet we still need to investigate why Thucydides in his own voice sees the Athenians and Spartans compelled to wage the war.

I suggest that when Thucydides speaks of the war as the outcome of compulsion, he points to the influence of certain psychocultural obsessions that resist even as they demand rational interrogation.[33] This understanding of political compulsion emerges most strikingly within what is arguably the most widely read portion of his work, the so-called Melian dialogue.

Imagination and Obsession in the Melian Dialogue

The Melian dialogue, occurring at the end of book 5, is often read as the paradigmatic acknowledgment of the influence of force exerted by material or military superiority. It is equally a testament to the power of political compulsions. The context is Athens's attempt to subdue the independent island city of Melos during the period of the Peace of Nicias, negotiated in 421 BCE. This assault is neither sudden nor, as Athens sees it, irrational. Much earlier, the same Athenian general, Nicias, unsuccessfully attempted to coerce Melos into the empire (3.91.1–3). There may be particular reasons why the Athenians wish to press this agenda again. Thucydides indicates that the peace exists in name only (5.25–26). He also suggests that Athenian designs on Sicily have intensified during the so-called peace (6.1.1–2). To the extent that the Athenians are contemplating the prospect of fighting two wars at once (7.28.3), firm control over the subject cities is essential. The perceived need to solidify the empire (5.91, 5.97) seems to drive the decision to subdue Melos.

The episode ends with the complete destruction of Melos; the adult males are killed, and the women and children are sold into slavery. As horrific as this action is, it is no different from what happens to the Chalchidean city of Scione after the negotiation of the peace (5.32.1–2) or from the initial decision about Mytilene (3.36.1–3).[34] What is particularly compelling in the Melian episode is what is said (cf. Connor 1984, 150). The form of what is said, the so-called dialogue between Athenian envoys and the Melian "leaders and the few" (5.84.3), is unique within Thucydides' narrative. However, calling this a dialogue is misleading, for the conversation is not discursively open with an equal privileging of voices, settled by the forceless force of the stronger argument (cf. Habermas 1996, 541 n. 58). The exchange is shackled from the outset by two exclusionary power moves. The first is that of the Melian leaders who prevent the Melian populace from listening to the Athenians (5.85). The second exclusion stems from the power imbalance between the two cities themselves. The Athenians insist that the conversation address only the issues that they introduce and that the Melians limit themselves to responding. Specifically, the Athenians exclude appeals to justice as pointless ("for just things are only decided through human speech [when directed by] equal compulsions [*isēs anankēs*]" [5.89]) and propose to focus exclusively on advantage, turning the conversation into a very limited kind of bargaining, settled before the fact by acknowledgments of power. In the presence of unequal forces, "the powerful do what they can, while the weak give way to them" (5.89).

In spite of these restrictions, the Melians treat the negotiation as a more open form of bargaining, for the Athenians' overwhelming power does not enable them simply to dictate the outcome.[35] The Athenians see themselves facing three basic alternatives, one far preferable to the other two. They strongly prefer that the Melians become part of the empire voluntarily, under conditions no worse than those imposed on the other subject cities (5.111). While they would reluctantly lay siege to Melos, they overwhelmingly prefer its voluntary submission to the sacrifice of blood and treasure that the second alternative requires (5.93). Either of these options is, however, preferable to allowing Melos to continue in its independence (5.95). The Athenians are capable of rejecting the last option unilaterally, but achieving their most preferred outcome requires the cooperation of the Melians. In spite of Athens's superiority in power, this engagement remains, at least at the outset, what rational choice theorists would see as a two-person game. However, the Melians' preference ordering is the reverse of Athens's. Their optimal outcome would have Athens agree to respect Melos's neutrality (5.94). Like the Athenians, the Melians would choose the second alternative, being besieged by Athens, over the third, voluntarily becoming a subject city within the empire. Similarly, the Melians can reject their least preferred outcome unilaterally, but can only achieve their most preferred result if the other side cooperates. The impasse arises because each side rejects the other's optimal outcome on principle. Laying siege and being besieged are rational choices for Athens and Melos, respectively, since each prefers this outcome over capitulation to the first preference of the other side.[36]

However, the two sides differ significantly over how the second option, the attempt of Athens to force Melos into submission, is to be described. For the Athenians, this will be an overwhelmingly unbalanced conflict ending in Melos's certain destruction. The Athenians insist that the Melians think of their advantage exclusively in terms of the survival of their city (5.87, 5.93). For the Melians, however, the conflict represents an unpredictable running of risks for both sides (5.102, 5.110). While the Athenians enjoy enormous superiority in immediately available military power, they should recognize that this advantage can be offset by the uncertain courses of war and by the prospective intervention of other powers (human or divine) (5.102). In light of these opposing descriptions of the second alternative, each side attempts to convince the other that the opposing preference ordering is irrational.[37] If the Melians truly face certain destruction at Athens's hands, refusal to submit is the height of folly (*pollēn alogian*) (5.101, 5.111). On the other hand, if the Athenians would run significant risks by initiating a siege, they should prefer to leave Melos alone and should choose the secure stability that Melian neutrality would provide (5.98). The coercive bargain that the Athenians attempt to enforce potentially becomes at least a kind of dialogue about the characterization of imminent practice.

Yet this dialogue never materializes because each side is as attached to its characterization of the alternatives as it was to its initial preference ordering.[38] The Athenians attempt to control these characterizations by dismissing the Melians' assessments as wishful thinking, grounded on hope in things inscrutable or invisible (*ta aphanē*) (5.103, 5.113). The Athenians represent themselves, however, as quintessential realists, taking their bearings from "things right before their eyes" (*tōn horōmenōn*) (5.113). Given the eventual outcome of the siege, it is understandable that many commentators have read this assessment as Thucydides' own. Whatever his moral judgments about the Athenian actions on Melos, he sees their speeches as undeniably "realistic" (cf. de Romilly 1963, 312; Ostwald 1988, 38, 55; Pouncey 1980, 104; for a dissenting overview, see Ahrensdorf 1997, 232–33). However, this assessment ignores the extent to which the Athenian position is also rooted in the belief in things not simply before one's eyes. Though the Athenians' rebuke does not include words that can be literally translated as "imaginary" or "imagination," it is clear that they contrast their own realistic perceptions of advantage and power with the fantasized scenarios of the Melians (cf. Crane 1998, 256–57). Yet the Athenians are also driven by what we might call a certain kind of political imagination. Appreciating the character and influence of that imagination, as applicable to both Melos and Athens, can extend questions about political rationality beyond strategy toward more fundamental questions of political purpose and cultural identity.

While the hopes of the Melians rest partially on the generally unstable character of war, they have more confidence in the predictable sources of assistance provided by the gods and the Spartans. "We [Melians] trust that, regarding fortune, through the influence of the divine, we shall not suffer, since we stand as pious men against those who are unjust, and regarding power, that the Lacedaemonians our allies will necessarily provide us with resources, if for no other reason than out of kinship and respect (*aischynē*)" (5.104). Implicitly, this statement resists the Athenians' stipulation that considerations of justice be set aside. The Melians reintroduce justice not simply because they perceive the desperateness of their situation but also because they accept a coherent vision of a world ordered by certain patterns of lawfulness and reciprocity in which it would be rational for the gods and the Spartans to come to their assistance.[39] Accordingly, political calculations ignoring questions of justice and obligation are radically distorting. Seeing this coherent picture as a kind of imagination does not mean that it is simply illusory. It seems instead to be a projection on experience that can be tested against and verified by practical outcomes. Reliance on the gods or fortune is validated in part by seven hundred years of Melian political independence (5.112). Expectations of support from the Lacedaemonians are justified by the Spartans' long-standing reputation as the emancipators of Greece, reinforced by Brasidas's apparent mission of liberation in the north (5.110).

As a coherent projection on experience, the Melians' political imagination also depends upon and reinforces sets of meanings embedded within a political-cultural identity. Melian rationality develops concurrently with kinship relations (5.104), a shared sense of honor and shame (5.104), and public practices of religion (5.104, 5.112). From this perspective, domestic or internal political relationships are not simply coordination or exchange relations among self-interested individuals, but psychocultural[40] processes through which memberships in communities of meaning become possible. This implies that conflicting political communities are not simply strategic agents pursuing interests, but cultural agents engaged in contests over meaning. Precisely because the Melians see the political cosmos as a realm where justice should affect both the standings and the fortunes of cities, they refuse to relinquish their own senses of shame and nobility as a condition for political bargaining (5.100), and they insist that the Athenians accord them a recognition cognate to that which the Athenians demand from them (5.92).

Thus understood, political imagination is a condition for, rather than a barrier against, rational political speech and action. The focus on psychocultural processes that create community memberships provides a way of moving between individual and collective levels of analyses that is less arbitrary than rational choice theory's characterization of a political community as a firm with a single preference ordering. The community is not the individual writ large, but the cultural context that makes particular forms of individuation possible. Likewise, the content of a regime's political imagination identifies an equilibrium that frames political projects and guides or limits political strategies.[41]

From this same perspective, however, Athens, no less than Melos, constructs its projects and organizes its strategies on the basis of a particular political imagination. The conflict between Athens and Melos is therefore one between two alternative political images. The Athenians frame their own bargaining with the image of Athens as a powerful, yet vulnerable, ruler of an empire in a world pervaded by competition and hostility. This image is consistent with the view of Athens articulated by Pericles in his three direct speeches represented in books 1 and 2. There are particular affinities with the last speech, in both its acceptance of the possible diminution of Athens's status (5.91; 2.63.2–3) and its recognition that, however unjust the empire might be, it is now dangerous to let go (5.99; 2.63). Driven by this image of the empire, the envoys can accept nothing less than Melos's subjugation, for its continuing independence would be interpreted as a sign of Athens's weakness, not only by the Spartans but also by the subject cities themselves: "[A]side from extending our rule, you would offer us security by being subdued, especially since as islanders, and weaker than the others, you should not have prevailed over the masters of the sea" (5.97).[42]

While the Athenian vision of the political world seems completely counter to the realm of piety and reciprocity imagined by the Melians, it, too, supposes an ordered cosmos, one where those who have the strength to rule do so. "For of the gods we hold the belief and of human beings we know, that by a necessity of their nature, where they are stronger, they rule. And since we neither laid down this law, nor, when it was in place, were the first to use it, we found it in existence and expect to leave it in existence forever, so we make use of it, knowing that both you and others, taking on the same power as we have, would do the same" (5.105). The Athenians thus also see themselves playing an established or necessary role in a lawful world. They respond to imperatives set not by reciprocity but by power and in a way they are as settled—or constrained—in their world as the Melians are in theirs.[43] While the Athenians may interpret their astonishing political success as reinforcing the validity of this world's principles, they are also compelled to maintain rule over the empire if they are to continue to occupy their role within this established order. Maintaining their position necessitates that they strive ceaselessly to solidify and to extend their power. Within a world ordered by this vision of strength and weakness, the only alternative to continuously active imperialism would be subordination or servitude (5.91.99). In this respect, the Athenian envoys' obsession with maintaining the empire mirrors Pericles' interpretation of Peloponnesian demands for the revocation of the Megarian Decree. "For the same enslavement (*doulōsin*) arises when either the greatest or the smallest requirement issues from a command given by an equal to an equal before arbitration" (1.141.1).[44]

Thus characterized, the Athenians' political imagination is as compulsive as the Melians'; yet it is a political imagination that the Athenians believe is consistent with the nature of things. The envoys' statement (5.105) that the rule of the stronger reflects a kind of natural law (*physeōs . . . nomon*) assumes that there are clear, noncontroversial measures of strength and weakness that can determine political relationships in unambiguous ways, such as the visible power of the Athenians as opposed to the invisible resources on which the Melians depend. From this perspective, various forms of political imagination can be tested comparatively against a harsh but clear standard set by nature. As Orwin comments, the "priority of the envoys' understanding of the human explains their most daring innovation in presenting the divine:

their subjection of it to the natural. In nothing else do they so foreshadow Plato.... The gods are not the first beings on which all else depends; they depend, like the others, on nature" (Orwin 1994, 106).

Here too, a number of commentators have read this Athenian statement as a reflection of Thucydides' own position (de Romilly 1963, 308–12; Pouncey 1980, 104; Crane 1996, 208; Crane 1998, 99–100, 310–11). From this perspective, Athens's compulsion is not an obsession capable of being examined by critical rationality, but a necessity set by its place in the natural order. Yet while this is certainly the envoys' position, it is less clear that it is Thucydides'. Even the Athenians' own statement eventually blurs the distinction between natural standards and human constructions. The language of necessity and nature gives way to the language of decision and legislation. If this law has been in some sense laid down (*keimenō*), it is not obvious that it has been in existence forever (*aiei*). The Athenians' tendency to derive their beliefs (*doxē*) about the gods from what is known clearly (*saphōs*) about human beings is also preceded by a tendency to determine what is known about human beings on the basis of the city's political imagination.[45] Theology may be an extension of anthropology (Orwin 1994, 106), but anthropology (the sorts of things that are said to be true of human beings generally) may itself be an extension of culture (the shared meanings that construct what is believed to be true about human beings generally). Thus, this Athenian statement differs dramatically from Thucydides' own conclusions about nature. Regarding the *stasis* in Corcyra, he notes that "with public life disordered to the point of crisis, human nature ruling over the laws, and accustomed against the laws to do injustice, took delight in showing that its anger was uncontrolled, that it was stronger than justice and an enemy to all distinction" (3.84.2).[46] Here, nature is not a harsh yet ordered hierarchy, but turbulence. Its characteristics are exhibited most clearly not in regularities but in extremes (3.82.2). And the very categories of strength and weakness seem themselves subject to disruption (3.83.3–4).[47]

Yet if conceptions of a cosmos ordered by the gods or by nature originate in, rather than measure, forms of political imagination, such conceptions ought to be susceptible to critique as alternative forms of imagination are developed and proposed. From this perspective, while *ta anankaia* are not simply psychic fantasies with no roots in tangible practice, neither are they simply acknowledgments of psychic or eternal imperatives. However, because both parties to the Melian dialogue construct visions of political order grounded in dogmatic extrapolitical foundations, theological or anthropological, they resist alternative formulations as untenable. The Melians are so willfully resistant to Athens's pressure because they cannot imagine a political cosmos without justice. The Athenians see the Melians as suicidal fools because tangible power is the only real measure of regime strength. When challenges are encountered, dogma silences. The Melian leadership fears the influence of the democrats' concerns for safety, so the majority is excluded from any "dialogue" with the Athenians. The Athenians begin the exchange by denying any Melian concern for justice.

However, while these powerful forms of political imagination are treated by their advocates as sources of strength and conditions for rationality, they eventually generate irrationalities that lead to disaster. The Melian disaster is more immediate. Athens responds to the dialogic impasse by laying siege; yet its power is not as overwhelming as expected and Melos for a time resists (5.116). Eventually, internal treachery helps the Athenians prevail. Commanded by a general named Philocrates (the lover of power), son of Demeas (*dēmos*),[48] the victorious Athenians are merciless.[49] Yet the apparent success of their harsh realism (never their first preference) is followed by their own disaster in Sicily, an invasion generated by the same political imagination that fostered the Melian expedition (6.1.1–2).[50] The calamitous end of the Sicilian campaign features the reappearance of voices ridiculed by the envoys; the embattled Athenian general Nicias, the first commander who attacked Melos (3.91.1–3), desperately hopes for aid, first from the gods and then from the Spartans (7.77.1–4, 7.85.1–2) (cf. Connor 1984, 155). Strategically, the invasion generates the very conditions that it was supposedly intended to avoid: prospects of the empire's dissolution and of Athens's falling under the rule of others (6.18.3; 8.1–2).

While the irrationalities of both Melian and Athenian strategic choices are signaled by disastrous outcomes, they are rooted in the more basic irrationalities of each side's political imagination. These are irrational in two related senses. First, their defining commitments to justice and power are specified so rigidly as to dismiss all challenges or reformulations before the fact.[51] The Melian conception of justice refuses to take the city's pragmatic disadvantages seriously, and the Athenian regard for power treats justice as irrelevant absent equal capacities to coerce. Second, illusions that these forms of political imagination are grounded in cosmic standards mask their cultural origins and diminish possibilities of cultural critique and political change. If the love of power is the son of *dēmos*, it has a cultural and not a natural origin, and *dēmos* may have other, gentler children. In light of these lurking irrationalities, each of these forms of political imagination takes on the character of a compulsion, understood neither as historical inevitability nor as natural necessity, but rather as a kind of psychocultural obsession, one that directs the application of subordinate forms of rational action, but which is itself resistant to rational criticism.[52] From this perspective, the importance of rationality is elevated beyond its significance within rational choice theory. Its role changes from the explanatory to the pragmatic. To describe our actions as rational when we do what we believe is in our interest considers only the bordered version of rational choice. Staying within that border is unworkable, for both its constitution (the relevant sense of equilibrium) and its coherence (the selection of appropriate strategies) depend on the rationality of the political imagination that conditions it. Consequently, the need to structure arrangements that allow self-interested parties to cooperate becomes subordinate to the need to render forms of political imagination less compulsive through the possibility of *logos*.

Dilemmas of Logos *in the Mytilene Debate*

Thucydides represents an attempt to revise Athens's imagination of its imperial identity in the debate between the citizen Diodotus and the demagogue Cleon over the fate of Mytilene, which has led the revolt of nearly the whole island of Lesbos against Athens in the fourth year of the war (3.2.1–3). Since Mytilene was exempted from the tribute imposed on the other subject cities (1.19), its actions inspire uniquely intense outrage. The Athenians subdue Mytilene with the help of the city's own *dēmos*, and the occupying Athenian general, Paches, sends the one thousand oligarchs thought responsible to Athens for trial, remaining himself at Mytilene to await the assembly's orders about the others. The assembly meets to determine the city's fate, and we are told only that it was decided to kill all of the adult males (democrats as well as oligarchs) and to sell the women and children into slavery (3.36.1–2). The next day, however, a majority of the citizens (*to pleion tōn politōn*) believe the initial decision was monstrous, and they successfully urge the assembly to reconvene. A number of citizens speak within the second debate, but only two speeches are presented. They are noteworthy not simply because they make the most influential cases for each position, but because they specifically address the nature of rationality and its relation to democracy. The implications of these speeches for assessments of democratic institutions will be discussed more fully in chapter 3. Here I concentrate on their respective claims about political rationality. Cleon's inflammatory rhetoric has unexpected affinities with certain elements of rational choice theory. In opposing Cleon, Diodotus offers a more complicating picture of the relationship between rationality understood as *logos* and democratic politics.

Cleon begins by doubting whether a democracy can successfully rule other cities (3.37.1–2); he claims that democratic institutions make the rational appreciation and pursuit of imperial interests impossible. Democratic decisions are always shifting (irrationality of outcomes) because of a passion for novel speeches (irrationality of process). The citizens who make up the assembly are often "simply overcome by the pleasures of hearing... and [behave] more like those who sit by and watch the displays of sophists than like those taking counsel (*bouleumenois*) about the city" (3.38.6). Cleon trivializes reconsideration of the decision on Mytilene as an example of this lack of seriousness. A more general implication of Cleon's attack is that a democracy's inability to rule an empire is simply a consequence of its inability to act effectively in its own interests because of the influence of democratic speech or rhetoric. Cleon opposes democratic speech by substituting a rationality more appropriate for imperial regimes.

In so doing, he appears initially to offer an extreme version of rational choice theory. We act rationally not simply when we do what we believe is in our interests, but when we have an undistorted conception of what those interests are and make effective calculations for securing them. For Cleon, then, modern rational choice theory's separation of means from ends is untenable. His conception of political rationality both presumes and demands an unassailable conception of the good.

This good is not, however, established on the basis of any sort of rational reflection. Rather, the content of our interests is communicated most effectively by the vehement passions that draw our attention to the compelling material interests of survival, gratification, and profit. Like the envoys on Melos, Cleon urges his audience to see what is most clearly before their eyes (3.38.5–6), achieved through the filtering lens of the passions. Cleon's speech is thus designed to re-create the fear (3.37.2, 3.40.5–7) and anger (3.38.1) experienced by the Athenians when they first learned of Mytilene's rebellion. The reliability of the passions as guides to the interests helps to resolve two paradoxes that frame Cleon's speech as a whole. Though Cleon appears to lead the *dēmos* through precisely the kind of rhetoric he condemns, his own speech escapes contradiction because it points to realities that are undistorted by rhetorical novelties.[53] And he can passionately assail the irrationalities of process and outcome fostered within the assembly, because his own passions of violence and anger are conclusive guides for what is to be done. The interests identified by the passions are unproblematic because they originate in urges so compelling that no rational case could possibly be made against them.[54]

Perceptions of the true or best political ends do not, therefore, require intelligence; in fact, it is often the supposedly intelligent who mislead the city out of their own ambition or pridefulness. The more ordinary or undistinguished (*hoi phauloteroi*) are better guides to identifying the city's interests than the more thoughtful (*hoi synetōteroi*) (3.37.3–4).[55] Yet though there should be no serious disagreement about the content of Athens's interests, the challenge lies in devising appropriate strategies to serve them, a task that it is rational for ordinary citizens to vest in experts such as Cleon. Therefore, Cleon does not so much argue for the elimination of distinction or intelligence altogether but revises the content of distinction so as to privilege strategic cleverness.[56]

For Cleon, the claim that true human interests lie in material accumulation and security achieved through power (3.39.8) draws on and reinforces a particular kind of political imagination that validates a conception of political equilibrium that exerts organizing control over rational choice's coordination and exchange relationships. Cleon's conception of Athens's political identity is contained in the statement that Athens is a tyranny (3.37.2). Commentators have pondered the differences and similarities between this claim and Pericles' contention in his last speech that Athens is "like a tyranny" (*hōs tyrannida*) (2.63.2–3).[57] In refraining from simply calling Athens a tyranny, Pericles reinforces his assertions (2.41.1–5, 2.64.5–6) that Athens must be esteemed for its brilliant achievements. To be sure, Pericles' vision ignores the fact that the subject cities may see little difference between Periclean and Cleonic rule. Still, the different statements underscore that Cleon's vision crassly excludes any sense of nobility.[58] For him, the exchange relation between Athens and the subject cities is one of material coercion and exploitation in return for Athens's withholding its capacity to punish (3.39.5–8). Thus, while Cleon begins by railing against the Mytilenes' injustice and demanding their punishment as a matter of right, he eventually asserts that Mytilene's injustices (*adikias*) are the harms (*blabas*) that it has done to Athens and that justice is simply retaliation (3.38.1–2, 3.39.6, 3.40.4).[59] In this respect, Cleon seems to go further than the envoys on Melos, for while they recognize a sort of justice that is separate from yet subordinate to interest, Cleon claims that whatever is in Athens's material interests is also just. In proclaiming the tyrannical nature of Athens's power, Cleon also anticipates Euphemus's strategy for coping with extended time horizons. By maintaining the harshest sort of coercive control, Athens strengthens its ability to deal unilaterally with possible defections in the future (3.40.8).

Yet Cleon's rhetoric cannot mask the contestable character of the interests that he says are obvious and the fragmenting consequences of the realities that he claims rational citizens should unite in recognizing. When he ridicules versions of the city's interests articulated by the thoughtful, he effectively acknowledges their continued persistence within public discourse. In attempting to foment a sense of fear and anger directed toward dissenters, Cleon attempts to orchestrate a sustained effort against those who argue that Athens's problems are more than strategic. He goes so far as to call the previous day's decision, which is simply a resolution passed by a majority of the assembly under his influence, a law.[60] Yet even the coordination that this sustained vigilance would require is called into question by the premises of his speech. Like rational choice theory, Cleon assumes that the most pressing individual concerns are formed exogenously to politics; they accompany physical existence, and any sensible person should be able to recognize their primacy without socialization. Any cultural self-understandings that diminish the importance of these interests (Pericles' funeral speech, for example) are mythologies that distort reality. In the presence of such interests, the advantages of any form of coordination are always subordinate to what might be gained by defection. Whatever political cooperation is achieved requires a recognition that predictably self-interested behavior needs to be controlled through the crafty use of rewards and punishments (indexed in Cleon's speech by greed and fear) on the part of the most influential political leaders. Yet since Cleon's description of human motivation applies equally to those occupying leadership roles, placing strategic decisions in their hands subjects ordinary citizens to their abuses in the name of material or power goods. Seen in this light, what looks like coordination may really be exploitation, the exposure of which may well make future coordination close to impossible (cf. Aristophanes *Wasps* 654–79). Possibilities for political rationality seem undercut by the substantive irrationalities that can surround strategies.

Cleon's implied premise that the rational examination of political ends is both unnecessary and impossible is challenged by Diodotus. In attempting to marginalize Diodotus's proposals before the fact, Cleon also reveals both the structure of and the stakes behind Diodotus's argument.[61] Cleon ends by warning the assembly against three errors (*hamartiai*) that are incompatible with ruling: pity (*oiktos*), the enjoyment of speeches (*hēdonē logōn*), and forgiveness (*epieikeia*) (3.40.2–3). Diodotus can only plead for moderation because there has been a certain degree of pity experienced toward defeated Mytilene. He proceeds to offer a subtle and therapeutic speech intended to encourage *epieikeia*. In this context Diodotus, too, relies on the influence of certain passions and emotions (*oiktos* and *hēdonē*), yet he does so in a way that opposes Cleon's conclusions. By implication, the passions are not as uniformly directed as Cleon had suggested. Moreover, by linking pleasure and speech, Diodotus suggests that emotions and rationality are related in more complex ways than in

Cleon's simplistic model, where the passions reveal goals and reason calculates strategies. Thus, while Diodotus's conclusions do not explicitly recommend Athens's surrendering its rule, they encourage a reassessment of what ruling requires.[62] Yet for all of his insistence on the importance of a noninstrumental rationality in politics, Diodotus eventually seems to despair of its prospects. Human beings need rationality desperately, even as they steadfastly refuse its assistance.

Diodotus begins by defending *logos* against Cleon's attacks. "I consider the two greatest opponents to good counsel to be haste and anger.... And as for speeches, whoever aggressively claims that they are not instructive as to action is either stupid or resists for reasons of his own" (3.42.2–3). This counterattack implicitly reverses Cleon's ordering of the passions and rationality and eventually challenges Cleon's understanding of rationality itself. For Diodotus, immediate anger is not an infallible guide to what is to be done, but a dangerous barrier against the counsel needed during periods of regime stress. The influence of the passions must itself be interrogated by a *logos* whose concerns go beyond strategy. Apparently, the shifting and problematic equilibria that condition strategies must themselves be continually revisited. Diodotus thus goes on to treat what seem to be the competing equilibria of interest and justice with a complexity that is unmatched by any of Thucydides' other speakers.

Initially, his proposals seem, if anything, to be radicalizations of Cleon's.[63] He insists that the decision about Mytilene should proceed exclusively with a view to Athens's interests. Even if the Mytilenes turn out to be guilty of injustice, Athens should punish them only if it is in its interests to do so. Conversely, even if they deserve mercy, it should be granted only if it would be "for the city's good" (3.44.1–3). However, in making these claims, Diodotus suggests that the city's interests are not obvious. He thus implicitly distinguishes his position from Cleon's in two crucial ways. First, he is not willing to convert justice into interest (as the response to injury). While interest may take priority, setting the two concerns against each other underscores the distinctive identity of justice. Second, Diodotus raises the possibility that mercy or forgiveness, determined according to a kind of justice, may be somehow connected to Athens's good. This cannot be true, of course, if Cleon's account of Athens's interests is compelling. Thus, Diodotus does more than offer an argument based on justice that parallels an appeal to advantage (Strauss 1964, 234; Orwin 1994, 151–55). He also implicitly urges rethinking the content of the city's interests based in part on an appreciation of the goods of justice. While justice is not reducible to interest and while the two may often be opposed, they may, while remaining separate, coalesce.[64]

The source and the content of Diodotus's understanding of justice are not immediately clear. He rejects Cleon's implication that justice is retaliation, yet he stipulates that justice is something different from the strategic calculation of advantage. Given Diodotus's utter silence about the gods, he is not relying on divine imperatives about just human practice. And in light of both Diodotus's and Thucydides' remarks about nature, searching for some sort of natural standard for justice seems futile. A more accessible source for Diodotus's beliefs about justice may be Athens's own institutions, the constructions or aspirations of a democratic society.[65] When the unnamed Athenians defend the city to the Peloponnesian allies before the war, they refer to the Athenian practice of giving greater degrees of equality to the subject cities than strict quantifications of power would require (1.72.2–3). To the extent that the Athenians show mercy to the Mytilene democrats, they will be more just than their power would require and so respect a form of equality constructed through political agreement.

Diodotus's appeal also includes a different imagination of the Athenian empire than what is offered by Cleon or the envoys. "If we subdue those ruled by force who naturally revolt for the sake of their autonomy, we think they must pay severely for their insolence. But we should not respond to rebellious free men with the harshest punishments; we should instead apply the most intense watchfulness over them before they revolt and through anticipation foreclose even the thought, and when we have put down revolts, we should bring the smallest number to account" (3.46.6). It is now clear both that Cleon was accurate when he forecast that his opponents would argue for *epieikeia* and that he was right in saying that forgiveness or evenhandedness clashes with his imagination of the empire. Diodotus is not simply counseling leniency toward the Mytilene democrats, nor is he simply recommending a more moderate stance toward defectors as a better strategy for managing the subject cities (3.47.1–2). What he implies is nothing less than the need to reimagine the practices and the identity of the empire itself.[66] Unlike the empire envisaged by both Cleon and the envoys, Diodotus's ruling takes the claims of those who call themselves free seriously (cf. 3.39.1–2) and finds arguments that justify their suppression on the basis of superiority in force to be inadequate. In this light, Athens's practices toward the subject cities should replace coercion with watchfulness. Yet if the primary posture of Athenian control becomes watchfulness, the advantages and goods of the empire need to be rethought. Thus, Diodotus suggests that the need to examine alternative forms of political imagination is the most important function of *logos*.

Of course, Diodotus's recognition of the significance of political rationality also intersects with a deeply critical assessment of the ability of democratic institutions to foster rational deliberation. A consideration of this aspect of Diodotus's speech will be deferred until chapter 3. At this point, let me emphasize the implications of the debate over Mytilene for rational choice theory. First, the opposing positions of Cleon and Diodotus reinforce insights that have arisen throughout Thucydides' narrative concerning the relationship between strategies and purposes. While rational choice theory separates questions regarding interest or benefit from the strategic calculations that comprise rational action, the opposing statements on Mytilene suggest that this is impossible. Separating ends and means limits the extent to which the effectiveness of strategic rationality can be judged. The comparative rationalities of Cleon's and Diodotus's proposals cannot be assessed on the strategic level alone, for they are driven by different conceptions of Athens's interests and identity. Absent a critical consideration of purpose, these opposing, contradictory proposals could each be seen as rational. A failure to consider the rationality of ends thus effectively diminishes the possibility of *rational* choice within the sphere of political action that determines what is to be done. Conversely, the assessment of strategies reflexively implicates examinations of ends. Diodotus cannot argue for the effectiveness of the moderate policy without pointing toward a conception of Athens's interests that departs dramatically from Cleon's.

Second, both Cleon and Diodotus offer descriptions of the cognitive status of the goals of strategic action that challenge their characterization within rational choice theory. The terms of these challenges make it clear why rational choice theory shrinks conceptions of politics and distances its formulations of political problems from those of political agents. Certainly, Cleon and Diodotus offer different views on the kinds of human purposes that should be identified as rational and, indeed, on the very grounds for determining rationality. Yet in spite of the substantial differences between their positions, neither sees the ends of rational action simply as preferences. For Cleon, the universally compelling nature of needs for security and profit makes it incorrect to imply that they can be replaced by other goals as tastes change. For Diodotus, the need to examine and defend our practical choices suggests that they are guided by priorities far more substantial than likes and dislikes. Our practical choices thus rest potentially on deep and extensive explanations of their purposes whose need for articulation becomes most apparent at moments of challenge. Rational choice theory's description of these purposes as preferences distorts both their nature and their importance.

Third, these distortions extend to understandings of politics and civic practice. For rational choice theory, politics is the context that enables and constrains negotiations over preference satisfactions. The Mytilene debate suggests that a more basic political function is to sort through the pressing question of where collective interests truly lie, engaging the content of what I have called a community's political imagination. To the extent that the most important civic task is working through these formulations, rational choice theory offers precisely the wrong guidance to citizens. While it attempts only to clear a space for the negotiation of preference claims, it specifies and constrains the political activities that that space should allow. In treating debates over the content of a political imagination as if they were competitive attempts at preference satisfaction, it offers a substantive account of the content of political practice. Yet by confining political activities in this way, it prevents political space from being put to other uses. The failure to engage questions of substantive rationality leads rational choice theory to diminish and therefore to misdescribe political rationality.

Yet in the end, Diodotus seems to despair that political rationality can guide political practice. Though human beings desperately require a rationality that takes political purposes seriously, they also continually resist it. The same psychological forces that mitigate the Mytilenes' behavior explain why arguments for mitigation might well fall on deaf ears. For Diodotus, human beings are continually driven to destructive overreaching by the force of the passions (3.45.4–5). No matter how dangerous the enterprise, *erōs* leads and hope (*elpis*) follows (3.45.5). From this perspective, both Diodotus's positive proposals and rational choice theory give rationality too much credit within explanations of political practice. The condition for rationality in politics would seem to be the control or the education of the passions, yet rationality seems inadequate to the task. Before the relation between politics and rationality can be seriously investigated, a case needs to be made for the possibility of, rather than simply the need for, a kind of *logos* whose concerns extend beyond strategy. We find these questions explored more fully in the Platonic dialogues.

The Uses and Abuses of Rationality in Plato

The Examined Life and Its Political Contexts

The value of a rationality that is more than calculated strategy is implicit in the Socratic image of the examined life (*Apology* 38a). While the meaning and value of this way of life are broad concerns within virtually all of the dialogues, I will focus particularly on the treatment of rationality within the *Protagoras* and *Charmides*. In different ways, each work suggests that strategic rationality needs to be understood in terms of its contributions to a coherent and choice-worthy way of life. What borders strategic calculation for Socrates is not simply an obsessive political imagination, but the pragmatic possibility for living well or badly (*Protagoras* 351b). To the extent that this is Socrates' focus, however, it may appear to have limited connections with the themes and conclusions of Thucydides. In its concern for living well, Socrates' discourse seems more optimistic (or cloistered?) than Thucydides' diagnoses of dark and violent obsessions. More generally, the two Platonic dialogues seem to pay far more attention to ethics (or virtue) than to politics (or power).

Yet these differences in tone and focus are not decisive. The Socratic concern to foster living well necessarily examines the complex psychological and cultural barriers that stand in its way. Neither the *Protagoras* nor the *Charmides* has a pragmatically positive ethical outcome. And what might be called human flourishing in both dialogues may require obsessions of its own, a willful endurance in the face of the pains and frustrations of uncertainty (in the *Protagoras*) or an *erōs* for the beautiful (in the *Charmides*). It is also clear that neither dialogue ignores the relationship between rationality and forms of political imagination. The sketch of the "science that would save us" in the *Protagoras* culminates in an argument concerning experiences of pleasure in a culture that valorizes the risk and even the sacrifice of life in battle. The belief in the *Charmides* that the virtue of *sōphrosynē* is a science of sciences anticipates the happiness of a city ruled by this kind of knowledge.

Dramatically, both dialogues are contextualized by political events associated with the war. The performative date of the *Protagoras* is 432 BCE, the year immediately prior to the war's outbreak. The *Charmides* begins with Socrates' return from the army laying siege to Potideia, one of the first Athenian campaigns indicted by the Corinthians (Thucydides 1.66–67). Though both conversations occur near the beginning of the war, there are images that point to the war's end. In the *Protagoras* when Socrates identifies the pains that might be associated with the pleasure of saving cities, he lists a series of evils associated with war; it ends with starvation, the condition of the Athenians defeated finally by siege (cf. Xenophon *Hellenica* 2.2.21–23).[67] Socrates' principal interlocutors in the *Charmides* are Critias and Charmides, two of the leaders of the Thirty who subvert Athens's democracy in 404 and rule the city with extreme violence for the next eight months (*Seventh Letter* 342c–d; *Hellenica* 2.3.1–4.43) Thus, the political turbulence surrounding each of these conversations is in part domestic. The *Protagoras* acknowledges the division between the few and the many, and its conceptions of the virtues cluster around these political cultural affiliations. The bracketing political events of the *Charmides*—the beginning of the war and the subversion of the democracy—may connect with deficiencies in *sōphrosynē*.[68]

In both dialogues, rationality is eventually represented as a perfecting rather than a strategic activity. To be sure, rationality—or knowledge (*epistēmē*)—is seriously praised in the *Protagoras* as a tool for calculating the pleasurable or painful outcomes of action choices. However, knowledge can play this instrumental role only as long as the good is identical with the pleasant and only as long as the pleasant and the painful experiences are measurable in ways that allow quantitative comparisons (cf. *Protagoras* 355e–56c). Useful calculation is only possible if there is clarity about purpose. Eventually, the dialogue suggests that such clarity is not available. Consequently, the meanings of both the pleasant and the good are problematized as potential obsessions, as distortions of, rather than guideposts for, rational action. Reason's task becomes sorting through these various meanings and confronting the obsessions that drive them.

The *Charmides* focuses more directly on the ends of action, understood not simply as ends in view but as the psychic condition of flourishing that is signaled by the active practice of the virtues, especially *sōphrosynē*. Within this dialogue, the identification and achievement of this condition is only possible through the discursive practice that Socrates calls philosophy. The initial focus of philosophy, thus understood, is a reflective interrogation of one's own practices or way of life. A person is fully rational not when she does what she believes contributes to her interest, but when she subjects beliefs about her interests to serious and careful criticism. For Socrates, such criticism is discursive for at least two reasons. First, in spite of its self-reflective character, this examination is not monologic, but requires the participation of at least two voices (cf. *Charmides* 172b–c). Second, all conclusions are subject to reconsideration in the face of question or challenge. To the extent that attachments to conceptions of self-interest are held monologically and dogmatically, they have the status of obsessions, and rationality remains at the strategic level. When such obsessions are partnered with drives for control, strategic rationality becomes the attempted exercise of power. In the *Charmides*, Socrates encounters the obsessive use of rationality as power in the person of Critias, whose speeches addressed to Socrates are a prelude to his practices toward Athens.[69]

The perspective on politics that emerges from both dialogues treats political reciprocity as something more than negotiation. Politics is also a context that can enable the interactive examination of interests. Politics or the city needs this sort of examination, for the consequences of being directed by obsessions are, as Thucydides and Plato both recognize, enormously destructive. However, while Plato seems more positive about possibilities for such rational conversations, both of the dialogues considered here recognize that politics does other things besides creating a context for cultural self-examination. Consequently, the relation of politics to rationality is always strained. Thus, while the *Protagoras* illustrates the dangers of subordinating critical rationality to political strategies, the *Charmides* dramatizes the dangers of subjecting politics to a certain kind of obsessive rationality. Unlike rational choice theory's insistence on the presence of an equilibrium as a condition for political rationality, the view emerging from the Platonic dialogues suggests that discursive rationality must maintain a skeptical and potentially destabilizing posture toward political equilibria of all sorts, even as it recognizes the pragmatic need for equilibria within a functional political life.

The Knowledge That Saves Us in the Protagoras

In the *Protagoras*, the value of rationality (the knowledge that would save us [356d]) is asserted within Socrates' attempt to compel the Sophist of the dialogue's title to agree that courage is a kind of science. The broader context is an argument between Socrates and Protagoras about virtue. On one level, this is the well-known problem of whether virtue is one or many, with Socrates apparently arguing for the so-called unity of the virtues.[70] Yet Socrates articulates this "moral theory" within a challenge to Protagoras's educational influence that is highly charged politically.[71]

Protagoras enters Athens as the most successful and renowned of the Sophists, promising to teach young men from the most eminent families "how they might order [their] own affairs better and become most powerful in the city whether in speech or action" (318e–19a). Protagoras thus accepts a psychology of interest that is at least broadly compatible with that presumed by rational choice theory. Individuals are principally motivated to pursue power and influence for the sake of furthering their own personal interests, of "winning" (cf. Downs 1957, 351; Riker 1962, 207–8). Politics is seen as providing both opportunities for and constraints upon self-interested agents. Protagoras teaches strategic skills enabling individuals to pursue their interests more effectively, to win.

Socrates' different view of education is apparent early in the dialogue when he is awakened by a young Athenian, Hippocrates, who is eager to be instructed by the eminent Sophist. He does not wish to become a Sophist himself; he would, indeed, be ashamed to present himself as one before the Greeks (312a).[72] He does, however, wish to be instructed in the things that would be suitable for a free man (*eleutheros*) to learn (*Protagoras* 312b). Eventually, Socrates tells Protagoras (without any challenge from Hippocrates) that the young man's goal is to make a name for himself in the city (316c) and that he wants to obtain the instruction that would further this ambition. Socrates, however, also warns Hippocrates that this sort of education poses great risks for his soul or his character, for souls are well or badly nourished by what they learn (313c). The strategies that Protagoras teaches thus presuppose and reinforce a more comprehensive view of the practices appropriate for a free human being. Socrates' assessement of Protagoras's education involves a critique of the conception of human practice that informs it, and his pragmatic goal in the dialogue is to counter Protagoras's influence among the young.[73]

After Protagoras says that he will teach Hippocrates how to order his own affairs better and become more influential in the city, Socrates redescribes this project as instructing young men in the political art (*politikē technē*) in order to make them good citizens (*agathous politous*).[74] While Protagoras sees no difference between this formulation and his own, Socrates' version gives priority to good citizenship, suggesting that political action or intelligence could be guided by something besides self-interest. On this basis, Socrates could attempt to replace the Sophist's teachings with a valorization of a moral culture fostering civic virtue. Yet Socrates is skeptical as to whether this kind of virtue (*aretē*) is teachable at all. The examples he uses as evidence are cultural, focusing on practices in the assembly and on outcomes of elite education. Socrates' preferred mode of education thus differs both from the sophistic and the cultural. However, the immediate consequence is a challenge to Protagoras's status. If doubts about the teachability of virtue are well-founded, Protagoras is either shamefully ignorant of what he claims he teaches or is a fraud.

This pragmatic contest affects the character of the exchange between the two interlocutors. Seeing this as a two-person game where each has the option of cooperation or defection is incomplete, absent indications of what each of these moves would mean practically. Since Socrates and Protagoras differ dramatically over the nature and goods of education, cooperation would require taking the views of the interlocutor seriously, being open to possibilities of persuasion by an alternative formulation. This would in turn require that views formerly settled and unquestioned become more tentative and less driving. Such cooperation would be manifest in a serious conversation that had as its primary focus the reaching of understanding. Socrates characterizes this conversation as one responsible to the *logos* rather than to interests or agendas (361a). Yet the conversation that does occur is eventually mocked by this same *logos* (361a). Socrates' and Protagoras's interactions are guided not by a commitment to reach understanding but by both parties' attempting to gain control. Protagoras thus calls this conversation a competition in speech (*agōn logōn*) (335a), and Socrates offers asides disclosing his own strategic moves (339e–40a). Their exchanges are marked by threats to defect (335a; 335c–d), and Protagoras ends the discussion by refusing to continue (361d–62a). Based on the experiences in the *Protagoras*, it appears that cooperation is only possible in the presence of agreement about some contestable good; yet attachments to personal goods (Protagoras's love of distinction, Socrates' love of questioning) make such agreements enormously difficult. A conception of politics as the cooperative negotiation of interests within shared institutional parameters thus obscures the greater importance and greater difficulty of investigations into the purposes of collective action.

The priority of this latter set of concerns is implicit in the dialogue's treatment of the virtues. Questions about virtue's teachability lead to the more basic question of what virtue is. In spite of his claim to be a master teacher, Protagoras has never theorized virtue in a serious way. Instead, he takes his bearings from the opinions (*doxa*) of the various cities he visits. From this perspective, the teaching of virtue is the function of cultural institutions (327e–28a). Where Protagoras rises above "all other human beings" (328b) is in his technical ability to impart standards of conduct previously determined. "[I]f there is someone even a bit distinctive in guiding us to virtue, we must give thanks. Such a one I take myself to be, distinguished among all other human beings in helping people to become noble and good" (328b). Protagoras is less master teacher than master strategist. This understanding of his practice suggests a way in which the autonomy of strategic rationality can be reconciled with the constitutive influence of culture. For Protagoras, culture provides authoritative templates for the content of the virtues. Yet strategic rationality is preeminent (and Protagoras deserves the high fees he charges), because neither strategic rationality nor Protagoras's distinctive expertise is subordinate to any higher form of reasoning. However, the problematic character of strategic rationality is eventually reflected in the ambiguous, even contradictory, character of Protagoras's strategic teaching.

In relying on conventions for substantive accounts of the virtues, Protagoras effectively discounts the possibility that virtue is controversial, that a nonstrategic *logos* might be needed to investigate more seriously the natures of "the noble and the good." While Socrates' arguments are often read as providing a conclusive theory of the unity of the virtues, they can also be interpreted as pointing to the need for a rationality whose structure is less systematic and whose discoveries are less conclusive.[75] What results is less a theory of virtue than an indication of why virtue needs to be taken seriously as a problem.

In response to Socrates' questions about whether virtue is one or many, Protagoras says that virtue is a single thing, with justice, moderation, and piety as its parts. In spite of the fact that these qualities are parts of a single, but complex, whole (analogous to the face), one can possess some but not others. Protagoras specifically claims that one can be brave but unjust, or just but not wise (329e). With these examples Protagoras adds courage and wisdom (the greatest [*to megiston*] of the parts) to the virtues already enumerated, and both are introduced in connection with the practice of injustice.[76] Protagoras thus acknowledges that the reliance on cultural standards for identifying the virtues is unreliable, for culture is neither consistent nor uncontestable. To the extent that justice condenses the virtues needed for political stability, wisdom and courage can be sources of disruption, in the name of either a subculture that rejects political equality or a powerful individual who asserts himself against the community. In one of the many ironies of the *Protagoras*, the conversation about civic virtue occurs in the presence of one of Athens's most violent oligarchs (Critias) and perhaps its most spectacular traitor (Alcibiades).[77]

Socrates relies on such tensions in his attempt to expose Protagoras's problematic status as an educator. In questioning Protagoras about the relationship among the parts of virtue, Socrates secures unjustified agreements—first, that justice and piety are closely related; and, second, that wisdom and moderation are identical. He then asks Protagoras about the possibility of being well-advised while being unjust (333b–c). Protagoras's reluctance to agree is disingenuous, since he has already offered the converse case—being just but not wise—as one instance of possessing some virtues but not others. The discussion turns heated when Socrates raises the broader question of how one fares well (*eu prattein*) (333d). I believe that Protagoras's anger stems from a recognition of the pragmatic dilemma that he confronts as one who claims to benefit his students as a teacher of virtue. If he teaches the best strategies for private advancement, he reinforces the suspicion that the Sophists undercut the civic culture (cf. *Meno* 91c). If he teaches obedience to the laws, he constrains his students' pursuits of personal benefit. Protagoras fails as a master strategist, because he is unable to accommodate two incompatible conceptions of the good, which generate two incompatible strategies. In this light, the autonomy of strategic rationality is itself compromised, for it requires and is complicated by a more reflective rationality capable of sorting through contradictory visions of well-being.

However, the autonomy of strategic rationality and, therefore, of Protagoras's strategic expertise could be preserved if human purposes could be understood so as to exclude deep controversy, through a reliance not on variable cultures but on a nature whose imperatives were too strong and too obvious to reject. This possibility is implicit in the argument in the last part of the dialogue.

After an extensive interlude in which the dialogic community of the *Protagoras* unravels and is then reestablished, Socrates and Protagoras return to an investigation of the virtues. By now Protagoras admits that while all of the other virtues are closely associated, courage somehow stands apart, for "you will find many among humanity who are unjust, unholy, licentious and ignorant, yet who stand out as being most courageous" (349d). Socrates, however, eventually compels Protagoras to agree that courage can be traced to a knowledge of the pleasurable or painful consequences of action choices (356d–57b). From one perspective, Socrates' proposal shrinks knowledge to an instrumental science of pleasant things. Yet it also preserves the power of knowledge as Protagoras understands it, for there is no other form of rationality (and no other rational person) to which strategic rationality (and Protagoras) is subordinate. The power of this form of knowledge depends, however, on the equation of a particular kind of pleasure with the good—namely, pleasurable experiences that can be measured and compared quantitatively (356a). As the discussion proceeds, this understanding of pleasure is exposed as incomplete and distorted.[78] Once other sources of pleasure are introduced, the nature of the good becomes more problematic, needing a different form of rationality if knowledge is truly to save us.

Socrates then turns the examination of the relationship between courage and the other virtues into a discussion of the good. Protagoras asserted earlier that goods are so fluid and various that no established conclusions about the human good, as such, were possible (334a). Now, however, Protagoras accepts statements about the good that apply to human beings universally. This good is the experience of pleasure and the absence of pain (354d–e). While Protagoras initially insists that this assessment needs qualification, that pleasures must be of the noble sort (351c–d), it becomes clear that the thesis asserting the identity of the good and the pleasant is Protagoras's own. To the extent that Socrates argues for the power of a certain kind of knowledge in relation to this good, he is revealing the basis and content of Protagoras's latent view of knowledge.[79]

The hedonist thesis that the good and the pleasant are identical is the basis of both an explanatory theory of motivation and a normative theory of ethical naming. In the first capacity, this theory of the good offers an account of the ends guiding action choices. A given action is rational if it successfully secures pleasure and avoids pain. Thus, the commonly expressed view, to which Protagoras first subscribes, that there can be base (*aischros*) or bad pleasures and admirable (*kalos*) or good pains, really means that some momentary enjoyments lead to greater pains (like drinking leading to hangovers) while some momentary pains produce greater pleasures (like exercising leading to health) (353c–54c). Socrates complicates analyses of the hedonic consequences of such action choices when he introduces "the saving of cities" and "ruling over others" (354b) as two of the pleasurable consequences of painful military training. This raises questions about how the individual and the community relate to one another as units of analysis for assessing experiences of pleasure and pain. It also introduces the possibility that there may be different kinds of pleasurable and painful experiences even at the individual level (the pleasures of anticipating the safety of one's fellow citizens or the glory of one's posthumous reputation versus those of physical safety and material gratification).[80] Yet Socrates and Protagoras obscure these complications when they agree that pleasures and pains can be calculated and compared along a single quantitative scale, where there is no unworthiness (*anaxia*) "in pleasure and pain except in excess or deficiency of one against the other, when one becomes larger (*meizō*), the other smaller (*smikotera*), or more (*pleiō*) and fewer (*elattō*), or greater (*mallon*) or less (*hētton*)" (356a).[81] This enables Socrates and Protagoras to recognize the preeminent value of a calculative science we might call hedonics (357a–b).

According to this utilitarian psychology, all forms of ethical naming (the good and the bad, the noble and the shameful) are tied to the contributions that action choices make to enjoyment or suffering (358b). Actions are noble or praiseworthy to the extent that they increase such pleasant experiences. Taken literally, Socrates' proposals would replace politics and culture with expertise. Politics is eliminated or marginalized, because the theory of motivation at work here is essentially monologic; it compares prospective outcomes of action choices not only according to a single scale, but also from the perspective of a single agent.[82] Unlike rational choice theory, Socrates' sketch of hedonics ignores interactions (exchanges, games) among self-interested individuals, each of whom is motivated to maximize pleasure. Problems of structuring cooperation or managing defections are not considered. Likewise, the cultural identification of practices as noble or shameful is now traced back to a natural standard. Because comparisons among pleasurable and painful experiences can, in principle, be quantified exactly, contentious claims about nobility and shame can be settled scientifically. Given Protagoras's pretensions, it is hardly surprising that he accepts the consequences of Socrates' argument enthusiastically (358a), for Socrates elevates strategic rationality as hedonics to directive status and identifies the Sophists as "the teachers of these things." Yet the argument has serious flaws.

Difficulties emerge when Socrates attempts to show that courage follows a particular application of hedonics. This argument depends on the strict reversibility of the claim that whatever is pleasant is noble into the claim that whatever is noble is pleasant. As noted, the first formulation reduces cultural designations of the noble and the shameful to individual experiences of pleasure and pain. From this perspective, if courage is to be seen as noble (as virtually all cultural sources attest), then its practice must result in the agent's experiencing a greater quantity of pleasure over pain. In order to be truly courageous, rather than ignorant or insane, an agent confronting intense danger must competently practice hedonics. From this perspective, cowardice is not a failure of heart or spirit (*thymos*), but a mistake in calculation (*logistikē*); cowards are ignorant of the pleasures to be experienced in such threatening situations as combat. If this reasoning is accepted, courage is not distinct from the other virtues but depends upon the effective presence of calculational knowledge, a *rational* choice. Yet this characterization of hedonics eliminates any attachment to a common interest compromising individual experiences of pleasure as a basis for true courage. If what matters most are individually experienced felt satisfactions, then it is difficult to see why anyone would sacrifice himself or herself to further the aggregate satisfactions of others, however close in blood or culture. If the relevant measures of comparability across pleasures and pains are quantities of experienced gratifications or sufferings, then the implied importance of other types of rewards, accessible via the praise of peers, for example, is a fabrication, psychic income as sucker's payoff.

Yet Socrates' reliance on the integrity of cultural designations within the second formulation (whatever is noble is pleasant) reintroduces the ambiguities that hedonics was supposed to eliminate. These complicate discoveries of both appropriate units of analysis and appropriate units of hedonic measurement. While the first formulation required that common goods or interests be reduced to individual experiences, the second makes the normative integrity of an ethical community dominant, for it is the community's standard of nobility that is the basis for assessing the pleasurability of an action choice. And while the first formulation presumed that the only basis for comparing experiences of pleasure and pain was quantitative, the second includes the possibility of qualitative variations as well. In light of these complications, neither the pleasant nor the noble seems any longer to be commensurable along a single scale. Consequently, the middle term common to both formulations (358d, 360a)—the good—moves from being transparent to being perplexing. Neither subjective perceptions of self-gratification nor cultural norms seem capable of settling the question of the good, for each perspective is vulnerable in principle to destabilizing alternative accounts. The apparent superiority awarded to Protagoras's strategic rationality is now shown to be only apparent, for the science that would save us cannot do so without a rationality that takes the perplexing character of the good seriously.[83]

This sort of rationality is not embedded in a science structured like hedonics, but in the discursive and critical practices of Socrates. Eventually, this form of rationality reveals the inadequacy of the science that Socrates has outlined. If virtue were (craft) knowledge, it could be taught, and Socrates remains attached to his earlier suspicion that virtue is not (in this way?) teachable (361a–b).[84] His response to this confusion (which is certainly experienced as a kind of pain) is to insist that he and Protagoras take up the question of virtue again. In this respect, Socrates' practice challenges the explicit conclusion of the argument, for he displays a kind of courage in the absence of wisdom.[85] While Protagoras declines the invitation, Socrates' commitment suggests that the rationality that would save us is not calculational knowledge, but a more discursive and less systematic form of philosophy. As discourse, this kind of philosophy respects politics and culture in a way that hedonics does not. Since this form of rationality depends on the interaction of dialogic partners, it cannot be a monologic form of calculation. And the interactions it requires are not negotiations of interests, but more comprehensive examinations of the purposes informing individual and collective actions.

However, there are also incongruities between Socrates' discursive rationality and the priorities of political culture.[86] The critical rationality practiced by Socrates reflects a continued refusal to be satisfied with apparently settled conclusions about human goods, virtues, and practices. Yet cultures effectively function in the presence of agreements on shared priorities, and politics is oriented toward collective decision. Consequently, there are limits to the compatibility of critical rationality with the practices central to common life. In this light, both critical rationality and politics may come to see each other's priorities as obsessions. To the extent that critical rationality is concerned to diminish this opposition, it avoids categorizing all constitutive political needs as obsessions, while not ignoring their obsessive potentials. Socrates' rational engagement with politics is, therefore, neither subordinate (like Protagoras's strategic instruction) nor hegemonic (like some readings of Socrates' science of hedonics), but ironic or critical. Here irony is the attempt to provide healthy reservations about the content of collective action without losing appreciation for its need and value. This ironic posture is applied even to the political activities that are most fundamental to Socrates' project. At the end of the *Protagoras*, what many would see as the premise of Plato's political philosophy, the teachability of virtue, is subjected to Socratic doubt. To the extent that Socrates subordinates strategic rationality to a more comprehensive rational investigation, then, it is a form of investigation characterized by irony. Yet this irony is neither psychologically disconnected from cultural education nor politically irrelevant to collective action.[87] These features of Socratic rationality are apparent within the dialogue *Charmides* as Socrates confronts a form of political rationality that is very different from the calculations of Protagoras.

The Dangerous Illusion of Control in the Charmides

The incompleteness of a strategic science of pleasure and pain could elicit an intellectual response very different from critical interrogation. This alternative would posit a directive rationality capable of guiding human practices in accordance with a definitive vision of the good. From a certain perspective, rational choice theory potentially *is* this kind of science, for it outlines the structure of a well-ordered society, rather than simply a functional one (cf. Buchanan and Tullock 1965, 306; Axelrod 1984, 126; Hardin 1995, chap. six; and Putnam 1993, 177–78). From this perspective, rational choice theory would deal with the border problem by overcoming rather than by engaging the limitations of strategic thinking.

At the same time, this aspect of rational choice theory also encounters challenges. It could, for example, be criticized for failing to acknowledge the scope of its intentions—namely, that it deals not simply, as it claims, with the effectiveness of means but also with the rationality of ends. To the extent that this is unacknowledged, rational choice theory's vision of a well-ordered society is left unexamined, even as it exerts significant intellectual force. More importantly, endorsing the rationality of substantive political goals or social arrangements displaces the political activities of citizens with the scientific or technical conclusions of experts. Though politics continues to involve the generation and application of power, political rationality is stripped of the language needed to scrutinize the public purposes that that power serves.

The dialogue *Charmides* represents Socrates' encounter with a directive rationality anticipated by the speeches and practices of the future tyrant, Critias. Unlike most of the voices within rational choice theory, Critias openly endorses a particular conception of a well-ordered society. Socrates' critique focuses not so much on making what is implicit explicit, but on showing why Critias's conception of substantive rationality dangerously remains at the strategic level, for Critias angrily resists all of Socrates' attempts to bring his substantive vision of the human good under critical scrutiny. In this respect, Critias's conceptions of human and social goods remain obsessions. These border rational choice not through limitation but through distortion. Socrates' alternative remains a rationality that critically examines ends or ways of life. The resulting conception of politics emphasizes not the authoritative control of the expert, but the rational scrutiny of the thoughtful citizen.

Like the *Protagoras*, the *Charmides* is Socrates' representation of an earlier conversation with an unnamed friend. Within that conversation, his interlocutors are his close companion, Chaerephon, and two of the men who become leaders of the Thirty, Plato's uncles Critias and Charmides. The explicit concern is to examine the nature and value of the virtue *sōphrosynē*, often translated (problematically) as "temperance" or "moderation." The dramatic context brings the dialogue closer even than the *Protagoras* to the narrative of Thucydides. Socrates has just returned from the army laying siege to Potideia, a colony of the Corinthians and a subject city within the Athenian empire. In this respect, Potideia may stand dramatically for the war itself. Yet Socrates moves quickly away from war stories to inquiries about the current condition of philosophy. This moves commentators such as Drew Hyland to suggest that the *sōphrosynē* praised by Socrates may be oblivious to human horrors (Hyland 1981, 28). A less severe reading of Socrates' concern is that it is an indication that war should be fought for the sake of peace and that wars are defensible primarily in light of the peaceful activities that they secure. In this light, Socrates' treatment of war differs from Thucydides' in both obvious and subtle ways.

Obviously, Socrates focuses on the educational activities of a political culture and on its support for what he calls philosophy as being "more worthy of speech" than the great motions or energies of war. Yet why philosophy is central to the peaceful activities of a political culture and, indeed, what philosophy itself means are no clearer in the first pages of the *Charmides* than the reasons for the war's importance are in the first twenty-three chapters of Thucydides. In parallel, Thucydides' treatment of the war's importance in book 1 moves from a reliance on Periclean criteria of motion and greatness to a focus on the destruction that Periclean rhetoric obscures.[88]

More fundamentally, Socrates and Thucydides might differ over both the content of and the path toward the deepest truths about human beings. For Thucydides, it is war, the harshest and most violent teacher, that reveals the destructiveness of human nature (3.82.2, 3.84.2–3). War exposes the inadequacies of rational choice theory by uncovering the obsessions that pathologize rationality. War's effectiveness at disclosing reality suggests, more generally, that the human condition can be most accurately discovered under circumstances of regime or cultural stress. One of the consequences of this stress is the destruction of cultural resources for conversation about the challenges that human beings continually face. For Socrates, in contrast, it is philosophy understood as discursive investigation that examines possibilities for nobility and traces the ways in which noble things are also useful (*Charmides* 175a–b). As such, philosophy reveals the incompleteness of rational choice theory by discovering the need to guide usefulness by a more reflective understanding of nobility or excellence. Because philosophy is discursive, it draws on cultural meanings that it examines and criticizes with the aid of cultural partners. For Socrates, then, the human condition cannot be most accurately characterized under conditions of political stress, but rather under those of a certain kind of cultural activity.

Yet Thucydides and the Socrates of the *Charmides* may not be as distant from each other as they first appear. One of Thucydides' most important purposes may be to create a cultural resource that can represent both the experiences and lessons of war, absent the hideous experience of war itself.[89] To the extent that certain cultural forms—for example, those that foster Athens's rule and Sparta's fear—contribute to the onset of war, Thucydides' project could be interpreted as a kind of cultural therapy, providing a text or a *logos* that works against these more damaging influences. Similarly, Socrates' practice of philosophy in the *Charmides* is bracketed by intense political violence. Just as Potideia condenses the war, the presence of Critias and Charmides images the defeat and the tyranny. To the extent that both war and tyranny emerge from political obsessions, a philosophy that envisages the practice of *sōphrosynē* may offer the faint prospect of an antidote.

However, insofar as Thucydides accepts the express content of Diodotus's speech on Mytilene, he seems to see possibilities for moderation and reasonableness as dismal, primarily because of the overwhelming influence of the passions. From this perspective, the development of reasonableness seems possible only under the unattainable condition of the silence of the passions. The *Charmides* suggests that such a demand is too severe, if not misdirected, for philosophy seems to require the presence of (and not merely control over) strong emotions. Consequently, while one of rational choice theory's errors may be to leave the influence of the obsessions unexamined, another may be to ignore or marginalize the kind of rationality capable of working constructively with the emotional dimensions of the psyche.

Although Socrates' express concern is with philosophy, the conversation's immediate surroundings have more to do with gymnastics and, eventually, with erotics. The narrated dialogue occurs in the palaestra where the adolescent Charmides' first appearance elicits fascinated gazes, especially from the boys. While Chaerephon acknowledges the beauty of Charmides' face, he tells Socrates that if he stripped naked he would appear altogether faceless, so striking is his figure or form. The responses of both the boys and Chaerephon appreciate Charmides' beauty in ways that depersonalize him. Socrates implicitly criticizes this attitude when he responds that Charmides would indeed be irresistible (literally, a male with whom no one could do battle) if he also has a beautiful soul. The concern with the soul turns the discussion back toward philosophy, yet this return presumes a continued influence of affect.[90] Socrates first says that he is incapable of measuring differences between the beautiful (154b). This is not because Socrates is insensitive to beauty, but because all who have reached this stage of life seem beautiful to him. As Socrates begins his conversation with Charmides, he sees beneath his cloak and gazes into his eyes. While the glimpse at Charmides' nakedness causes Socrates to catch fire, it is his eyes (the windows of the soul [*Phaedrus* 255c]) that rivet him (155c–d).[91] Socrates' conversational or philosophical attempt to identify the quality of Charmides' soul is thus accompanied by a continued fascination with his beauty in all of its complex manifestations. By the dialogue's end Socrates is ambiguously disposed toward him, and apparently only a form of coercion can continue their association.

In this light, Socrates' practice reflects a circularity between emotion as fascination with beauties and rationality as judgment about souls. Emotion here is not simply a prompt or call for rationality (a need to cope with potential sources of obsession, the beauty against which no battle can be waged) but a constitutive focus that gives rationality its substance. The conversation is about whether Charmides' soul is as beautiful as his body. Socrates' judgment is not a disinterested verdict on Charmides's soul, but a way of managing ongoing interactions that must be understood at least partially in affective terms. Insofar as the point of such interactions is some good, that good cannot be disconnected from emotional experience. The good of acting with knowledge is to do well and to be happy (173d). At the same time, Socrates' emotions are capable of instruction or improvement in light of the outcomes of judgment. Socrates' attraction to Charmides is influenced by what he discovers in conversation, suggesting that the attractiveness of others can be enhanced or diminished (*as* attractions) by our thoughtful discoveries or judgments about them. Beauty is as beauty does. Affections or passions that are less erotically focused, such as anger, fear, pride, or ambition, are thus potentially subject to the same kind of education or criticism (righteous anger, baseless pride). Thus, when Socrates asks Charmides to form an opinion about the *sōphrosynē* that may be within himself, he is not simply asking him to provide an intellectual characterization of a psychic condition that persists before and after the intellectual effort that engages it. Rather, this effort has at least the potential of influencing the character of that psychic state. The sense that whatever *sōphrosynē* we have in our souls needs to be reflexively perceived and examined is one way in which its character can be improved. Socrates examines the meaning of *sōphrosynē* first with Charmides and then with Critias. Charmides' formulations are derivative, relying either on cultural templates or on the opinions of his guide, Critias. These initial proposals also dissolve any connection between *sōphrosynē* and intelligence. Appropriately, Charmides exhibits very little willingness or ability to defend his opinions in serious question and answer. Critias's more sophisticated formulations originate in a confidence about his own abilities and powers. While his understanding of *sōphrosynē* begins with doing (*prattein*), he moves very quickly to knowing (*gignoskein*) or science (*epistēmē*), and *sōphrosynē* becomes a kind of rationality.

Socrates follows his wondering whether Charmides' soul is as beautiful as his body by asking him about the quality of soul that Critias says he possesses. The uncertainty about both Charmides and *sōphrosynē* is premised on the suspect nature of high cultural categories. In a subculture that valorizes genealogy, Charmides' noble descent would be sufficient proof of his excellence (157d–58a).[92] Yet the possibility exists that Charmides might be lacking (*endeēs*) in virtue despite his lineage (158c). At the same time, Socrates' question does not imply that completely conclusive answers about either the virtue or the person are available. Indeed, the discussion continues because of strong uncertainty (on Charmides' part) with regard to both questions (What is *sōphrosynē*? Can I find it in myself?). Within the dialogue, this uncertainty is prompted by the conflicting opinions of the surrounding culture. If Charmides says that he does not possess *sōphrosynē*, he will be effectively calling Critias and the "many others" (*allous pollous*) who say he does liars. If he does claim to possess the virtue, he will praise himself, and so seem oppressive (*epachthes*) (158c–d). Socrates redescribes this conflicted external direction as an internal dissatisfaction with set opinions and therefore as a promising beginning to a joint (*koinē*) inquiry or dialogue.

Charmides' first definition of *sōphrosynē* is "quietness" (*hēsychiotēs*), and his second is "modesty" or "edification" (*aidōs*). L. B. Carter makes a convincing case that both endorsements reflect Charmides' close attachment to Spartan values (L. B. Carter 1986, 56ff.).[93] Socrates refutes both almost as quickly as Charmides expresses them.[94] One reason for his success may be that Charmides' attachments to the qualities identified are extremely tenuous. In each case, the proposed definition is agreed (by Charmides) to be incompatible with nobility (*to kalon*). Regarding quietness, Charmides agrees that physical and psychic activities done quickly and intensely are more noble (*kallion*) than those done quietly and slowly (159b–60b). Regarding modesty, Charmides is dissuaded by being reminded of the noble (*kalos*) statement of Homer's Telemachus that *aidōs* is not good (*ouk agathē*) for a needy man (*kechrēmenō andri*) (161a).

Charmides thus takes his bearings from a certain understanding of nobility that needs to be inferred from his own situation and responses. He himself is characterized by a striking beauty (*to kalon*, as well) that allows him to stand out from among all of the other males at the palaestra, and Critias says that Charmides is distinctive in both wisdom and beauty (154e–55a). This sense of *to kalon* as conspicuous attractiveness also informs Charmides' own sense of the noble. Doing things quickly and therefore nobly is the basis of someone's being held worthy of praise (*epainou axios*) (160a). Thus, even though Charmides has not succeeded in perceiving and articulating the sense of *sōphrosynē* as it might be found within himself, he does reveal his own attachment to virtue understood as the collection of qualities that make one stand out as praiseworthy. In one respect, of course, this disconnects Charmides from cultural conceptions (vaguely Spartan) of *sōphrosynē* as quietness or reverence. Yet this understanding of nobility also reflects Charmides' positioning within an Athenian subculture that values both beauty and achievement. Thus, there are also broadly political implications attached to this conception of nobility. Intriguingly, the general context of the quotation from Homer is Odysseus's prospective fight to the death with the suitors over control of Ithaca, a home that must be retaken by force (*Odyssey* 17.347). Within the future turbulence within Athens, it is likely that Charmides and Critias would see themselves and their colleagues in the places occupied by Telemachus and Odysseus, with the democrats playing the roles of the usurping suitors (cf. *Seventh Letter* 324c–d). Accordingly, nobility would emerge as an aristocratic quality, with *aidōs* belonging properly to the chastened many.

The source of Charmides' final definition of *sōphrosynē* is initially more mysterious than either the manners and morals of convention or the sayings of the poets. Charmides has heard someone say that *sōphrosynē* is the doing of one's own things (*to ta heautou prattein*) (162b). There is an immediate, provocative connection with the *Republic*, for this is the definition of justice on which Socrates and Glaucon agree in the second half of book 4 (443c–44a). Socrates' response to Charmides raises the question that could properly be asked about the *Republic*'s definition: What precisely is the nature or content of one's own? The discussion in the *Republic* points to the locus of one's own as the soul.

In the *Charmides*, however, Socrates' initial perplexities stem from observations about the practices of various arts. It would be ridiculous if individuals were expected to weave their own clothes, cobble their own shoes, and so on (162e). The obvious alternative is to have artisans produce specialized goods both for themselves and for others through exchange. Thus, Socrates points to need as the origin of communities, a claim made more explicit in the story of the beginnings of the first city in speech in book 2 of the *Republic*. In the *Charmides* Socrates says that a city in which specialization and exchange occur is well-ordered (*eu oikeisthai*). In a way, this would be a more developed version of the *Republic*'s first city, and insofar as either requires a form of government, it would most likely be a basic democracy (Glaucon would call it a primitive or a swinish one) of relatively equal craftsmen/householders. Charmides does not recognize that in important respects each of these specialized craftsmen still does "his own." Consequently, his borrowed third definition is now ridiculed as something offered by "some fool" (162a). Finding this insulting, Critias intervenes.

Socrates conciliates by suggesting that the definition might be seen as a riddle (*ainigma*) (162b). From a Socratic perspective, this could be high praise, for riddles can stimulate, even as they perplex. Critias, however, treats this as a challenge, signaling that differences between his and Socrates' attitudes toward conversation are central to the dialogue's pragmatics. Socrates tells the *hetairos* to whom this conversation is being narrated that Critias had for the longest time been bristling for competition, lusting after recognition or honor (*palai agōniōn kai philotimōs*) (162c). This passion immediately distinguishes Critias from the modest craftsmen who would inhabit Socrates' well-ordered city. Socrates' different attitude toward conversation will suggest that there are needs other than those for material security or competitive distinction.

Consistent with his concern for preeminence, Critias responds to Socrates' concerns about the craftsmen doing "their own" by shifting the focus of the discussion to the differences between doing (*ergein*) and acting (*prattein*), on the one hand, and making (*poiein*), on the other. "Hesiod. . . . too held that making (*poiein*) is something other than doing (*prattein*) and working (*ergein*), and although a thing made sometimes becomes a disgrace (*oneidos*) when it does not come to be along with the beautiful, a work (*ergon*) is never a disgrace at all. And things made (*poioumena*) beautifully and advantageously he called works (*erga*), and such makings he called workings and doings" (163b–c). The political structure consistent with this distinction is a society characterized not by general equality but by strict hierarchy. However, the basis of the distinction is not as straightforward as it appears. Initially, Critias seems to subordinate making to doing and acting. In terms of the classes of citizens in the *Republic*'s best city, this elevates the activities of the guardians over the functions of the craftsmen. But Critias eventually wishes to turn those "makings" (*poioumena*) that come into being along with the noble or the beautiful (*to kalon*) into standards for identifying true doings and workings (163c; cf. Hyland 1981, 22–23, 84–85).[95] This creates, in more tangible terms, grounds for distinguishing between the shameful (*aischra*) arts, such as shoemaking, salt fish selling, and prostitution, and those makings that come into being along with the noble (163c). Under these circumstances, it is less likely that the well-ordered city would be egalitarian with transfers of products occurring through exchange. The hierarchy of makers implies that the practitioners of the lowly arts would furnish their products to the makers of the noble. And it would presumably also exclude shoemakers, salt fish sellers, or prostitutes from enjoying things beautifully made. Like Thrasymachus's just citizens in book 1 of the *Republic*, the practitioners of the lowly arts work for another's good (*Republic* 343b–d).

Critias implies more generally that a well-ordered city is supervised by the best maker. While Critias indicates that such an arrangement would be good owing to its conformity with some external standard of the noble or the beautiful, Socrates says that Critias's understanding of the beautiful (and the good) is drawn from his conception of his own interest (*Charmides* 163d). What Socrates wishes to press, however, is the role that intelligence plays in such an ordering. Critias agrees that no competent artisan could be ignorant of the benefits that his art provides (164a). Socrates eventually represents this awareness in radically perfectionist terms, proposing that craftsmen such as doctors must "of necessity know" (*gignōskein anankē*) when their treatments will be advantageous and when not (164b). This knowledge of the best maker excludes vulnerability to ill luck. In a way that reflects his tendency to see the noble and the good through the prism of his own interests, Critias calls this kind of intellectual power self-knowledge (*to gignōskein heauton*), so that the good that (for example) the doctor knows in treating a patient is really his own (164d). Even Thrasymachus in book 1 of the *Republic* had seen the prudent doctor practicing not one art but two: medicine and moneymaking (*Republic* 346b–c). Critias's enthusiasm for this sort of self-knowledge bespeaks complete confidence in the powers of the highest intelligence to know both its own good and how to secure it, an architectonic science of ends and means. Consequently, he does not read the inscription at Delphi,"know thyself" (*gnōthi sauton*), as an *ainigma* as most do, for he has supreme confidence in his own ability to detect its meaning (*Charmides* 164d–e). Perhaps it is reasonable to see some inabilities to predict as culpable, such as Critias's and Charmides' failure to see that they might play the suitors' roles to the democrats' Odysseus.

The conception of rationality informing Critias' revised account of *sōphrosynē* thus seems strikingly different from the strategic intelligence portrayed in the *Protagoras*. Critias's science is not instrumental but directive. The superiority of Critias's rationality does not rest on the fact that the only realms of experience standing above it resist investigation by any form of reason. Rather, Critias's rationality is capable of penetrating all forms of experience so that no *ainigmai* remain. Consequently, while Protagorean reason is destined to serve affections susceptible to stimulation or affliction, Critias's rationality is defined by agency. Standards for practices and deeds are set by acts of making. Finally, while Protagoras's understanding of rationality was unable to negotiate conflicts between the few and the many, Critias's implies a societal hierarchy that both separates and regulates noble and shameful forms of making. In this respect, the deficiencies of Protagoras's strategic rationality are overcome by a more substantive or teleological reason, not one that questions the purposes of strategy, but one that settles them.

Yet this understanding of rationality shares at least two deficiencies with Protagoras's. It is, first, a monologic rationality whose discoveries are accessible to isolated and gifted practitioners. Second, it is informed by compulsions that its monologic character insulates from critical scrutiny. Socrates exposes both deficiencies when he endorses a self-critical form of rationality within an interactive discourse in which Critias is asked to participate. Critias reinforces Socrates' criticism in his own responses, for he constantly attempts to absorb Socrates' objections within an ever expanding realm of controlling rationality and attacks Socrates' commitment to discursive self-criticism as an obsession of its own.

Socrates' challenges to Critias's views on *sōphrosynē* focus on the problems associated with calling it a science (165c).[96] All of Critias claims are driven by the premise that *sōphrosynē* is a structured and systematic body of thought enabling control. The emerging Socratic view, however, is that *sōphrosynē* is a reflective and interrogatory intellectual activity insisting on self-criticism.[97] These two different understandings of rationality thus generate two different visions of the common good or two different implications for what I have earlier called political imagination. At one point, Socrates hypothesizes that if we knew both what we knew and what we did not know, we would be much more capable of ordering not only our own lives, but also those of the people we ruled. Ordering in this case involves assigning suitable tasks to the appropriate practitioners, a top-down rather than a bottom-up version of the *Republic*'s discovery of the value of having one person do one job (*Republic* 370b). This ordering would be perfectly reliable, removing or abolishing error (*hamartia*) or, from another point of view, correcting one of the fundamental ills of the human condition (*Charmides* 171d–72a) (cf. Hyland 1981, 128). Critias enthusiastically endorses this description of the healthy common life in which Socrates uses a variant of ruling (*archein*) or leading (*hēgeomai*) four times in fifteen lines of the Loeb Greek text. Critias's own political future as leader of the Thirty suggests a kind of ruling and leading that is rigidly structured and, when necessary, violently applied. Using the language of rational choice theory, the equilibrium that arranges this polity is not reached through the negotiation of individual political agents, but through the application of a controlling and coercive political science. Socrates' response proposes a version of knowing both what we know and what we do not know that makes both the nature of our good and what it means to know or not to know it into explicit problems. This requires an openness to learning that is intricately linked to the practice of interrogation. "And now I say that this is what I am making (*poiein*), an investigation of the argument mostly for my own sake, but perhaps also for the sake of my other associates. Or don't you think that the common good (*koinon agathon*) for almost all human beings is that each of the things that are should come to appear as it really is?" (166d).[98] Here, equilibrium is understood neither as the result of individual acts of bargaining nor as the product of applied political science understood as definite making, but as the continued and revisable process of sorting through proposals about the content and value of collective choice under conditions of agreement and difference.

Critias elevates rationality to this level of control because he ignores or dismisses the question that Socrates had seen as crucial in his first exchange with Charmides: the question of the quality of the individual's soul or moral identity. Eliminating any puzzles about the soul's or the individual's good makes it easier for Critias to interpret self-knowledge as knowing what one does and does not know, an appreciation of and thus a power over intellectual resources. Since no other form of self-knowledge stands above a knowledge of capabilities, perfectly known and executed capabilities can support beautiful makings that do not require rational criticism. Control is an unexamined obsession. To the extent that Socrates is able to reveal the ignorance behind Critias's position, he potentially turns attention back toward *sōphrosynē* as a problematic condition of the soul and therefore toward the need for a rationality that is dissatisfied and questioning rather than confident and powerful.

Socrates says that by calling *sōphrosynē* a science, Critias implies that it has, like the other sciences, a proper object and a distinct outcome, in the way that medicine deals with the organism to produce health (165c–d).

From Critias's perspective, this acknowledgment would turn *sōphrosynē* into one science among many and potentially construe its power as derivative and instrumental. Critias therefore rejects the analogy, instead likening *sōphrosynē* to the more conceptually precise sciences of calculation or geometry (165e). Socrates counters that even these sciences have numbers and figures as foci. By itself, this response likewise ignores the question of *sōphrosynē*'s benefit. Were its concern identified as the soul, however, its benefit might be seen (in a way analogous to medicine's) as a certain kind of therapy or education (cf. *Gorgias* 504b–e). Critias himself takes this direction when he claims next that *sōphrosynē*'s concern is with itself. Yet in continuing to see *sōphrosynē* as a science, Critias effectively characterizes the self as the repository of technical capacity and therefore indicates that this self's perfected science can be used architectonically as a precise measure to test other forms of knowing. While *sōphrosynē* is therefore the science of itself and of the other sciences (166b–c), it is only superficially turned inward, for there is no sense in which its concern for itself is puzzled enough to prompt self-examination. Yet Socrates doggedly insists on retaining a problematizing inward focus, for he now doubts the possibility of the self-reflexivity that the science of self (*as* science) presupposes. All of Socrates' questions imply that *sōphrosynē* is self-reflexive only if it is understood as a quality or character of the soul. This reminder of the importance of the soul, were it to succeed, would not make the possibility of self-reflexivity transparent as much as it would show why the question of self-reflexivity is so crucial for our well-being, for self-reflexivity is the condition and the practice of the examined life (cf. Hyland 1981, 124). All of the examples that Socrates uses to suggest the impossibility of self-reflexivity—sight, hearing, all of the senses, desire, wish, love, fear, and opinion—can be understood as activities of the soul.[99] And the problem that Socrates identifies within the absurdity of Critias's proposal (if something is stronger than itself, it is also weaker than itself) is clarified in the *Republic* by a reflection on the soul (430e–31a). Yet the discovery that the soul is "that which has by nature the power to relate to itself" (*Charmides* 169a) identifies the soul as a problem or a question (How can it be both stronger and weaker than itself?) and therefore diminishes the extent to which a conclusive science of the soul could be hegemonic over the other sciences.

Socrates follows by questioning how the hegemonic science of sciences that Critias envisages can benefit human beings (171d). If taken seriously, Socrates' question would lead to a searching examination of what human benefit involves and to the identification of the soul as the most important locus of benefit and harm. However, this sort of examination would require a form of rationality very different from the model upon which Critias relies. As a standard that tests scientific credentials, *sōphrosynē* as Critias characterizes it can only determine whether a given practitioner thinks scientifically (or not), but it cannot distinguish the scientific practitioner of medicine from the scientific practitioner of justice (170b) or, for that matter, the scientific practitioner of rhetoric who pretends to be a doctor from the scientific practitioner of medicine itself (171c; cf. *Gorgias* 456a–c). This means that the knowledge of the good provided by medicine or justice will be provided by the relevant science itself, without the contribution or supervision of a science of sciences (*Charmides* 174c). *Sōphrosynē* could apparently provide benefits of its own if it were specifically focused on good and evil, so that it now might be characterized as the science of the good. Yet its claim to this title would seem to require surrendering the claim to being a science of sciences (174b–c). Critias responds to this problem not by acknowledging the puzzling character of *sōphrosynē*'s concerns, but by proposing that it preside also over the science of the good (174e). But in expanding the scope of *sōphrosynē*'s control, Critias contributes to its evanescence, for the advantageous is now provided by the science of the good, just as health is provided by medicine (174e–75a). If *sōphrosynē* is to benefit, apparently it must be decoupled from Critias's obsession with control. While the *Protagoras* reveals the need for strategic rationality to be guided by a more comprehensive form of intelligence, the *Charmides* discloses the illusions and the dangers attending proposals for scientific hegemony.

In the *Charmides*, as in the *Protagoras*, Socrates practices a third form of rationality, different from both the strategic and the hegemonic. Less obsessed with control and more aware of its own shortcomings, it relates to other human practices in a way that is dialogic. Through the interactive use of question and answer, this form of rationality both learns from and challenges the practitioners of the other arts. "Will not such a person examine others about the things that he has learned more nobly, while those who make such searches absent this learning will do so more feebly and poorly?" (*Charmides* 172 b). Its concerns are not to determine whether such practitioners adhere to an undifferentiated standard of formal rationality, but to inquire about the goods and limitations of their various practices. In this connection, the concerns of dialogic rationality would extend to comparing these different goods, such as health, victory, and justice. Eventually, dialogic rationality treats the relation between the different goods or practices as an inevitable problem or question. Toward the end of his conversation with Critias, Socrates says that because health is the outcome of medicine and advantage the outcome of the science of the good, *sōphrosynē*, as the science of sciences, provides us with no identifiable, discrete benefit. However, this criticism presupposes an understanding of *sōphrosynē* as a ruling (*archousa*) science that commands (*epistatei*) all of the others, each of which generates its own proper outcome. Yet if *sōphrosynē* is envisaged as a more open and more questioning kind of rationality that inquires about the content of and relationships among overlapping and potentially conflicting goods, its beneficial character emerges.

This revised understanding of *sōphrosynē* informs a less definite but also a less obsessive vision of politics, in part because it encourages the examination of obsessions. By investigating *sōphrosynē* in a context that closely follows Potideia, Socrates counsels a moderation of the Athenian obsession with empire that plays a compelling role in causing the war. And if Socrates somehow succeeded in moderating Critias's obsession for control, he might diminish those impulses underlying his leadership of the Thirty's subversion of the democracy. At the very least, the open embarrassment of Critias as a mentor may undercut the influence that he exerts over the potentially powerful audience of gentlemen in the palaestra.

In the dialogue, as in the real world, however, things turn out differently. Socrates' confession that he is in a state of embarrassing vexation (*panu aganaktō* [175d]) about *sōphrosynē* is met by Critias' ordering Charmides to submit himself to Socrates' charms (176b-c). This demand mirrors in practice the intellectual impulse of the science of sciences to control the science of good and evil without itself knowing what good and evil are. In this connection, Socrates will apparently function as a certain kind of artisan, while Charmides himself is ordered (*epitattei*) to play the schizophrenic role of student/enforcer. As proposed by Critias, this hierarchy is a perversion of the *Republic*'s relationship among philosopher-king, guardian, and craftsman, for the real philosopher is compelled to function as an agent of the controlling tyrant, educating while also remaining under the control of a pathologized guardian. One of the most damaging aspects of the tyrant's control is the destruction of rationality.

Yet Critias's ambition for control is incomplete. Socrates' final statement in the *Charmides*, that he will not resist (176 d) the proposed use of force, is shown to be only partially true—that is, ironic—under the rule of the Thirty. In the *Apology* Socrates contends that when Charmides helped to construct a real enemies list (*Charmides* 161d),[100] including the name of Leon of Salamis, Socrates refused to be drawn into collaboration (*Apology* 32c-d). Yet rationality's success in resisting the application of control is, at best, partial. Socrates' refutation of Critias no more prevents the Thirty's tyranny than his passive resistance rescues Leon of Salamis. Rationality cannot counter political obsessions without assistance from nonrational aspects of or practices within political life, the accidental accession of philosophy to political power imagined in the *Republic*, or the partnership between dialogue and rhetoric hinted in the *Gorgias* or the *Meno*. As political practice, Socrates' discursive rationality is rescued from the Thirty by the returning democracy that also eventually condemns him. Yet, for Plato, a recognition of rationality's problematic yet inextricable relationship to politics is both more accurate and more valuable than attempts to limit rationality to strategic calculation or to elevate it to a controlling status.

The Borders of Rational Choice

In spite of significant differences between them, Thucydides and Plato each point to the shortcomings of rational choice theory by identifying what I have called its borders. These borders are not the conceptions of equilibrium that cohere and structure interactions among rational agents. They are, on the one hand, the broader and deeper psychocultural and political forces that generate different conceptions of equilibria and thus constitute different practices as rational. They are, on the other hand, the pragmatic possibilities that can be arranged into distinctive ways of life that need to be subjected to critical scrutiny. Any investigation of the role of rationality in politics must examine rather than presume such constitutive influences and pragmatic outcomes.

A number of Thucydides' characters (both cities and individuals) thus practice and defend strategic forms of rational calculations that draw upon and contribute to forms of political imagination, visions of the priorities and challenges that constitute the identities of political agents and cultures. Far too often, these forms of political imagination emerge from obsessions, individual or collective commitments resistant to the scrutiny of rationality. For Thucydides, the form of rationality needed to confront such damaging obsessions is critical rather than strategic. Yet one of the most damaging consequences of obsession is its ability to block self-criticism. Within human affairs, generally, *erōs* leads, and hope follows (3.45.4–5).

While Thucydides' critical posture grows out of his own engagements with war's harshest teachings, Plato's begins from the interactive conversations that Socrates calls philosophy. For Socrates, too, the antidote to expertise in the service of compulsion—or rationality in the service of irrationality—is a self-critical form of rationality that is imaged by his own dialogic practice. Like Thucydides, Socrates is all too aware of the barriers against individual or collective exercises of this form of critical reason. Yet he seems more hopeful about prospects for this activity for at least two reasons. First, Socrates does not see passion or emotion as the inevitable enemy of rationality. Emotion and judgment may function as partners within attempts to choose well in ways contributing to human happiness. Second, Socrates seems more hopeful that resources supporting critical rationality can be found within democratic political cultures. His rejections of both the strategic rationality of Protagoras and the hegemonic rationality of Critias implicitly point to a more discursive alternative, epistemologically more tentative and politically more open and multivocal.

In spite of these differences, the intersecting texts of Thucydides and Plato agree that the central problem or question for political well-being concerns the ways in which determinations of collective action can be made more open to the contributions of rationality. In so doing, they make the examination of compulsions the most important task for political rationality. And by questioning a reliance on political expertise, they also place whatever rationality politics allows in the hands of political agents or citizens.

Yet must we return to classical political philosophy to discover a more discursive alternative to rational choice? Such a prospect seems available within the framework of deliberative democracy. Deliberative democratic theory denies rational choice's inclination to treat political interactions as types of economic bargaining. And interests are seen not as tastes or preferences, but as practices that can be explained, justified, and criticized through rational interaction (Benhabib 2004, 12–13; Habermas 1996, 108; Young 1997, 399). It is to this perspective that I next turn.

3

Deliberating Democracy

Introduction: The Institutions and Ethics of Deliberation

While the rational choice perspective offers an explanatory framework that in principle applies to all forms of social interaction, deliberative democratic theory provides an expressly normative treatment of how discursive interaction and democratic politics reinforce each other. Understood as the best procedure for making collective choices where members of society have different resources, positions, and conceptions of the good, deliberation is most effectively institutionalized within a properly functioning democracy. And healthy democratic institutions are privileged because they respect and are guided by the goods of deliberation. The ethical priority awarded to deliberation provides a normative argument for arranging democratic institutions so that all affected parties may examine the merits and drawbacks of policy alternatives interactively, privileging or diminishing no voice because of power or status (Cohen and Arato 1992, 348; Habermas 1993, 49–50; Habermas 1996, 108; Young 1997, 394–95; Estlund 1997, 190–91; Warren 2001, 67).

In a way that is at least formally similar to classical political philosophy, deliberative democratic theory also rests its political prescriptions on an ethical theory: discourse ethics (Habermas 1975, 89; Habermas 1990, 43–115; Cohen and Arato 1992, 345; Benhabib 2004, 12–13; Warren 1999, 327). While this framework admits important variations, it is committed to at least two general principles. First, the justificatory structure of ethics, generally (what one might call the formal level of moral argument) is set by the normative expectations implicit within communicative reasoning, where partners are committed to respect sincerity, truth, and normative rightness (cf. Habermas 1990, 86–94; Cohen and Arato 1992, 347; Benhabib 2004, 130). Jürgen Habermas has earlier characterized this condition as an ideal speech situation (1973, 17; cf. 1990, 58–59). More recently, Mark Warren grounds the case for democracy on the value of individual and political autonomy (2001, 61, 226; cf. Cohen and Arato 1992, 356–57). Thus, discourse ethics does not presume an independent moral order accessible apart from or prior to the rational agreements of appropriately motivated discourse partners—some sort of natural law position, for example. And because discourse ethics requires the involvement and contribution of all affected parties, moral imperatives cannot be identified monologically (Knight and Johnson 1997, 279; Cohen and Arato 1992, 348; Habermas 1990, 65–66).

Second, the support of discourse ethics for particular practical decisions (the substantive level of moral argument) recognizes how historical and cultural circumstances constitute the situations that interactive discourses engage (Habermas 1993, 86, 98–99, 103). Attempts to establish substantive moral principles in abstraction from the pragmatic conditions that give rise to moral choices are highly suspect. While discourse ethics does not surrender itself to historical or cultural standards of value, it does not presume to determine in advance which aspects of a given situation will seem most important to moral agents or how those agents will in fact interpret and respond to those circumstances (Habermas 1990, 103; Cohen and Arato 1992, 362). To this extent, discourse ethics is open to substantive instruction from the moral deliberations of particular communities.[1] Yet this also means that discourse ethics' own guidance for conduct focuses heavily on the procedures through which possibilities for action are considered (Habermas 1990, 103).[2] Thus, in spite of formal similarities with classical political philosophy, deliberative democratic theory aggressively rejects any teleological framework. For Habermas, the characteristics of partners within communicative interactions do not depend on what he repeatedly dismisses as a metaphysical conception of the person, but rather on the requirements of the pragmatic need for rational agreement in the face of difference and uncertainty (Habermas 1993, 103; cf. Benhabib 2004, 13; Warren 2001, 66; Cohen and Arato 1992, 358).

The priority of discourse ethics requires that deliberation and democracy be understood in ways different from their meanings within the rational choice paradigm. Deliberation is not a strategic process of calculating how stipulated goals are to be achieved, but a reflective practice through which prospective goals can be constructed and criticized. Insofar as deliberative activity engages multiple and conflicting conceptions of purpose, it demands the meaningful involvement of a plurality of voices. Even construed solely as epistemic process, deliberation presumes a polyvocality that challenges the settled equilibria that frame rational choice. Similarly, democracy is not seen simply as an institution structuring cooperation among parties with established interests, but as one that allows a thorough examination and critique of both individual interests and public purposes. Iris Marion Young characterizes deliberative democracy as the replacement of "competitions among self-regarding interests, in which each seeks to get the most for himself" with "a process of discussion, debate and critique that aims to resolve collective problems" (1997, 400). The possibilities of democratic deliberation may therefore include transforming individual or group identities so as to diminish self-aggrandizement and parochialism and enhance generosity and openness (Warren 1992, 8–23; Young 1997, 384–85). From this perspective, a full analysis of democratic institutions cannot be confined to an examination of how political structures further or frustrate negotiations among self-interested individuals or firms. It also requires a broader sociological understanding of the institutional and cultural forms that allow all affected groups to participate in the deliberative examination of public purposes and enable democratic citizens to be open to possibilities for self-transformation. Such analyses allow the critical scrutiny of social forms and practices that contribute to or detract from possibilities for collective autonomy (Habermas 1996, 489).

Thus characterized, this perspective seems preferable as *democratic* theory to the rational choice approach for several reasons. In differentiating between types of rational processes and social forms, deliberative democratic theory conceptualizes social practice in a way that does not convert all forms of public choice into market behavior (cf. Elster 1997, 10–11; Warren 2001, 164–65). In insisting that political deliberation involve the examination of ends as well as the calculation of means, deliberative democratic theory seems more capable of taking the possibility of significant political change seriously (Warren 1999, 336). For both of these reasons, deliberative democratic theory also seems more compatible with the self-understandings of democratic political agents (cf. Warren 1999, 340–41).

Yet for all of its strengths, the perspective is also beset by shortcomings that limit its effectiveness as a resource for the very activity it deems central. When examined in light of the texts of Thucydides and Plato, the significance of these shortcomings becomes particularly apparent. Though this critique does not simply reject the position taken by deliberative democratic theory, it does suggest that the position is seriously incomplete. Problems in three areas seem particularly noteworthy.

First, deliberative democratic theory is too hasty in renouncing its connections with a certain kind of teleology. While it rightly criticizes dogmatic and rigid claims about the content of the human good, it fails to recognize the value of more dialogic forms of teleological reasoning for its own project. Indeed, deliberative democratic theory effectively presupposes a substantive and controversial argument about why the social and psychological dimensions of a deliberative society are goods for members of democratic communities. The need for and challenges encountered by this argument are shown by the continued presence (in both democratic theory and democratic practice) of alternative visions of democracy and of the individual and social goods that they produce.[3] Thus, when Habermas argues that neither classical liberalism nor civic republicanism offers an adequate account of modern democratic society, he is implicitly relying on the teleological arguments that he repeatedly dismisses.[4] Though discourse ethics denies any connection with a supposed metaphysics of the person by focusing on the interactive pragmatics of rational communication, it presumes an argument showing why this form of interaction is a more suitable ethical base than interactions more characteristic of the market or the church. Absent this functional equivalent to teleology, Habermas's own endorsement of the priority of communicative autonomy itself seems problematically metaphysical, precisely because it calls for the sort of rational justification and critical defense that is left unstated.[5]

By severing connections with teleology, deliberative democratic theory constrains its treatment of the virtues. To be sure, deliberative democrats are very concerned to identify the virtues needed for rational communicative interaction (Habermas 1996, 461–66; Warren 2001, 70–77). Yet this cannot be all, for the focus on self-transformation suggests a need to move beyond an instrumental concern with the virtues supportive of functional democracy to a fuller examination of how democratic citizenship relates to those virtues connected with more expanded forms of human flourishing. Communicative rationality is valued not simply for its effectiveness but for the desirable forms of life that it both reflects and enables.

Second, deliberative democratic theory is limited by its overriding focus on procedures and the accompanying reluctance to engage questions of substance or outcome.[6] Its major concern is to determine how well democratic institutions enable all affected parties to engage in full and open deliberation about the direction of public policy. It has much less to say about the substantive content of possible policy directions. This reticence stems from a respect for the discursive autonomy that deliberative politics presupposes and from a rejection of the apparently antidemocratic claim that desirable political outcomes can be identified prior to the exercise of deliberative politics itself (Knight and Johnson 1997, 279; Warren 2001, 53; Shapiro 2003, 65–66). Deliberative democrats also remind their critics that normative rightness must be one of the commitments governing partners who interact according to the framework of discourse ethics (Habermas 1990, 93). Insisting on the need for independent consideration of the substantive merits of deliberative outcomes is, according to this view, both dangerous and unnecessary.

Closer scrutiny suggests that deliberative democratic theory's attempts to negotiate between procedure and substance are more problematic. This perspective effectively gives any substantive decision made under authentically deliberative conditions the presumptive status of normative rightness by virtue of its having been made in a procedurally correct way.[7] Critics who wish to challenge the normative status of outcomes deliberatively agreed to are therefore left with no theoretical resources, as distinct from historical or cultural ones, that could be employed within substantive debates. Yet deliberative democratic theory is hardly, qua theory, as agnostic about political outcomes as it pretends. Its procedural formulations are replete with assumptions about the expected decisions of properly functioning deliberative institutions.[8] And its claims about the transformative influences of those institutions are hardly noncommittal with respect to the worthiness of the alternative ways of life that such transformations involve. In fact, deliberative democratic theory's normative affiliation with particular outcomes suggests that the anticipated results of deliberative procedures provide one basis for the endorsement of those procedures. If so, a principled approval of substantive political choices becomes part of the argument marshaled in favor of deliberative institutions.[9] When such positions are unacknowledged or tacit, arguments endorsing these institutions become either pragmatically circular, convincing only to those who share attachments to certain political goals (cf. Shapiro 2003, 24–30), or radically misleading, pressing for controversial political ends in the guise of a more analytic argument for fair procedures.

Third, if deliberative democratic theory combines an analytic comparison of political processes and institutions with an unacknowledged privileging of certain political outcomes, it threatens to replace rather than to respect the pragmatic activities of democratic citizens. Insofar as broad questions of purpose are tacitly settled, the more significant political debates become matters of institutional design or organization, questions answered more appropriately by experts.

Deliberative democratic theory encounters these difficulties in part because of the way in which it conceptualizes the practice of political theory. Its analytic side has close intellectual ties to the rigorous forms of social theory developed in the postpositivist movement of the last quarter of the twentieth century.[10] While there is no necessary connection between employing the conceptual tools developed by postpositivist social theory and privileging deliberative democracy, the two perspectives have affinities. Both resist conceptualizing society in holistic or totalizing terms; both affirm the need to differentiate among social forms and the functions they perform (cf. Warren 2001, 5–6; Cohen and Arato 1992, 372–73). Both also refuse to confer autonomy on the economic realm (or markets), seeing instead possibilities for controlling the social consequences of economic practices through political means (Habermas 1975, 83; Habermas 1996, 297–99; Elster 1997, 26). Finally, both reject the possibility of a neutral social science and endorse social analysis with a practical intent (cf. Habermas 1996, 329–30; Putnam 1993, 63). Buoyed by discourse ethics or by cultural analyses that see the principles of deliberative democracy validated in the templates of contemporary Western political culture (cf. Rawls 2005, 223), social theory's mission becomes the specification of how the interactive social forms of modern society enhance or diminish prospects for deliberative political communication (Warren 2001, 3). Any attempt on the part of political theory to comment on the quality of public outcomes in abstraction from the operation of democratic political processes would thus seem to require similarly rigorous forms of analysis threatening to displace democracy (cf. Habermas 1996, 278–79; 298–99; Shapiro 2003, 65–66).

However, deliberative democratic theory never explains why political philosophy must be understood in this way. It relies for validation on the emerging features of a developing intellectual perspective that combines a professionalized and sophisticated social science with the normative privileging of a certain kind of democracy. This perspective refrains from offering substantive judgments about the merits of political outcomes because it presumes that such statements would only be possible on the basis of a rigorous analysis that settled matters of practice and left politics with nothing to do.[11] Yet a political philosophy more continuous with the practices of political agents can engage in a reflective examination of ends in ways that, while less precise and more tentative, are no less rational than the conceptual analysis that characterizes postpositivist social science. This approach would not eliminate deliberative democratic theory's contributions to social analysis, but it would contextualize such efforts by critically examining the values and limitations of a variety of public ends. Judging the normative character of political outcomes would be acknowledged as playing a central role in the assessment of political processes, yet these normative conclusions would emerge not as a product of theory but through the reflective interactions of intelligent human beings drawing on political thought as a resource.

In this chapter, I will try to develop this position by considering how Plato and Thucydides address two concepts essential to deliberative democratic theory's treatment of institutions—political trust and democratic judgment. A relevant form of trust must accompany a healthy, differentiated civil society, where social bonds both enable and are strengthened by deliberative institutions. Political judgment is the outcome of properly functioning deliberative forms. Within a deliberative context, the political goods of trust and judgment are therefore mutually reinforcing. I suggest that deliberative democratic theory reveals the importance and dimensions of both of these concepts in ways that go beyond treatments provided by other conceptual and normative frameworks, such as classical liberalism and civic republicanism. Yet placing deliberative democratic theory's treatment of trust and judgment in conversation with the contributions of Thucydides and Plato identifies difficulties that call for more adequate treatment.

The Goods and the Pitfalls of Political Trust

Varieties of Political Trust

While most democratic theorists note that trust is essential to a democratic community's well-being, there is considerable disagreement about what political trust means and why it is valuable. For both classical liberalism and rational choice theory, political trust means willingness to cooperate with others in undertaking the risks of collective action (Hardin 1999, 24–26). Trust is built by institutions that provide predictable and effective means for influencing and monitoring public policy. Political trust is thus an instrumental good that helps political actors achieve individual or group goals (Luhmann 1979, 88–89). Political mistrust is an unwillingness to cooperate because institutional supports are absent or ineffective. Those writing within the broadly communitarian tradition, in contrast, often see political trust as growing out of shared membership in a moral community (cf. Bellah et al. 1985, 275–77; Elshtain et al. 1998, 6; Fukuyama 1995, 336). Here, political trust reflects confidence that one's associates share conceptions of the good and value the same qualities of character. While liberalism and rational choice theory see political trust fostered most effectively by appropriate institutions, communitarians rely on more encompassing cultural forms such as shared traditions or religion (Bellah et al. 1985, 248–49). Political mistrust grows out of suspicions that one's fellow citizens are too fragmented in their value orientations to articulate or to act upon a meaningful understanding of the common good (cf. Elshtain et al. 1998, 4–6).

Deliberative democratic theory provides an account of political trust that differs from both liberal and communitarian variants. Like liberalism and rational choice, deliberative democratic theory conceptualizes political trust as the willingness to place oneself under the power of others in order to engage in collective action (Warren 1999, 311). These perspectives also agree that political trust is enabled by institutions that make the actions of those trusted subject to careful scrutiny (Warren 1999, 338–40; Hardin 1999, 29–30). However, deliberative democratic theory intersects with communitarianism in its focus on the importance of participatory agency and in its appreciation of how political and social interactions enhance citizens' interpretations of their interests. Because of its focus on self-transformation, this perspective also maintains that involvement in deliberative interactions helps to build social trust by encouraging citizens to become less parochial and more tolerant (Warren 1992, 8–23; Young 1997, 384–85). Finally, deliberative democrats are more expansive than liberalism and rational choice theorists in their treatment of what counts as warranted or justified trust. For the liberal and rational choice perspectives, trust is warranted whenever institutions ensure that it is in the trusted's interests to be trustworthy (Hardin 1999, 26). In addition, the deliberative democratic perspective requires that a society's normative regulations themselves be ethical as determined by the broad guidance supplied by discourse ethics (Warren 1999, 327). Yet deliberative democrats do not see political trust depending on the strong moral agreement required by the communitarians. To do so would be to move illegitimately from an inherited community of norms to normative ethical prescriptions (Warren 1999, 327; Habermas 1996, 279). For deliberative democratic theory, then, political trust means that there are legitimate grounds for believing that both elites and ordinary citizens will sincerely follow communicative procedures in determining and executing collective decisions. This belief is supported not only by sanctions that punish violations but also by norms that foster behavior patterns or qualities of character that make the participants trustworthy (Offe 1999, 70–72).

While deliberative democratic theory provides a treatment of political trust that is more comprehensive and nuanced than those offered by either liberalism and rational choice or the communitarians, incongruities and omissions are also apparent.

Consistent with its premature dismissal of teleology, deliberative democrats need to say more about why trust is a good for democratic communities. While they can show why political trust contributes to the functioning of deliberative institutions, they are less forthcoming in clarifying why a deliberative democracy that nourishes a healthy sense of trust is good. This incomplete treatment of the goodness of political trust is accompanied by a limited treatment of the virtues. Deliberative democratic theory's institutional focus is on political and sociological forms that enhance citizens' capacities for monitoring the trustworthiness of elites and for participating in trusting and trust-building relations with one another (Habermas 1996, 287–88; Offe 1999, 73–76). However, while deliberative institutions must support qualities needed to establish the communicative bases of trust, these institutions also presuppose intellectually responsible and morally decent citizens socialized by a wider array of influences. In this connection, deliberative democratic theory is more involved than some of its proponents might wish with the communitarian issue of how cultural norms influence the development of certain virtues.[12]

Deliberative democratic theory's treatment of political trust is also limited by its preference for engaging procedural questions over conversations about substance. This shortcoming particularly affects the treatment of warranted trust. In examining the ethical nature of the normative precepts and regulations of the society itself (Warren 1999, 327–28), the deliberative democratic view potentially involves itself, in a way that rational choice theory does not, with the purposes or ends of democratic practices. Beyond determining how closely political agents adhere to procedures fostering publicity and transparency or how sincerely they respect cultural standards that endorse or discourage certain types of behavior, a test for warranted trust is the ethical character of the collective actions involved (Warren 1999, 327). Though deliberative democratic theory wishes to rely on the resources of discourse ethics in determining this ethical content, I have suggested that it cannot assess the character of particular collective-will formations without engaging the substance of those political decisions more directly. This difficulty can be seen in David Estlund's (1997, 173–204) attempt to argue for a kind of epistemic proceduralism as the grounding for democratic authority. Epistemic proceduralism identifies conditions under which democratic deliberation would be most likely to take seriously the rational (rather than simply the preference-based) grounds for public choices. It is offered as an alternative to both fair proceduralism, which is "insensitive to reasons," and correctness theory, which, like some versions of teleology, ties the legitimacy of a democratic decision to its conformity with a substantive standard identified in procedurally independent ways. Yet in appealing to the *epistemic* status of proceduralism, Estlund points inevitably beyond procedures to determinations of content—to what it is reasonable to decide and to who reasonable political agents are.

Deliberative democratic theory's rejection of teleology and confidence in procedures also distance it from the ways in which democratic citizens assess the trustworthiness of their political communities. Estlund sees democratic theory as focused principally on questions of legitimacy. Since judgments about legitimacy cannot be held hostage to controversial views about correctness, democratic theory must decline to comment on correctness except through the filter of epistemic proceduralism. Yet there is no reason to limit democratic theory's concern exclusively or primarily to questions of political legitimacy. Theorizing democratic politics as the enhancement of particular individual and social goods (as in Warren 2001, 63) involves political theory in critical assessments of the policy directions that democracies follow, going beyond while still recognizing the importance of legitimacy. This expanded democratic theory would resemble the perspective of thoughtful citizens who may challenge the correctness of policy choices without denying the legitimacy of the procedures or the administration that determined them.

Deliberative democratic theory's treatment of political trust can be enhanced by continuing the interpretations of Thucydides' presentation of the Mytilene debate and the Platonic dialogue *Protagoras* that were initiated in chapter 2. As read here, each text considers the question of why particular forms of trust are good for political communities, particularly those guided by democratic deliberation. Thucydides' treatment of the Mytilene debate indicates that political trust is central to the quality of political life in a democratic community because it allows its members to engage difficult and controversial questions about the good. According to this view, political trust is good for democracies in a way that goes beyond its instrumental contribution to collective action. Plato's dialogue extends this discussion to suggest that warranted trust in the outcomes of these engagements requires the presence of citizens who practice certain virtues. These are not the virtues reflective of a homogenous moral community, but rather those that emerge from a critical engagement with cultural norms. Consequently, a healthy democratic polity also requires a kind of mistrust that goes beyond the institutional monitoring of elites to include the kind of rational mistrust that makes cultural self-criticism possible. This means that theorizing the procedures of democracy must be supplemented by critical investigations into what democracies do. By offering these corrections, the texts of Thucydides and Plato do not displace democratic politics, for they suggest that political trust is an important yet problematic democratic good that requires careful civic attention.

The Fragility of Trust in Thucydides

I have focused earlier (in chapter 2) on the importance of the Mytilene debate for an examination of Thucydides' treatment of political rationality. The exchange between its two antagonists also addresses the intersection of trust and deliberation within democratic politics.

Cleon's skepticism about Athens's (or any democracy's) ability to rule an empire is rooted in a criticism of the trust relations that hold the city together. He says that the Athenians' openness toward one another generates an unjustified and dangerous trust in others that makes it more difficult for the city to practice the harshness needed for imperial control (Thucydides 3.37.1–2). This naive form of political trust also makes the assembly's discursive or deliberative practices potentially destructive. In response, Cleon tries to engender ever widening circles of mistrust, first against the move to reconsider the first decision about Mytilene, then against any speakers who might argue for a policy of moderation, and ultimately against the political institutions that make such a reexamination possible. As an alternative, he recommends very different forms of seeming trust that encourage neither deliberation nor democracy.

Sounding (oddly) like Socrates in Plato's *Gorgias*, Cleon assails the assembly for being vulnerable to deceptive rhetoric. In chapter 2, I outlined Cleon's critique of rationality and his alternative reliance on the passions as conclusive guides to interest.[13] Applied to conceptions of political rationality, Cleon's speech endorses strategic thinking that calculates how best to achieve the goods of security, wealth, and power. His treatments of political trust and mistrust are conditioned by these understandings of interest and rationality. Trust among the citizens (horizontal trust) is simply the common recognition of the priority of material interests and the agreement to cooperate in their pursuit. Vertical trust awarded to leadership is understood as deference to those who are adept and reliable sources of strategic guidance. Maintaining agreement about the good requires vigilant mistrust toward those who argue for conceptions of interest (being just as a part of one's well-being) or courses of action (leniency toward Mytilene) that challenge truths that are plainly seen (Thucydides 3.38.5–6). Common citizens should distrust the more thoughtful and, instead, invest horizontal trust in one another and vertical trust in Cleon (3.37.4, 3.40.4).

In chapter 2 I also suggested why Cleon's efforts to create these more focused forms of political rationality are undercut by the psychology that his speech presumes. The same fate befalls his approach to trust and mistrust. Cleon's rhetoric appeals initially to a collective Athenian understanding of the city's interests. Yet it is difficult to see how such a solidarity can be maintained in light of the unrelenting attack on virtually all extant forms of trust. Cleon does not simply try to replace an inadequate sense of collective trust with a more adequate version, for his political principles drive a wedge between "ordinary" and "thoughtful" among the citizens (3.37.3–4). Moreover, in light of the psychological assumptions behind Cleon's vicious policy proposals, there are no reasons why those within the more ordinary class of citizens should trust one another except to recognize the universal dominance of selfish motives. Trust lasts only as long as collective selfishness aggregates atomistic selfishness. Displaying the thin character of civic trust also reveals the vulnerabilities of ordinary citizens to the abuses of trusted experts. It is surely appropriate to interpret Cleon's public rhetoric in light of Thucydides' own assessment of the motivations of those who attempted to succeed Pericles as "foremost man." Far from being guided by concerns for the city's good, all were spurred by individual drives toward honor and gain (2.65.6–7). Given the selfish motives of these experts or leaders, any trust invested in them is inevitably based on some degree of deception. Cleon pointedly addresses the more ordinary citizens in terms of their mistrust (*apistountes*) of their own intelligence and characterizes them almost exclusively in terms of deficiencies in learning and power (3.37.4–5).

Cleon's ridicule of any argument that challenges the appeal of ends that should be obvious to all is paralleled by a demonization of anyone who opposes the partiality and viciousness of those ends. His own perverted version of trust is thus accompanied by a dangerous form of mistrust. Instead of counseling a healthy skepticism about controversial interest claims, Cleon reinforces a thoughtless acceptance of the most immediate interest claims and a mistrust of deliberative institutions that could provide a venue for self-criticism. Cleon's conception of human interests and his proposed rearrangement of political interactions reveal not conditions for trust, but the complete pervasiveness of mistrust.

Diodotus's response implies alternative visions of rationality, politics, and political trust. However, his position is subject to significant interpretive controversies due to the complexities of his own rhetoric, especially with respect to his treatment of democratic institutions. These controversies generate very different views of Diodotus's relevance for democratic theory.[14] Commentators such as Peter Euben (1990, 180–82) and Josiah Ober (1998, 94–104) see Diodotus's speech as damaging democracy by relying on deceptive rhetoric. For Clifford Orwin (1984, 320; 1994, 158–62), however, Diodotus's critique emphasizes the need for a political leadership that accepts the permanence of democratic institutions but recognizes the need to control their functions and outcomes through a rhetoric that compromises democratic capabilities. This implies that Diodotus secures trust only by violating the ethical requirements of deliberation. Arlene Saxonhouse, in contrast, sees Diodotus as the true democratic theorist of antiquity (1996, 75; cf. 2006, 156–64). My own interpretation sees insights and omissions in all of these views. Euben and Ober downplay the extent to which Diodotus's deception is employed in the name of a democratic good. Orwin's careful tracing of the intricacies of Diodotus's rhetoric exaggerates the degree to which the creation of political trust requires the suspension of rationality (1994, 160). What complicates Saxonhouse's assessment is Diodotus's degree of skepticism about achieving the goods or mitigating the vulnerabilities of democratic political life.

As noted in chapter 2, Diodotus secures a moderation of the initial decision about Mytilene by arguing for an exclusive attention to Athens's advantage apart from any consideration of justice (3.44.1–2). I have suggested that this treatment of justice is not simply dismissive and that one of the most important implications of Diodotus's speech is that conceptions of interest need to be rethought in light of the imperatives of justice. However, Diodotus appears to serve justice by reinforcing the political-cultural distortions that subvert the processes of deliberative democracy, for he begins his speech with the claim that anyone who wishes to benefit the city must deceive it (3.43.2–3). This apparently cynical perspective seems validated by the final outcome of the debate, where the moderate position loses votes once both sides have been heard (compare 3.36.5 with 3.49.1–2). And Diodotus's plea that the thousand oligarchs "whom Paches thought to be guilty" should be tried again calmly goes unheeded when the assembly votes to execute them on Cleon's motion (compare 3.48.2 with 3.50.1). In this light, we might conclude that the Mytilene *dēmos* is saved from, rather than by, deliberative democracy.[15] Habermas could interpret this conclusion as evidence of the inadequacy of the premodern institutions and culture with which Diodotus must cope (1996, 300–301). But Diodotus himself traces his problems to basic human characteristics that challenge the effectiveness of any institutional arrangements.

Like Cleon, Diodotus indicts the deliberations practiced in the assembly. Yet his characterization of and complaints about democratic processes are different. While Cleon criticizes the assembly for encouraging too much talk, Diodotus focuses on how the assembly's practices frustrate deliberative rationality and, thus, he bases his critique of practice on the assembly's own normative possibilities. He begins by insisting on the need to reconsider the directions of public policy in light the contributions of a thoughtful *logos* (3.42), implying that political trust can extend beyond strategic cooperation to an openness to engage in a mutual conversation that examines goals. Yet his recognition of the distortions that the assembly imposes on thoughtfulness plausibly drives him to a deception that pursues deliberative goods through nondeliberative means. Orwin explicitly connects his interpretation of this aspect of the speech to questions concerning trust and mistrust in democratic regimes (1984, 313–25; 1994, 160–63). While Orwin's Diodotus recognizes the salutary features of healthy political trust, his criticism of democratic society requires replacing deliberative rationality with a rhetorically generated trust in the guidance of intelligent and reassuring leaders (1994, 158, 160, 162). True democrats thus see Diodotus establishing a rhetorical hierarchy ("cryptic and mendacious" [Ober 1998, 102–3]) that undercuts further the prospects for deliberative interactions (cf. Euben 1990, 182–83). For Orwin, however, deception is the only plausible response to the more sinister varieties of image politics that always plague participatory democracies (Orwin, 1994, 158). Diodotus also offers a deep explanation for the diseases of deliberation by pointing to the force of the passions (3.40.5–6). The self-transformation thesis of the deliberative democrats collapses when confronted by the passions, which oppose not simply transformation but even educability.

However, this pessimistic conclusion is softened by Diodotus's own practice, which implicitly encourages a rational reevaluation of interests that is compatible with what is best in democratic culture. To the extent that Diodotus encourages the Athenians to be more just than their power requires, he is employing rhetorical deception to foster a good connected with democratic equality.[16] Performatively, while his speech acknowledges the power of the passions, his speech-act recognizes possibilities for an education that his argument seems to rule out. He presupposes the normative potentials of a thoughtful deliberation that his harder institutional and psychological diagnoses would appear to disallow (3.42.1–2).[17] The immediate rescue of the Mytilenes opens onto possibilities that are too ambiguous to be simply the products of an image politics.

To the extent that educability is a pragmatic possibility, Diodotus also leaves room for the development and influence of a form of democratic political trust that supports rather than opposes rationality. Rather than being simply an instrument in the collective pursuit of material success or an affective alternative to reasoned deliberation, this form of political trust would be a continuing partner within attempts to determine the best direction for collective action within a democratic context. While Diodotus's speech implicitly appeals to the most thoughtful Athenians, he does not attempt to use that category either to privilege or to marginalize any particular class of citizens. Disagreements about the good set the pragmatic context that makes political trust both necessary and desirable, even as these disagreements represent the strongest barriers against establishing meaningful forms of trust.

Diodotus's speech-act could therefore be interpreted as identifying both the inevitable need for and the substantial barriers against confronting disagreements about the good in a deliberative democratic context.[18] At one level, his position could be read as a warning against subjecting deliberative institutions to immediate political pressures (cf. Habermas 1996, 311–14). The damaging impacts of these pressures are apparent within the Mytilene debate as practical rationality gives way to political necessity. If what Diodotus says about the power of the passions is true, no one involved in the rebellion can be justly executed. Yet near the end of his speech, his references shift from the innocent and the guilty to the democrats and the oligarchs (3.47.1–2), inevitably accepting the executions to be decreed on Cleon's motion. Diodotus is led here not by personal callousness or political partisanship but by the recklessness that is potentially embedded in the assembly's own practices. The immediate pressures for decision coupled with the residual influences of anger make quietness (*hēsychia*) impossible.

Nonetheless, for Diodotus the greatest impediments to healthy deliberative institutions and a strong sense of warranted trust are not so much institutional as psychological, imaged by the hope that always follows in the wake of *erōs*. His implicit treatment of deliberative democracy thus courts paradoxes of its own. His view of the passions makes any prospect for what the deliberative democrats call self-transformation virtually impossible, yet his own pragmatics presuppose the possibility of a more limited educability. Diodotus's rhetoric can thus be read as a complex and conflicted response to his understanding of the needs for and barriers against democratic trust. In so doing, Diodotus also potentially expands the scope of the discussion beyond narrow political institutions to a broader set of cultural forms whose function is to educate the citizens. This possibility can be accessed by revisiting the *Protagoras*.

Trust, Mistrust, and the Virtues in the Protagoras

In chapter 2, I suggested that the *Protagoras* is structured around the examination of different approaches to moral education. Varying relationships between educational possibilities and conceptions of political trust are implicit in Socrates' initial response to Hippocrates' demand that he be taken to meet Protagoras. Under Socrates' questioning, Hippocrates acknowledges that he does not wish to turn himself into a

Sophist (*Protagoras* 312a). Socrates could exploit this sense of shame and return Hippocrates to the care of the culture, sowing seeds of mistrust in educational innovation on the basis of a conservative trust in established conventions. Instead, Socrates proposes that they visit and question Protagoras together. Within this initial exploration, three alternative forms of education arise: that provided by specialists, that transmitted by the guidance of the elders, and that which can occur through interactive dialogue. Each has a political parallel. The reliance on specialists is compatible with a politics of strategic rationality. The recourse to the elders implies a more general view of the need for enculturation within a community of memory. The development of individuals through discursive interaction most closely parallels a politics of deliberation.

These approaches to education are also cognate to particular conceptions of trust: the training of specialists to a trust in experts, the guidance of elders to a trust in cultural norms, and the involvement in discourse to a more complicated trust in practices that allow the interrogation of strategies and hierarchies. Within these forms of trust only the third requires continuous involvement with mistrust. While the first two exclude or dismiss mistrusted sources (amateurs or outsiders) before the fact, discursiveness functions by continuously juxtaposing trust and mistrust; it relies upon a trusted activity to examine both the content and the sources of apparently conclusive decisions, which are thus, to a degree, mistrusted. Yet unlike deliberative democrats who see institutional arrangements successfully balancing trust and mistrust within democratic communities (cf. Warren 1999, 339–40; Offe 1999, 72; Habermas 1996, 172), Socrates' experience suggests that the relationship between trust and mistrust involves inevitable and unresolvable tensions.

Politically, while a number of commentators commend Protagoras's democratic inclinations,[19] my reading argues that Socrates' relation to democratic regimes is potentially the more positive.[20] Protagoras dismisses Athens's complex political sociology in his own apologia for his sophistry. Within the house of the wealthy and well-born Callias, he says that attempts to disguise his identity as a Sophist would not deceive "those among human beings who are most capable of action in the city," though they would escape the notice of the many, "who, so to speak, are aware of practically nothing" (317a).[21] With respect to trust, Protagoras implies that the many can simply be trusted (predicted) to follow the political guidance of the few.

However, Protagoras is forced to acknowledge that democratic political culture is more complex. His claim that his instruction will enable Hippocrates to order his own affairs better and to "become most powerful in the city whether in speech or in action" (318e–19a) is redescribed by Socrates as teaching the political art that creates good citizens (319a). If Socrates' description is accurate, Protagoras would be able to make those whom he educates politically trustworthy; the trust invested in the privileged would be warranted on the basis of their having learned the skills necessary for good citizenship. If there is a preexistent community of interests between the many and the few, Protagoras could teach experts who would be particularly adept at identifying effective strategies for furthering the city's good. Yet this possibility has already been challenged both by Socrates' description of Hippocrates' motivations (that he is anxious to become individually distinctive [316c]) and by Protagoras's unreconstructed statement about the benefits of his teaching (the sensible ordering of one's own affairs and the exercise of the greatest power in the city). Alternatively, Protagoras could apply a more reformative political education to the powerful, creating good citizens by making their interests more compatible with the good of the community. Yet this would require Protagoras to revise his initial political judgment and praise the excellences of the few because they contribute to the well-being of the democracy.

Socrates offers a more basic challenge to Protagorean education when he says that he does not think that civic virtue is teachable (319a–b). He supports this claim with observations, first about the practices of the democratic assembly and then about educational outcomes among the young elite. Socrates says that the assembly's practice points to the absence of any political art. While there are technical experts who advise on means, there are no equivalent policy experts who speak to ends (319b–d). At this point, Socrates makes no express reference to the quality of democratic decisions. One possibility is that they are made in ignorance, but this conclusion is justified only if there is no available political intelligence beyond an expertise modeled on the arts. He also says nothing about how these epistemic confusions contribute to the justice or injustice of collective action. However, the subsequent criticism of elite education is expressly ethical. The city's best cannot hand down their virtues to their sons, and the first named example of this failure is Pericles (319e–320a).

Both friends and critics of Plato have interpreted Socrates' treatment of the assembly as a complaint about democracy's incapacity for knowledge or inability to recognize it.[22] Yet his assessment can also be read as a more complicated treatment of democratic politics, revealing, like Diodotus's speech, both its potentials and its dangers. While Socrates hardly suggests that the democracy is the "best" regime, his treatment of the democracy is more favorable than the subsequent examination of elites. His characterization of the assembly implies that it keeps experts available while allowing citizens equal access to deliberations about public choices (319d). According to this view, expertise as particular craft knowledge could be the basis for a limited sort of vertical trust, while egalitarianism and publicity would foster the understanding that one may speak openly and receive the full consideration of one's fellow citizens. The institutions held together by horizontal trust would deal with more purposive questions and serve as sources of oversight, preventing abuses of vertical trust by experts trying to overstep their bounds. The possibility that a less rigid form of vertical trust might emerge is neither affirmed nor denied. For example, Socrates could accept the difference between thoughtful and vulgar citizens, yet deny that they could be distinguished by broad class (educational, social, or economic) markers.

However, as a description of the assembly's deliberations, this account fails. First, the separation between technical and policy questions is impossible to sustain in light of Socrates' own examples of *technai*. References to buildings and ships bring to mind the walls, the harbors, and the navy, the material infrastructure of the Athenian empire. Such technical discussions within the assembly are inevitably politicized (cf. *Gorgias* 455d–e). To the extent that they are presented as exclusively technical questions, their politicization is concealed. Second, the influences of both supervised expertise and egalitarian discursiveness can be undercut by rhetorical appeals to the passions. In the *Gorgias*, the title character claims that the power of rhetoric can eclipse both expertise and deliberation (456b–c), and Socrates himself associates the abuses of rhetoric with democratic institutions (503b). Here, in front of those most likely to be suspicious or contemptuous of democracy, Socrates offers a potentially more positive assessment of democratic deliberation, implying (in agreement with at least a part of Diodotus's speech) that destructive rhetoric is a treatable pathology rather than a fatal defect.[23] Socrates is much harsher in his criticism of the education of the elite sons of the wisest and the best of the citizens. If transmitting virtue to the young requires moral guidance, the deficiencies of the young must be traced much more directly to the deficient character of the elders.

Building upon this dramatic reading, it appears that Socrates insists that analyses of political trust be conducted in light of two broader recognitions. The first is that the character of political trust can never simply ignore disputes over power positions. The creation of trust negotiates, but it does not neutralize (and should not disguise) the continued presence of conflicts within society. Second, the creation of political trust necessarily requires attention to the virtues of the citizens. In a way, this conclusion emerges from a comparison of the Socratic position with that of Diodotus. To the degree that Diodotus despairs of the possibility of warranted trust, he does so because he effectively despairs of the possibility of virtue, understood as thoughtful rationality (Thucydides 3.42.1–2), in light of the overwhelming force of passion. From this perspective, virtue's relevance for political trust is not confined to premodern communities held together by homogeneous traditions. Rather, the creation of trust in any kind of society seems impossible without the presence of appropriate forms of virtue. In the *Protagoras*, Socrates does not attempt to discover the content of a human virtue that exists prior to politics. But he also does not confine himself to examining the potentials for virtue that are embedded in particular political cultures. Instead, he proceeds by treating human virtue and political virtue as mutually enriching and problematizing questions.

Protagoras responds to Socrates' skepticism about the teachability of virtue with a more general statement about politics that is part myth and part argument. Yet his attempt to show that the virtues are teachable ends by clustering the virtues along psychological and political lines in ways that heighten possibilities for conflict and mistrust. Protagoras's myth about the origins of cities begins with the premise that a struggle for survival is the fundamental natural condition (*Protagoras* 320e–21b). Originally, he says, human beings responded to their physical vulnerabilities by associating, but they fought continually among themselves (322b–c). Out of a desire to preserve the species, Zeus instructed Hermes to endow all human beings with justice (*dikē*) and deference (*aidōs*), qualities allowing basic levels of peaceful cooperation.[24] The existence of any political community requires the effective presence of justice, moderation, and piety, condensed into the "manly virtues" (*andros aretēn*) (324e–25a). For Protagoras, this mythical ethology can be applied to solve the first of Socrates' puzzles about political virtue in Athens. Everyone is entitled to address policy concerns in the assembly because the political virtues needed for cooperation are shared by all members of society. Protagoras then explains the apparent failures of education among the young by implying that Socrates has set his sights too high, failing to realize that even those whom society fears and punishes as criminals are far less menacing than the utterly asocial (327c–d). With typical cautiousness (317b–c) Protagoras avoids rather than engages the specific Socratic criticism of those who think of themselves as the wisest and the best.

Thus explained, the civic virtues based on *dikē* and *aidōs* enable minimal degrees of horizontal trust (confidence that one's fellow citizens will respect basic civility) fostered by and supportive of political stability. Because of the continuous need to resort to punishment, however, this sort of trust seems hardly distinguishable from social coercion, made necessary by the tendency of human beings to pursue their own interests in disregard of justice. Initially, this prospect is hidden by the universal terms of association based on the general distribution of *dikē* and *aidōs*, for this would also be a society devoid of factional subcultures and hierarchies. Once this account is revised to include the possibility of social divisions, however, it serves to heighten the possibility for civic disruption that the distribution of *dikē* and *aidōs* was supposed to counter.

These difficulties emerge in the exchanges between Socrates and Protagoras over the virtues. In response to Socrates' query (Is virtue one or many?), Protagoras says that virtue is a single thing, with a number of valorized qualities as its parts—specifically, justice, moderation, and piety (329d). In response to further interrogation, he then adds courage and "the greatest" of the parts, wisdom, emphasizing on his own initiative that one can be courageous without being just or just without being wise (329e). In effect, these additions reveal Protagoras's own reservations about the virtues originating in *dikē* and *aidōs*. The virtues necessary to hold society together do not necessarily include the intelligence and daring that enable the most-impressive personal achievements.[25] There are parallel disruptions to possibilities for political trust. If the virtues of the distinguished work against civic equality and political stability, they cannot elicit trust from the majority. While this sort of mistrust may generate internal trust within the contending subcultures, these outcomes originate in resentment or fear and are reinforced by aggression or resistance. In different ways, all of Protagoras's societies—the mythical community saved by Zeus, the minimalist community held together by harsh education, and the pragmatic community that surrounds his own professional activity—are characterized by the absence of meaningful trust.

The moral and political hazards of particular forms of both mistrust and trust emerge in the dialogue's final examination of courage. The conversation has reached the point where Protagoras is willing to admit that while all of the other virtues intersect, courage still stands apart (349d). From one point of view, Protagoras's willingness to associate wisdom with the more social virtues reintroduces the possibility of warranted vertical trust. Yet by isolating courage, he acknowledges the possibility of deep mistrust between the community as a whole and its most effective and most necessary defenders. In separating courage from the other virtues, Protagoras also changes the context of political conflict from that between competing groups (the Thirty as led by Critias?) to that involving opposition to common mores on the part of daring individuals (the manipulations and betrayals of Alcibiades?).[26] Consequently, any expanded horizontal trust within societies can be seen even more clearly as mutual fear that unites the community against predators. And prospects for horizontal trust among the conspicuous diminish, too, for there are no grounds upon which the distinctively courageous (Alcibiades and Brasidas?) should trust one another.

In compelling Protagoras to agree that courage can be reduced to knowing the pleasurable or painful consequences of action choices (356d–57b), Socrates relies, as I have suggested in chapter 2, on a fallacious conversion from "the pleasant is the noble" to "the noble is the pleasant." What invalidates the conversion is the illegitimate move from individual affective experiences that define the pleasant to the cultural standards of praise that constitute the noble.[27] In effect, this move images the potential conflict between the good of the individual and that of the community, a conflict that has shaped the dialogue's argument and drama from the beginning. This problematic identification of the noble and the pleasant also reveals the inadequacies of forms of trust generated by either individual self-interest or communal devotion. If the first statement, "the pleasant is the noble," is an adequate account of motivation, consolidated priorities of ethical communities must be rejected in favor of individual gratification. Under the second statement, "the noble is the pleasant," individual interests are now seen through the filter of cultural interests and norms; affective trust merges with civic commitment. That these two claims stand in such opposition, even though they are treated as convertible, is an indication of the dangers and the inadequacies of both, for each position involves a potentially serious form of instrumentalization that threatens the possibility of moral choice and warranted political trust. If the individual experience of pleasure sets the standard for the noble, political interaction becomes the aggressive pursuit of one's own material interests in a way that rejects the normative claims of any other individual good or any common good (Cleon).[28] If cultural understandings of nobility shape all individual goods, then rationality becomes the pursuit of common purposes designed to further the standing or reputation of the community (Pericles).[29] The consequences of either of these conceptions of politics for the development of warranted political trust are severe. In the first case, the dominance of selfish interests requires the ultimately paralyzing vigilance of both vertical and horizontal mistrust. In the second, representing the nobility of civic devotion as the source of personal gratification establishes a misleading sense of affective trust that obscures dangers and demonizes criticisms.[30]

In this light, the undermining of warranted trust seems traceable to mistaken understandings of the relationship between the noble and the pleasant and ultimately to a reliance on problematic sources of knowledge about the good. The reduction of the noble to the pleasant reflects the belief that we can know the good simply by consulting our inclinations.

The absorption of the pleasant by the noble implies the validity of cultural or subcultural valorizations. As I have noted in chapter 2, Socrates' response to both of these distortions is not a grand theory that links appropriate understandings of pleasure and nobility to a lucid knowledge of the good but discursive philosophy as practiced ironically by Socrates. The identification of the noble with the pleasant is surely intended to undercut the self-satisfaction of the attending elites, who see their own distinctive activities, focused on politics and war, as setting the standard for nobility. In replacing this standard with a pleasurable gratification enjoyable by anyone, Socrates effectively democratizes conceptions of the noble. At the same time, dissatisfaction with the argument that reduces noble courage to the calculation of pleasurable experiences is reflected in the persisting doubt that virtue can be taught as a form of expertise. Socrates' alternative is to invite Protagoras to continue with him as they try to work through the question of virtue again. In offering this invitation, Socrates indicates that his own mode of discursive interaction combines elements of both mistrust and trust. He mistrusts the immediacy of inclinations, the authoritative standing of cultural meanings, and even his and Protagoras's own previous agreements. Yet he also offers to trust Protagoras as a discourse partner as they consider alternatives. Though Protagoras declines and the dialogue ends, this unfulfilled partnership provides insights about political trust.

There are both analogies and discontinuities between the discursive philosophical relationship proposed by Socrates and the characteristics informing political, particularly democratic, trust. The first analogy clarifies the pragmatic context that makes political trust both necessary and desirable. The practice of discursive philosophy suggests that the need for trust is generated not simply by discrepancies in power positions but by controversies over the good. The philosophical interaction in the *Protagoras* has its political parallel in Diodotus's insistence that what is good for Athens is not as obvious as Cleon says and that discovering the good requires serious investigation and thought. Dissenting from the communitarian notion that trust presupposes substantial agreement about the good, both Plato and Thucydides imply that trust is a political requirement precisely when agreement on the good is lacking. Consequently, this perspective also deepens and expands the treatment of trust offered by deliberative democrats. The practical need to engage questions about the good helps to explain why individuals are willing to place themselves under the power of others if the subsequent collective deliberation will help contribute to greater clarity about public direction. And since the stakes in disagreements over the good are so high, we can more fully understand why power discrepancies within determinations of collective action are so troubling. Finally, the central importance of engaging the good and bad aspects of political purposes makes it questionable whether deliberative democratic theory can offer constructive assessments of political deliberations without going beyond an attention to procedure to deal, in Estlund's terms, with correctness as well as with legitimacy. In connecting examinations of deliberation and discourse with critical judgments concerning conceptions of the good, both Socrates and Thucydides imply that political theory should enhance, rather than either abstract from or stop short of, the substantive concerns of thoughtful citizens.

The second analogy between discursive philosophy and democratic politics is that trust is one of the constitutive goods of a decent political partnership. From this perspective, trust is neither simply an instrumental good that furthers the achievement of individual or group aims nor an encompassing good that reflects comfortable membership in a strong moral community. Instead, political trust, understood as the willingness to work with others to engage controversial questions about collective actions and purposes, is one of the goods that helps to constitute the value of a partnership of human beings who share similarities but also recognize the presence of differences. Consequently, the deliberative democratic position needs to be amended to allow it to discuss political trust in ways that are broadly teleological, understanding trust as one of the benefits fostered by a democratic community that is functioning well.[31] Far from ignoring differences within complex societies, this teleological understanding of trust contributes to a more discriminating assessment of democratic goods. In addition to being a *constitutive* democratic good, political trust is also related to a number of other societal goods in noninstrumental ways. As an *enabling* good it contributes to mutuality among different individuals and subcultures. As a *reinforcing* good it helps to maintain equality, allowing individuals and subcultures to relate to one another on terms of openness and fairness. And as a *signaling* good it points to the presence of those virtues that make this society's members able to trust and to be trusted.[32]

This last function points to a third analogy between discursive philosophy and the development of political trust within democracies. In order to flourish, both require the presence of appropriate virtues that each practice must strive to develop. Unlike Cleon, Protagoras clearly recognizes that stable political communities require virtues fostering basic civility. Yet Protagoras sees these virtues as desirable solely for their contributions to political security. Precisely because they represent the basic qualities needed to hold societies together, he believes that it is easy to understand what these virtues are. But Socrates forces Protagoras to admit that recognizing the virtues is difficult and controversial. He thus insists that the development of the virtues is an integral, rather than simply a preliminary, concern of politics. Good politics provides an education that extends beyond the development of peaceableness. This teleological investigation of the conditions that further or frustrate the development of relevant political and human virtues takes us beyond deliberative political institutions to deeper realms of cultural norms and practices. An attention to the virtues relevant to the creation of warranted political trust is not an alternative to focusing on political institutions and political culture but, rather, a more complete elaboration of that focus.

Yet there are also incongruities between the role of trust within Socratic discursive philosophy and its place within democratic politics. While both practices rely on interactions between trust and mistrust, Socratic philosophy awards a greater priority to mistrust than any politics possibly could.[33] Socrates' philosophical project presupposes the unsettled character of agreements about the good and thus the need to revisit these questions repeatedly.[34] Politics, in contrast, must presume some level of basic agreement about shared values and must be conscious of the need to make conclusive decisions.[35] There is thus clearly a sense in which Socrates' continued questioning of shared meanings and resolved decisions works against the inherent priorities of politics. This complexity helps to explain why Socrates' engagements with political questions must be ironic. One of the many functions of this form of irony is to oppose tendencies to convert Socratic discourse into a political program (Alcibiades' project in the *Symposium*) or to consign Socratic philosophy to political irrelevance (Callicles' project in the *Gorgias*). To be sure, this sort of ironic discourse requires a differentiation of social institutions analogous to those identified by deliberative democrats. Yet Socrates' ironic discourse also complicates the perspective of deliberative democratic theory by suggesting that its recommendations to balance political trust and mistrust through institutional arrangements can never be altogether successful. Institutional design must be frustrated by discourses that are politically relevant but ironically articulated, in part because ironic speech necessarily falls both within and outside of all discursive spheres (Markovits, forthcoming). Thus, Socratic irony raises questions about its own premises in a way that deliberative democratic theory does not. While deliberative democratic theory relies on the priorities of discourse ethics to generate a normative sociology that identifies institutions conducive or damaging to deliberation, Socrates closes the *Protagoras* by restating his doubts about what many would (reasonably) see as the normative basis of Plato's political philosophy, the teachability of virtue (361a). This treatment of political trust therefore opens onto the deeper question of the place of critical judgment within democratic communities.

Political Voice and Judgment in Democratic Communities

Democratic Voices

Democratic communities can be distinguished from other forms of political organization because they depend so heavily on the continuing political voices of their citizens. Like political trust, democratic voice can be conceptualized and assessed in a variety of ways. Classical liberalism and rational choice theory construe political voice mainly as interest articulation (what could be called political voice as making demands or, when frustrated, outcries), while communitarians focus on political voice as an eloquence that constructs and ennobles common purposes, binding the members of a democracy into a more substantive moral community. For deliberative democratic theory, in contrast, political voice is best interpreted as a certain kind of judgment. I will suggest that while deliberative democratic theory's treatment of political judgments seems the most fruitful of the three, it is hampered by a series of omissions.

Conceiving political voice as the continuing pressure or reaction produced by the demands of citizens is a consistent feature of liberal political theory extending from Locke's early insistence that political authority depends on citizen consent to the more recent conclusions of Robert Dahl that constitutional government is grounded in institutions allowing representation and contestation (Dahl 1971, 9). This conception of political voice has supported significant, though problematic, developments in empirical and positive political analysis. Since individuals make political demands known through the activities of interest or pressure groups, the pluralist model continues to be one of the most important empirical frameworks for the study of democratic societies.[36] The basic premise of liberal contractarianism also lends itself quite easily to the construction of various economic theories of democracy. In the early 1960s these conceptual approaches contributed substantially to the normative political theory of democratic elitism in which elites handled public affairs efficiently with the largely passive approval of the voters (cf. Berelson, Lazarsfeld, and McPhee 1954, 313; Almond and Verba 1989, 339–44).

Yet these advantages appeared to many as deficiencies. Critics charged that reducing politics to competitions for economic goods effectively made real politics disappear (cf. Berns 1962, 55–57). Both pluralist political sociologies and economic theories of democracy thus seemed much more capable of explaining political continuity than political change (Arendt 1958, 297–300; Wolin 2004, 281–82). Such conceptual or empirical reservations were paralleled by a number of normative objections. Critics of the pluralist model pointed to the ways in which established legitimation processes prevented the political empowerment of marginalized populations (Schattschneider 1960, 35; Wolff 1965, 47). And deeper objections were made to the narrow scope and crass character of political interests understood exclusively as quests for economic gain (Barber 2003, 34–35; Sandel 1996, 5–7; Wolin 2004, 271; Young 1997, 400).

By contrast, the civic republican alternative emphasizes the distinctiveness and preeminence of political phenomena.[37] Within this context, political voice is an eloquent call to transcend narrowly egoistic and material concerns in the name of something more encompassing and worthwhile. Benjamin Barber thus contrasts the paltry talk of thin or pluralist democracy to the fullness of promise of strong or participatory democracy (2003, 173–74).

Critics of this ethos often suggest that eloquent calls for public service must be seen through to discover the narrower individual or group interests that motivate them.[38] Moreover, even when sincere or authentic, appeals to the beauty of community (in Benedict Anderson's phrase in B. Anderson 1991, 141–44) often have harder edges than their supporters are comfortable recognizing. The exemplary writers and communities that often inform the civic republican tradition, Machiavelli and Rousseau, Sparta and republican Rome, display political commitments characterized by high degrees of aggression.[39] Even if there is no necessary connection between civic energy and violent political competition, civic republicans often use the strength of communal attachment as a proxy for regime health or move immediately from recognizing the constitutive influence of cultural forms to endorsing the norms of communitarianism (Hardin 1995, 24). Finally, critics of all sorts point to the hazards that civic republican institutions can impose on possibilities for rational autonomy or critical judgment (cf. Habermas 1996, 286; Villa 2001, x–xii; Warren 2001, 23–24).

Theories of deliberative democracy are accordingly dissatisfied with both contractarian and civic republican conceptions of political voice and instead endorse a view of political rationality supportive of the individual agency and critical judgment that democratic theories of collective action presuppose (Habermas 1996, 146–47, 298–99; Warren 2001, 62–63; Cohen and Arato 1992, 354, 411). Consequently, of the three competing positions, deliberative democratic theory's treatment of political voice is the most consistent with the complex premises of democratic politics, understood as a process for collective decisions binding individual members while respecting citizens as the originators and critics of public choice.

Yet deliberative democratic theory's treatment of political voice also faces some of the same conceptual limitations that compromise its treatment of political trust. Its skepticism about teleology constrains its ability to defend the good of a democratic society governed by the judgment of citizens. Its parallel suspicions of conceptions of human virtue limit its examination of the institutional and cultural resources needed to support healthy judgment. And its exclusive concern for procedure means that it praises democratic judgment without providing any separate guidance for evaluating its substantive determinations. Together, Thucydides and Plato create a context for examining the phenomenon of democratic judgment that is more complicated and more substantial. Yet they do so without displacing the critical independence that such judgment presupposes.

Political Judgments and Misjudgments in Thucydides

The importance of judgment for Thucydides is apparent both in the pragmatic concerns of the *History* as a whole and in the individual treatments of democratic political practice that extend throughout the narrative. Cynthia Farrar suggests that Thucydides' possession for eternity is not a timeless causal analysis of the human condition, but a historically sensitive resource in support of political judgment (1988, 158), needed because of the erosion of the community templates that had previously guided Athenian political choices (1988, 154). For Farrar, this resource is offered particularly in the narratives of the speeches and practices of Pericles that together construct a model for a political rationality built on the careful interpretation of events and a disciplined moderation of destructive passions. As a resource for education, this example encourages human thought (*gnōmē*) that can resist the onslaughts of passion (*orgē*) so as to manage better the fluctuations of chance (*tychē*). (Farrar 1988, 159–65; cf. Edmunds 1975, 52, 56, 193, 209; Price 2001, 24; Parry 1981, 154, 156).

In her interpretations of Pericles' three speeches, Farrar traces a consistent concern to develop the Athenian capacity for civic judgment in service of the city (1988, 163; see also Balot 2001, 144–47; Edmunds 1975, 193, 211; Price 2001, 237, 260; Yunis 1996, 79–80; and Parry, 1981, 188). There is considerable textual evidence in support of this claim, for all three speeches link private with public welfare (Thucydides 1.144.3–4, 2.43.1–2, 2.61.2–4). And Pericles' concern to foster thoughtful moderation among the Athenians is reinforced by Thucydides' glowing appreciation for Pericles' statesmanship and scathing assessment of those who followed him as leaders of the democracy. "Whenever he perceived that [the people] were arrogantly bold against what the times warranted, he confounded them into fearfulness by his speaking, and again, when they were irrationally afraid, he restored them to confidence. And what was said to be a democracy was in fact a rule by the first man. Those who came later, in contrast, since they were much more like one another and each was extending himself to become first, [they] gave over the affairs [of the city] to the pleasure of the *dēmos*" (2.65.9–11).

Yet aspects of Pericles' speeches also prompt reservations about the character of his leadership.[40] These speeches are highly complex rhetorically, and each has been carefully interpreted by a number of fine commentators. Let me focus on two continuous features that problematize Farrar's assessment.[41] First, Pericles is consistently guided by a conception of Athens's well-being that is heavily influenced by his own conception of the human good.[42] This vision is forcefully summarized in the last speech (2.60–64), where a concern for how Athens will be remembered plays an ever more prominent role. Though it is in the nature of all things to be diminished, what is to be cherished most is reputation or the greatest name (*onoma megiston*) won by daring achievement. While Athens's project of self-assertion may well end with the disappearance of its material accomplishments under the ravages of time (cf. 1.10.2–3) and while it will certainly engender resentment among its immediate competitors and subjects, "hatred does not persist for long, but the brilliance of the instant and repute (*doxa*) therefore remain in eternal memory (*aieimnēstos*)" (2.64.5–6). This speech condenses Pericles' opposition to the cramped and crass political ambition of lesser regimes. What motivates Athens is the pursuit of reputation or distinction that defeats death. Consequently, Pericles extends the funeral speech's recognition (2.43.3–4) of the boundless fame awaiting those conspicuous men who have the whole earth as their tomb or monument to the city itself. In one sense, this repoliticizes an individual love of reputation that might otherwise treat the city's well-being as instrumental to selfish achievements.[43] Yet it also treats Athens as if it were the conspicuous man writ large, mapping the priorities of the daring individual in love with fame onto the community as a whole.[44]

A second continuous theme across the three speeches is that this vision of the human good and thus of Athens's well-being is politically contested. The source of what Pericles characterizes as Athens's "greatest name" is that "we as Hellenes ruled over the most Hellenes, sustained the greatest wars against them, both individually and united, and lived in a city that was in all ways best provided for and greatest" (2.64.3–4). This encomium to Athens's competitive energy and imperial reach encounters resistance and challenge from numerous cultural quarters ranging from the grieving families of the dead (2.44–45) to those who oppose this project in defense of their own political independence (1.143.5) or in support of an alternative vision of Athens's good (2.64.4–5). Pericles' rhetoric is crafted to combat such dissenting voices. In his first speech, he absorbs all concerns for private well-being within a more expansive vision of the public good, while at the same time characterizing that public good in demanding terms. "[O]ut of the greatest dangers (*megistōn kindunōn*) emerge the greatest honors (*megistai timai*) for both city and individual" (1.144.3–4), he says, as if prospects for the greatest honors drove every individual to run the greatest risks. When the funeral speech builds toward the exhortation that all citizens "really pay regard (*theōmenous*) each day to the power of the city and become her lovers (*erastas*)" (2.43.1), it simultaneously acknowledges and diminishes concerns for more private conceptions of well-being as useless (*achreia*) (2.40.2, 2.44.4).[45] And though the final speech begins with Pericles' portraying the city as the guardian of private security (2.60.2–4), it ends with the eloquent praise of Athens's power and brilliance and a dismissal as do-nothings of those who refuse to contribute to Athens's eternal reputation (2.64.4–5).

From this perspective, Pericles' rhetoric seems less like the promotion of judgment (*gnōmē*) as a civic good in itself and more like the elicitation of civic commitment in service of a political image that will live (forever [*aiei*]) in memory. In this respect, Pericles' inspiring memory seems less friendly to rational criticism, which now appears as the resentful whinings of the useless and the inactive. This characterization of Pericles' project makes it less obvious that Thucydides' own assessment of Pericles' leadership is an unqualified endorsement. While Pericles' response to the plague ("the sole thing among all others that has happened beyond our foresight" [2.64.1]) is to reaffirm the eternal permanence of Athens's name owing to the facts of its spectacular and beautiful achievements, Thucydides' positioning of the plague narrative after the funeral oration provides a basis for remembering the sordid and ugly consequences of the war.[46]

Thucydidean reservations about Pericles' accomplishments and legacy can be detected even within the encomium on Pericles' career.[47] While commentators justifiably emphasize Thucydides' dramatically different assessments of Pericles and his successors,[48] there is a disquieting continuity between Pericles' role as first man in a regime that was democratic only in name and the subsequent competition among his successors over who would be the next one to be first. Might the

Thucydidean Pericles speak as if his rule was itself out of time, from the vantage point of imagining eternity, dismissing the need to take the temporality of politics into account?[49] Thucydides' praise of the regime of the Five Thousand as the "Athenians'.... best government at least in my lifetime" (8.97.2–3) may not outline an institutional approximation to Periclean virtue (as for Farrar 1988, 186), but instead serve as a pointed criticism of the Periclean example. As praised by Thucydides, the regime of the Five Thousand is not a democracy in name, yet it is in fact very far from the *archē* of any *protos anēr*.[50] Oddly put, it is a regime that is distinctive in its moderation (Thucydides 8. 97). And in spite of the praise of Pericles' prudential foresight in recommending strategic restraints of efforts to expand the empire in wartime, the assessment ends by implying that his prediction about Athens's eventual success in the war was hubristically distorted: "So great were the resources Pericles had at that time, enabling his own prediction that the city would easily prevail in the war over the Peloponnesians alone."[51]

Revealing the strengths and weaknesses of Pericles' *gnōmē* may thus be a part of a larger educative attempt to develop a more nuanced form of civic judgment. In this light, it is valuable to assess Thucydides' representation of the judgment of other citizens, acting within regimes that are not simply democratic in name. Of particular importance is the juxtaposition of two compelling and ambiguous democratic voices, both expressed within debates over collective action in the face of frightening civic crises. These are the speeches of Diodotus, opposing Cleon, in the Mytilene debate and of the Syracusan democrat Athenagoras, opposing the statesman Hermocrates, in the dispute over Sicily's response to the apparently imminent Athenian invasion (6.33–41). Both speeches expressly underscore the vital connection between judgment and democracy. Rational judgment is the form of political voice most appropriate to democracy, and its effective exercise is both crucial for democratic collective action and problematically related to democratic political forms.

The circumstances and consequences of Diodotus's speech have been outlined earlier. In opposition to Cleon, he has argued for the critical importance of rationality in the determination of public policy (3.42.1–2). Yet rationality is threatened by two dangerous hazards. The first is posed by the passions of anger, fear, hope, and *erōs* that afflict the human species (3.45.1–6). The second is found in political and cultural practices that foster competitions and jealousies poisonous to collective deliberation. Though the normative premise of the assembly seems to be deliberative rationality, its actual operations exploit and intensify the passions that undercut judgment. Diodotus's implicit response to a position such as Habermas's is that institutions supporting the forceless force of the stronger argument are tragically self-undermining. Intersecting with the violence of the passions, they only seem to make things worse.

As I have suggested earlier, however, this critique of the assembly is made in the name of a vision of the appropriate outcomes of discursive politics. While Diodotus moves from the historical failure of punitive measures to control crime to an inference about the futility of punishment in principle (3.45.4–7), he makes no such claim with respect to the possibility of educating the passions through some form of *logos*. If the success of such an argument is not impossible, then Diodotus's recourse to deception is a contingent strategy responsive to immediate political pressures, not an inevitable consequence of the political impotence of *logos*.

At the same time, Diodotus's characterization of deliberative practices goes beyond suggesting that healthy democratic institutions need to foster honest discourse. His criticism of the current deliberative environment within the Athenian assembly is that "it has come to such a pass that good advice spoken out of honesty is no less suspect than bad, so that it is equally required that the one who wishes to bring the many to the most terrible decisions must resort to deceptions to persuade them, just as that one whose speeches are better must lie to be persuasive" (3.43.2–3). Apart from its immediate importance within the *History*, Diodotus's critique can also be read as implying that a more complex framework than that provided by deliberative democratic theory is needed for the theoretical assessment of democracy. Institutions can enable or pervert honest and inclusive discourse. Speakers can be truthful or deceptive. The policies they recommend can aim at what is better (*ta ameinō*) or can counsel the most terrible things (*ta deinotata*) (3.43.2). These pairings are not always congruent. Truthful speeches offered in contexts of complete openness can persuade audiences to act viciously. There can also be noble lies and noble liars. From this perspective, the openness of a discursive process and the truthfulness of speakers (cf. Habermas 1993, 86–94, 136–37) do not assure the goodness of decision, and theorizing democracy needs to do more than track or systematize democratic processes (Habermas 1996, 321–28; Warren 2001, 226). Diodotus's speech thus suggests the need for more consideration of how the processes and outcomes of democratic deliberation intersect. His own choice of a good outcome deceptively achieved over a terrible one openly agreed to rejects the valorization of processes. Yet his speech is hardly insensitive to the political importance of discursive procedure. Cleon's impressive though execrable performance shows that decent processes and healthy outcomes can be threatened from the same sources.

Beyond this, while Diodotus's speech implies that a healthy democratic theory should inform political deliberations from a vantage point that overlaps but extends beyond institutional deliberative spheres, expanded theorizing is no replacement for the deliberative practice that institutional spaces make possible. Consequently, Diodotus's speech as a citizen cannot be simply generalized into political theory because it is embedded in the distortions that political judgment must necessarily encounter. In this respect, Diodotus's political judgment is both more and less than a democratic political theory (cf. Saxonhouse 1996, 75). It is more because it partially depends upon insights about healthy democratic outcomes that cannot be validated solely on the basis of an appreciation of democratic processes. It is less because it must take seriously nests of political motivations and demands that a theorized account of democracy's normative possibilities would often ignore. Diodotus's intention is to elicit mercy for Mytilene's democrats and a quiet reconsideration of the fate of its oligarchs. He must settle for saving the democrats while leaving the oligarchs to Cleon's justice. Though the complete narrative of his practice is a problematic basis for either a critique or an endorsement of deliberative democracy, it is difficult to deny that as a citizen faced with a wrenching political dilemma where no outcome is innocent, Diodotus judges, if not well, at least, as well as he can.

From a vantage point more removed from the practical immediacies, democratic judgment can now be seen as partner of trust within functional democratic institutions. Trust is both a condition for and a consequence of healthy democratic judgment. As partners, both are threatened by hazards besetting those institutions. The nature of these hazards is seen more clearly within the speech of Athenagoras, who praises judgment even as he sows the seeds of mistrust.

Occasioned by rumors of the imminent Athenian invasion of Sicily, the speech is a response to what seems initially to be a strategic proposal made by Hermocrates, the notable Syracusan. Treating the rumors as certainly true, Hermocrates urges an aggressive confrontation of the Athenian fleet at Tarentum, intercepting the invaders before they can establish any foothold in Sicily (6.34.3–4). This advice is clearly more than strategic, for it draws upon a controversial vision of Sicily's possibilities, what I have called, in chapter 2, a kind of political imagination. At one level, Hermocrates envisages strengthening Syracuse's immediate influence (6.33.4). Yet the material advantages of power are less important than the opportunities for enacting the most noble deeds (*kalliston dē ergōn*), appropriately rewarded by glory and reputation (6.33.4). In this respect, Hermocrates' political imagination envisages Syracusan achievements that rival and eventually surpass those of the Athenians.

Deliberating Democracy

This vision of Syracusan achievement cannot be realized, however, unless the city abandons its "characteristic quietness" (*to synēthes hēsychon*) in favor of a more daring disposition (6.34.4). The success of Hermocrates' proposals, both narrowly and broadly understood, depends on his ability to foster a new, more Athenian, sense of Syracusan political identity. In calling for such radical changes in self-conception, Hermocrates implicitly presents himself as a leader whose achievements do not simply parallel Pericles', but go beyond them. He is Periclean insofar as he argues for the attractiveness of the noblest deeds against the voices of those who treasure peace and quiet. In striving to consolidate widespread alliances against an Athens now playing the Persian role (6.33.5–6), Hermocrates' aspirations resemble Themistocles' (1.93.3–5). And his earlier (4.44.3) attempts to forge a modern Sicilian identity may be cognate to the founding accomplishments of Theseus in Attica (2.14.2).

The political cultural implications of Hermocrates' proposals make Athenagoras's response more intelligible and consistent than it otherwise might seem. Understandable distaste for the person of Athenagoras can lead to a premature dismissal of his speech's importance. Pouncey sees this as Thucydides' only "deliberately wasted" speech, inviting "the reader's scorn for the fatuity of its content" (1980, 14).[52] Far from sharing this assessment, I suggest that Athenagoras's speech and practice play important roles within Thucydides' treatment of democratic judgment. Athenagoras moves from a skepticism about the alleged invasion to an affirmation of the egalitarian principles of democracy and a praise of judgment as democratic voice. These claims are related, for he ascribes the falsity of the rumors not to error or fear but to the machinations of oligarchs determined to seize power.

Athenagoras justifies his skepticism about the invasion by referring to the predictable behavior of "clever [or sensible] human beings [educated by] numerous experiences" (*anthrōpoi deinoi kai pollōn empeiroi*) (6.36.3). The behavior expected from such people is not daring aggression but prudent caution. Since the invasion rumors are baseless, they must be traced to seditious attempts to manipulate public opinion. While Hermocrates had focused on the rational fear that would drive the smaller Sicilian cities to align with Syracuse, Athenagoras points to the irrational fear that would lead the Syracusan majority (*to plēthos*) to surrender control to the few (6.38.2). Athenagoras thus situates the debate about the invasion within domestic contests (*agōnas*) or wars (*polemious*) that threaten to end in oligarchy or tyranny (6.38.3). These concerns are intensified by Hermocrates' urging a proactive strategy requiring considerable changes in Syracuse's habitual practices. What Hermocrates (or Pericles) might see as exemplary energy is interpreted by Athenagoras as a source of oppression. Yet though he resembles Cleon in his distrust of the few or the notables (cf. Connor 1984, 171; cf. Saxonhouse 2006, 176), Athenagoras's response differs in at least two important respects. First, while Cleon intensifies feelings of division in a way that could lead very quickly to bloodshed (3.37.3–4), Athenagoras offers the possibility of a reconciliation. His strategy for dealing with the oligarchs combines refutation and surveillance with education (*didaskōn*) (6.38.4). While Cleon is said to be the most persuasive (*pithanōtatos*) and most violent (*biaiōtatos*) of the citizens (3.36.6), Athenagoras is characterized only as "the popular leader who seemed most persuasive to the many" (*hos dēmou te prostatēs hēn kai en tō paronti pithanōtatos tois pollois*) (6.35.2). Second, while Cleon exploits the assembly's uncertainty to insult democracy (3.37.1–2), Athenagoras approvingly places the determination of public policy with the many, whose specific political virtue is the ability to judge things for the best (*krinai . . . arista*) (6.39.1).[53]

Athenagoras's praise of the many's capacity for judgment is offered as a reply to his own representations of oligarchic theories of political equality and justice. The oligarchs argue for a kind of proportional equality where possessions or property signal the ability to rule well (6.39.1). Athenagoras responds with a claim about the salutary contribution that the many can make to the formulation of public policy. While the rich are the best guardians of possessions and the more intelligent the best counselors, the many, after having heard everything discussed, are the best judges (6.39.1). Consequently, the rich, the more intelligent, and the many, understood either as a separate part of society or simply as the different types of individuals who comprise the civic body as a whole, ought to enjoy the equality that is appropriate to a democracy (6.39.2).

On the basis of this argument, Athenagoras goes well beyond Aristotle's preliminary definition of democracy as the rule of the poor majority in its own interests (*Politics* 3.7). For Athenagoras, the many justly rule not on account of power or numbers, but because of a certain ability or virtue. He does not expressly maintain that this virtue is equally distributed among the individual members of the many but simply that the many's collective judgment is likely to produce the best decision for the community. Indeed, Athenagoras's definition of the many seems purposefully vague. From one perspective, they can be distinguished from the rich and more intelligent as the poorest and least-educated class of citizens. Yet the many can also include individual members of the rich and educated social classes, so that democracy means an arithmetical political equality within the assembly and before the law. In a sense, Athenagoras makes not simply the clearest and most comprehensive (cf.

Strauss 1964, 169), but also perhaps the best case for democracy and for its own particular political voice.

However, while Athenagoras praises judgment as a democratic intellectual virtue, his own speech is more notable for its lack of judgment.[54] He is wrong about Athens's intentions with respect to the invasion; this error is traceable to his mendacious searching for sinister motives behind calls to take the Athenian threat seriously. These failures in judgment are not simply personal deficiencies. While Orwin rightly condemns Athenagoras as a fool and a scoundrel, I believe he goes too far in concluding that Thucydides' representation "could hardly have presented the case for democracy more disparagingly" (1994, 186). Instead, Athenagoras's speech reveals the best possibilities for democratic voice, even as his speech-act reveals hazards that can interfere with its practice. In some respects, it is the very case for democracy that most clearly reveals Athenagoras's political vices.

One reason for Athenagoras's errors is that his assumptions about human behavior are smugly pedestrian.[55] He sees no essential difference between the kinds of things that rational human beings desire. All sensible people pursue the material satisfactions that the rich succeed in achieving. Experienced or mature human beings pursue these goods progressively and cautiously, securing one before moving to the next. Therefore, regimes are not to be distinguished by the particular values or priorities they identify as good. Oligarchies and democracies differ only in their relative distributions of risks and rewards (6.39.2). Desires for preeminence and status and readiness to court danger to achieve them are signs of inexperience and immaturity. The rich may be rational in wishing to spread the risks of acquisition while hoarding its rewards, but the young are foolish in wanting to rule before the appropriate time (6.38.5). This simplistic assumption about the character of human desires prevents Athenagoras from taking prospects of an Athenian invasion seriously, for he fails to recognize the motivating force of the love of fame and reputation. He treats the cautious civic identity urged on the Athenians by Nicias (6.11–13) as if it were an accurate description of Athens's civic priorities, and he cannot envisage the sensible Athenians falling under the influence of an Alcibiades (6.18.6–7). For the same reasons, he fails to take seriously the political imagination underlying Hermocrates' vision for a new Syracuse. He therefore groups the powerful with the young (6.39.2), dismissing the ambitions of the powerful as immaturities that will be cured by experience, and groups the best with the rich (6.39.1), denying any claim to distinction beyond wealth. Here, Athenagoras's claim that the intelligent are the best counselors but the many the best judges can be read as referring to strategy. The wise, like the Sophists, provide options for achieving those things that every mature person desires. The many are best positioned to select among these proposed options, perhaps basing their decisions on the relative distributions of risks and rewards.

For Athenagoras, judgment is not, therefore, faced with sorting out relative merits of competing goods, for the content of the human good properly understood admits no controversy. If the good is material prosperity, regimes should be judged according to their abilities to make it accessible to the largest number of citizens (6.40.1) and not in light of their efforts to develop ennobled or enhanced conceptions of well-being. Democracy is the best regime because it offers the broadest distribution of material rewards and not, as in Pericles' formulation, because it elicits the widest array of individual achievements (2.37.1–2). Judgment as political voice confirms rather than interrogates the material goods of democracy.

Athenagoras thus construes political judgment as nonproblematic in two senses. First, it is not faced with any teleological dilemmas, for questions about the good are in principle resolvable by maturity and experience. Second, the exercise of judgment is not impaired by any passions that cannot be diminished or tamed through maturation. Democratic regimes are not challenged by their need to rely on the rational judgments of their citizens; nor is the development of capacities for rational judgment a pressing political cultural problem in need of intelligent attention. Yet Athenagoras's own speech-act problematizes judgment in precisely these two ways. The immediate presence of Hermocrates and the progressive advance of the Athenians signal visions of the good very different from that pursued by Athenagoras's sensible man. And Athenagoras's own blinders (treating Hermocrates as an adolescent and seeing democratic Athens as a replication of Athenagorean democracy) obscure a much more turbulent political field that both demands and complicates the healthy functioning of judgment.

If Athenagoras ignores the complexities of and barriers against judgment, Diodotus dwells on them. In insisting that Athens's decision about Mytilene be guided by advantage rather than by justice, Diodotus recognizes the prospective influence of two priorities that are neither reducible to one another (Cleon) nor commensurable according to a single unit of measure (Protagoras). In his indictment of contemporary public deliberation, he reveals persisting conflicts between private and public interests that need to be somehow negotiated. And in emphasizing the overwhelming power of the passions within an argument for rational moderation, he raises but does not resolve the vexing question of how intelligence and desire relate. Yet while Athenagoras's praise of judgment is undercut by the very difficulties he ignores, Diodotus's express pessimism about the possibility of political judgment is mitigated by his appeal to it.

We should note, however, that this appeal (which is only partially successful, in any case) is made by a figure whose presence in the assembly is curious. Lying beneath Diodotus's speech and practice is his mysterious identity. In this respect, he is linked in a literary way with Athenagoras, for it is plausible that both are dramatic creations of Thucydides (cf. Forde 1989, 40 n. 34; Palmer 1992, 125, n. 22; Saxonhouse 1996, 75). No known historical source provides independent evidence of their existence, and both are named in ways that are intrinsically connected to their thematic importance. Though Athenagoras is a Syracusan, his speech is a condensation of the strongest case that could be made for democratic governance. The preeminent democracy in Thucydides' narrative is Athens, and the most extended space for the expression of democratic voice is the *agora*. As Connor notes, "We have traveled to Syracuse and found Athens" (1984, 171). Yet if this assumption about Athenagoras's dramatic significance is accepted, then the deficiencies of his speech-act (which undercut his simplistic understanding of democratic judgment) are perhaps themselves products of the political culture of democracy, particularly its suspicion of serious attempts to engage teleological dilemmas as masks for oligarchy or repression. It is up to Diodotus to recognize that democratic judgment is both essential and problematic. His response to this condition draws on both the possibilities implicit in democratic institutions and the resources that somehow extend beyond them. If Diodotus is, as *his* name suggests, a gift of the gods (or Zeus), then his presence cannot be confidently assumed on the basis of an acquaintance with democratic culture and, indeed, with political culture generally. Thus, though Diodotus's speech offers an implicit critique of Athenagoras's, that critique is not made in the name of political arrangements that Athenagoras opposes. A critique of Athenagoras is not equivalent to a rejection of democracy. Instead, the distinctive practices of democracy make Diodotus's contributions possible. While the seemingly frank speeches of the oligarchic sympathizers of 411 work to silence democratic voice (8.53.3, 8.66.2–5), the admittedly deceptive speech of Diodotus provokes it.

Despite his limited success in arguing for moderation toward Mytilene, however, Diodotus effectively maintains that prospects for institutionalizing democratic voice are remote indeed. In this sense, Diodotus's speech anticipates the implications of Athenagoras's speech-act; only a gift from the gods can remedy the condition that the speeches of Diodotus and Athenagoras, in different ways, reveal. We find this discouraging conclusion moderated in a surprising way by the Platonic Socrates.

Judging the Gorgias

Socrates' most sustained examination of democratic voice is found in the *Gorgias*. On the surface, the Socrates of the *Gorgias* is even more despairing than Diodotus of formulating public policy through rational deliberation. He implies that democratic assemblies and juries are ignorant and licentious. Concerned only with gratification, they are vulnerable to the flattery of scheming rhetoricians and potentially threatening to those seriously concerned with civic improvement (*Gorgias* 521d–22a). This pessimistic conclusion about democratic institutions seems continuously interwoven with a contempt for democratic voice in which interactions between orators and citizens reflect the vices of both eloquence and outcries.[56] The verbal relation is between an orator who is "without knowledge" (*anepistēmos*) and an audience made up of "those who do not know" (*tois mē eidosin*) (459a–b); the result is persuasion without teaching. In the dialogue, the teacher of rhetoric, Gorgias, takes this result as a sign of the rhetorician's (eloquent) power. However, Socrates eventually argues that this exercise of power is only successful because the rhetorician praises and blames the things that gratify the ignorant. Eloquence turns into flattery and power into dependency very quickly. But since the many are fawned over and not educated, their capacity for responding even to proposals concerning their narrower interests is gradually corrupted. Eventually, they will come to see cooks and vintners as trainers and physicians, and will "cry out" (*anaboēsai*) against anyone who attempts to impose beneficial but painful treatments (522a).

The alternative that Socrates seems to offer, however, is not any kind of democratic voice, for such an instruction would rely upon the unrealistic possibility of the many's becoming somehow knowledgeable. What Socrates sketches instead is a therapeutic rhetoric that aims at improvement by appealing to the desires, a rhetoric executed "with a view to the best" (*pros to beltiston*) (502e–3b) by a "philosophic statesman" dealing with a crowd of persons who have "but little intelligence."[57] The result of this exercise, then, is not intellectual judgment but moral virtue, construed in the *Gorgias* largely as a certain kind of moderation (504d). This moral improvement seems, however, to be achieved by eliminating rather than improving democratic voice. According to this view, the democratic assembly is turned into a group of good listeners. This listening is less Barber's political listening (in which the "empathetic listener becomes more like [an] interlocutor and [the speaker and listener] bridge the differences between them by conversation")[58] and more the respectful listening of a congregation to a sermon. Within this latter form of listening, edification and compliance predominate more than reflection and criticism.

Most critics, both friendly and hostile, have taken this Socratic attack as accurately reflecting Plato's position on democratic political institutions. Defenders of democracy have responded counter-Platonically by reaffirming the democratic speech that Socrates condemns or by challenging the intellectually hegemonic politics that seems to be the alternative.[59] These responses remind us of both the contestable character of Socrates' criticisms of the democracy and the difficulties inherent within what looks to be his own proposal. Yet each response is also problematic. The first tends to discount the hazards of popular democracy much too preemptively. And the second fails to consider the dramatic form of the Platonic dialogues, in which Socrates' speeches are crafted with a view to particular interlocutors and situations and, indeed, in which Socrates himself speaks with what the *Republic*'s Thrasymachus calls "habitual irony" (*eiōthuia eirōneia*). The irony of Socrates' literal attack on democratic politics is hinted at when Socrates later (*Gorgias* 521d) calls himself the only practitioner of the political art (*politikē*) in Athens, even as he refuses to become involved in official or institutional politics. What it means to be a democratic citizen now becomes uncertain. In this light, Socrates' attitude toward democratic politics is considerably more complex.[60] A reconstruction that improves democratic politics in a way consistent with democracy's own priorities or presuppositions may be more of a possibility than a literal reading of Socrates' statements would suggest.

In the *Gorgias*, prospects for reconstruction hinge on the possibility of democratic voice as judgment. Such prospects are implicit in the dramatic circumstances of the dialogue. The speeches of the five speaking characters—Socrates, Chaerephon, Gorgias, Polus, and Callicles—are witnessed by a number of nameless citizens whom Gorgias wishes to impress and whom Socrates no doubt wants to influence. These men never speak as individuals, though they sometimes express collective preferences. At crucial junctures, however, Socrates attempts to elicit judgments from Callicles, a man who in some respects represents and in others stands apart from the larger group.[61] Callicles' opportunities, responses, and eventual rebuke illustrate the promises of and the limitations to democratic judgment. The structural dimensions of this kind of judgment emerge subtly as the dialogue unfolds. The results can be more systematically rendered by sketching six interactive aspects that, in course, arise.

First, democratic political judgment is situated between private and public realms. In his interrogation of Callicles about different forms of political rhetoric, Socrates asks whether the most influential leaders of the democracy, past or present, have spoken to improve the citizens or merely to flatter them. (502d–e). As stated, the question is immediately much more complicated than the now standard question addressed with great frequency to the American electorate, originating most explicitly with Ronald Reagan during the 1980 U.S. presidential campaign: "Are you better off now than you were four years ago?" While Reagan's question requested a verdict on one's own personal situation, Socrates' demands a personal reflection on political or cultural conditions. This reflection involves more than a simple balancing between private interests and the common good. It suggests, rather, that private interests or benefits are necessarily intertwined with the health of the political community. To the extent that Socrates' listeners belong to the Athenian public, they are asked to draw their conclusions based in part on their own experiences. Yet because they must judge the effects of political rhetoric upon the civic culture generally, they must compare their own reactions to those of others, present and past, or supplement introspection with cultural and historical awareness. However, because Socrates is also asking for a reflective personal conclusion, the respondent cannot simply answer as a typical or representative member of the Athenian regime. The democrat capable of legitimate judgment must stand both among and apart from his or her fellow citizens.[62]

The difficulty of achieving this individuated sense of common responsibility is suggested by the fact that neither of the two principal interlocutors in this discussion succeeds in practicing it. Gorgias's opening praise of rhetoric's power implies that skill in speaking enables both personal success and civic freedom (452d). This compatibility is fractured as Polus and Callicles progressively undermine respect for the community by appeals to private advantage. Socrates responds by eventually calling himself the only statesman (*politikos*) in Athens, thus making his philosophy into a publicly beneficial discourse. The strategy he employs is to unmask the fact that Callicles' principal concern is with security rather than with gratification and to frighten him into privateness by revealing the dangers of public crime both while alive and in the afterlife. Socrates emerges at the dialogue's end as the private philosopher who is also a kind of statesman, while Callicles appears as the aggressive politician who is anxiously, if not obsessively, self-protective.[63] Each of these conversions underscores by implication the dangers resulting from a failure to keep the public and the private in proper proportion. Reducing the one to the other causes diverse forms of destruction, ranging from the destruction of philosophy (by publicizing it into statesmanship) to the destruction of politics (by privatizing it into deadly quarrels among aggressive predators and fearful victims). In the context of this discussion, we can appreciate how these dangers also beset the democratic voices of outcries and eloquence; conceiving democratic voice as the expression of outcries or demands sees through and thus eliminates the public (Cleon), while interpreting it as eloquence threatens to overwhelm the private (Pericles). One of the advantages of judgment is that it avoids both distortions. To the extent that judgment scrutinizes competing goods like the (publicly) noble and the (privately) pleasant, it insists that public deliberation or public policy respect priorities or goods that extend beyond personal gratification. Yet by remaining individual, judgment also insists that the rational person be guided by more than communally focused appeals of public eloquence.

The principal concern of this form of judgment is illustrated by a second difference between the Reaganite and the Socratic questions compared earlier. While Reagan's question immediately focuses the listeners' attention on narrowly conceived economic interests, and thus provides a readily accessible answer to the question of well-being, Socrates' makes what it means to be well-off into a problem. From this perspective, democratic judgment is pragmatically teleological; it is focused upon the need for and the content of human improvement. Articulating this teleological concern likewise seems beyond the reach of outcries and eloquence. Socrates' denial that the good and the pleasant are identical (495e) makes it impossible to claim that human well-being is simply personal gratification. And by asking Callicles his own opinion about the contribution that political culture makes to the well-being of citizens, Socrates insists that a rational person's pursuit of the good must include a critical scrutiny of publicly valorized symbols.

Political voice understood as judgment can exercise its choice making and critical functions only if personal rationality can be constitutive of choice, rather than simply instrumental or subordinate. To the extent that political voice is construed as outcries, its articulations become strategic devices serving the passions or, less dramatically, the preferences. The subservience of rationality to desire is implicit in Gorgias's contention that rhetorical skill can be employed so that the rhetorician will not have less (changed by Polus and Callicles into having more) than practitioners of the other arts. Similarly, construing political voice as eloquence threatens to enclose rationality within a rush of common feeling or a festival of public symbols. Socrates comments ironically on his own reactions to such speeches within the *Menexenus*, a dialogue devoted to a rewriting of Pericles' funeral speech. "[The orators] praise so beautifully (*kalōs*) . . . that they bewitch (*goēteuousin*) our souls and praise the city according to every fashion and they praise those dying in war and all of our ancestors from former times and ourselves now living, so that I, Menexenus, being praised by them feel altogether ennobled (*panu gennaiōs*) and each time I stand listening and enraptured, I am led immediately to become greater and nobler and more beautiful . . . and this feeling remains with me for more than three days, so persistently does the speech and the voice of the speaker ring in my ears that it is only on the fourth or fifth day that I recollect myself and perceive that I am here on earth, and not, as I thought before, on the Isles of the Blessed" (*Menexenus* 234c–35c).

This ironic description of the effects of such orations reveals both the power and the deficiencies of public eloquence in ways that are directly relevant for understanding democratic judgment. Such speeches are enormously powerful insofar as they prompt those who hear them to forget their own vulnerabilities and shortcomings. By eliciting an unrealistic sense of superiority, eloquent orations block access to the kind of intelligent self-criticism that a teleologically oriented judgment requires. Yet for the same reasons, such eloquence is also debilitating, because the vulnerabilities and shortcomings that it obscures persist. Pericles' speeches do not make Socrates less ugly. In this respect, Socrates is better-off than most of his fellow citizens, for while his ugliness is literally as plain as the nose on his face, the Athenians are surrounded by apparent confirmations of their power and nobility.[64] It takes something as unrelievedly ugly as the plague to upset these certainties. But while rationality cannot remove physical ugliness or provide immunity from disease, it is capable of helping human beings recognize the hazards and injustices connected with amassing wealth or attempting political domination.

Yet such a conception of rationality, precisely on account of its potentially directive role, seems authoritative rather than democratic, political voice as imperative, rather than as judgment. This impression is softened by three subsequent features of political judgment that emerge implicitly within the *Gorgias*.

Socrates does not, in this dialogue, present himself as an expert of any kind. He is, instead, a partner in dialogue. This emerges most clearly in the conclusion when he assails his interlocutors and himself for their shameful lack of education (*apaideusia*), shown by failure to come to better conclusions about the most important questions. Indeed, the only *logos* that remains unrefuted is that doing injustice is to be avoided far more than suffering it (527b). In making this claim, Socrates does not enshrine this conclusion as a dogma or certainty with no need of further rational defense. Rather, he invites his interlocutors (and himself) to attempt the discovery of a better *logos*, one that will be supported by a positive agreement rather than simply by the absence of convincing refutations.

In insisting that the benefits of justice be established dialogically, Socrates thus indicates his support for a discursive (rather than a demonstrative or didactic) model of political reasoning. From this perspective, political judgment cannot be practiced or completed monologically with its results communicated to a waiting audience. Instead, its expression requires discursive interactions with identifiable others in question and answer. This focus on dialogue as an alternative to rhetoric suggests a parallel between Socratic practice and the discourse ethics upon which deliberative democrats rely. Yet the parallel extends only so far in light of the rejection of teleology by discourse ethics and its consequent leanings toward proceduralism. Socrates' continued allegiance toward teleological questions is shown by his insistence that the value of political choice in a democracy be assessed in light of its contributions to the character development of citizens. This contribution should not be seen as instrumental, since the ability to examine thoughtfully how our practices relate to a well-lived life is itself excellence (*Apology* 38a). Thus, for Socrates, the value of procedures associated with deliberative rationality cannot be decoupled from an assessment of the outcomes that deliberation reaches. Rationality is marked by substantive commitments, not simply by procedural legitimacy.

That such a rationality must remain discursive rather than authoritative is underscored by a fifth distinctive feature of Socratic political judgment. It is nuanced or contextual rather than generalizing and rule-governed. Endorsement of this form of rationality is implicit even within Socrates' seemingly most categorical assertions in the *Gorgias*. In spite of his direct attacks on the incompetence and vice of the Athenian politicians, he exempts Aristides, who was called "the just." The general accuracy of the conclusion that "from among the powerful are the human beings who have become especially wicked" does not prevent Socrates from noticing the particular justice of one politician (*Gorgias* 525e–26b). The accuracy of this particular exception aside, Socrates' noticing fundamental differences among his interlocutors thus seems to be one of the permanent features of his conduct throughout the dialogues.

The ability to see texture and particularity amid patterns and generalities seems to associate the Platonic conception of political judgment with the turn away from universalizing moral rules and toward an appreciation of the "concrete other" that characterizes some positions within contemporary feminism or with the more general ethical position called moral particularism.[65] To this extent, however, the Platonic position may seem more relevant for moral than for political discourse.

For while a judgment "which is more contextual, more immersed in the details of relationships and narratives" (Benhabib 1992, 149) may be a marked improvement over cold formalism within moral life, it seems less valuable or appropriate within the more constraining and less personal realm of politics. As Socrates says in the *Apology*, his interrogations of individual Athenians do not extend into formal politics (31c ff.).

But while commitments to a more contextual form of judgment might be limited for those exercising the highest form of political leadership, similar constraints do not affect the practice of reflective democratic citizenship. To the contrary, political activities such as voting (for candidates or on questions), jury service, or membership on local boards of various sorts continually require judgments that are not categorical but particular. While such judgments may involve prior reflection on the content or importance of political principles (such as equity or responsibility) or prior recognition of generalized procedural constraints (such as prohibitions against conflicts of interest or requirements that guilt be proven beyond a reasonable doubt), the practical conclusions that result are not simply specifications of principles or applications of rules. Nor do they serve only as sources of enhanced or alternative general priorities, the function of reflective judgment in Ronald Beiner's interpretation of Kant or, as critically assessed by Stephen Salkever, in the commitment to care in Carol Gilligan's work.[66] Neither does judgment's attention to particularity play the role that it does for Benhabib, offering a salutary counterweight to an overstated but reasonable concern for impartiality (Benhabib 1992, 187–89). Rather, the sort of practical judgment implicitly endorsed by Socrates is an enriching actualization of practical generalities: actualization because practical generalities by themselves play only abstract roles, enriching because such judgments inevitably reveal nuances and singularities that fall outside of what can be captured by any generality. From this perspective, voting, jury service, or even thoughtful letters to the editor are constitutive of, rather than simply vehicles for, democratic political voice. Thus, in spite of the Platonic Socrates' overall abstention from formal political life, everything he does with his fellow Athenians is in a way political. It is perhaps this form of rationality, which is different from some sort of science of the good and which is more than the simple expression of a generous disposition, that allows Socrates to say (*Gorgias* 521d) that he is Athens's only real practitioner of *politikē*.

Yet Socrates' affective connections are not simply irrelevant to his political judgment. The presence of dispositions or affect within healthy political voice is a final defining characteristic of the Platonic model of democratic judgment. This characteristic differentiates the Platonic treatment of political judgment from those treatments that focus largely on judgment's cognitive or discursive aspects. However, this focus on affect also introduces a fundamental difficulty concerning the ultimate appropriateness of the Platonic model for guiding contemporary democratic practice.

Socrates' own practice is a constant reminder of the crucial importance of affect for democratic voice. At the beginning of his exchange with Callicles, Socrates says that they can communicate with each other because they share experiences or feelings (*pathēma*) (481c–d), certain kinds of love (*erōs*). Callicles loves both Demos, the son of Pyrilampes, and the Athenian *dēmos*, while Socrates loves both Alcibiades and philosophy. Close to the end of the dialogue Socrates traces Callicles' inability to be persuaded to a particularly intense form of *erōs*, his love of the many (513c–d). Implicitly, healthy political judgment cannot be practiced in the absence of a psychologically deeper affective orientation. The political importance of emotional connection is apparent in the *Apology* when Socrates says he interrogates his fellow citizens because they are more closely related to him (*Apology* 30a). From this perspective, Habermas's model of communicative democracy, which focuses on a virtually unencumbered capacity for critical rationality,[67] is simply too abstract or distant to provide either truly adequate characterizations of, or fully useful guidance for, democratic practice. The dramatic course of the *Gorgias*, in which Socratic appeals for rationality founder against Callicles' persistent *erōs*, is a pragmatic counterexample to the deliberative democrats' reliance on the forceless force of the stronger argument.

Recognizing the essential importance of affect for practical judgment implies that a political culture can only contribute to the development of thoughtful citizens by influencing character, understood as the qualitative configuration of appetites and aversions that individuate human beings. In this respect, the institutions needed to support the active practice of deliberation extend beyond deliberative institutions narrowly understood. Yet the creation of institutions molding character seems to work against both the fundamental principle of classical democracy, the priority of freedom or the desire to live as one likes (cf. *Republic* 557b), and the broadly Kantian premise of deliberative democracy, the need to respect the rational autonomy inherent in each human being (cf. Warren 2001, 63–65; Richardson 2002, 67–68).

The problem emerges with particular acuteness in the *Gorgias* when Socrates refers to his refusal to accept the unconstitutional proposal within the trial of the generals accused of widespread negligent homicide after the battle of Arginusae (cf. Xenophon *Hellenica* 1.7.14–16). Within the context of the *Gorgias* the implication is that the Athenian assembly would have acted more moderately and rationally had it respected the city's own judicial institutions. Yet the dialogue also suggests that the Athenian democrats could have respected the city's institutions only if they had, in fact, been more moderate and rational. To foster such a moderation and rationality, institutions beyond those that supply procedural safeguards are necessary. If judgment is the preferred form of democratic voice and if the capacity for judgment depends upon the presence of a certain kind of disposition or character, then democratic politicians who share these Socratic concerns face the problem of nurturing character within a cultural context that views political attempts to do so with suspicion and hostility.

We can outline this problem by specifying the different ways in which institutions could contribute to the emergence of a character capable of democratic judgment. Such institutions can be differentiated in terms of their educative, enabling, or elicitive influences. *Educative* institutions (secondary schools, churches, popular literature, newspapers, film, television, music, the Internet, and other forms of culture) contribute to the shaping of an intelligence capable of reflecting upon private and public priorities and of a character able to meet the challenges that anger and fear could pose. *Enabling* institutions (voting or the participation in interest-group politics) permit and request, but do not require, the exercise of political judgment.[68] Voting can be the result of the thoughtful formation of political opinion, but it can also reflect narrow personal responses to economic conditions or emotional attachments to highly charged symbols (Berns 1962, 3–62). *Elicitive* institutions, however, depend for their essential integrity on the exercise of judgment. Jurors or members of local school boards pervert those institutions when their decisions on cases or policies are influenced by personal gain or prejudice or when they fail to pay sufficient attention to facts or fair procedures out of carelessness or laziness.[69]

From this vantage point, political institutions supportive of democratic judgment must interact to perform all three functions. It would be inadequate to focus primarily on the enabling function, as theorists informed by Dahl do when they emphasize the contestative role of interest or pressure groups within democratic politics. Nor is it satisfactory to rely, as deliberative democratic theory often does, on the impacts of the elicitive institutions of parliamentary bodies and political public spheres. While the exploration of alternative institutional designs is beyond my purposes here, the institutional issue in general helps to clarify the problems involved in fostering democratic judgment. In particular, democratic theorists need to identify an educative function devoted to supporting the virtues within a political context committed to freedom and equality.[70] The *Gorgias* responds to this problem both intellectually, within Socrates' observations about the impacts of political culture on individual development (the explicit "political theory" of the *Gorgias*), and pragmatically, as a text written and read within a democratic culture.

The dialogue's theoretical response is that all cultural practices exert educative influences on their members. Human beings are individuated in particular ways through distinct forms of enculturation. When Socrates examines the effects of democratic rhetoric on Athenian culture, he goes beyond rhetoric's capacity to engender an ethic of freedom (one of Gorgias's claims [*Gorgias* 452d]) and speaks, instead, of the consequences of a rhetorical culture on the affective conditions of the character or the soul. Within this examination, freedom itself emerges as a trope whose deeper reality is the ability to achieve desired goods through the exercise of various forms of power. Rhetoric's predictable psychic effects reinforce the sovereignty of experiences of pleasure (gratification) and pain (deprivation) and thus the status of power as the most significant primary good. Citizens educated within such a culture encounter strong reinforcements for the priority of want satisfaction, all too easily aggregated into the powerful moves of an appetitive and aggressive society (472a–b). From this perspective, the valorization of freedom is an alternative treatment of character rather than an enlightened alternative to moralizing obsessions about character. Considering the ubiquitous influence of enculturation, the relevant critical question looks not simply to the degree but to the kind of educative influence that culture exerts. Thus, a rhetoric applied with a view to a more healthy psychic condition endeavors to displace a passionate desire for gratification with a more thoughtful appreciation of moderation (508c). At the same time, the danger for democracy is that the success of such a therapeutic rhetoric would support political voice by influencing the priorities of a settled psychological identity whose validity judgment simply confirms.

We find an example of this kind of rhetoric within the counter-Periclean vision of the funeral speech in the *Menexenus*. Here Socrates repeats for the young Athenian Menexenus the funeral speech that he has supposedly learned from Pericles' mistress, Aspasia. The rhetorical complexities of this presentation are numerous. While Socrates identifies Aspasia as the source, he also indicates that she has taught a very different oration to Pericles (236a–b), suggesting the content of his speech may be traceable to his own participation. Moreover, while the cultural function of funeral speeches is to provide occasion for public affirmations of a city's identity, this speech is clearly one that will never be given in any public context (cf. Salkever 1993, 136). Its educational effects will be more particularly attuned to the needs of Menexenus, and its broader political impacts will be more subtle and less direct. For all of this, however, the oration of the *Menexenus* offers a strikingly different vision of Athens's political-cultural identity from that affirmed in the parallel speech of Pericles. Whereas Pericles focuses on the priority of daring innovation and the superior achievements of the current generation (Thucydides 2.36.1–4), Socrates stresses the need to respect Athens's traditional civic identity and ancestral deeds (*Menexenus* 238b ff.). Pericles effectively equates education with the exercise of power (Thucydides 2.41.1–3), and war is implicitly seen as the context enabling the greatest risk, thus providing opportunities for the most enduring fame (2.41.4–5); Socrates demands that power should be applied in the name of education (*Menexenus* 248d) and offers a reading of Athenian history that shows the city making war only under duress (242c–d).[71] Pericles proclaims that the noble deeds (*erga*) of the Athenians shine so brilliantly as to make any speeches (*logoi*) about them derivative or superficial (Thucydides 2.41.4); Socrates' greatest respect for the Athenian dead is shown by giving them voice (*Menexenus* 246d ff.). In effect, the Athenian identity envisaged by Socrates replaces energy with balance and power with education, exhibiting a rhetoric executed with a view to this ordered conception of the best.

In the *Gorgias* Socrates avoids even a fictive practice of a public rhetoric that would improve rather than flatter. Still, the conversations with Gorgias and the rest are more open than the intimate philosophical exchanges that Callicles rejects as adolescent and ineffectual. These interactions become part of the cultural lifeworld when the *Gorgias* is engaged as a text.

Socrates presents his own assessment of Athenian culture late in the dialogue (*Gorgias* 507d ff). Applying his critique of rhetoric to the broader culture, he condemns its various expressions, because they flatter but do not improve (502b–c). Socrates specifically indicts various forms of *musikē*, the lyric and the tragic poets (502e ff.). This damning verdict prevents Socrates and Callicles from envisaging any prospects for cultural reform (like those considered by Socrates and Adeimantus in books 2 and 3 of the *Republic*). From this perspective, the Athenian lifeworld seems altogether resistant to speeches that would improve as well as please.

Oddly, this critique of culture leaves out comedy. In various ways, the *Gorgias* thematically anticipates Socrates' indictment and trial (for example, 521c–22a), and in the *Apology* Socrates says that a comic poet (Aristophanes) is the source of the most deep-seated and long-standing prejudices against him (18c–d, 19c). Consequently, his omission of comedy from the cultural critique of the *Gorgias* is puzzling. The puzzle becomes more curious in light of the many connections between the *Gorgias* and a number of the surviving comedies of Aristophanes.[72] Nightingale's (1995, 187–90) illuminating reading focuses particularly on parallels between Callicles' *erōs* for the many and the personification of Demos and his political lovers in Aristophanes' *Knights*. Beyond this particular parallel there are provocative intersections between the *Gorgias* and Aristophanic comedy that can provisionally be sketched.

Socrates is accompanied in his confrontation with Gorgias by Chaerephon, the sidekick who assists in managing the *phronisterion* in the *Clouds* (*Clouds* 104). Yet while the Aristophanic Socrates of the *Clouds* subverts cultural standards by teaching the unjust speech of self-advancement (*Clouds* 112–19), the Platonic Socrates of the *Gorgias* articulates what the *Clouds* (961–83) offers as a just speech (*dikaios logos*) supporting the laws of the community against self-seeking opportunists and valorizing the healthy virtues of justice and moderation against the predatory powers of cleverness and daring (491c–e). Socrates also confronts Callicles in a way that implies a parallel opposition to the protagonist of the *Clouds*, Strepsiades. In the comedy, Strepsiades wishes to learn the unjust *logos* to defend himself against his creditors and proposes to hire a Thessalian witch to bring down the moon to prevent the onset of the beginning of the month, when the bills come due (749–52). In the *Gorgias* Socrates warns the champion of the conventionally unjust *logos* against the dangers of bringing down the moon like the witches of Thessaly (513a). To this extent, the Socrates of the *Gorgias* and the Aristophanes of the *Clouds* engage the unjust *logos* as a common opponent.[73]

Like Aristophanes' comedies, the *Gorgias* tracks the course of the war (cf. Benardete 1991, 7). Callicles, who praises self-advancement over public spirit and rhetoric's self-serving manipulations over respect for the community's norms, resides in the deme of Acharnae (495d). Aristophanes' Acharnaeans are praised both for their heroic civic spirit at Marathon (*Acharnaeans* 180) and for their support for the comic poet's opposition to the rhetoricians (630–35). The differences between Aristophanes' civic Acharnaeans at the war's outset and the self-promoting Acharnaean Callicles at the war's end reinforce Thucydides' observation that the course of the war saw a gradual erosion and fragmentation of Athenian political culture (Thucydides 2.65.10–13).[74] To the extent that Acharnae images the painful beginning of the war (*Acharnaeans* 509–12; Thucydides 2.19.1–2), it also serves as a symbol of the devastating consequences of the Athenian empire as one of the war's causes (compare *Acharnaeans* 523–54 with *Gorgias* 519a–b).

As the end of the war approaches, social fragmentation is visible within the anger- and grief-driven Arginusae trial (*Gorgias* 473e–74a).

Socrates' references to pilotage and swimming as arts of (mere) survival (511c–12b) recall the massive shipwrecks and drownings at Arginusae, suggesting that even knowledgeable practices of such arts carry no guarantees. This accompanying denial that life is the highest good closely precedes the *Gorgias*'s mythos about the afterlife. Images of Arginusae likewise frame Dionysius's and Xanthias's journey to the underworld in Aristophanes' *Frogs* (33–34, 48–51, 190–91, 245–49, 361–62, 416–19, 588, 693–94, 700–2, 1195–96). Both visions of the afterlife center on judgments. In the *Frogs*, Dionysius judges the competing merits of the deceased poets Aeschylus and Euripides (785–86) and decides to send Aeschylus back to Athens because of his superior ability to reweave the city's tattered moral fabric (1070–74, 1195–96, 1419–21, 1471). In the *Gorgias*, the fearsome judges Minos, Aecus, and Rhadamanthus determine the virtuous or vicious character of the souls before them according to the standard of psychic health (523e3–8). The verdicts reveal that the politicians or the powerful are the most likely practitioners of the destructive vices that not only mark an incurably diseased soul (526b) but also foster abuses leading to political catastrophes (*Gorgias* 518e–19a). While the *Frogs* enlists poetry in the service of a morality that distrusts Socrates (1491–92), the *Gorgias* crafts a poetic image warning of the dangers of power, recommending Socratic discussions as an antidote (*Gorgias* 527a ff.).

Regarding democratic institutions, Callicles views the assembly and the law courts not as contexts for communicatively selected collective action, but as arenas for manly competition and self-assertion (*Gorgias* 485d–86a). Callicles is himself driven by an intense obsession with competitive manliness, often expressed through an anxious anandrophobia (485d). The personal object of Callicles' manly eroticism is Pyrilampes' son, Demos (481d), known in all quarters of the city for his striking beauty (*Wasps* 98). Socrates, whose philosophic practices are condemned by Callicles as unmanly (485d–e), is the lover of Alcibiades (481d), described by Aeschylus in his contest with Euripides in Hades as a lion nurtured by the regime (*Frogs* 1431–32). Those whom Callicles believes are most at risk from the democratic culture of equality are called "young lions" (*Gorgias* 483e). Though Socrates challenges Callicles' praise of manliness as a pathologized misunderstanding of the best life (527e), eventually Callicles' practice reveals that his obsession with the assembly and the law courts is rooted in a fearful concern for self-protection (521a–b).[75]

Aristophanes reinforces criticisms that the law courts have become spaces for pursuing individual or class vendettas (*Wasps* 574–75). And, as noted by Nightingale, he satirizes the Athenian Demos as susceptible to the continuous manipulation of demagogues, ending with the gratification purveyed by a sausage seller (*Knights* 143–44, 1102–8), a criticism resembling Socrates' comparison of rhetoric with cookery (*Gorgias* 465c).⁷⁶ Yet in his scrutiny of democratic institutions, Aristophanes finds not only opportunities for manipulation but also possibilities for reform. The sausage seller of the *Knights*, whose name is revealed as Agoracritus (the chosen—or the pick—of the agora [1257]), eventually practices an art that improves while gratifying (cf. *Gorgias* 504d–e), restoring Demos to a youthfulness and vigor opposing political flattery (*Knights* 1356–57).

Criticism of the educational outcomes of politics is implicit in Socrates' harsh judgment of Pericles (*Gorgias* 515d–16a), which parallels the Aristophanic Aeschylus's criticism of Euripides (*Frogs* 1010); the Athenians have become more vicious under Periclean and Euripidean care. Yet Socrates also relies upon Euripides in rejecting Callicles' claims about the best life, for one may, with Euripides, question whether our familiar existence driven by compulsions of pleasure and pain is truly living (compare *Gorgias* 492e with *Frogs* 1082, 1477). Regarding the wider poetic culture, Aristophanes continually ridicules the dithyrambic poet Cinesias (*Frogs* 153; *Clouds* 333; *Birds* 1379; *Assembly of Women* 329–30); Socrates seconds this attack and goes one better in assailing Cinesias's father, Meles, whose voice neither improves nor pleases (501e–2a).⁷⁷

However, even though Callicles and the institutions and practices he celebrates represent everything that Aristophanes despises within Athens's political culture, Aristophanes seems as contemptuous as Callicles of things associated with the unmanly. The tragic poet Agathon, whose speeches are compared to Gorgias's by Socrates in the *Symposium* (198c2), is ridiculed for his effeminacy in the *Festival of Women* (171–72, 204–5).⁷⁸ While Socrates and Aristophanes may each resist the destruction of civic virtue through the agency of the rhetoricians, they have different conceptions of that virtue in mind (cf. *Symposium* 191e–92b) and therefore different visions of the meaning and value of philosophy.

The intersections and collisions between the *Gorgias* and the Aristophanic comedies suggest the intriguing hypothesis that the *Gorgias* may inhabit the Athenian cultural lifeworld as a certain kind of comedy, a form of speech that can improve while also gratifying.⁷⁹ The dialogue is replete with comic elements, both superficial and deep. Gorgias's terse answers to Socrates' question at 449d ff. comically illustrate his boast (449b–c) that he is an expert at providing long or short answers. Polus's dismissive ridicule of Socrates collapses almost immediately, as he stupidly cooperates in undercutting his own argument concerning the opposition of evaluative categories of good and bad and noble and shameful (474c–d, 474e ff.). Polus's posturings thus image the inadequacies of rhetorical speech by providing a comic caricature of its encounter with critical rationality. These inadequacies are revealed as Polus accedes to

Socrates' outrageous reversals of the accusatory and defensive capacities of rhetoric. In contending that a well-used rhetoric accuses oneself and one's friends while protecting one's enemies from prosecution (480a ff.), Socrates provides a comedic revision of the functions of the just and unjust speeches of *The Clouds*.[80] Callicles' manly ridicule of Gorgias's and Polus's deference to conventional shamefulness (482c) is undercut by his shame over the mention of the catamite (*kinaidos*), perhaps the most contemptible cultural image of the unmanly (494e).[81] And Socrates himself becomes comic when he responds to Callicles' refusal to continue by conducting a "dialogue" with himself (505e ff.). Is dialogue characterized by complete agreement laughable?[82] The threatening myth of judgment and punishment becomes potentially comic with the introduction of Thersites, a rogue (*ponēros*) not yet incurable because of his status as a private person (*idiōtēs*), into the myth's afterlife (525e). Thersites is punished by Odysseus in the *Iliad* to the great amusement of the soldiers (*Iliad* 2.264–70). In the *Republic*'s myth of Er, it is Thersites who opts to make a monkey out of himself in his next life (620c).[83]

As a kind of comedy, the *Gorgias* gratifies its audience by making those who see themselves as the wisest of the Greeks (527a–b) look ridiculous (cf. *Apology* 33b–c).[84] Yet a reflection on the dialogue's action also has the capacity to improve the judgment of the audience by asking its members to be more critical of the public speeches to which they are often subjected (compare with *Acharnaeans* 632–35), perhaps including the public speeches of comedy.[85] To the extent that the *Gorgias* exhibits elements of comedy, it invites a critical voice that is particularly democratic. Publicly performed tragedies provide open contexts for democratic education, and so transmit as well as presume images connected to Homer and the myths (*Frogs* 1108–14). If anything, comedy is potentially more open to all.[86] And unlike rhetoric, whether well or badly used, comedy seems authentically respectful of the audience's capacity for judgment. For Gorgias, the power of rhetoric would be proven conclusively by his convincing an ignorant audience he was a doctor (456a–c). By contrast, comedy relies on a certain active intelligence among the audience. "Getting" the joke, and thus the success of the comedic narrative, demands that author and audience interact as equals through a certain mutual recognition and respect. Unlike Gorgias's rhetoric, which reinforces and directs the many's exercise of power (452e), the *Gorgias*'s text warns those who are fascinated with power's benefits (468e). By participating in a comedy drawing on the city's lifeworld, Socrates (*Apology* 30a) thus seems more hopeful than Diodotus about prospects for civic improvement in a democracy. And insofar as he is the author of a comedic text with a capacity to educate,

Plato does not share Thucydides' darkest intimation (3.82.2) that war as the most violent teacher reveals the heart of things.

Yet this form of comedic discourse can also be differentiated from rhetoric in a more unsettling way. The impossibility of controlling comedy's political effects challenges Gorgias's illusions about the rhetorician's capacity to control political outcomes. Yet this same unpredictability accompanies the public performance of comedy in contentious political circumstances. Does Aristophanes' lampoon of Socrates escape his control when it becomes part of the hostile atmosphere surrounding Socrates' trial?[87]

Consequently, the *Gorgias* is hardly a comedy in any simple sense. Comedy and tragedy are not mutually exclusive; tragic poets can also write comedies, though the reverse may not be true (*Symposium* 223d).[88] Whatever humor the dialogue offers is darkened by the shadows of the seemingly endless war and the ominous images of the trial and execution of Socrates. Socrates' comedic representation of his bumbling performance in front of the assembly (*Gorgias* 473e–74a)[89] points backward to the disaster of Arginusae and forward to his fatal collision with the empowered democracy. By enclosing the Gorgias's comedy within a horizon of tragedy, Plato may offer the audience a reminder of the stakes involved in political decisions and of the consequences of subordinating political judgment to the passionate and reckless exercise of power.

Finally, there is also a sense in which Socrates subverts the completeness of his own (and Aristophanes') just speeches by revealing their inadequacies and dangers. In Socrates' direct speech to Callicles, the best life is represented as a calm moderation in the face of psychic and political instabilities (*Gorgias* 507a); good laws and responsible public speeches should aim at establishing psychic order or health in the soul, analogized to the regular and balanced functioning of the body (504b–d). Yet this vison of psychic health offers a radically incomplete picture of human excellence and happiness. The moderate life represented in the image of full jars, whose owners can now "have quiet" (*hēsuchian echoi* [493e]), is as remote from the continuously destabilizing philosophy of Socrates as it is from the turbulent sensuality of Callicles' fantasies. Socrates' encomium to the "completely good man" (*agathon andra einai teleōs*) identifies his virtues in a way that pointedly excludes wisdom (507b–c). To this extent, Socrates' endorsement of the political-cultural forms that can develop virtuous citizens encounters its own limitation in the full context of the *Gorgias*.[90] There are senses in which this ambitious project of psychic formation would threaten the development of capacities for critical judgment.[91] Just as philosophy requires a continued mistrust of seemingly settled conceptions of the good, critical judgment functions most effectively when it interrogates rather than validates dominant conceptions of moral order.

This kind of judgment would appreciate the limitations as well as the benefits of a rhetoric executed with a view to what is best. Critical judgment thus discovers the shortcomings of political speeches such as that offered by Socrates in the *Menexenus*. Though the speech that Socrates "repeats" is a political speech that is intended never to be given publicly, the genre of this fictive *logos* is still *political*. It therefore retains elements or appeals that critical rationality might well oppose. The most striking example of an appeal that both represents and problematizes politics is Socrates' reliance on the aggressive cultural construction that posits a radical separation between Greeks and barbarians (245c–e). This distinction seems necessary to support attachments to Athens's mission of defending and liberating the Greeks in the face of external aggression (239d ff.). It also serves to reinforce the sense of gentleness that the speech fosters among the Hellenes (243e–44a). From one perspective, gentleness within can require externally directed hostility. Yet, as Cleon (of all people) acknowledges, domestic gentleness may also soften harsh and exclusionary postures toward the strange or the other. To the extent that gentleness is appropriate among the combative Greeks, it is more difficult to deny the possibility of extending it to those called barbarian (cf. *Republic* 471a–b). What would separate Greeks and barbarians absolutely would be categories of difference found not in culture but in nature. Socrates thus contends in the *Menexenus* that those who are truly Greek are endowed with a natural purity that exposes as pretenders those who are merely Greek in name or by convention (245d). Yet this claim is challenged at the outset when Socrates comments on the intense but misleading psychic impacts of funeral speeches, cultural constructions that cause the listeners to revise upward their impressions of their own characteristics, both natural (height) and cultural (quality of birth) (235a–b). While funeral speeches blur the categories of nature and culture (height as beauty), their status as cultural constructions reinforces an awareness of separation, for their appeals to nature point to an evaluative framework extending beyond the merely cultural. These inherent tensions within the form and content of Socrates' speech underscore rather than resolve complicated questions concerning harshness and gentleness, nature and convention, one's own and the other. To the extent that political needs (commitment to Athens's distinctive ethical identity) require ignoring such complications, they subordinate the demands of rationality to societal imperatives. By contrast, an insistence on the priorities of philosophy or *logos* reveal the distortions and dangers of accepting cultural requirements as the sole standard for judgment. The *Menexenus* strikingly represents a speech that privileges such cultural judgments, even as it simultaneously reveals their shortcomings. To this extent, it offers a deep and subtle contribution to Menexenus's political education.

The critical judgment of the *Gorgias's* audience is similarly challenged by portraits of both the disordered democratic society that distorts it and the ordered cosmic community ("heaven and earth, gods and human beings" [507e–8a]) that absorbs it. Insofar as judgment is an essential expression of the human capacity for *logos*, a disordered and distorting democratic arrangement may be preferable to the ordered and absorbing one that construes the most perfect rationality as geometry (508a).[92] At the very least, the contrast between disordered and ordered societies shows what is gained and lost under both arrangements and, therefore, the possibilities and dangers of democracy in particular. Socrates' nuanced connections to democratic culture are suggested at the end of the dialogue when he holds all previous conclusions up to the test of critical judgment applied within a discursive context (527b). In this respect, judgment recognizes the political indispensability of the just speech, while maintaining control over the ability to criticize.[93]

Classical Theory and Deliberative Practice

Thucydides' and Plato's treatments of trust and judgment can thus be read reconstructively as appreciative criticisms of the perspective that informs deliberative democratic theory. They are appreciative in maintaining that healthy public choice is guided not by the attraction of material interests (Cleon's justification of the empire) or political cultural pride (Pericles' vision of an Athens living in eternal memory) but by the counsels of rationality. They emerge as implicit critics, first of all, by underscoring the need to investigate why deliberative institutions and practices are in fact good for political communities. The attempt to construct an evaluative framework through a discourse ethics that rejects teleology simply obscures the continued importance of critically examining the merits and hazards of conditions embedded in democratic political forms. This in turn constrains deliberative democratic theory's treatment of the practices and institutions that can foster the virtues needed both for a deliberative democratic society's well-being and for the flourishing of its members as human beings.

A second emerging difficulty is found in both authors' going beyond deliberative democratic theory's focus on procedure. For both

Diodotus and Socrates, the value of deliberative processes is determined in part by the kinds of outcomes that these processes tend to generate. This is not to see deliberative processes in purely instrumental terms. Diodotus's own rhetorical victory is recognized by Diodotus himself as incomplete and perhaps even as dangerous on account of its deception. And Socrates' refutations of Protagoras, Gorgias, Polus, and Callicles fail, in spite of their substantive political benefits, to stand up to the scrutiny of a more adequate logos (*Protagoras* 361a; *Gorgias* 527a) that may emerge not as an abstract possibility but as an outcome of continuous reflection on the dialogues themselves. Still, ignoring outcomes within an assessment of procedures implies either a tacit privileging of results not subjected to critical scrutiny or a limitation of political theorizing to the tracking and assessment of process. Either way, political theory loses much of its critical edge.

Finally, by excluding a critical focus on goods and outcomes, deliberative democratic theory disconnects itself from the most important concern of democratic citizens, the determination of what is to be done, and vests too much confidence in experts mapping intricate connections among various levels of social institutions, often employing highly technical vocabularies. By contrast, both classical authors offer their observations through the representation of different forms of democratic practice.

For all of this, I have also tried to discourage reading these texts as efforts to undercut deliberative democracy.[94] To be sure, Diodotus's despair regarding the predictable functioning of the assembly and Socrates' harsh criticism of rhetoric seem to endorse a more directive, less discursive form of political rationality. Yet I have suggested that both authors can be read in a different way, as sketching the political and psychological dangers that threaten democratic deliberation. The deliberative democrats of classical political theory act within an ecology that is only partially supportive. They must also confront the damages and exhilarations that make rationality both more necessary and more remote. In a way, both authors assess the dangers of democracy in light of democracy's characteristic goods. While Plato and Thucydides may seem more pessimistic than contemporary theorists of deliberative democracy, theirs is a healthy pessimism that attunes democratic citizens to dangers within their most treasured public practices and to damages that may darken their most noble public accomplishments.

4

Culture's Justice

Introduction: The Cultural Turn in Democratic Theory

The normative sociology developed by Habermas in support of deliberative democratic theory relies on what is called the lifeworld to provide the "reservoir" of societal meanings that surround and enable communicative action (1996, 22; cf. 1996, 354). His concentration on how political crises can engender stronger democracy leads him to emphasize two particular functions of the lifeworld. It is the site at which systemic problems first become tangibly present for citizens (1996, 359). And it constitutes the informal but structured communicative networks that allow discursive interactions among the differentiated spheres of complex societies (1996, 558–59).

For those who see democratic political culture as playing a constitutive role for democratic theory, the lifeworld becomes the surrounding condition for political practice, the source of its coherence and the grounding of its norms. For this kind of democratic theory, the dominant templates of a modern pluralistic and constitutional society enable both the explanation of political forms and the evaluation of political alternatives.

Certainly the most visible and influential example of this cultural turn within contemporary democratic theory is the position of John Rawls in *Political Liberalism*. Rawls's appeal to the shared principles of liberal democratic culture represents at the very least a sharp difference in emphasis from the more universalist aspirations that informed *A Theory of Justice*. In *Political Liberalism*, the constructed principles of justice that Rawls affirms are not universal imperatives valid sub specie aeternitatis (1971, 587), but developments of the "fundamental political ideas viewed as implicit in the public political culture of a democratic society" (2005, 223).

This cultural turn has at least three important consequences for democratic theory. First, within this framework the endorsement of democratic institutions and the assessment of particular democratic alternatives would not need to be based on any controversial foundational or (in Rawls's terms) comprehensive philosophical or moral doctrine. Rawls's alternative lies in the idea of the overlapping consensus, the notion that liberal political institutions can be broadly supported because they are consistent with a plurality of comprehensive positions (2005, 144–45, 170–71).

Second, Rawls's concern to identify principles of justice compatible with a liberal democratic culture tempers calls to universalize liberal values and practices. Such projects become suspect because of their apparent reliance on an untenable metaphysical mode of thought and their potentially dismissive or oppressive attitude toward cultural particularity. Accordingly, Rawls's liberal theory of justice is not a call for reforming the diverse variety of nonliberal societies along liberal lines, but an attempt to respond to our own political and social dilemmas in ways that are most consistent with our public identity (2005, 44–45).

Third, by connecting theorizing with the discovery of commitments implicit in our fundamental political cultural ideas, Rawls insists that the character of democratic theory is substantive as well as procedural (2005, 192). Rawls therefore moves beyond Habermas's concern to identify the conditions under which public deliberation will be truly democratic (Habermas 1996, chap. 7) and toward indicating what democratic public action should try to accomplish.

For all of its differences with *A Theory of Justice*, *Political Liberalism* is written very much within the conceptual and stylistic framework of analytic Anglo-American liberal political theory. Yet its underlying approach is also linked with perspectives on social inquiry and epistemology that challenge the epistemic groundings of analytic philosophy and the completeness of political liberalism. These challenges sketch the contours of a form of democratic theory that radicalizes elements of Rawls's cultural approach.

If Rawls's political cultural turn is to be understood as something more than the convenient defense against the charge that his theory of justice is itself illegitimately based on its own comprehensive understanding of the good,[1] it must rely on a more explicit argument about the significance of culture in human life. These explicit arguments are found notably within the hermeneutic approaches to social science supported by Peter Winch and Charles Taylor and the methodological premises of Clifford Geertz's cultural anthropology. While there are important variations and disagreements between these positions, they concur that social science is essentially interpretive, modeled more on the activities of the literary critic than on those of the analytic philosopher or positive scientist (Taylor 1971, 5–6; Geertz 1973, 9).[2] This interpretive/narrative approach to social science is made necessary by the constitutive role that culture plays in creating human identities (Geertz 1973, 82–83; cf. Geertz 2000, 211–12). Social practices are therefore explained when they are situated within a coherent and evidentiary narrative that clarifies their places within a surrounding context of cultural meanings (Taylor 1971, 45; Geertz 1973, 15–16).

Those who articulate the basis and implications of this understanding of culture more fully than Rawls would therefore see his cultural turn as a problematic half turn, with both methodological and substantive complications. Although Rawls explicitly wishes to focus on public culture as distinct from what he calls background culture (2005, 14), his assessment of the content and requirements of political liberalism would seem to require a broader contextualizing background. For example, the historical creation of political liberalism presupposed fundamental changes in cultural conceptions of the role of religion in society. These changes were made possible by the growing influence of secularism and Enlightenment science in Western Europe (2005, xxii–xxiii). This cultural account of political change differs, however, from Rawls's assertion that the emergence of a society structured by political liberalism was "the work of free practical reason within the framework of free institutions" or, more strikingly, "the inevitable outcome of free human reason" (2005, 37) and not simply one historical shift among many. From this perspective, Rawls declines to make the full cultural turn because of a continued allegiance to certain elements of comprehensive liberalism. It is the focus on the workings of free reason rather than any cultural interpretation that seems to support Rawls's crucial claim that it is not the fact of pluralism per se, but the fact of *reasonable* pluralism that most fully describes the public culture of political liberalism (2005, 36). Consequently, Rawls's attempt to clarify the self-understandings and practices that create the cultural conditions for political liberalism should be appreciated insofar as it reinforces the local nature of the project, but corrected if it proposes anything universal as grounding its priorities (the inevitable workings of free reason) or extending their influence (political liberalism as a model for structuring relations in other cultures).[3]

Rawls's turn toward culture is complicated even further by the second broad framework to which his later approach is methodologically tied; this involves treatments of the constitutive role of language, extending from Winch's readings of Wittgenstein through Richard Rorty's postmodernism. For Winch, epistemology and sociology share the task of clarifying the broadly linguistic conditions that make forms of practice or knowledge possible (1961, 86–87). From one perspective, this means that treatments of political cultures should aim as much as possible at understanding societies and cultures in the terms in which they understand themselves, clarifying the significance of the social meanings that are embedded in their institutions, rituals, games, and so on. While shared normative templates may allow the intracultural evaluation of social acts according to accepted norms, there is no metalanguage that would enable the comparison of norms across cultures.[4] In this respect, attempts at cross-cultural evaluation too often end in the imposition of one set of cultural norms on other communities of meaning.[5]

While Winch (1961, 102–3) and Geertz (1983, 42–43) conclude that this prospect demands a neutral interpretive social science, Rorty and Taylor deny, for very different reasons, that any such neutrality is possible, owing to the inevitable involvement of understanding with efforts to cope with the problems that surround us.[6] Consequently, no social science can be neutral, and projects of clarification cannot be separated in principle from pragmatic efforts to establish preferred forms of coping. From this perspective, Rawls cannot chart the transition from a nonliberal to a liberal public culture without becoming involved in a pragmatic attempt to establish the priorities of this political culture in the face of competition from alternative possibilities. *A Theory of Justice* and *Political Liberalism* become intellectual resources within broader and more combative efforts to establish the terms that will guide the development of the just democratic society.

Once Rawls's concern with political culture is connected with more extended attempts to examine the constitutive role of culture, the strengths and weaknesses of democratic theory's cultural turn become more apparent. The acknowledgment of the contingency and pragmatics of cultural forms supports a political theory that is constructed in response to social problems or conflicts. The democratic cultural perspective also reinforces, in one sense at least, the modesty and gentleness of liberal aspirations. Doing without universalist pretensions, liberalism becomes less committed to establishing its political culture among populations governed by very different societal norms (though theoretical allegiance to the principles of liberalism has rarely been the main reason for Western colonization and imperialism). Of equal importance, democratic theory's cultural turn can remind democratic citizens that their own guiding cultural templates are susceptible to historical criticism and revision, introducing resources that can counter the prideful confidence that too often masks imperfections and dangers.

Yet this perspective also generates problems or hazards that become particularly apparent in connection with the pragmatics of democratic collective action. There is a sense in which the characteristics of contingency and localism work against the imperatives of pragmatism and criticism. Contemporary interactions ranging from the political and cultural to the economic and technological increasingly tend to blur distinctions between the local and the global. This blurring is in general bidirectional, and it is perhaps most problematic in concerns over human rights. The term itself challenges the localism and contingency implicit in democratic theory's cultural turn. The claim that humans qua humans have rights points to imperatives for action and implies standards of evaluation that challenge locally controlling cultural norms. Both the intelligibility and the moral force of human rights claims make it more difficult to ignore abuses in different societies once they are called to our attention by the interconnection of modern systems of economic production and intersocietal communication. Conversely, our own political experiences suggest that human rights concerns are not easily escaped within local controversies over capital punishment, same-sex marriage, or the treatment of defendants accused of terrorist crimes.

The moral continuum that links the local with the global or cultures with the species is reinforced by the intellectual difficulties encountered by those wishing to frame social inquiry exclusively through the categories of culture. Rawls's own efforts clearly reveal an essential dependence on trans- or cross-cultural conceptions of human activities and goods, the priority of reasonable pluralism as the outcome of the progress of free reason. The more radically cultural and contingent views of Geertz and Rorty still rest on general theses about human beings or human nature. Geertz's humans are incomplete animals driven to complete themselves by cultural constructions (1973, 218). Rorty's are contingent beings who are inevitably faced with the daunting and exhilarating prospect of creating and re-creating themselves and their communities through the power of broadly understood linguistic practices (1989, 23–28).

Democratic politics is complicated in different ways by attempts to tie all forms of theorization or rationality to political affirmation or resistance. In this respect, Rorty's intellectual guide is less John Dewey or William James (cf. Rorty 1982, 160–61) than it is Michel Foucault.[7] To the extent that democratic politics must, like all politics, be seen through to detect the power relations at its core, it becomes more difficult to see how various political forms (democratic and nondemocratic) can be evaluatively compared. To be sure, there are structural or cultural variations in the distribution and exercise of power. But the ubiquity of power contests, which underlie all forms of supposedly rational argument, frustrates any attempt to assess their outcomes in terms beyond factual success. In one respect, tying culture to power encourages critical practice by multiplying recognition of sites of oppression and resistance.[8] Yet, in another sense, it undercuts the integrity of rational criticism by seeing it as just another power move.

These difficulties with democratic theory's cultural turn are particularly problematic in assessments of the role of cultural meanings in questions having to do with justice. From one point of view, the shared meanings that constitute a culture can make conversations about justice possible. Yet this reliance on culture has limitations as well. While most disputes over justice may originate locally, it is far from obvious, as the examples connected with the category of human rights suggest, that it is either possible or desirable to address them purely (whatever that might mean) in local terms. And while all conceptions of justice endorse or assail particular proposals for distributing and applying power, seeing these conceptions simply as strategies within power conflicts undercuts possibilities for assessing their rational validity. Two more specific problems therefore emerge. First, how can cultural investigations of justice proceed in ways that escape the limits of the cultural without embracing a universalism that is invalid and threatening? Second, how can the inevitable connection of justice with power be acknowledged without reducing all attempts to institutionalize justice to Foucauldian technologies of power? Democratic theories grounded in the constitutive role of democratic culture can be faulted not for failing to "solve" these problems but for contributing to their disappearance as ongoing sources of theoretical concern. Rawls's appeal to templates of liberal public culture seems mistaken in the belief that problematic connections with comprehensive doctrines have been avoided. And those who link theorizations about justice with pragmatic concerns for power generally do so not for the sake of justifying a coldly neutral science of power, but in the name of a particular conception of political justice that often remains implicit and therefore unexamined.[9]

In what follows I suggest that the texts of Thucydides and Plato are valuable precisely because they help us to rethink and extend our understanding of these questions. It is not that they somehow resolve the converging dilemmas of how culture relates to nature or justice to power, but because they keep these questions alive and deepen our sense of them as problems.

The Suppression and Persistence of Justice in Thucydides

Intersections of Culture and Nature

One barrier against contemporary political theory's appreciating the continued importance of broader human questions within its treatment of cultural conceptions of justice is that the alternatives are often stated in such polarizing ways. For those committed to interpreting culturally embedded discourses about justice, the alternative seems to be a universalism that runs roughshod over local knowledge and particular attachments. Conversely, those who insist on the need to ground political and cultural investigations on a deeper or more foundational conception of human nature often condemn any serious cultural turn as incoherently and irresponsibly historicist. There are a number of polemical sources that could easily be cited. But this tendency is visible even within the most intellectually sophisticated and nuanced offerings. Leo Strauss sees the decisive change between classical philosophy and modern social science reflected in "the fact that whereas for classical philosophy the comprehensive theme of social science is the best regime [thus requiring an understanding of those political things that are according to or against nature], the comprehensive theme of modern social science is civilization or culture [representing a turn against nature and toward history]" (Strauss 1989, 102). Clifford Orwin's reading of Thucydides seems informed by a similar commitment. In an important note, Orwin equates a recognition of the constitutive influence of language on political identities with the thesis that human beings are radically historical creatures (1994, 177 n. 10).

These alternatives are unnecessarily radicalized. The antinatural voices not only rely on functional equivalents to naturalism (Rorty's self-creating or Geertz's incomplete animals), but also ignore the ways in which certain forms of universalism or naturalism can serve as critical resources, revealing the deficiencies or dangers that lurk in the acceptance of cultural norms. And while I share Orwin's instincts in rejecting radical versions of historicism that dismiss conceptions of human nature as unintelligible before the fact,[10] his own challenge to this position (as well as the Straussian perspective on which it draws) may represent a paradoxical acceptance of its formulation of the choices. What seems needed instead is a framework in which language/culture and essence/nature can be treated as problematic and interactive fields.

From one perspective, however, Plato and Thucydides could be read as two of the originators of this polarization. Strauss's comments are telling: "For Thucydides the cause of the wisdom which found its home in Periclean Athens is Periclean Athens. For Plato, Periclean Athens is merely the condition, and not the cause, of Athenian wisdom. Thucydides, we may say, identifies condition and cause; Plato distinguishes between condition and cause. Hence politics is of decisive importance for Thucydides and not for Plato" (Strauss 1989, 101).[11]

Nowhere does the Platonic privileging of a nature that overrides culture seem clearer than in the *Republic*. Socrates exposes deep contradictions within conventional or cultural views of justice, apparently replacing them with a rationally grounded conception of a justice according to nature (435b, 433a–e, 443c–44a). The attack on culture is particularly intense in the cave story that begins book 7. There culture is imaged as a construct resting on a series of cognitive distortions and physical coercions. Human beings educated in cities are compared with cave dwellers compelled to face a wall illuminated by a fire burning behind them. The light given by the fire allows artificial figures carried by (apparently) unfettered human beings walking behind the fire to cast shadows on the wall. The bound cave dwellers mistake these shadows for reality and believe that the echoes of the sounds made by those carrying the figures are the voices of the shadows. Though the immediate sources of these distortions are the error-prone senses of sight and hearing, the enabling context is a surrounding community held together by force. As against this cultural distortion—called a lack of education (*apaideusia*)—Socrates envisages an education that occurs once some individual is released from bonds (something that Socrates says happens by nature [*physei*])[12] and is compelled to move upward from the cave and toward the light above. Since the person who has followed this path rejects what the cave dwellers take to be reality and yet, on returning, fails to perceive the cave's contours because of difficulty in readjusting to the darkness, any further attempts to release the prisoners are violently opposed (516e–17a).

While the Platonic Socrates seems to assail existing culture as a perversion of nature, Thucydides appears much more attentive to the constitutive role of cultural forms. Many of the voices represented by Thucydides are named not as individuals, but as regimes. In a sense, Thucydides individuates the Corcyreans and the Thebans as political cultures by revealing their characteristic priorities and activities. The narrative's most important regimes, Athens and Sparta, are represented continuously in terms of what seem to be their distinctive political-cultural commitments: the daring activity of the Athenians and the cautious moderation of the Spartans (cf. 1.70.1–9). Thucydides' concern for the character of regimes is so pronounced that Gregory Crane sees him constructing a polemical discourse in which "the city-state is predominant"

(1996, 111, 139; cf. Crane 1998, 140).[13] Yet in spite of Crane's criticism of what he sees as Thucydides' reductive cultural analyses (1996, 50, 56; 1998, 324–25), the Thucydidean focus is not obviously reifying or simplistic. Few of the cultures given voice are as they represent themselves on first hearing. While many misrepresentations are strategic, the deepest deceptions are often self-deceptions.[14] The Spartans' belief in their own severe respect for justice obscures the close connection between what they say is just and what they calculate is advantageous (Thucydides 5.105.3). Likewise, none of these cultural forms is stable. Spartan cultural solidarity is challenged by the individual projects of Pausanias (1.128.7, 1.130.1–2) and Brasidas (4.108.7, 5.116.1). And the most pronounced aspects of Sparta's political culture are both reinforced and threatened by the dangerous presence of the Helots (1.101.2–3, 4.80.2–5). Apparently stable cultural identities are thus created through the waging of continuous culture wars. Alcibiades and Nicias attempt to shape Athens's political identity on the basis of opposed visions of praiseworthy forms of collective action and ways of being (6.13.1–2, 6.18.6–7).

The place given to regimes or cultures is also central within Thucydides' rich explorations of his individual characters. Far from displacing or obscuring individual practices, the conditioning boundaries of culture make them intelligible. Pericles, Cleon, Alcibiades, and Themistocles are certain kinds of Athenians, just as Archidamus, Sthenelaidas, Brasidas, and Pausanias are certain kinds of Spartans.[15] Yet this intelligibility requires continued acknowledgment of the elusive and contested character of culture; characterizations of Thucydides' cultural focus as a static and mechanically reproduced national character mislead.[16] It is perhaps more valuable to see his approach to the relation between regimes and individuals as psychocultural, recognizing that human beings are individuated within cultural practice and that the dynamics of cultural processes are carried forward by the fluctuating and conflictual activities of enculturated members.[17] Archidamus's strategic recommendation of a cautious response to Athenian aggressiveness shows both the strengths and weaknesses of Spartan education. Brasidas's love of distinction pragmatically contests the Spartan norm of deference. Pericles' funeral speech attempts to create an ethos of activity within a conflicted culture (the continuing need to oppose the apragmonists) rather than simply describing that ethos within a cohesive one.[18] Even the proliferating strategies of self-interested individuals, which many see as book 8's thematic and stylistic innovation,[19] are only intelligible in light of their positioning within cultural stresses. From this perspective, the Thucydidean focus on culture is less a reductive explanatory concept than it is a field that invites and demands the activities of the interpreter.

Both Platonic nature and Thucydidean culture play the roles they do through ongoing involvement with the conditions that they seemingly oppose. Postmodernists might see both nature and culture as constructions whose intelligibility and normative force depend on the continuous presence of their others.[20] However, culture (for Plato) and nature (for Thucydides) play different and more complicated roles. While the postmodern other is seen as an artificially stable and reified presence that reinforces the standing of its originator,[21] neither the Platonic understanding of culture nor the Thucydidean representation of nature is guilty of such oversimplification. For both authors, the meaning and significance of each of these concepts are continuing puzzles that can be engaged only if they are seen as dynamically ambiguous.[22]

Socrates' Cultural Conversations and Nature

For the Platonic Socrates, investigations into the nature of the just or the good depend continuously on the possibility of philosophy. This philosophical investigation is not a purified engagement between the mind and the ideas but a much more embedded encounter with opinions and therefore with cultural practices, both enabling and problematic.[23] Cultural or subcultural realms provide loci of meanings that make conversations about the just and the good possible. In book 1 of the *Republic*, Cephalus draws on both religious and social templates to construct his definition of justice as paying back what one owes. Polemarchus extends this proposal, through the contributions of poetry and a certain kind of politics, to contend that justice is helping friends and harming enemies. While Socrates challenges and eventually undermines both claims, he does so not on the basis of a formal understanding of justice abstracted from all immediacies, but through recognizing the complications raised by other social and cultural experiences. When Thrasymachus violently confronts the interlocutors, he not only endorses yet another cultural view (justice is the advantage of the stronger) but also makes clear that examinations of justice inevitably implicate power relations. Appropriately, Socrates' response is not only an attempt to show that Thrasymachus's definition of justice is incoherent (with much of the evidence coming from recognized cultural practices and needs), but also an effort to gain discursive control (cf. 352b–54a).

The attempt to discover what justice is thus presupposes a prior effort to construct a city or a political culture in speech (369a). As this proceeds, all apparent closures are undone by difficulties given voice within the dialogue's own discursive community. These objections draw on a variety of cultural meanings, including opinions equating material enjoyment with happiness (419a), the political acknowledgment of the need for defense (422a), a respect for the institutions and place of the family (449c), and suspicions about the uselessness or dangers of philosophy (487b–d).[24] Consequently, the construction of the city in speech is a series of continuous reconstructions that inscribe responses or accommodations to culturally generated concerns. Apparently, a city that is founded according to nature is at some level impossible without the continuing contributions and challenges of culture. Thus, the image of the cave as culture does not simply reveal how the education of human beings by nature is distorted by convention, but offers a more complicating image of our nature itself (514a). The experiences of the cave dwellers imply continuities as well as tensions between culture and nature. The movement from the shadows to the light originates within the shadowland itself (515c), just as the road upward from the depths to the light is difficult yet somehow continuous (515e–16a). Indicting the cave culture as a lack of education depends upon discoveries to which this culture itself somehow contributes, for the movement upward does start within the cave. That this education is not simply against *our* (that is, our human) nature (*tēn hēmeteran physin*) is reinforced by the complete reversal of the human perspective (529c) that is both required and fostered by the more strictly philosophical education described in book 7, where these people, too, are said to be led up to the light (521c). Perhaps human nature with respect to education and lack of it is revealed by the insights and inadequacies of both of these images.

All of this suggests that the *Republic* presents the relationship between nature and culture as one that is continually ambiguous and mutually complicating. Culture is not simply a distortion or a pathologization of nature, and nature is not simply a purified standard that designates culture for overcoming or control. Cultural meanings and practices seem necessary not only for the intelligibility but also for the effective creation of conditions that are according to nature. Yet nature is not simply a generalized version of the most common or influential cultural practices. Relying on a conception of nature as a standard for the evaluation of culture involves continued revisions in the understanding of what is by nature in light of cultural corrections or requirements. Nonetheless, perceiving the benefits and dangers of particular cultural arrangements is structured by a concern for how they are according to or against nature, *kata physin* or *para physin*. Nature is not an illusory universalist vantage point but rather a realistic pragmatic frame of reference.

Culture, Nature, and Power in Thucydides

Thucydides' attention to the constitutive role of cultural forms emerges not as an alternative to but as a consequence of his understanding of nature. However, crafting a politics with a view toward nature does not mean, as for Socrates, founding a city that is as far as possible *kata physin*, but rather establishing a political community *para physin*, fundamentally opposed and resistant to natural ravages. In Orwin's assessment, "For Thucydides ... the gravest problems of politics ... attest to the power of nature in human life, opposing and overshadowing that of convention. ... The political task accordingly remains the suppression of nature (in part through the enlisting of its power)" (1994, 177 n. 10). While Orwin is clearly right that reflections on nature are essential to Thucydides' project, the characterization of Thucydidean nature (vindictiveness, power) and the assessment of the role of politics (suppressing nature) require further comment.

On first view, identifying Thucydides' vision of nature and its imperatives seems easy, for there is a consistent position on this question taken by a number of his most striking characters. The Athenians at Sparta (1.76.2–4), the Syracusan statesman Hermocrates (4.61.5–7), the Athenian envoys to the Melians (5.105.2), and the Athenian negotiator at Camarina, Euphemus (6.85.1–2; 6.87.4–5), all acknowledge the universal practice of the stronger controlling the weaker. None of these figures describe this control as a matter of simple oppression. It can be a calculated pursuit of interest (Euphemus) or an anxious one (the Athenian envoys on Melos), or simply what human beings do when opportunities allow or necessities dictate (the Athenians at Sparta, Hermocrates). The speakers contemplating the harshest deed (the envoys) offer what seems to be the most explicit and comprehensive speech. Their stated understandings of gods and human beings (and thus of the cosmos) reveal that the strong are naturally compelled (*anankaias*) as if by law (*tōn nomōn*) to rule when empowered. In light of this general agreement, it is small wonder that de Romilly has concluded that this collection of remarks points to a Thucydidean position: "In the final analysis Athenian imperialism is the only perfect example of a common experience whose nature is governed by universal laws" (1963, 312).[25]

As I have suggested earlier, we should be cautious in inferring Thucydides' position from the speeches of his characters.[26] All of these men speak from within powerful regimes, imperial Athens and Syracuse, the daring innovator of the west (8.86.5). Thus, while these speakers may be right to insist on the continuing importance of beliefs about nature, they all represent particular cultural priorities or advantages as if they were reflections of natural arrangements. At one level, these distortions may stem from the same general inclination or need that works in the reverse direction, interpreting natural occurrences in light of their human significance (1.23, 2.54, 3.89, 7.50, 7.79, 8.6). Yet even if this tendency to collapse the natural and the cultural reflects a human inclination, the significance of even the most basic needs for survival and security is heavily conditioned by cultural influences. While the need for security may explain the origins of politics (1.8.3–4), its interpretation depends on varying cultural templates. The Melian leaders view security as civic independence to the degree that political servitude is worse than civic death (5.92). The Athenian envoys respond by defining their own security as the continuation of Athens's empire (5.95, 5.97). Even within cultural communities, the meanings attached to survival are contested. Alcibiades argues that the only antidote to civic deterioration and death is eternal competition (6.18.6–7). He is opposed fundamentally by Nicias, who finds security in the enjoyment of the wealth and reputation won by achievement. Conversely, even the most pathologically destructive and obsessively self-regarding passions apparently look to cultural forms for validation. Neither the desperate pursuit of physical pleasure in the face of the plague (2.53) nor the ruthless love of gain and honor behind *stasis* (3.82.8) can do without the valorization of nobility (*to kalon*) that culture offers.[27]

Likewise, human beings may construct beliefs about the gods in accordance with their own hopes and fears (2.54.4–5). Yet such anxieties are sufficiently indeterminate to require the more substantial contributions of shared meanings for articulation. Thus, the striking religious differences between the Athenians and the Spartans reflect and reinforce distinctive regime identities. In light of the Corinthians' characterizations of the Athenians as daring innovators and the Spartans as diffident traditionalists, it is no surprise that the Athenians dismiss as irrelevant Spartan attempts to discredit Pericles because of his genealogical connection to an earlier pollution (1.127.1–2)[28] or that Spartan anxiety over an alleged breaking of the truce festers continually until the period of the Sicilian invasion (7.18.2–4). Interpreting these responses as reflecting differences between a secular and a religious society is misleading. The sophisticated Athenians respond to oracles (2.54.3–4) and seers (7.50.4; 8.1.1–2) and have more confidence in the pious Nicias than in the accomplished but hubristic Alcibiades (6.15.4).[29] In a way not altogether distinct from that of the Spartans, the Athenians' political commitments are intensified by their connections to religious practices and symbols. The mutilation of the statues and the alleged profanation of the mysteries are seen as attacks on the city's religious and political identity (6.27.3). Yet Athens's response to these acts is motivated at least as much by the democrats' fear of tyranny (6.15.4) as by outrage at impiety.[30] The city invests its own political identity with a kind of sacredness. While resources from public and private religious dedications and ceremonial practices are fair game for transfer into the city's war chest (2.13.4–6), the Athenians sequester one thousand talents in the acropolis for the defense of the city itself and will punish anyone who proposes another use with death (2.24.1).[31] And just as Athenian sophistication fails to banish religious influences, Spartan religiosity is linked to the pragmatics of its political culture. Its cautious reluctance to reach beyond its own borders is reinforced not only by a fear of the consequences of hubris, but also by the much more immediate need to control the Helots (1.102.2–3, 4.80.1–3). The Spartans are not above concealing treachery behind ritual (4.80.3–5) or interpreting sworn oaths according to the dictates of advantage (2.72.1–3, 2.74.2–3).

From this perspective, culture emerges as the field that provides the range of human impulses or needs with their conditions for tangible expression and meaningful presence. Consequently, what de Romilly sees as the perfect expression of a nature governed by universal laws is one cultural specification among a number of those that are possible.

Yet none of this means that Thucydides abandons the possibility or need for serious attention to nature. He provides such attention in his own voice within his extended reflections on the Corcyrean *stasis* in book 3.[32] At one level, this disastrous civil conflict, exhibiting all the worst excesses of savagery (3.82.1) and overthrowing all civic and familial ties (3.81.5), seems explicable by structural factors: the class divisions between the many and the few that are exploited for strategic purposes by the Athenians and the Spartans (3.82.1). As I have suggested in chapter 2, there are also significant political cultural factors, particularly the Corcyreans' complete disregard for institutions enabling collective action and political and social trust.[33] Yet Thucydides deepens his explanatory framework to encompass influences belonging to human nature, providing a general vision of nature. His express causal statements focus on how overreaching (*pleonexia*) and the love of honor (*philotimian*) (3.82.8) pervert civic language and institutions to foment and intensify political conflict. Though they fight over material and status goods, both parties mask their aggression with spurious pretenses to public benefit. The democrats say they are committed to equality before the law for the majority, the oligarchs that they embrace a moderate aristocracy. Such ideologizations legitimate and intensify partisan agendas, making their adherents even more aggressive. Thus far, Thucydides' diagnosis of the causes behind the Corcyrean *stasis* seems consistent with de Romilly's positing a lawlike nature where aspirants for power positions struggle in ways that lead eventually to the rule of the stronger. Thucydides complicates this, however, in suggesting that one of the consequences of the *stasis* is a disruption of the very meanings of strength and weakness: "The meaner in intellect were more often the survivors; out of fear of their own deficiencies and their enemies' intelligence, that they might not be overcome in words (*logous*) and become the first victims of plots issuing from the others' intelligent deceptions, they daringly embraced deeds (*erga*). And those who contemptuously believed they would know all in advance, and that they need not seize by deed what would come to them by intelligence, were taken off their guard and perished in greater numbers" (3.83.3–4).[34] From this point of view, nature seems understood less as power than as a turbulence that continually resists or undercuts efforts to understand or control it.[35] In this respect, cultural disruption is caused not by the intrusions of identifiable natural imperatives (as in Glaucon's and Callicles' criticisms of the origins of convention in the *Republic* [358e–59a] and the *Gorgias* [483b–e]), but rather by nature's frightening and chaotic indeterminacy.[36] Consequently, nature can be best understood not through collected examples of a universal experience but through extreme cases that arise only under severe stress (3.82.2).[37]

In light of this emerging picture of Thucydidean nature, it is too simple to characterize culture's response as attempted suppression. Instead, culture's function can be understood in part as the organization of turbulence so as to create various forms of coherence. Culture's enlisting the power of nature (Orwin's formulation at Orwin 1994, 177 n. 10) may presuppose a prior cultural organization of turbulence into forms of power. Consequently, the consolidation and exercise of power on the part of the strong now seems not according to nature, but against it, for it is one manifestation of efforts to control the devastating flux that nature represents. On this reading, power is not natural but cultural, and nature's resistance to culture is not an expression of power but an attack on it. In this respect, Thucydides' understanding of power seems intriguingly consistent with Foucault's, for constructed power seems to be an essential aspect of all cultural forms and a necessary condition for all human projects, ranging from the consolidation of rule through the creation of knowledge.[38]

Yet Thucydides' treatment of the relation between culture/power and nature/turbulence anticipates more complexities than do Foucault's genealogies of power and knowledge. These complexities allow Thucydides to engage in two intellectual projects that elude Foucault. First, Thucydides' assessment of the ways in which power is established and applied is evaluative in a way that does not seem possible within Foucault's genealogical accounts. Thucydides acknowledges that culture's efforts to organize nature will continually involve culture—if not with nature's power, then at least with its materials. The cultural imperative of controlling the passions is achieved not by educating or moderating their content, as proposed by Plato and Aristotle, but by channeling or focusing their expressions. This means that cultural forms can intensify as well as limit natural disruptions. The passions that contribute to the creation of culture and stability—the love of power and the love of gain (1.8.3)—reappear as the root causes of the political cultural suicide in Corcyra (3.82.8). Though both would deny that anything called nature can serve as a positive standard for guiding human practice, Thucydides' appreciation of culture's appropriate mission allows him to distinguish between constructive and destructive power moves in a way that Foucault cannot. While Foucault's framework confines him, in Thomas McCarthy's assessment, to producing "simply another power move in a thoroughly power-ridden network of social relations" (1990, 445), Thucydides' provides him with the cultural grounding for a certain kind of moral evaluation: "In Corcyra, then, many of these things were first dared; those acts of retaliation committed by those ruled arrogantly rather than moderately once they are given the opportunity to revenge themselves; those [acts] that might be committed against justice when, in order to escape their constant poverty and mostly on account of their suffering, [men] strive eagerly to gain what their neighbors possess; those savage and pitiless attacks against those who stand on equal footing, launched not for the sake of gain but driven by unrestrained fury (*apaideusia orgēs*)" (3.84.1–2).[39]

Second, while Thucydides may claim that power is a condition for all forms of social and intellectual coherence, he does not claim that anything that presupposes power is reducible to it.[40] Here condition is not cause. Cultural and intellectual discourses made possible by power configurations can in principle be turned against their enabling conditions. The thesis that cultural achievements derive their identities from their originating power is proclaimed by Pericles in the funeral speech. Athenian culture is represented at one level as being remarkably heterogeneous and comprehensive. Athens encloses goods or practices that are scattered across the other Greek cities. And it fosters these practices in a way that avoids what are elsewhere inevitable deficiencies. Athenians are courageous without being brutal, and they can philosophize without becoming weak or "going soft" (2.39.1–3, 2.40.1–2). Yet for Pericles all of these civic or cultural goods are defined rather than simply enabled by the distinctive power of Athens's empire. Athens's being an education to the rest of Hellas is made manifest by its power, so that education is equivalent to influence (2.41.1–3). The city is "most self-sufficient," because its military and naval capabilities provide access to the goods of others (2.38.2). The dominating role of Athenian power also imposes limits on the kinds of cultural expressions presented as legitimate. In separating Athenian philosophy from softness, Pericles banishes the sort of philosophy that would foster civic gentleness, in effect anticipating the attitude toward philosophy promoted by Callicles in the *Gorgias*.[41] Not surprisingly, Pericles' praise of Athens's political cultural identity thus attempts to privilege action (*ergon*) over speech (*logos*), the faculty perfected with philosophy and poetry (2.41.4). Eventually, Pericles' listeners are exhorted to relate to the regime emotionally (as lovers) rather than critically (as citizens participating in the mutuality of ruling and being ruled). Membership in Athens's political culture thus requires sharing in both the benefits and the risks of its exercise of power.

Numerous commentators have noted that the Periclean vision of Athenian power is undercut almost immediately by the devastation of the plague, reminding Thucydides' readers of the limitations of cultural and political power in the face of natural disruptions.[42] Yet Thucydides' narrative also points to the ways in which cultural forms may resist the control of the power that enables them. It is Thucydides' authorial decision to narrate the plague where and how he does that makes the city's vulnerability apparent.[43] And whereas the plague's disruptions are destructive, cultural disruptions, which include Thucydides' representation of the plague, can be beneficial.

Thus understood, Thucydides' own *logos* is both beneficiary and critic of Periclean political culture. Athens's material prosperity and military reach allow the leisure and cosmopolitanism that are unavailable to—indeed, forbidden by—the disciplinary ethos of the Spartans (1.6.4–5). And Periclean standards of value provide the initial criteria that are used to determine the significance of events (1.1.2). However, Thucydides' narrative is not limited to repeating or ennobling the citizen-lovers' praise of Athens's power. Instead, the gaze he turns on Athenian culture/power is more reflective and critical, allowing a deeper investigation of what it means for Pericles to say that Athenian power has left lasting memorials of harm and good everywhere (2.41.4–5). In framing his critical vision, he draws on a variety of cultural sources in a way that respects the comprehensive aspirations of Periclean Athens but does not limit itself to the priorities sanctioned by the more determinate templates of the Periclean ethos. Consequently, while this discourse is enabled by power and while it would, if taken seriously, revise or supplant Periclean power, it bases its validity claims on human practices that power enables but does not simply control. From this perspective, culture's resources can do more than attempt to suppress nature; they can also provide the bases for critiques of cultural power. This critical possibility informs Thucydides' complex treatment of justice.

Justice and Political Culture in Thucydides

Thucydides offers no definition of justice in his own name. The meanings of justice emerge through the argument and rhetoric of his characters. In nearly all cases, justice is understood in juxtaposition with its alternatives or opposites: the display of power or the pursuit of advantage. For the Athenian envoys to Melos, just relations are fundamentally different from those in which the powerful dispose and the weak accede (5.89). Even the harshest characterizations of justice as retaliation (by Sthenelaidas [1.86.7], Cleon [3.40.4], and Gylippus [7.68.1]) presuppose a case against some prior commission of injustice, understood as the reliance on violence or aggression when alternatives were possible.[44] Diodotus's stark but misleading premise in his speech on Mytilene is that he will consider only advantage or disadvantage and not justice or injustice. Though all these assessments treat considerations of justice as secondary to those of power (the envoys) or interest (Diodotus), justice retains its own intelligibility and voice. Consequently, considerations of justice do not simply disappear under harsher scrutiny. Accordingly, Thucydides' characters often speak in ways that take the symbol of justice seriously. Accusations of injustice (the Corinthians' charges against Corcyra) and defenses against charges of acting unjustly (the Spartans' account of the siege of Plataea) are rhetorically significant within political contests.

Generalizing cautiously, Thucydides' political agents claim to act justly when their behavior toward one another is constrained by some consideration of the other's condition or status according to criteria validated by the relationship itself. The weak can expect to be pushed around, but not that their condition of weakness will have any constraining influence on the behavior of the stronger. Parties bound together by mutual interest have reliable expectations only as long as interests intersect.[45] By contrast, a commitment to behave justly reflects being vested in a relationship that the practice of justice reinforces.

As Thucydides assesses them, such relational standards of justice are not grounded in any order or imperative external to the relationship itself. I have suggested that appeals to natural standards or divine imperatives made by Thucydides' characters are culturally rooted. Criteria for just practices, worldly or religious, are embedded in certain kinds of regimes. Thucydides' narrative focuses particularly on two competing cultural possibilities, the Athenian and the Spartan, recognizing that these designations extend beyond particular cities to identify certain styles of practice and thought.

On first view, the Athenians appear to see the requirements of justice as far less compelling than do the Spartans. For Pericles, the empire may have been unjust to take up, but it is dangerous to put down (2.63.1–2). For Cleon, insofar as justice recommends anything less than punishing Mytilene with the greatest severity, it must be ignored unless one opts "to surrender the empire and act the decent man without running risks" (3.40.4–5). For Diodotus, a passionate attachment to a justice demanding retribution must give way to rational calculations about interests (3.44.1–3). For the envoys to Melos, any appeal to justice is irrelevant in the face of Athens's military superiority (5.87). However, though all of these men admit that considerations of justice recede when faced with necessity or advantage, none goes so far as to deny the intelligibility of justice claims. How is justice made intelligible within Athenian culture?

Within the speeches of the generalized (and therefore thematically linked) "Athenians" at Sparta and on Melos, what initially distinguishes justice as a form of political practice is the recognition of a certain form of equality (1.76.3–4, 5.89). Connecting justice with equality is at one level consistent with the broad though ambiguous democratic commitment to recognizing the equality of citizens before the law (2.37.1). Extended to relations among cities, a certain kind of equality informs the first stages of the Ionian alliance against the Persians instituted by the Delian League (1.96.1–2). Under these conditions, it seems culturally consistent for these two separate groups of unnamed Athenians to connect their articulation of the meaning and the reach of justice among cities to notions of equality. Yet the characterizations and consequences of equality vary considerably across the two speeches. The envoys on Melos connect justice with equality in a way that dismisses the relevance of justice for the decisions taken about Melos. The Athenian speakers at Sparta point to a practice of Athenian justice that is understood as the equal treatment of the subject cities. Though the two speeches appear to take very different stands on what equality means and how it influences political practice, both end by underscoring the fragile character of interpolis equality and any attendant justice in the face of Athens's imperial rule.

For the envoys to Melos, the equality that frames justice is measurable by equal necessities (*isēs anankēs*), understood as balancing quantities of material power (5.89). Consequently, just behavior is not the advantage of the stronger but the outcome of recognizing that no party possesses superior strength. Under these circumstances, however, it becomes difficult to distinguish a respect for justice from prudential restraint engendered by fear. In their petition for Spartan assistance at the beginning of book 3, the rebellious Mytilenes admit that only fear keeps suspicious allies yoked together (3.11.1–2). In a sense, then, the envoys move not only to restrict the circumstances in which considerations of justice apply, but also to recharacterize justice simply as the acknowledgment of equivalent force. For this reason, justice is never voluntary, for it is either required by balanced necessities (as the Mytilenes contend) or made moot in light of unequal distributions of power (as the envoys insist). And while one can be blamed (as the Melians are) for foolishly refusing to defer to superior power, no one can really be praised for being (sensibly) just.

The Athenians at Sparta represent equality in a different way from the envoys to Melos and draw different conclusions about the voluntariness and praiseworthiness of justice. For them, the equality relevant for justice is not a consequence of equal power but a counter to power imbalances "so that those who deserve to be praised (*epaineisthai te axioi*) are the ones who, giving way to the natural human need to rule others, nonetheless behave more justly than their power [allows]" (1.76.3). Here justice seems the advantage of the weaker, for those deficient in power are given more regard than their inferior capacity alone would warrant. The just or restrained behavior of the powerful is therefore voluntary, and just practice elicits admiration. This account of justice seems nobler and more generous than the one sketched by the envoys.

Yet other aspects of this Athenian rhetoric complicate these assessments. As represented in the speech at Sparta, the condition for Athens's voluntary justice is its overwhelming power; its juster than necessary treatment of the subject cities is yet another sign of its ability to act as it wishes, leaving, as Pericles will claim in the funeral speech, memorials of harm and good everywhere (2.41.4–5).[46] The absence of material imperatives requiring Athens to be just is implicitly taken to mean the absence of imperatives simply (1.76.2–3). There are no binding institutions or agreements that set the content or duration of Athenian justice beyond Athens's discretion. Consequently, the Athenian spokesmen both dismiss and resent the subject cities' anger when they are treated with less equality than they expect. Pride in Athens's justice is consistent with the speakers' broader intention "to reveal how great the power of their city was" (1.72.1).

Moreover, if Athens's practice of justice is undertaken for the honor it garners, it also rests on a kind of compulsion that paradoxically works against its voluntary, and thus its praiseworthy, character. The Athenian speakers have attempted to exonerate the creation and expansion of the empire by appealing to the compelling or overwhelming motives of fear, honor and interest, revised on second statement to give honor first place.[47] If these motives are truly compelling, then it is highly questionable that behaviors traceable to their influence can be understood as voluntary and praiseworthy. From this perspective, the Athenian love of praise compels them toward a liberality that generates as a by-product behavior that looks like justice.

Thus, while commentators continue to wrestle with the question of Athenian deterioration over the course of the war,[48] the Athenian statements at Sparta and on Melos can be read in ways that reveal continuity.[49] To the extent that the Athenian justice praised at Sparta stems from the regime's magnanimity, it appears as a gift that can be offered or withdrawn as Athens sees fit. The envoys' understanding of compelled or fearful justice is eventually surpassed by the valorization of a more generous or daring justice, linked to the nobility (*to kalon*) of those who accomplish things while running risks (5.107). In this respect, both speeches connect Athens's understanding of justice to its own political cultural identity in ways that eclipse the initial ties to equality, for they each eventually articulate some version of an Athenian exceptionalist thesis. For the Athenians at Sparta, Athens's just behavior distinguishes it from regimes that would exercise their superior power more despotically (1.76.4). The envoys contrast noble and risky justice (5.107) to the self-serving practices of those (like the Spartans) who are obsessed with safety and who therefore "regard what is pleasant as noble and what is advantageous as just" (5.105.3). If Athens encourages the subject cities to demand greater equality (1.76.3 to 1.77.1–4) by being juster than it has to be, it runs the noble risk of encouraging defections from the empire. Yet it is largely the concern with the defection of the subject cities that underlies the attempt to subdue Melos (5.99). To this extent, the Athenians seem no longer willing to run such noble risks. However, it is also unclear whether this reluctance stems from a fear of the empire's dissolution (recalling Pericles' caution that it is now dangerous—or risky [*epikindunon*]—to let the empire go) or the prospect of the even nobler risk of the Sicilian expedition (Thucydides notes at 6.1.1 that the Athenians intended to subdue all of Sicily "if it were possible" [*ei dunaito*]). Consequently, both speeches link Athenian justice to the Athenian empire in a way that leaves the supposed generosity of that justice highly uncertain. The contention that justice toward others is purely discretionary could easily be interpreted as a mark of tyranny, an assessment of Athens's rule virtually conceded by Pericles (2.63.2) and defiantly affirmed by Cleon (3.37.2). The association of justice with a noble running of risks reinforces the Corinthian image of Athens as the regime that neither enjoys any peace itself nor leaves anyone else alone.

Claims of exceptionalism notwithstanding, Athens is hardly the only city that interprets the requirements of justice in light of political cultural priorities. Spartan justice, too, is understood as a radically distinctive mode of social practice. While the Athenians tie their beliefs about justice to multiple and problematic conceptions of equality and affirm their city's comprehensive ability to control how just they are, the (broadly) Spartan view relies on hierarchical social and kinship relations reinforced by piety. Within this hierarchy, parties remember their established claims and responsibilities and promise to respect and fulfill them by means of oaths sworn in the presence of the gods.

This enculturated justice appears first within the speech of the Corinthian ambassadors, who oppose the proposed Athenian alliance with Corcyra. Corinth is just because it has fulfilled obligations incurred by virtue of its place within the norms of responsibility and reciprocity set by Hellenic culture. What underlies the Corinthian sense of justice, then, is a vision of a structured and stable hierarchy of relations that make common life possible.[50] A centerpiece of the Corinthian argument is an appeal to the "things that are just . . . according to the laws of the Hellenes" (*dikaiōmata . . . kata tōn Hellenōn nomous*) (1.41.1). These are not simply the legislative or adjudicative laws or customs of this or that city, but the constitutive cultural "institutions" (Smith's translation of *nomous*) or foundations of Hellenism. They are constitutive not only because they create conditions for stable social interactions, but also because they shape conceptions of interest (the Corinthians' status that the Corcyreans insult) and create imperatives for action (Corcyra's obligation—violated—to help its own colony, Epidamnus) and restraint (Athens's obligation to refuse the Corcyrean invitation to ally).

I have suggested that this same reliance on a stable social and indeed cosmic order underlies the Melians' defiance of the Athenians. Confronted by the apparently overwhelming military power of Athens, the Melians hope for assistance from the gods and the Spartans. I have also suggested that even though the Athenians dismiss this vision of an ordered cosmos as imaginary, they replace it with their own conception of order, one that is equally problematic.[51] Still, Melian order is strikingly different. While Athenian order is dynamic and innovative, Melian order is settled and traditional, relying on respect for long-standing obligations to reinforce patterns of social interaction, creating obligatory ties that will govern future practice. Justice becomes a recognition of one's (or one's community's) obligations and entitlements overseen and enforced by just gods. From one perspective, the psychic consequence of this sense of justice is a kind of fearfulness, the anxious concern to recognize and to fulfill obligations. Yet in another, it is the confidence that entitlements will be respected and virtue rewarded.

The Spartans themselves proceed to ignore the Melians' plight and to allow their destruction at the hands of the Athenians. The final account of Melian resistance (5.116) is appropriately juxtaposed with yet another example of Spartan dilatoriness. While this simply seems to validate the Athenian envoys' dismissal of Spartan justice as the pursuit of interest behind the mask of rectitude, the cultural reality is more complex. The Spartans' disregard for what the Melians see as obligatory does not bespeak a general Spartan disregard of justice or piety. Indeed, the Spartan behavior described at 5.116 concerns a planned invasion of Argive territory that is aborted due to unfavorable sacrifices. Throughout Thucydides' narrative, the Spartans repeatedly abandon or limit projects that seem to be in their strategic interests because of suspected divine disfavor (cf. 5.16.1–3). They view success suspiciously, looking ahead with trepidation for eventual reverses, and they respond to failure accusingly, looking back to detect the cowardice or mendacity of individuals (2.85.1–2) or the transgression or impurity that crossed the gods (1.27.1–3). In spite of Sparta's long-standing political independence and stability (1.18.1–2)[52] and its reputation for invincibility in ground combat (5.75.2–3), the regime's civic ethos is characterized much more by fear than by confidence. Spartan fear (one of the two principal causes of the war) seems inextricably connected with the fundamental social conditions of the regime, particularly the relatively small number of ethnic Spartans (4.38.4–5, 5.68.1–2) and the menace posed by the institutionally enslaved Helots (4.41.3). Sparta's piety is thus informed by a sense of vulnerability, reinforced by the perceived oversight of judgmental gods whose verdicts are tangibly expressed through rituals (134.3–4), oracles (5.16), and portentous natural events (1.128.1–3).

The fearfulness that penetrates Spartan political culture has two major consequences for the regime's conception of justice. First, it turns Sparta's political cultural attention inward, specifically with the mission of developing an effective sense of civic commitment among Spartan citizens. In his defense (1.80–85) of the Spartan regime against the Corinthians' complaint that its caution and inwardness give Athenian aggression free play, the king, Archidamus, reminds the Spartans gathered together that the city's political freedom and notable reputation have been secured by the effectiveness of the regime's educational institutions (1.84.1–3).[53] Chief among these are the laws themselves, which discourage hubristic senses of individual cleverness and distinction. Spartan justice fosters an equality of submission to codes of behavior that keep Spartan citizens in their place (cf. 1.6.4). Yet this comprehensive defense of the benefits of Spartan severity does nothing to deny—indeed, it may reinforce—the Corinthians' charge that Sparta's domestic trust (*pistis*) prevents the regime from responding to the threatening actions of enemies or the legitimate requests of friends (1.68.1).[54]

Second, to the extent that Sparta *is* worried that its own behavior toward others is not just, it focuses on avoiding blatant violations of oaths or duties, surety being literal compliance with external forms. Sworn promises are treated as formally obligatory commitments, but their precise imperatives depend on how oaths are remembered. Thus, in spite of Archidamus's standing as the model of Spartan virtue, he is not above interpreting oaths or obligations in contorted ways that favor Spartan interests. When the besieged Plataeans recall the promises of independence sworn to them by Pausanias in return for their heroic stand against the Persians (2.71.4), Archidamus responds (strikingly, for a Spartan) by looking not to the past but to the present and the future. The Spartans' oath is valid only if the Plataeans cooperate in resisting the Athenians, to whom the Plataeans themselves have sworn allegiance (2.72.1).[55] When Plataea eventually falls, the Spartans tell the defeated citizens that none of them will be executed against justice (*para dikēn*) (3.52.2–3), but justice means simply the rendering of a judgment after Plataean responses to an unanswerable interrogatory (3.52.3–5).

From this perspective, what the envoys on Melos characterize as the Spartan inclination to see the pleasant as the noble and the advantageous as the just is not calculated hypocrisy, but a deep-seated characteristic of the regime. Conceptions of justice and their supporting practices are heavily infused with Spartan fear; there are important senses in which the regime's interests are both constituted and contorted by the culture's justice. This is made particularly apparent by the influences of cultural shame on Sparta's political identity and collective actions.[56] Archidamus gives the sense of shame (*to aischron*) a central role within the education that fosters civic commitment. "We have become warlike (*polemikoi*) and well-counseled (*eubouloi*) through our [being] well-ordered (*eukosmon*), warlike because deference (*aidōs*) has the greatest share in moderation (*sōphrosynēs*) and shame (*aischynēs*) in courage (*eupsychia*); well-counseled because we are educated with too little learning (*amathesteron*) to disdain the laws and with too much moderation (*sōphronesteron*), bred by severity (*chalopotēti*), to disobey them" (1.84.3).

Spartan order is manifest psychologically in the citizens' ability to blend moderation (*sōphrosynē*) and courage *(eupsychia)*, virtues that might separately foster the dangerous conditions of slavishness or savagery (cf. *Republic* 410d ff.; *Statesman* 310d–e; *Politics* 7.7). Paralleling

Pericles, Archidamus contends that his regime succeeds where others fail in securing incompatible goods. Yet while Pericles says that Athens succeeds by encouraging a dazzling variety of differences (2.37.1–2), Archidamus traces Spartan success to its creation of a psychic uniformity that emerges from and reinforces senses of cultural shame. If Pericles' Athens is the multihued cloak that Socrates uses as an image of the democracy in the *Republic* (557c), Archidamus's Sparta is the single-colored fabric, so well dyed that no lye or alkali can fade it, that is the metaphor for the city in speech's political courage (429d–30b). Thus, the defining core (or base color) of Spartan *sōphrosynē* is not self-possession or sound-mindedness, but a deeply felt *aidōs*, the sense that the self must subordinate or redefine its own interests in the face of a just and pious social arrangement. Spartan *sōphrosynē* is therefore a kind of *aischynē*, an anxiety about offenses that might threaten this divinely sanctioned order.[57] Archidamus sees *sōphrosynē* infused with *aischynē* as the strongest support for the courage that Spartan warlikeness requires. Consequently, the good counsel (*euboulos*) of the Spartan polity does not bespeak the role of public deliberation and therefore the need for citizen rationality in determining the direction of public choice, but rather reflects the success of an enculturation establishing pervasive cultural shame through its own harshness.[58]

However, in part because of its ubiquitous presence in cultural practice, the shame that both supports and is validated by Spartan justice generates destructive outcomes. This is clearest in the response to the defeats at Pylos and Sphacteria during the seventh year of the war. Strategic mistakes in dealing with an Athenian incursion into Pylos (in the southwest Peloponnese in the area of Messenia) have led to a substantial number of Spartan hoplites being isolated on the nearby island of Sphacteria. No longer able to resist Athenian attack, the hoplites request guidance from the city and receive a typically Spartan reply: "The Lacedaemonians tell you to do whatever you wish [as long as you] do not do anything shameful (*aischron*)" (4.38.3). To the surprise of most observers, the hoplites on the island surrender, and Spartan policy is thereafter focused obsessively on securing their release. Once the negotiated settlements of the Peace of Nicias (5.18.7) arrange the hoplites' return, the Spartans strip them of political rights, fearing (*deisantes*) that they might attempt some change in the regime owing to their fear of suffering some diminution (*elassōthēsesthai*) because of "what happened" when they "gave up their arms" (5.34.2). Here the anticipated outcome of Sparta's shaming culture intensifies rather than lessens the regime's fearfulness. Expecting that the returning prisoners will fear the shaming that is at some level deserved,[59] the Spartan regime itself fears that their response will be aggressive. It therefore moves to diminish the returnees' influence by preemptively dishonoring them. The shaming that the returnees expect follows not from discipline but from fear. And the shame and fear that are intended to hold the regime together create sources of potential fragmentation.

Spartan culture is vulnerable to the adverse consequences of its particularly severe sense of justice in part due to another cultural characteristic celebrated by Archidamus. In educating its citizens to be suspicious of any learning that erodes respect for the laws, the culture stifles—and, indeed, tries to root out—sources of self-criticism.[60] The behavioral alternatives available to Spartan citizens are disciplined conformism or subversive expressions of individuality. The nonconforming Spartans within Thucydides' narrative are regarded with unease (Brasidas [4.108.7]) or suspicion (Pausanias [1.95.7]). And Sparta itself recognizes that the effectiveness of its disciplinary education depends heavily on its ability to observe and punish. The most culturally problematic behavior is correlated with distance from the regime's control.[61] Yet many of the departures from Spartan discipline are generated or intensified by the culture itself. In attempting to crush individual desires for possessions and reputation, Sparta may pathologize them. Both Plato (*Republic* 550d–e) and Aristotle (*Politics* 2.9) suggest that Sparta's open denigration of wealth leads to secret hoarding. The obsession with avoiding shame can be extended to the love of honor; the Spartans contribute to Brasidas's desire for preeminence by choosing him as the first to be commended for daring in the war (2.25.2–3).[62] The story of the Spartan king Pausanias's abuses is told in parallel with an account of the career of the Athenian, Themistocles (1.126–38). While these chapters have sometimes been read as an undisciplined digression, commentators increasingly appreciate them as contributions to the broader examination of Spartan and Athenian regimes (cf. Connor 1984, 48–49; Debnar 2001, 199–200; Orwin 1994, 76 n. 14). In spite of attempts to foster austere civic devotion, Sparta can produce a Pausanias, whose luxury and hubris undercut Sparta's standing with its allies (1.96.1) and threaten its security from within.

By contrast, Athenian culture supports a greater range of resources for self-criticism by offering a number of inherent bases for challenging conceptions of justice tied so closely to Athenian power.[63] To the extent that the Athenian political culture takes equality seriously, it can be troubled by claims that its relations to the subject cities represent a kind of tyranny.[64] Alternative sources of justice can be articulated and examined because of the culture's valuing of *logos*. There are obvious ways in which possibilities for the rational interrogation of public choices and the prospects for a justice that limits the exercise of power are related. *Logos* offers a pragmatic example of a basis for human interaction other than force; just institutions that diminish the influence of power enhance possibilities for effective *logos*. Yet although Thucydides sees this intersection of *logos* and justice as an Athenian possibility, he also identifies cultural and cross-cultural factors that work to diminish its practice.

Paradoxically, the strongest attempt to argue for the value of *logos* within public deliberations is linked directly to the proposal that seems most in disregard of justice. In arguing for moderation toward the Mytilene democrats, Diodotus underscores both the need to base public decisions on careful deliberation (3.42.1–2) and the imperative that such deliberations focus exclusively on the city's interests (3.44.1–3). Both commitments are responses to elements within Cleon's previous speech urging severity. As we have seen, Cleon's case is based on a warning against the deceptiveness of speech as compared with the clear guidance of the passions and is infused with a moralizing rant that condemns Mytilene for betraying Athens (3.39–40).

Diodotus responds to this partnering of passion and justice with a support for rationality in the service of interest. As I have tried to show earlier, however, neither of Diodotus's commitments is straightforward.[65] The initial case for rationality is muted by pessimistic diagnoses of the political and psychological barriers against it (3.43.3–4). In emphasizing the presumed deceptiveness of his own speech, however, Diodotus complicates the apparently ruthless focus on interest. Thus, his speech can also be read as an argument for the justice as well as the advantage of mercy and thus for a kind of compatibility between justice and interest that differs markedly from Cleon's formulation. Since neither justice nor interest is simple, each demands the attention of *logos*.

Justice and Cultural Criticism

In securing a relatively more moderate decision toward Mytilene, Diodotus encourages the Athenians to be juster than their power requires. His practice is therefore consistent with the *logos* about Athens's justice provided by the Athenians at Sparta. Yet the kind of justice consistent with Diodotus's speech proceeds not from haughty generosity and a confidence in power, but from thoughtful concern and an appreciation of the uncertainties of power. In this respect, the contention that justice means treating others more equally than quantities of force require implies the prior choice of taking equality seriously as a political good and investigating its merits and complexities through interactive rationality. To the extent that justice originates in a recognition of the good of equality, it is both voluntary and worthy of praise.

This kind of justice thus seems consistent with the democratic cultural priorities of equality and deliberative rationality. Yet Diodotus's reliance on deception also signals the vulnerability of these priorities to the characteristics of democratic politics exploited by Cleon. In spite of, or perhaps because of, his deception, however, Diodotus's speech matters. Though Cleon succeeded in bolstering much of the wavering support for harshness, Diodotus's pleas for leniency "prevailed" (*enkratēse*). However skilled, Diodotus could not have succeeded without the appropriate political space. This includes not only the formal institution of the assembly, but also the broader political cultural practices that legitimate revisiting decisions taken earlier. While both of these conditions create possibilities for abuse, they also provide opportunities for reexamining seemingly settled decisions because of the availability of new or disconcerting information or for correcting mistakes.[66] Though such practices may often be overwhelmed or captured by the passions (fear or anger, sympathy or remorse), they also provide opportunities for reflectively examining the passions' urges and consequences. Parts of Cleon's argument for severity—that the oppressed can be excused for resisting their oppressors and that the Mytilenes have been driven on by reckless hopes and desires (3.39.1-2)—are reconsidered as part of Diodotus's case for leniency.[67]

In this respect, the outcome of the debate on Mytilene can be compared with the outcome of the debate on Plataea narrated very shortly thereafter. Though these speeches occupy more text than those represented in the Mytilene debate, they only confirm that Spartan judgment is predetermined. In this context, the speeches have nothing to do with a deliberate reconsideration, however imperfect, but reflect instead the desperation of the Plataeans and the resolute vehemence of the Thebans. "In virtually every respect, it was on account of the Thebans that the Spartans turned so thoroughly against the Plataeans, thinking the Thebans useful to them in the war that had just now begun" (3.68.4-5).[68] *Logos* subordinates the formalities of justice to advantage.

Yet Athens's openness to a *logos* capable of challenging the regime's conception of justice is an unfulfilled promise in the rest of the narrative. Just as the restraint showed toward the Mytilene democrats is followed by the execution of the Plataeans and the cycles of violence in Corcyra, Diodotus's appreciation of the value of *logos* is followed by its increasing instrumentalization to power (in the Melian dialogue) or interest (in the speech of Euphemus). Diodotus explains the causes behind the diminution of rationality when he points to the overwhelming influence of the passions (3.45.4–7). These comments clarify why cultural attempts to control nature may well lead to an intensification of nature's disruptions. While culture may enable discourses that can turn a critical eye on culture's own practices, it may also intersect with the passions to pathologize culture's own worst possibilities. The envoys to Melos organize nature's turbulence into a law that justifies Athens's exercise of power. And as numerous commentators (see, for example, Connor 1984, 167–68; Edmunds 1975, 121; and Orwin 1994, 162 n. 32) have noted, Diodotus's claim that humans overreach because *erōs* leads and hope (*elpis*) follows is spectacularly confirmed in the narrative of the launching of the Sicilian invasion (6.31.1–6, 6.32.1–2).

Consequently, while Thucydides does not abandon in principle the possibility of a critical *logos* that draws on culture's best resources, his treatment of this possibility is informed by doubts about the sufficiency of Athenian (or any) cultural resources for effectively guiding human improvement. Thucydides, "an Athenian," represents what seems to be the best of Athenian voices through a character who may be his own creation and whose very name, Diodotus, suggests a gift from Zeus. In this light, critical cultural voice may provide only an exposure of hypocrisy or injustice. Speaking in his own name in book 8, Thucydides uses the episode of the Athenian oligarchs' efforts to entrench their power by establishing oligarchies in the subject cities to comment on the character of the empire. Creating an oligarchy in Thasos leads not to closer ties between Thasos and the oligarchs, but to an attempt to throw off Athenian control altogether. "And it was the same, it seemed to me, among the other subject cities; for the citizens having taken on a moderation [of governance] and having more security for their own actions [aimed toward] freedom entirely, no longer taking seriously the hollow good order [alleged by] the Athenians" (8.64.5). This assessment is culturally conditioned, for it relies seriously on the evaluative criteria introduced rhetorically by the Athenians at Sparta; Athens provides good order and is worthy of praise because it treats the subject cities more equally than its superior power requires. Though the speakers implied that this behavior is another sign of Athens's power, Thucydides now (in book 8) treats it, in a way that is consistent with the spirit of Diodotus's speech, as a constructed discourse that recognizes equality as a certain kind of good. Though this discourse could not have been articulated absent Athenian power, its function extends beyond service to that power. The character of equality is examined as a priority that democratic culture insists be taken seriously. Its critical usage envisages an alternative political order that is not simply hollow. Yet the narrative offers little promise for realizing that alternative vision. In calling his work a possession forever, Thucydides may look toward a more positive consequence of his own *logos*. Yet this prospect may be led, if not by an *erōs* resistant to rationality, then by a hope that rationality cannot altogether support.

The Problematic of Justice in Plato's *Republic*

Discourse and War

Plato's *Republic* likewise examines connections between justice and political power, but its conclusions, perspective, and tone seem fundamentally different from Thucydides'. At the end of the dialogue Socrates affirms the positive connection between individual happiness and justice (621c–d). Along the way, he has outlined arrangements that would make political justice a reality. However, any optimism seems purchased only at the cost of a radical distancing of Platonic *logos* from the realities of the Thucydidean world. Socrates eventually admits that the city that has been the focus of so much of the dialogue cannot really exist anywhere on earth; it is a pattern in heaven that can help the motivated individual found something similar within himself (592a–b).

Plato's conclusions thus seem to require what Nietzsche characterizes as a turning away from the world.[69] This assessment is shared by a number of modern commentators who have set Thucydides' approach against Plato's (de Romilly 1963, 362, 365; Crane 1998, 325). To the extent that interpretations such as these are accurate, comparing what Plato and Thucydides have to say about justice is of limited value.

As I have suggested earlier, claims about Plato's disconnection from reality are challenged by the dramatic character of the dialogues. The dialogues may not be suffused with savageries and horrors, but they are situated in turbulent historical circumstances and populated by individuals with passionate identities and interests. The dramatic date of the *Republic* cannot be identified precisely, but the conversation must take place within the broad period of the war.[70] The presence of Polemarchus, Lysias, and Niceratus points to the war's end, to the defeat of Athens and the subversion of the democracy by the Thirty.[71] In spite of the dialogue's supposed focus on the city in speech at rest or at peace,[72] there are a number of important and complicating references to war (or motion) that intersect provocatively with the narrative and concerns of Thucydides.[73]

Within the city in speech, the very creation of the class of guardians, which eventually generates a class of philosophic rulers, responds to prospects of interpolis conflict. While these conflicts seem to be material quarrels over scarce resources, the interpretations of the involved parties are more ambiguous. Once the city that Socrates, Glaucon, and Adeimantus are founding turns from moderation to luxury, it can no longer support its population with its own produce and livestock: "Then we shall have to cut off a portion of our neighbor's land if we are to have enough for pasture and ploughing" (373d). While the expansion of this city originates in what seems to be necessity, this condition only emerges after a change in the regime. The luxurious city soon finds itself on the defensive, threatened by aggressive neighbors who "abandon themselves to the pursuit of wealth without limit, exceeding the boundaries of necessity" (373d). In spite of the attempt to separate defensive from aggressive wars, it would be understandable if the city's greedy neighbors also saw themselves driven by necessity, just as they might interpret the needful expansion of the city in speech as the pursuit of wealth without limit. In this respect, what appears to be necessity is set in part by the nature of the regime, and what looks like desperation to one party might appear as overreaching aggression to another. These considerations are not so removed from Thucydides' claim that the truest causes of the war were Athenian greatness and Spartan fear, both called necessities or responses to necessities, and both tied to the characters of the regimes.

As the city in speech is constructed, questions about war continually arise. Near the beginning of book 4, Adeimantus wonders how this city will be able to wage war without the great wealth its institutions forbid (422a). This echoes one of Archidamus's reservations as he attempts to restrain the Peloponnesians from undertaking reckless action against Athens (1.83.1–3). Adeimantus's question also intersects with Pericles' confidence in Athens's overwhelming material advantages (1.141.2–7, 2.63.1–2, 2.65.12–13). Socrates' reply is that the moderate city could defeat not one but two rich ones, just as a well-trained and conditioned boxer could easily overcome two overfed amateurs. Their city will succeed by pursuing a strategy of divide and conquer (422b ff.); when confronted with a single opponent it can prevail by exploiting the social enmity between the oligarchs and the democrats that makes every existing city "not one, but two" (422e–23a). In this respect, the city in speech shares in the disciplined priorities of Sparta and sets itself quite decisively against an indulgent city such as Athens. In pointing toward the defeat of the wealthy city, Socrates contests the Periclean focus on resources as assuring military success. Yet in another way, the Socratic city is frighteningly unique, for it adopts as a deliberate policy the replication of Corcyrean *stasis* among its neighbors, using factional allegiances to disintegrate other cities as a prelude to overpowering them. Its singular success requires generalized chaos.

Though this city is allegedly constructed to help find justice in the soul, the focus of the dialogue shifts in book 5 to examining whether it is possible or desirable to make this city real.[74] After Glaucon agrees that this city (whose institutions now include a common military education for men and women and common spouses and families) would be altogether desirable, he presses Socrates to show its possibility (466d). Socrates responds initially with a long excursus on how the city would fight (466d–e ff.) in a way that inscribes experiences of the Peloponnesian War within the dialogue. However, it does so in ways that challenge not only the perspectives of the major Greek combatants but also of that of Thucydides himself. And the excursus ends not with a strategic plan to foster disorder, but with the prospects of more humane restraints on conflictual behavior. In a sense, this could be read as a prelude to the imminent introduction of philosophy as the condition for this city's coming into being.[75]

Socrates begins by indicating that exposing the young to the sights and sounds of war is an essential part of their early education (466e–67a).[76] This way of passing wars onto one's children is not viewed as a frightening prospect to be avoided, as it is by Archidamus (Thucydides 1.81.6), but as an opportue necessity to be wisely exploited. The rigorous training of the warriors occurs within a severe military culture that mandates (among other things) that those who voluntarily surrender their arms are to be left behind as the victors' prisoners (*Republic* 468a–b). This education, if anything, intensifies the shame culture employed in Spartan training, for it implicitly condemns both the Spartan hoplites who gave up their arms at Pylos (4.38.3–4) and the Spartan leadership who obsessed continually over their return (4.41.3–4, 4.108.7, 5.15.1–2).[77] Fallen warriors are praised and buried in ways (468e–69b) that outdo the rhetoric and ritual of Pericles' funeral speech. Yet Socrates adds that the same honors are appropriate for those dying of old age (marginalized by Pericles) who have lived exceptionally good lives (469b). Finally, Socrates focuses extensively on the differences between wars among Greeks and those fought between Greeks and barbarians. He compares Greek wars to a sickness (*nosos*), the response to which is an attempted healing through the moderation of hostilities (470e–71a). Such conflicts are therefore properly called factions (*staseis*), not wars (*polemoi*), and their resolution is not destruction of conditions of civility, but "compelling the guilty to do justice by force of the sufferings of the innocent" (471b). In saying that *stasis* is a kind of *nosos*, Socrates associates the disruptions caused by homicidal civil strife (as in Corcyra) with those arising under the intense pressure of the plague. Yet in holding out prospects for returning the Greeks to health, Socrates denies that *stasis* is the truest reflection of the human condition (Thucydides 3.82.2) and suggests that such illnesses can be treated as well as described (Thucydides 2.48.3).[78] Consequently, the sufferings of the innocent are not seen as marks of war's inevitable and limitless inhumanity (1.23.3–4), but as abuses whose remedy both justifies and limits war-making. Socrates therefore concludes with prospects for more general moderation. Thucydides' narrative concludes with the return of the Persians (8.109); the involvement of the barbarians will exacerbate violence among the Greeks (8.5.4–5, 8.46.1–2). Socrates' excursus suggests that since the Greeks should fight with the barbarians in the way they now fight among themselves (*Republic* 471b), they may come to treat the barbarians in the gentler or more forgiving way they should treat each other.[79]

While acknowledging that savageries and horrors are part of his audience's political-cultural experience, Socrates responds not by departing for the realm of ideas, but by positioning these dark occurrences against other human possibilities. Both the dramatic setting and the thematic focus of the *Republic* bespeak a civic condition that is neither altogether peaceful nor constantly embattled.[80] The relative priority accorded to the question of how cities and human beings can be just when stable or at rest suggests, like the conversation in the *Charmides*, that the activities that the city performs or enables at peace or at leisure are more valuable and significant than those it performs at war or under compulsion. Within the *Republic*, those peaceful activities are conversations about justice or those practices that Aristotle says (*Politics* 1.2) make human beings political. While Thucydides examines the origins and foci of the forms of justice established within particular political cultures as part of a larger inquiry into how these cultures make war, Socrates encloses his treatment of how war is waged within a dialogic investigation of justice[81] and how it is related to happiness. At the same time, however, no vision of how the city can best perform its appropriate function when at peace can altogether neglect the necessities that may initiate war. These necessities may include both authentic threats from without and unexamined compulsions from within, such as a desire for wealth that is interpreted as a requirement for survival. The proper response to the latter is a critical rationality that examines sources of political obsession so as to distinguish legitimate need from greed or hubris. The proper response to the former is vigilance and, where necessary, assertiveness. In extreme cases, the need to meet external aggression may severely compromise higher peaceful possibilities. Yet this realization should not lead to the mistaken conclusion that the need to respond to threats or acts of aggression drives all conceptualizations of political practice.[82]

From this perspective, Plato differs from Thucydides not primarily because he is obsessed only with ideas, but because he understands the political world in a different and more recuperative way. Building on a similar insight, a number of commentators have disputed the epistemic basis of interpretations like those of de Romilly and Crane,[83] and argued that Plato's work draws heavily on the meanings and practices of democratic culture. For Peter Euben, for example, while the *Republic* appears to level a devastating attack on tragic poetry, the dialogue and tragedy have parallels. For Euben, what makes the intersection between Platonic dialogue and tragic poetry both possible and necessary is the contextualizing influence of Athenian culture (1990, 236). Sara Monoson draws similar conclusions about the connection between Socratic philosophy and the experience of the theatergoer in the Athenian democracy (2000, 206–38), expanding this to the relation between philosophic education and democratic practice generally (2000, 13).

While I am in considerably greater agreement with Euben and Monoson than with de Romilly and Crane, the interpretation of the *Republic* that I develop in the rest of this chapter is indebted to, yet differs from, both views. The de Romilly/Crane interpretation is complicated by Socrates' failure to discover a definition of justice and an arrangement of the just society that escape either the continued influence of opinion or the ongoing possibility of injustice. And while Socrates is constantly engaged with the meanings and practices of democratic culture, his investigations of justice in the city and the soul require resources that go beyond those provided by democracy. These resources are not the insights of pure intellection, but the outcomes of critical reflection on both human and cultural possibilities.

City, Soul, Culture

The importance of culture within Socrates' examination of justice goes well beyond the exposure of the inadequacies of various conventional opinions in book 1. The extended attempt to prove that justice is good for itself is a response to the articulate challenges of Glaucon and Adeimantus that begin book 2. Their concerns are prompted in part by the ambiguous, even contradictory, status that justice occupies within the city's educational institutions. Glaucon develops the case for the attractiveness of injustice by indicating what "they say" (358c) justice is and where it came from. What follows are the famous counter-Hobbesian interpretation of the social contract and the revised Herodotean story of the ring of Gyges' ancestor.[84] Both stories suggest that humans are naturally inclined toward injustice; all want more than their share of material, status, and power goods, and attempts to get them are restrained only by personal weakness or social coercion (360b–d). Glaucon uses these stories to reinforce the alleged opposition between vigorous nature and fearful convention. Yet it is far from clear that he succeeds. While the cultural suppression of the strong by indoctrination is said to be against nature, convention's success in controlling the impulses of the powerful attests to its own strength and thus to its natural superiority. And Glaucon's stories themselves rely on what cultural opinions ("they") say and teach about justice. Culture's power is pragmatically revealed by its control over how nature appears.

Glaucon frames his challenge to Socrates by positioning constructed visions of just and unjust men (which Socrates compares to statues [361d])[85] within a hypothetical cultural context. The society in which Glaucon positions his representative men intensely loves justice and passionately hates and fears injustice, but it has significant difficulty telling which is which. Culture's errors are exaggerated by the crafty deceptions of the unjust man and the puzzling ineffectiveness of the just one. The unjust one is a clever craftsman (*deinos demiourgos*) of injustice, able to display the behavior that is considered just while gaining all the rewards of injustice (360e6–9). As for the just man, "though doing no injustice, let him have the reputation for the greatest crimes. So that he may be tested [tortured] regarding justice by not giving way to [being softened by] bad reputation and other consequences coming out of it" (361c). The just man is so firm in his practice of a justice that is reputedly unjust that he is eventually subjected to hideous tortures (361e–62a). It is easy to see why the clever practice of injustice would include the ability to beat the system by manipulation and deceit, but it is harder to understand why Glaucon portrays the nightmarish situation of the just man as a perfection (*teleion*) of his identity (360e). He is not simply someone who minds his own business, for he comes to public attention as (mistakenly) unjust. Yet his justice is so ineffective that it is seen as its opposite. But perhaps there should also be serious reservations about the surrounding culture. Its hatred of injustice is unaccompanied by discerning intelligence, and if the noticeable practices of the just man draw such hatred, we should be skeptical about whether this culture's priorities are truly just.[86]

Glaucon's unusual representations are followed by Adeimantus's interpretation of how justice and injustice are treated within more-familiar cultural contexts. He traces concerns such as Glaucon's to deficiencies in the education offered by the Athenian public culture, particularly by the poets. While justice is praised as noble (*kalos*), it is also said to be hard and laborious; injustice, on the other hand, is represented as pleasant and easy, shameful (*aischros*) only by opinion (*doxa*) and law (*nomos*) (363e–64a). These images are reinforced by social practices that honor the rich and powerful despite their vices and dismiss the poor and the weak, disregarding their virtues. Culture's inadequacies are particularly apparent in its treatments of the gods, who are represented as doling out benefits and harm in ways that are at best inattentive to moral qualities and as being susceptible to toadying and bribery via charms and sacrifices (364b–65a). The intelligent young man who puts all of this together concludes the following: "[T]he consequences for me of being just, if I also don't seem to be, are, they say, not advantages, but toils and obvious penalties, but if [I am] unjust, and I have a reputation for justice, it is said that a godlike life awaits" (365b).

Like Glaucon's images, Adeimantus's interpretation raises more questions about culture than he intends. If culture itself creates the opinion that injustice is shameful only by law, much of what is offered as a part of cultural education is transparently self-undermining. At one level, Adeimantus's critique reinforces the existence of a consistent or reified cultural presence. Private citizens and poets all sing their song as if with one mouth (*pantes gar ex enos stomatos hymnousin*) (364a). Yet this song contains contradictory lyrics, especially as they are heard by those who are shown, or are savvy enough to detect, inconsistencies. Culture's educational contradictions thus create puzzles about the effectiveness of social power. To the degree that enculturation generates attachment to the appearance rather than to the reality of justice, it fails to achieve its goal of producing thoroughly just citizens. Yet as the source of Glaucon's statements about the relative attractions of just and the unjust lives, it exerts a powerful influence over moral belief. The contestability of culture's influence seems itself to originate in cultural sources. While culture seems to try to reach beyond itself to construct socially useful stories about the gods, it is unable to maintain control over how those stories are interpreted. Culture's content (its express and tacit messages) and membership (its valorized representatives and its independent thinkers) reflect similar degrees of fragmentation. In ways that are consistent with such multivocality and contestability, the speech-acts of Glaucon and Adeimantus point to a third and less definite response to culture's flawed attempts at socialization. Plato's brothers are neither convinced by surface exhortations to justice nor corrupted by tacit envy of the rewards of injustice. Because it is neither as consistent nor as powerful as it might be, this cultural configuration reinforces both the need for and the possibility of a critical thinking that is not simply limited by cultural templates or stymied by cultural contradictions. Socrates comments on the brothers' questions by praising their natures (367e). They request a defense of the goodness of justice that presumes the soul rather than simply the culture as the appropriate frame of reference; Adeimantus insists that Socrates defend the goodness of justice while bracketing references to the culture's gods (366e–67a).

Socrates' subsequent attempt to convince Glaucon and Adeimantus of the good of justice itself (367e) is therefore contextualized more broadly by questions concerning the relationship between the soul and the city. Initially, the city is introduced for analogical reasons; supposedly, we can see justice in the smaller thing (the soul) more clearly if we can first discover it in the bigger one (the city). Socrates illustrates the positive uses of the analogy by comparing it to improvements in the ability to see smaller letters by first seeing them writ large (368d–e). This is a surprising possibility for anyone who has ever taken an eye test, for the benefits only follow if seeing the larger letters improves vision. In this context, finding justice in the city reveals it in the soul only if a discussion of political justice contributes to a kind of self-knowledge. Consequently, working through the analogy is not simply the skillful use of technique, but an aspect of liberal education (cf. Ferrari 2005, 75–82). To this extent, Socrates' interactions with Glaucon and Adeimantus in one way support, in another challenge, the city's educational mission. Like the city, Socrates will argue for the good of justice, yet he will do so by going beyond the templates of the city (justice will be defended as something good for itself and not simply for its consequences) and he will treat the city or the culture not as a presupposition, but as a problem. Glaucon's and Adeimantus's continued attachments to justice (368d) in the face of cultural inadequacies and misdirections may be largely traceable to Socrates' influence. While this education is culturally permitted, it is not culturally sponsored, and certain elements within the society view it with deep suspicion.

The analogical method is only effective if city and soul suitably resemble each other. Socrates tries to establish resemblance by pointing to various features of language. The first is the example used to initiate the analogy: two identical letters of different sizes. These cannot invariably be lowercase and capital letters, since the form or look of capitals is not always simply a larger version of the lowercase. The similarity is supported, instead, by the cultural use of language. "There is, as we say (*phamen*), a justice of a single man (*anēr*) and of a whole city?" (368e). Here the similarity between the city's larger justice and the man's smaller justice is indicated by applying the same predicate to both subjects. This convention reflects and reinforces broader social experiences, since communities insist that their members be just as conditions of association (351c ff.), and the justice of the city is a fundamental concern of (and often a source of contention between) the citizens (338d–39a).[87] What the culture says about the justice of cities and men therefore enables further discourses about these forms of justice and about the general nature of justice. Part of what takes place within this subsequent discourse, however, is an examination of the adequacy of its own enabling condition or the validity of cultural education.[88] Thus, after identifying the virtues, and therefore justice, in the city, Socrates prefaces his investigation of the soul by questioning the completeness of the analogy itself. "We supposed that, if we found the larger thing that contained justice and first put the effort into regarding (*theasasthai*) it there, we should easily behold what it is in the single human being (*en eni anthrōpō*). And it seemed to us that this larger thing was the city, and so we constructed the best one we could, well believing that [justice] might be found in the good one. What we believe we saw there should be brought back to the individual and if they agree, all is well. But if something different (*ti allo*) appears in the individual, we will go back again to the city and test it there and it may be by looking from the one to the other and rubbing them upon one another, as we do with fire sticks, we may make justice burst forth and, when it has become evident, secure it for ourselves" (434d–35a). Beginning with the resources supplied by the culture's construction of justice, we need to use our critical abilities to establish a fuller understanding.

Socrates begins an alternative account of "what justice is and where it came from" with the origins of the city, constructed because "each of us is not self-sufficient but in need of much" (369b). Society originates not in power but in need. At the same time, the functioning and development of society reshape human needs and thus the terms of human association in fundamental ways, as marked by the transition from basic needs to luxurious ones and from the healthy city to the feverish one (372e–73a). In this respect, Socrates' position is neither that of the rational choice and social contract theorists, who see the most important human needs existing exogenously to society, nor that of Geertz and the interpretive anthropologists, who see everything human as a cultural construction (Geertz 1973, 82–83; 217–18). For Socrates, there is a sense in which psychology is (theoretically) prior to culture (the city does have its conceptual origins in identifiable human needs); yet culture is also indispensable for providing the psyche with different paths for individuation (human needs seem capable of a range of specifications, enabled by different cultural forms). Thus, although Socrates says that we explain variations in the characters of regimes on the basis of their being populated by individuals of certain types, those types have also been shaped by differing cultural influences. "Must not we ... necessarily agree that the same forms and characters as are set in the city are also in each of us? ... Surely they didn't come there from any other place.

It would be ridiculous to think that spiritedness doesn't come into the cities from those private individuals alleged to have this quality, as [is ascribed to] the Thracians and Scythians and just about the whole northern region; or the love of learning which could most be ascribed to our region; or the love of money, which would seem to be the case not least among the Phoenicians and those in Egypt" (435d–36a). The private persons (*ta idiota*) who are the sources of these qualities in regimes are in one sense individuals whose characters and types cohere as a culture. Yet precisely because all of these forms and characters are in each one of us, individuation seems dependent on the influence of cultural memberships. Culture can be according to nature not only because natural standards or functions are appropriate vantage points for cultural assessments, but also because the creation of culture is one of the most indispensable human activities by nature. Perhaps nature can become a standard for assessing different cultural forms only because culture makes natural achievement or debasement visible. Self-sufficiency is a precultural standard for assessing regime quality, but different possibilities for human self-sufficiency become available only on the basis of cultural constructions. Moreover, the fact that spirit, the love of learning, and the love of money are distributed within as well as across cultures (the love of money is found "not least," i.e., not exclusively, in Phoenicia and Egypt) suggests that no cultural construction is simply homogenous.[89] Together, the range of cultural practices map possibilities for each community. And each, to some degree or other, is capable of drawing upon all. Cross-cultural comparisons and, thus, some glimpse into the range of human variations possible by nature are achievable within internal cultural conversations, whose richness and breadth are themselves culturally variable.

That cultural and psychological phenomena must be examined interactively is suggested by the failure of attempts to elevate either to preeminence. Temptations to do so represent two different abuses of the analogical method.[90] The first, literally seeing the individual as the city writ small, derives all psychological identities and activities from cultural templates. The second, seeing the city as the individual writ large, configures culture according to some controversial model of the psyche.[91] Thus, in saying that there is a similar justice of a whole city and of a single *anēr*, we privilege the virtues associated with maleness (rather than humanness) in inevitably problematic ways. Though they stem from opposite impulses, these abuses oversimplify and therefore distort the needs and practices involved in a self-sufficient life.

One basis for defending the analogical method in the *Republic* is the thesis that culture is constitutive of individual senses and practices of justice. The individual's justice, like the Thracians' spirit or the Phoenicians' cupidity, is a microcosmic version of the regime's identity. Pervasive attempts at socialization are assumed within Adeimantus's critique of Athenian education; incoherent or debased individual beliefs about justice reflect broader cultural inadequacies and pathologies. Appropriately, Socrates' attempt to orchestrate sweeping educational reforms of the city in speech in books 2 and 3 are instigated primarily with the cooperation of Adeimantus. Together, they envisage a radical purge of what the poets are allowed to teach, especially with respect to the representation of the gods and the heroes. The scope of these reforms expands when Socrates enlists Glaucon to advise in the censorship of musical modes (399a ff.). Whereas Glaucon had earlier prompted the transition from moderation to luxury in the description of how the citizens of this regime would live (372c), he now assists in what Socrates describes as "purg[ing] the city that a while ago we said was luxurious," affirming, "[t]hat's because of our moderation" (399e).[92]

Yet what is striking about these attempts to instill a penetrating ethic of moderation (extending from poetry and music through sculpture and architecture [401b–d]) is their eventual failure. All require a more fundamental grounding in the noble lie (supplied ironically by the money-loving Phoenicians) that represents this education as a dream experienced while the various classes of citizens—rulers, auxiliaries, craftsmen—were being formed in the earth (414d–e). Culture needs the sanctioning of nature, but natural validation is provided by a deliberately constructed lie. In one way, the lie explicitly problematizes culture by portraying its educational influence as a dream, yet it also empowers it by making its influences invisible.[93]

However, the lie's influence will not guarantee that the guardian class will see itself as protective brother to the rest, for this class must be isolated in material poverty; none of them is allowed even a drink from a silver or golden cup for fear that the whole project will disintegrate (416d). The military power (the deceived and isolated children of the earth are armed) of these auxiliaries needs a much more encompassing social power that further tames or normalizes the members of this class, as if it were an animal breed. The attempt to shape human beings by powerful cultural norms ends by eliminating significant aspects of humanity altogether. The culture of guardianship can only function within a concentration camp for watchdogs (cf. 416a).

Adeimantus himself challenges this outcome at the beginning of book 4 when he reminds Socrates that he is in no way "making these [guardians] happy" (419a ff.), in effect confronting the radicalized political good of civic virtue with the individual or natural good of happiness.

Socrates' response is that their concern is with the happiness of the city, generally, not that of (simply) one of its parts (420b). The inadequacy of this response has been noted by numerous commentators, beginning with Aristotle (*Politics* 2.5). However, what is most striking in this context is that Socrates attempts yet another form of cultural control through the political colonization of the category of happiness. The political role of the guardians now sets limits around the kind of happiness appropriate for them (420d–e), so that happiness itself seems as much of a cultural outcome as justice.

This exchange is followed by Socrates' serial attempts to locate justice first in the city and then in the soul. This elicits still more objections that force Socrates to consider the possibility of establishing the city in speech as a reality. The question of this city's possibility eventually intersects so decisively with the psychological inquiry that motivated the regime's construction that Socrates reverses completely the earlier obsession with culture and contends that "the city is best governed [when it] is most like single human being" (462c). Only under this condition does it seem reasonable to apply the predicate "happiness" to the city in a way that legitimately subordinates or instrumentalizes the apparent happiness of one of its major parts. The individual human being is, however, now understood in a way that construes the soul on the basis of the functions and experiences of the body. The paradigmatic individual activity is neither justice nor thought, but physical pleasure and pain (462c–d). This perspective requires the city's social partners to be reimagined as an organism's physiological members. Consequently, there is no civic or cultural home for the different; the only relevant categories are one's own or the other (462c).

Seeing the city as if it were the individual frames all of the educational, marriage, and child-rearing proposals that Socrates outlines in book 5, ending with the assertion that the only way the best city can be actualized is through the rule of philosopher-kings (473c–e). While the philosopher-kings are introduced initially as the required condition for this city's being happy and well-governed, the entire purpose of the regime is soon recast as providing the context for the education of philosophic rulers. This revises the paradigmatic activity of the single human being who provides a model for the best city from the physiological to the intellectual, so much so that material conditions or physical attachments become distractions (485d). Since the city is seen as the human being writ large, it can choose to suppress or eliminate those of its own practices that interfere with its pursuit of the good. The elimination of the conventional family and household are the social consequences of a diminution of their originating desires in light of the overwhelming attractiveness of philosophy (485d–e). While the radical cultural reforms of books 2 and 3 produce a city resembling an armed camp, the philosophic turn of books 5 through 7 ends with one fulfilling a theorist's fantasies.[94] Yet both visions abstract from the more ordinary human needs and practices that make the city necessary and help to define the self-sufficiency that makes it desirable. The soul is capable of activities other than philosophy, just as there are pleasures and pains beyond physical experiences.

Socrates' own use of the analogy potentially works against both of these abuses. It draws on cultural practices and human possibilities in a way that recognizes both interaction and tension. In focusing on interaction, Socrates declines to follow either the rational choice or the interpretive anthropological treatment of the relationship between culture and psyche. And in revealing tensions rather than contradictions, he goes beyond postmodernism's inclination to see all forms of human interaction as power contests.

Political Imperatives and Cultural Complexities

Socrates' treatment of justice in the city is based on the fundamental principle that each member or citizen should do his own work, performing the single function for which he—or she—is most suited (370b). In the first and healthiest city, this simplicity is a reflection of the different individual talents that contribute to economic production and exchange (370a–b). These capacities are evidently precultural and belong to each individual by nature; the formation of the city organizes but does not create these differences in talent. The relevant practices of this city's inhabitants seem confined to their following their occupations (*erga*), and their interactions consist of repeated patterns of production, exchange, and consumption. Their lives also seem stable or unhistorical; as long as the healthy city persists, no fundamentally new needs emerge.

Glaucon contests this picture of health and satisfaction by accusing Socrates of describing a city of pigs (372d). In response, Socrates proposes the construction of a much more complex society, characterized initially by an expansion of the arts and crafts. Since this richer but needier community is more likely to engage in conflicts with other cities, Socrates adds the specialized cohort of guardians, requiring the supervision or control that marks the first appearance of politics. This increasing social complexity is paralleled by a developing psychic complexity; the first mention of the soul (*psychē*) during this founding period occurs (375b) after the creation of the guardians.[95] Thus, while the soul is not simply a social construction, it is apparently unable to develop its own potential ranges of complexity without the contributions of culture. In the immediate sequel, however, complexity seems more a source of corruption than of enrichment. The complex society of differentiated craftspeople reinforces a desire for luxury that leaves the community vulnerable to the aggression of the spirited warriors (375b–c). The ensuing political cultural reforms (in the treatment of poetry and the other crafts) are intended to restore the moderate simplicity that the city's growing luxury had undermined. This concern is extended to representations of the gods, "for the god [must be portrayed as] altogether simple and true in deed and speech" (382e). Anything to the contrary in Homer must be excised or rewritten; complexity is condemned as deceit or falsehood. Yet the simplicity at which these reforms aim is not the recognition of any kind of natural purity or health but the product of cultural manipulation through the exercise of power over educational discourse. Eventually, Socrates conceals this cultural effort behind the natural facade created by the noble lie. To the extent that Socrates and his interlocutors attempt to represent the cultural as if it were natural, they too practice a form of deceit, implying that the political simplification that this city requires originates in complexity. If this is so, then complexity reflects more than corruption, for the deceitfulness of Socrates and his cofounders aims, albeit problematically and unsuccessfully, at establishing political health. Consequently, while social complexity generates the potential for injustice that political simplifications aim to remedy, such simplifications themselves create potentials for accompanying injustices that the complexities of culture need to identify and challenge.

The city and the soul as investigated through the analogical method have both moved far beyond the simpler and healthier originating society. Their degrees of complexity are shown in part by the fact that neither city nor soul can be explored without essential reference to the other. While the treatment of the city is prior to that of the soul, references to the soul eventually are critical to the discovery of the city's virtues. Conversely, while the treatment of the soul is intended to follow the same formal pattern used in the examination of the city, elements of the soul cannot be fully grasped without substantive references to political or cultural influences.

When Socrates attempts to say where the virtue of *sōphrosynē* can be found in the city, he departs from the earlier practice of locating each virtue within single classes (wisdom in the rulers, courage in the guardian/auxiliaries). *Sōphrosynē* is a special problem, because common usage treats it as both reflexive and relational, as when an individual is said to practice *sōphrosynē* by being master of himself. "Yet isn't the phrase 'master of himself' ridiculous? For he who is master of himself would also be subject to himself, and the one subject to himself would also be master" (430e–31a). Socrates makes sense of this by referring to that state of the soul, already understood as a kind of complexity, where the worse part is ruled by that which is naturally better (*to beltion physei*). As the condition for psychic complexity, culture thus allows, though it hardly guarantees, the development of what is better by nature. Unlike wisdom and courage, *sōphrosynē* extends throughout the regime, manifesting itself differently within different social groupings and contributing to a complexity that is also a coherence (431b–d). Though the analogy with the city is intended to clarify the virtues of the *psychē*, discovering *sōphrosynē* in the city requires attention to its function in the soul.[96]

Conversely, the investigation of the soul presumes a complexity that only develops under cultural influences. When Socrates characterizes the individual desires found within the appetitive part of the soul, he focuses on their appropriate sources of satisfaction; hunger is the desire for food, thirst for drink, and so on. He rejects a proposal to qualify these as the desires for *good* food and *good* drink on the grounds that all human beings desire the good (437e; cf. 439a). From one point of view, this suggests that the desires themselves are neither good nor bad and that they therefore require the guidance of reason to determine the degree and quality of satisfaction appropriate in particular cases.[97] Yet insofar as the desires are individuated exclusively with reference to their cognate sources of satisfaction, there seems to be no rational basis for criticizing any desire qua desire as bad. The suspicion that the objects of one's desires may not be good, prompting the discovery of the calculative faculty that scrutinizes and when necessary opposes them (439c–d), pointedly arises when cultures identify some gratifications as noble and others as shameful. This is one implication of the story Socrates tells about Leontius, son of Aglaion, "who was going up from the Piraeus when he noticed corpses lying by the public executioner. He desired to look but at the same time was disgusted and turned away" (439e). Socrates uses this story to clarify how the third faculty of spiritedness cooperates with reason to oppose desire (440a).[98] Yet the story itself is far more than illustrative, for the narrative relies upon the formative influence of culture on psychic configurations. Simply as an object of vision, the dead body of an executed criminal elicits no distinctive perceptual response; the sight itself only becomes meaningful within a political cultural context (cf. Allen 2000, 245). Similarly, while the reaction of Leontius to the sight of the corpses may originate to a degree in a natural or biological response to mortality, that reaction is specified within a cultural environment that provides, through the laws, templates for behavior and, through punishment, sanctions against violators.[99] In this respect, cultural standards are the conditions for the complexity even of desire itself; Leontius experiences both attraction and disgust in light of his responses to different and partially contradictory impressions constructed by cultural forms.[100] What Allen (2000, 254) calls the differentiation of *orgē* into *epithymia* and *thymos* is, therefore, a cultural as well as a philosophical or intellectual outcome. Consequently, the city is not simply an analogical resource for mapping the formal structure of the justly ordered parts of the soul, but also a constitutive influence on the development of the parts themselves. Yet the context of the story also serves to raise questions about that very influence. The narrative is based on culture's failure to foster practices compatible with sociality; otherwise, there are no crimes or criminals, and, in this context, it is striking that Socrates never considers whether those executed were condemned justly or unjustly (cf. *Gorgias* 468e). Culture's being a condition for the complexity of the soul does not mean that it maintains either effective or justifiable control over the soul's activities and projects.[101]

The political regime's relation to the soul is therefore not simply constitutive and nurturing, but also potentially distorting and conflictual. Socrates' just city reflects and manages social complexity through the structure of the three classes. Yet the focus on classes as the primary units of analysis works against the deeper complexities that characterize enculturated individuals. Even within the deceptively simple framework of the tripartite soul, each member of every class must be characterized by degrees of reason, spirit, and appetite.[102] Yet the class divisions cluster everyone around the dominance of some one of each. Apparently, the only way of enforcing the principle of one man, one job, is to shoehorn every individual into one of three classes that are themselves exclusively defined by their functions. However, this class-based sociology seems no more able to flatten psychic complexity than the cultural reforms of books 2 and 3 were able to domesticate desire. Even though the elaborate system of educating the guardian class in book 5 aims at turning this group into even more of a herd (459e), it cannot suppress—indeed, it relies upon—the passions for individual recognition and gratification. "And don't you [Glaucon] agree that the one who has excelled and is well regarded shall first be crowned by his comrades in the campaign, by the lads and the boys each in turn. . . . and that he should kiss and be kissed by each?" (468b).[103] The philosopher-kings needed for the best city's realization flagrantly violate the provision of one man, one job, that defines the city's justice. Far from simplifying the class of rulers, the addition of philosophy complicates it to the point of contradiction.

From this perspective, though politics as the arrangement and exercise of power can be understood as a move toward social simplification, culture fosters a wider possible set of psychic and practical complexities.

The political arrangement in the cave binds all of the members in their places, yet interactions among them can also lead to a release from bonds and upward movement. The establishment of justice or order through politics thus always includes as a parallel outcome the creation of possible forms of injustice. Even the most elevated representation of the best city is unable to avoid this outcome. Philosopher-kings are made to suffer a kind of injustice when they are forced to rule when a better life is possible (519d). The resiliency of cultural complexity against even the most relentless attempts at political simplification suggests that one of culture's most important functions is to provide a resource for the discovery and critique of political injustices. Attempts to link defensible political conceptions of justice to broader cultural meanings may give too little regard to the tensions between politics and culture that become particularly apparent in the simultaneous presence of justice and injustice. In light of culture's openness to indeterminate forms of complexity, it seems misleading to characterize culture as a relatively closed semantic system (Geertz) or as a restricted collection of firmly established sociological facts (Rawls). To do so mistakes the political treatment of culture with general cultural functions. Because of culture's contributions to the development of complexity in the soul, examining variations in cultural complexity may be a part of, rather than an alternative to, investigations into human nature. Possibilities for interrogating political justice and criticizing political injustice in light of what is according to nature are enabled, and not replaced, by thoughtful attention to culture. This is part of what is implied when Socrates begins the cave story by asking Glaucon to make an image of our nature (514a).

Clashes between the political imperative for simplification and the need to examine politics in light of the possibilities that are according to nature are particularly pointed in the references to war within the development of the *Republic*'s various cities.[104] As the city's social structure becomes more complex and its character more feverish, the likelihood of wars increases. From one perspective, the creation of the guardian class generates additional social complexity. The guardians represent not simply another social class, but one that can threaten rather than cooperate with the others. The pressure created by this source of potential destabilization demands a political cultural simplification that can develop loyal soldiers. However, the very mechanisms designed to reduce the hazards posed by the guardians' natures increase the power of a social structure that threatens the guardians not only with injustice, but also with a diminution of their humanity. The culture that Socrates attempts to create within this city would be oblivious to this prospect, but the culture established by Socrates with his interlocutors detects it.[105]

This dialogic community enables Adeimantus and Polemarchus to challenge the noble lie's naturalization of culture in the name of biological generation within the family.[106]

As the cities in speech develop, the need to provide for the common defense does not settle the question of how wars are to be fought or the place of fighting within human interactions. Socrates considers these questions at two crucial junctures. At the first (422a–23a), his assessment of how poor cities can fight with rich ones makes it clear that examinations of how wars are waged cannot be undertaken absent a deeper understanding of the nature of the regime and its education. Eventually, this understanding reinforces the benefits of a political culture encouraging material moderation and therefore one less likely to mistake the desire for wealth with the demands of necessity (cf. 373d ff.) At the same time, Socrates' ruthless strategic guidance may well threaten the moral foundation upon which this city rests. Can this city really orchestrate the Corcyreanization of its neighbors without pathologizing itself?[107] At the second juncture (470–71) he raises the question of how one fights with one's own (i.e., other Greeks) versus how one fights with the other (the barbarians). In opposition to the divide-and-conquer strategy asserted earlier, Socrates now underscores the need to recognize that quarrels among the Greeks are curable, emphasizing not potentials for separation but opportunities for reconciliation. The need to rethink how one fights with one's own also implies the need to reconsider how one fights with others and perhaps the need to reconsider the basic difference between the other and one's own.[108] In both cases, war teaches by revealing the harshest realities confronting humanity and by providing a particularly intense reminder of the tensions between the pressures for political simplification and the critical potential of cultural complexity.

If war reminds us of the pressing character of these problems, democracy offers possibilities for unusually rich and complicated responses. Culturally, democracy is the fairest of regimes, because it encloses the largest number of possible arrangements of human experience. "This is the most beautiful of regimes ... ; as a garment of many colors, decorated with many hues, so this, decorated with every type of character, would seem most beautiful.... And it is a suitable place in which to search for a regime.... [O]wing to its richness (*exousia*), it includes all kinds of regimes, and it seems likely that anyone who ventures to found a city, as we are just now doing, must go to a city ruled democratically and select the sort that pleases him, as if in a bazaar of regimes, and after choosing, establish his own" (557c–d).

In characterizing the democracy this way, Socrates is not suggesting that democracy's political organization is incoherent, for the location of power is not at all in doubt. In book 6, Socrates makes it very clear that democratic power is exercised when the many (*hoi polloi*) come together in public fora such as the assembly, the law courts, and the theater and make their wishes known by acclamation (492b–c). Socrates' evaluation of democratic control seems altogether negative; he calls the *dēmos* acting collectively the greatest sophists (*megistous sophistas*) and says that the corruption of which the "private sophists" are accused pales before the damage caused by the *dēmos* itself. Yet it is important to note that Socrates' objections here focus less on the political consequences than on the educational consequences of this empowerment. "In such cases, how do you think the youth's heart, as the saying is, is set? What private teaching do you think will be held to and not be swept away by blame and praise and carried away on its current, so that he will say that the same things are noble and shameful, and will act in the same ways as they act, and be like them?" (492c). These objections to the *dēmos* acting politically concern its attempt to control the content of education by punishment (492d). Like all political forms, then, democracy attempts a definite form of cultural simplification that is both threatened and resisted by a more complex culture.

When Socrates says that the democracy is a bazaar of regimes, he seems to be describing its broader culture rather than its narrower arrangement of political power. The regimes (*politeiai*) involved indicate alternative ways of life, not just various structures of power. Understood in this way, democratic culture emerges as a particularly rich resource for life choices. If complexity belongs to culture generally, then democratic culture is a complexity of complexities. This is implicit in Socrates' observation that "where there is such an *exousia*, it is also [the case] that everyone would privately construct his own life for himself in a way that pleases him" (557b). Shorey and Bloom translate *exousia* as "license," a term that seems appropriate in light of Plato's presumed objections to democratic disorder. Yet *exousia* is surely one of democracy's contested symbols, for it can also represent the capacious richness captured in the image of the multihued garment. Intersecting with the social freedom allowed to the citizens, democratic culture offers a broad variety of life choices or ways of describing human possibilities not available in other regimes (cf. *Gorgias* 461e). Thus, the individuals whom Socrates describes in book 8 as living lives that parallel the five distinct regime types (aristocracy, timarchy, oligarchy, democracy, and tyranny) all seem to have grown up in a single city: the democracy as the bazaar of constitutions (557d). Consequently, their ways of life are affected by the offsetting influences of other possibilities.[109] The timocrat and the oligarch are less obsessively devoted to honor and wealth than the regimes they parallel.[110] Socrates' construction of the various cities in speech draws upon and contributes to this particular cultural richness. When Glaucon is asked to look to a model for establishing a regime within himself, it is the model of the best city, simply, a regime that exists nowhere on earth, though it does have presence through the speeches articulated in the *Republic*. And this founding will be that of a city within the soul, rather than some political alternative to the democracy (557d, 592b).

Socrates' philosophic activities are likewise enclosed by democratic culture's *exousia*, for he claims (e.g., *Crito* 53c–d; *Phaedrus* 230d) that he cannot examine his own life or those of his fellow citizens (*Apology* 30a) anywhere as well as in a democracy. Does this mean that Socrates' philosophic activity is enabled by democratic culture? Yes and no. Yes, because democratic *exousia* provides the social space and cultural resources that Socratic philosophy requires. No, or not simply, because of two important qualifications. First, there is the important difference between democratic political organization and democratic cultural possibility. While the latter may provide and be open to the sort of complexity that Socratic inquiry demands, the former is infused with the drive toward simplification that characterizes all political forms. Consequently, interpretations such as Euben's and Monoson's may assimilate features of democratic culture into democratic politics too indiscriminately.[111] Within the Platonic dialogues, Anytus's judicial attack on Socrates is motivated by a hostility toward and a fear of the influence of philosophy on democratic education.[112] Commentators such as Eva Brann (1978, 19–20) interpret this prosecution as marking the inevitable conflicts that arise between the city's shared meanings and philosophy's disruptions. Yet another way of interpreting Anytus's indictment is as an attempt to establish political control over complex cultural meanings and practices. From this perspective, while Socrates' defiant attachment to philosophy may arise from his own conviction that the unexamined life is not worthwhile for a human being (characterizing his situation in terms of species rather than cultural membership), it is also consistent with the unusually rich complexities of democratic culture. Democratic complexity can include an openness to critical thinking that extends the complexities of democratic culture even further while also resisting the efforts of democratic politics at establishing cultural control. This means that Socrates' frequent criticisms of Athens's imperial political agenda (cf. *Gorgias* 518e–19a) are made from a perspective informed by possibilities both human (the examination of one's ethical and civic practices is the most worthwhile life for an *anthrōpos*) and cultural (responding to the opportunities for political critique implied by democratic *exousia*). The conflict between Anytus and Socrates is a kind of culture war.[113]

Yet this does not mean that Socrates' critique of democratic politics is offered simply in the name of supporting broader democratic cultural priorities. The second qualification of the enabling relation between democratic culture and Socratic philosophy is that not every activity that democracy allows is simply consistent with its broad cultural meanings. Democratic culture parallels democratic politics in its understanding of freedom. Both culturally and politically, freedom is the ability to live as one likes (557b). This conception of freedom is politically institutionalized in the practices of the *dēmos* as it rules by decree (cf. *Apology* 32a–c). This form of democratic freedom shapes the other democratic cornerstone, equality, as the equality of votes in the assembly and the law courts, aggregated to create the sovereignty of the *dēmos*. Culturally, the priority of this understanding of freedom means the ability to order one's life in the way that is most pleasing (*areskos*) (557b). And all pleasures, from whatever source, are awarded equal status as gratifications that are open to pursuit as the mood strikes (561a–c). In this respect, democratic *exousia* does seem more like license; pleasure and pain (or preferences) become the standards for public and private choices. To this extent, democratic culture seems, at the very least, deeply suspicious of perspectives that suggest the need to move beyond democratic conceptions of freedom to a deeper understanding of virtue as the most important concern for a human being. When Socrates challenges these political and cultural understandings of freedom, equality, and happiness (557b, 558c, 560e–61b), he is, then, appealing to priorities or goods that go beyond and may even dispute those valorized by democracy, broadly as well as narrowly understood. One of the outcomes of Socrates' continued interrogations about virtue is a denial of the view that individuals and communities should order their lives and practices simply according to what pleases. Consequently, determinations of what is just may go well beyond—indeed, may offer substantial challenges to—a clarified or purified statement of cultural priorities. Socrates' admittedly exaggerated statement to Glaucon close to the end of the myth of Er emphasizes the value not of cultural clarity but of individual rationality, the only really effective way of negotiating "the whole risk for a human being."[114]

However, for all of this, Socrates does not translate his political cultural critique into the formulation of any realizable alternative to political democracy. Among the various regime types sketched in *Republic* 8 and 9, democracy seems mired in the fourth place out of five, superior only to tyranny (580a–b). Yet it needs to be remembered that this ordering of cities is constructed to influence Glaucon's choice of the just over the unjust life (cf. 347e). Both of the inferior regimes held to be superior to democracy, the timarchy and oligarchy, are vulnerable to substantial criticisms that make their relative preferability as forms of political organization very questionable.[115] The principal political implication of this ordering seems to be that the democratic conception of freedom understood as license is dangerously close to tyranny and thus a threat to democracy itself. In book 6 of Thucydides, Euphemus's equation of a ruling city (*hē polei archēn*) and a tyrannic man (*andri de tyrannō*) is followed closely by Alcibiades' speech in Sparta, in which Alcibiades, suspected by the Athenians of aiming at a tyranny (6.15.4), speaks as if he were himself a city (6.89.1–4). In a way, the claim that imperial Athens neither enjoys peace herself nor leaves anyone else alone (1.70.9) can prompt self-criticism as well as external suspicion.

Wherever one stands on the complicated interpretive question of the Platonic Socrates' assessment of democracy, one can sketch a Platonic response to the cultural turn in democratic theory signaled by Rawls's later work. Whereas Rawls treats particular aspects of democratic political culture as established facts that ground the articulation of a democratic theory of justice, Socrates sees democratic culture as a complexity of complexities that can be characterized in a variety of ways. Rawls therefore needs to make an argument that what he treats as the most obviously compelling features of democratic political culture should, in fact, be seen as such. Absent this argument, Rawls can justly be faulted for articulating a conception of democratic culture that is not political, but politicized, under the direction of a problematic form of simplification. In this respect, Rawls's contention that no political culture is neutral in its influence over the ways of life of its members (he calls this a commonsense fact of political sociology [2005, 193]) should not foreclose, but initiate, examinations of the meaning and significance of this claim. For Socrates, then, democratic culture needs to be investigated as a problem (the fascinating and ambiguous character of democratic *exousia*), not treated as a clear template for resolving all basic controversies about democratic political justice. The embeddedness of justice within culture means that questions or problems about them need to be investigated together. A more unsettling version of Rawls's commonsense sociological fact is that no institutionalization of justice can be free of parallel forms of potential injustice.[116]

Moreover, the open character of cultural complexity suggests that it is both unnecessary and impossible to conduct examinations of political cultural priorities according to narrowly cultural categories. That human needs and possibilities emerge and develop within cultures suggests that cultural horizons and species characteristics dynamically intersect. And the fluid, semipermeable character of cultural boundaries make cross-cultural encounters continuous realities. Thus, Socrates' alternative to a reliance on limited cultural meanings is not an ascent to some supracultural vantage point, but rather an engagement with cultural resources and cultural limitations so as to investigate and discover salutary or necessary truths about the human condition. As in the cave image, our education (or development) as human beings is inseparable from the presence of enhancing or retarding cultural forms. And the myth that concludes book 10 constructs cultural images that revise the fates of the Homeric heroes (in a way that differs from the rewriting of the *Iliad* and the *Odyssey* envisaged in books 2 and 3) to underscore the perplexing and continuing character of the whole risk for a human being.

Culture, Nature, Power

For all of their differences—indeed, because of them—Thucydides and Plato provide a richer treatment of the questions that arise out of democratic theory's cultural turn than those provided by more current approaches. For both authors, questions about justice and injustice need to be posed and addressed within more encompassing and challenging investigations into the character of regimes. And culture itself, both generally and in its particular expressions, provides the resources that enable such investigations to proceed. In neither case, however, is the focus on culture an alternative to or a substitute for a deeper inquiry into the potentials and liabilities of the human species. This does not imply the simple assertion of nature contra culture, but rather a recognition that attempts to examine the benefits and hazards of cultural memberships inevitably connect with more encompassing human questions. Consequently, attempts to close off questions about nature for the sake of an exclusive attention to culture are either self-limiting, for attempts to understand cultural functions without including their relation to the possibilities of the species would be incomplete, or self-defeating, for the concentration on human cultural practices may treat culture as the outcome of certain forms of species development or as a kind of nature. Instead, culture's contribution to the development of an indeterminate human complexity suggests that culture enables practices and languages that move beyond its own explicit templates to create an intellectual and critical perspective that is explicitly cross-cultural and thus relevant for the general concerns of human beings.

Likewise, both Thucydides and Plato recognize the connections between power and the cultural institutionalization of justice. This connection is both necessary and problematizing. It is necessary because turbulent nature requires organization to create conditions for stability (Thucydides) or because the tasks and threats confronting complex institutions call for political simplification (Plato). Yet the connection is also problematic, because the interconnections between culture/power and natural disorder can intensify the most violent features of political culture (Thucydides) or because political simplifications create possibilities for both justice and injustice (Plato). However, neither author suggests that the problematic involvement of power with justice reduces all discussions about justice to power relations.

For Thucydides, the rationality fostered by some cultural forms is capable of exposing the discrepancies between what is said to be justice and what is practiced as policy (the hollowness of Athenian good order). Yet even those forms of rationality able to escape power's debasing influence are generally confined to identifying and exposing the practices that critical cultural discourse at its best ought to condemn as injustice. War exposes self-serving power moves for what they are, yet it also undercuts any illusions about the naturalness of justice.

For the Platonic Socrates, culture is more than an attempt to organize or to control nature; cultural institutions enable the development of a human complexity that always stands in a problematic relation to natural possibilities and dangers. The simplifications that result from the necessary arrangement of power by politics are therefore both conditions for and contested by the complexities of culture. A justice that is according to nature is less a definite standard than a critical imperative that insists on assessments of the character of political cultural institutions. Within this framework, the experiences or images of war are not the teachers of what is conclusively true, but reminders both of the necessities that demand political simplifications and of the dangers of misreading necessary simplifications as noble complexities.

Consequently, both Thucydides and Plato respond to continuing dilemmas about the relation between culture and nature and power and justice not by proposing ways in which such problems can be conceptually solved, but by clarifying their statuses as problems. There is no confident dismissal of nature in favor of an exclusive focus on culture, yet nature is only accessible by drawing on and investigating cultural resources. While the articulation of a theory of justice that does not itself create other forms of injustice is in principle impossible (unlike for Rawls), neither are all efforts to establish justice equivalent only to power moves (as they are for Foucault). Plato does not strive to create an idealized intellectual reality, and Thucydides does not simply reproduce the savageries and horrors of the world. Instead, they attempt to create cultural resources that can nourish the reflections and practices of those citizens of (particularly) democratic societies who aspire also to be thoughtful human beings.

5

Proximate Others

Introduction: Postmodern Democratic Theory and the Other

If the turn toward political culture is problematic because it promises to settle things prematurely, postmodern democratic theory understands itself as a practice that is continually unsettling, multiplying contestation and self-criticism indefinitely. For postmodern democrats, impressions that democratic political culture is stable or cohesive are undercut by the challenges and enrichments of dynamically revisable individual and social identities. Recognition of this variety means more than tolerating the unconventional or the previously marginalized; it also expands possibilities for democratic action. For William Connolly, expanding a commitment to traditional liberal pluralism into what he calls an ethos of pluralization allows "the [critical] pluralist temper [to foment] multiple possibilities of micropolitics, collective assemblage, cross-national movements, pluralization, and responsiveness" (1995, 198). This characterization of politics rests on a deeper social ontology of identity formation that treats the self as a social construction and social forms as politicized and politicizing sources of regulation (Butler 1997a, 79–80; Butler 1997b, 14–15, 132; Connolly 1990, 82; Honig 1993, 13; Mouffe 2000, 99). The focus on the inevitable contestation among social forces means that assessments of cultural stability are intellectually illusory and politically suspect. So, Connolly reads Rawls's cultural turn not as providing a basis for resolving fundamental political institutional questions, but as identifying a field in which permanent solutions are rejected in principle as incompatible with democratic politics (Connolly 1990, 60; cf. Honig 2001, 31).

  This perspective radicalizes the liberal pluralist model of democratic politics that attained currency in the middle of the twentieth century. One of the common critiques of more traditional models of pluralism is that they impose conservative restrictions on the sorts of group identities that can be recognized as legitimate and thus limit possibilities for significant social change (Wolff 1965, 47; Schattschneider 1960, 35). By contrast, pluralization multiplies pragmatic experiments in living that demand to be taken seriously, extending possibilities for political action (Butler 1997a, 15; Connolly 1995, xix; Honig 1993, 208; Mouffe 2000, 101–3).

Postmodernism's reliance on this ontology of social agonism also rejects claims that ways of living can be understood—and criticized—for their actualizing or debasing essential human potentials. Critical pluralism especially resists what Connolly calls "fundamentalisms," efforts to establish dominant conceptions of the human good based on some "absolute, singular ground of authority" (Connolly 1995, 106). In privileging this singular authority, fundamentalisms construct and demonize "others" who threaten the goods that authority valorizes.[1] In the hands of critical pluralism, however, "others" provide "critique and destabilization," rightly focusing on the coercions and contradictions of fundamentalist claims (Butler 1997a, 140–41; Connolly 1995, 106; cf. Honig 1993, 4–5). The demise of fundamentalism allows demonized others to be seen as interesting representations of difference that can both challenge and enrich social life. Yet because a welcoming attitude toward the different itself requires a structured institutional context,[2] postmodernism acknowledges the threats posed by at least one "other" that is not a pathological construction—namely, any social arrangement that would stamp out pluralization to establish rigid and violent fundamentalist societies, what Richard Rorty (1982, 166) calls "the dark." Critically pluralist societies protect themselves from these others by enforcing general civilizational prohibitions against invasions of privacy or the imposition of undeserved suffering (Connolly 1995, 194; Rorty, 1989, 63–64). From this perspective, the attitude of a decent politics toward the other is bifurcated into an inclusion that welcomes previously demonized forms of otherness as interesting difference and an exclusion that opposes dogmatism and repression. Either way, a democratic politics informed by an ethos of pluralization is a realm where the phenomenon of otherness disappears as a political-cultural dilemma.[3]

In spite of rejecting most forms of intellectual closure, then, critical pluralism becomes something of a mirror image of the fundamentalism it rejects. Both positions imply that healthy politics can only occur once problems concerning the other have been resolved. They bear similar mirroring relations toward questions about the content and the influence of claims pointing to characteristics belonging essentially to human beings. For fundamentalists, a sure knowledge of what it means to be human issues clear-cut imperatives for practice. For postmodernism, all claims about the content of human nature are to be seen through and dissolved in light of a diagnosis of the power moves that lie behind them. For both, questions about what it means to be human lose their puzzling and disconcerting character.

Debates over political and social practices are constant reminders that such dilemmas are not easily resolved in either direction. Controversies over the justification of abortion, capital punishment, or same-sex marriage, for example, draw much of their force both from continued questioning about the grounds separating the decent or civilized from the depraved or barbaric and from challengeable but unavoidable claims about the meaning of the human and the senses of limit and dignity that an understanding of the human condition implies. If continuing problems or puzzles about the other and the human are embedded in the dynamics of political life itself, perhaps we should see democratic politics not as requiring a space cleared of distorting claims about the other and the human, but as the form of politics that is most suited to grappling with them.

Critical pluralism's vision of a healthy democracy is beset by at least three difficulties emerging from these dynamics. First, there is more to social criticism than the defense of the different against attempts to demonize it as the other. We are called repeatedly to make collective judgments on the qualities of varying expressions of difference. Since difference is valued not simply because it champions possibilities for self-expression but also because it can reform collective action, varying forms of difference need to be substantively assessed on the basis of a fuller inquiry into the merits of their proposals. In this connection, the tropes "fundamentalism" and "fundamentalist" lack nuance. If the category of fundamentalism is assigned simply on the basis of the committed style of political claims, figures as different as John Cardinal O'Connor, Ronald Dworkin, the Ayatollah Khomeini, Martha Nussbaum, Pat Robertson, and Jesse Jackson are all fundamentalists in the strict sense. This inattentiveness to relevant substantive differences between varying political commitments distorts the character of particular attempts at social criticism and delegitimizes on purely formal grounds important arguments within the reflective examination of public choices. For example, Nussbaum's case against female circumcision argues that it destroys certain valuable experiences that belong naturally to human beings.[4] Critical arguments in the death penalty debate likewise draw much of their force from claims that the practice affronts the respect for dignity that is essential to our humanness. Ignoring what alleged fundamentalists claim *is* fundamental and the reasons why they do so both misrepresents and impoverishes important debates about collective action.

Second, the need to delve beneath the simple categories of difference, otherness, and fundamentalism reinforces the need for critical judgment in politics. Yet by focusing so heavily on innovative or contestative political *enactments*, the ethos of pluralization threatens to redescribe judgment as simply another side of conflict.[5] Relying exclusively on contestative political enactments to determine appropriate directions for democratic action threatens to transform inquiries about the content of political proposals into strategic competitions and to substitute factual success in power contests for the substantive conclusions of political judgment.[6]

Third, because the ethos of critical pluralism essentially describes a context for political competition, it offers democratic citizens little guidance for exploring the substantive advantages and limitations of proposals for collective action. For some commentators, this represents an admirable refusal to replace the processes of democracy with the conclusions of theory (Honig 1993, 2; cf. Shapiro 2003, 65–66). Yet by confining itself to clearing space, postmodernism declines, at least explicitly,[7] to provide any substantive resource for what occurs therein.

These difficulties suggest that, despite strong claims to the contrary, proposals for a more critical pluralization have not avoided two of the illusions that compromise more traditional forms of pluralism. The first is an illusion of civility or the belief that pluralistic institutional and cultural norms can establish frameworks for pragmatic experimentation without imposing problematic forms of suffering or injustice. The second is an illusion of closure or the belief that pluralizing institutional or cultural forms represent what Rorty approvingly calls (1989, 94–95) the last word in social organization. To the extent that it falls victim to these two illusions, an ethos of pluralization may itself depend on a kind of fundamentalism, the confident and aggressive *assertion* of the value of a distinctive way of life and the civilizational structures that make it possible.

In this light, critical pluralism may constrain rather than inform a democratic politics that presupposes the permanence rather than the resolution of dilemmas rooted in uncertainties about both the other and the human. This insight is expanded by the interpretation of the Thucydidean and Platonic texts that I offer here. For some critics, of course, these two authors may seem guilty of thoughtless or sinister constructions of the other, due either to a Thucydidean worship of Hellenic culture or to a Platonic dismissal of the incoherent world of diverse opinions. Yet I suggest that both writers thematize the figure of the other in ways that depend on deeper cultural and psychological investigations and thus offer more extended possibilities for political self-criticism. Thucydides' and Plato's different but surprisingly related treatments of otherness imply that no political-cultural arrangement is capable of making the problem of the other disappear. In Thucydides' narrative of the atrocity at Mycalessus in book 7 of the *History*, the opposing images of Greekness and barbarianism reveal a form of brutality that can easily infect both cultures while being other to human aspirations for decency and civility. If that which is other to civilized communities does not simply lie outside of valorized cultural boundaries, members of those communities must be able to recognize and to counter ways in which this otherness arises within their common life. In Plato's *Symposium* we encounter a constructive form of otherness in Socrates' practice of philosophy, one that contributes to the critique of dangerously aggressive conceptions of individual or collective action by pointing to very different human possibilities. Likewise, though both authors also insist on the need to examine the question of the other within a broader consideration of the meaning of the human, neither practices the fundamentalism that Connolly criticizes, for the content of the human is the source of continuing questions, not settled certainties. Consequently, classical treatments of the other introduce a complicated vision of politics that is more directly continuous with the thoughtful interactions of democratic citizens than are those of either the postmodernists or their fundamentalist adversaries.

Thucydides' Mycalessian Narrative: The Other in Ourselves

Thucydides' narrative of the slaughter at Mycalessus initially seems to rely upon and reinforce the otherness of barbarianism to Greekness. The incident involves the destruction of a small Greek city in Boeotia by a force of Thracian mercenaries hired by Athens. "[T]hirteen hundred peltasts from the Dian tribe of knife-wielding Thracians" were recruited for the army sent to reinforce Nicias's increasingly vulnerable position at Syracuse. However, they arrived too late and were sent back toward Thrace, commanded by an Athenian named Dietrephes with instructions to harm the Boeotians (allies of the Spartans) along the coast. The attack on Mycalessus (7.29.3–5) follows:

> At night [Dietrephes] camped undetected near the shrine of Hermes about sixteen stades from Mycalessus, and at dawn he assaulted the city, which is not large, and took it by falling upon people who were off guard, not expecting that anyone would come in so far from the sea and attack them; their wall was

weak, partly fallen down also, partly built low, and their gates open in their belief that they were safe. Rushing into Mycalessus, the Thracians destroyed houses and temples and slaughtered the people, sparing neither the oldest nor the youngest, but all they encountered, killing women and children and even beasts of burden and any other living creature they saw. For the race of Thracians, like the most extreme barbarians, is most bloodthirsty when emboldened. And on this occasion general disorder and every form of destruction prevailed, and attacking a boys' school, the largest in the city and one the boys had just entered, they killed them all; this disaster was inferior to none that had befallen a whole city, being beyond others unbelievable and terrible.

Both in the presentation of the details ("killing children and women and even beasts of burden and any other living creature they saw") and in the identification of the causes ("the race of Thracians is.... most bloodthirsty when emboldened") Thucydides seems to underscore the bestiality of the Thracians, who are explicitly marked as non-Hellenes ("like the most extreme barbarians"). Here characterizations of act and agents are mutually reinforcing. Only the most bloodthirsty barbarians could commit an atrocity that, even within this war, is flagrantly horrific. And the details of the massacre reveal that the core of the barbarian's identity is a lust for blood. In using these tropes, Thucydides appears to be part of the cultural practice that Edith Hall calls the invention of the barbarian, the "polarization of Hellenism and barbarism" that plays an essential role within the self-definition of Hellenic, and particularly Athenian, culture by projecting vile traits onto the barbarous other (1989, 105, 161). Thucydides' concluding assessment that this "disaster was inferior to none that had befallen a whole city, being beyond all others unbelievable and terrible," could even be read as softening condemnations of Athenian cruelties. For all of their brutality, the Athenian atrocities at Scione (5.32) and Melos (5.116) seem less bestial (only the adult males were killed) and more rational (some strategic purposes were at work). Read in this light, the narrative perhaps continues what Price sees as Thucydides' claims about Hellenic exceptionalism (2001, 339–40).[8] I agree that this narrative should be read in light of Thucydides' overall examination of the differences between Hellenes (particularly Athenians) and barbarians. However, unlike Hall I believe that his treatment of this incident goes well beyond a repetition of the familiar trope of barbarian savagery. And, unlike Price, I see Thucydides' comparison of Hellenism and barbarianism not only as the recognition of a unique cultural achievement but also as a diagnosis of dangerous cultural pathology. While Thucydides maintains the distinction between Hellenism and its other, he also problematizes the distinction by discovering this same form of otherness lurking within Hellenism and particularly Athenianism itself. Thucydides may write within a tradition that constructs distinctions between Greeks and barbarians and between the Athenians and other Greeks,[9] but his own treatment problematizes these categories.[10] If Thucydides validates a form of the Hellenic table of opposites, he does so not by projecting its vices onto a distant identity but by employing its construction of the barbarian as part of a much more reflexive cultural criticism.

The first chapters of book 1 of the *History* thus trace the emergence of a Greek culture while also underscoring crucial similarities between Hellenes and barbarians. Thucydides first claims (1.1) that the magnitude of the war is shown by its impact not only on the Greeks, but also on "a large portion of the barbarians—one might say most of humanity," reminding his readers that particular cultural differences can be eclipsed by the more encompassing category of humanness. The importance of this expansion is developed within the two different explanations of the war's importance found in the *History*'s first chapters. In writing (1.1) that the war will be the one "most worthy of being talked about" (*axiologōtaton*) due to the impressive size and character of its motion, Thucydides seems to validate the broadly Periclean criteria associated with energy and daring (cf 1.70, 2.41, 2.64). In 1.23, however, he suggests that this war was the "greatest action," eclipsing that of the Persian wars, because of the great sufferings (*pathēmata*) that it imposed, specifically by Hellenes and barbarians destroying so many cities. Thucydides not only points to the human cost of daring, but also implicitly identifies the ways in which Periclean criteria of value may be problematically culture-bound.

The associated treatment of Hellenism portrays it as a fluid construction, not as a reflection of distinctions that are either mandated by nature or firmly established through cultural achievement. "Hellas" marks a linguistic homogeneity (1.2–3) that enables a shared symbol system. Yet this Hellenic identity was also a constructed form of power that created a capacity for collective action. Together, shared language and consolidated power enabled the Hellenes to separate themselves from those called barbarians (1.3).

This sketch of Hellenism's contingent origins is accompanied by ambiguities about its cultural content. Greekness accommodates the vastly different cultural systems of the luxurious Athenians and the disciplined Lacedaemonians (1.6). While contemporary barbarian societies may resemble those of the early Greeks (1.6), Hellenic cultural progress is not universal, and many of its features are nonexclusive. Both Hellenes and barbarians had an early history of piracy; residues of those earlier practices can still be found in the customs of some contemporary Greeks (1.5). There are cognates both to Athenian wealth and power and to Spartan military prowess among the barbarians (2.97).

As Pericles' funeral speech suggests, of course, a constructed culture's achievements can generate a sense of enormous accomplishment (2.41–42). Yet the trajectory of Thucydides' narrative underscores the fragile character of those achievements. It anticipates the eventual disappearance of both Athenian and Spartan regimes, with only their deteriorating (and misleading) material traces remaining (1.10). The wartime suffering caused by barbarians and Greeks reduces some Hellenic cultures to levels below the primitive societies that Hellenism supposedly surpassed. Athenian lawfulness disintegrates under the extreme stress of the plague (2.53); the besieged Potideians eat each other (2.70).

Thucydides' characterization of the Thracians at Mycalessus thus employs a cultural symbol that the work as a whole problematizes. However, its use within this portion of the narrative is also unique within Thucydides' text, for it is the only occasion where "barbarian" is employed in a strongly evaluative—indeed, condemnatory—way. Elsewhere, the term marks peoples not speaking Greek[11] or provides an alternative characterization of the Persians or the Medes.[12] Here, equating the Thracians to "the most extreme barbarians" expressly trades upon an image of violence that isolates barbarianism from Greekness. In light of his emphasis on the constructed natures of both cultures, Thucydides' reference to barbarians in the context of Mycalessus employs a stereotype so as to emphasize its stereotypicality,[13] both acknowledging and problematizing its significance.

More pointed contrasts set the Mycalessus narrative against the controversial image of Athenian distinctiveness. From one perspective, Pericles' portrait of Athenian completeness (2.39–40) suggests that Athens is culture, perfected, whose completeness is shaped by its distinctive energy (cf. 1.70). In the funeral speech, Pericles proves that Athens is an education to Hellas by pointing to the city's power, itself a sign of the city's virtue and daring (2.41). Alcibiades intensifies this vision of Athenian uniqueness by claiming (as he reinforces the decision to invade Sicily [6.18]) that only ceaseless competition (*aiei agōnizesthai*) prevents stagnation and decrepitude. The account of Mycalessus effectively challenges such images of Athenian culture and activity; it follows an account of Athens's spectacular image among the Greeks by disclosing something that otherwise might remain hidden, and the story itself connects the image of barbarian bloodthirstiness with that of Athenian daring.

The broader events surrounding Mycalessus are Athens's invasion of Sicily, particularly the siege of Syracuse, and the Spartan fortification of Deceleia, which establishes a continuous hostile presence in Attica. After commenting on the stresses of these events, Thucydides summarizes (7.28.3) the impressions that the Athenian responses have made on the Hellenes:

> And it affected [the Athenians] most of all that they had two wars at the same time and had developed such a love of victory that anyone who had heard about it would not have believed it before it happened, that when they themselves were under siege by the Peloponnesians, they did not withdraw from Sicily, but should be there attacking Syracuse in the same way, a city in itself not inferior to Athens, that they did something that was so unbelievable to the Hellenes due to their power and daring, and that at the beginning of the war some thought that they would survive a year, some two, and no one more than three if the Peloponnesians invaded their land, as coming to Sicily in the seventeenth year after the first invasion, already worn-out by the war, and taking on another war no smaller than the one already facing them. . . .

The resulting impression of Athens is a turbulent mixture of fear and admiration. Orwin is, therefore, right to say (1994, 133–34) that this statement is no simple encomium to Athenian energy; yet neither is it simply a diagnosis of Athens's dangerous proclivities. Instead, it strikingly represents the city's image among not only the Greeks but also among any others who saw or heard of its actions.[14] The spectacle of Athens's fighting two wars at once is extended to her unbelievable (*paralogon*) tenacity over the seventeen years since the war's beginning. This assessment reinforces Thucydides' earlier contention that the war was continuous (5.26). Yet it also overstates the intensity of the war's pressure on the Athenians, implying that the Spartan threat in Attica was constant since the war's onset. Perhaps another way in which the Athenians are remarkable is that they generate exaggerated impressions of how remarkable they are.

Read in this way, Thucydides' account of Athens's reputation seems to confirm the boast made in Pericles' last speech (2.64.3–6) that

> Athens has the greatest name among all human beings because of not yielding to misfortune but expending the most lives and labor on war, and has acquired certainly the greatest power known up to this time, of which it will be forever remembered by those who come after, even if we now give way somewhere

(for it is in the nature of all things to be diminished), that we as Hellenes ruled over the most Hellenes, sustained the greatest wars against them, both individually and united, and lived in a city that was in all ways the best provided for and greatest. Though the inactive (*apragmōn*) might condemn this, anyone who wishes also to be active will be emulous, and whoever has not made such acquisitions will be envious. To be hated and pained for the moment has been the situation for all alike, whenever any have claimed to be worthy of ruling over others, but whoever accepts this jealousy for the sake of the greatest things is rightly counseled. For hatred does not persist for long, but the brilliance of the instant and glory thereafter remain in eternal memory.

This claim seems to reaffirm what Ober (1998, 84) sees as the funeral speech's tendency to subordinate all forms of *logos* to magnificent action (*ergon*). Yet Pericles also attempts to establish the control of *logos* over events, for he represents reality in ways that ruthlessly dismiss unsettling presences (family grief in the funeral speech) or strategically co-opt them (civic anger in the final speech). Thus, his speeches also strive to reshape reality, for they constitute as much as they draw upon Athenian power.[15] By following the representation of the amazement Athens commands with Mycalessus, Thucydides' *logos* poses a critical challenge to this nexus of rhetoric and power.

Divulging the events at Mycalessus thus requires a narrative form different from the one preceding. Thucydides is now an investigative reporter, ferreting out as many details as possible about an atrocity in Boeotia. Initially, these details confirm the differences separating Mycalessus from Deceleia and Syracuse. The spectacular invasions have some strategic purposes, and both involve substantial risk due to the estimable character of the adversaries. By contrast, the attack on Mycalessus is pointless. Though the Athenians have told the Thracians to harm enemies along the coast, the assault requires a considerable march inland, the city being "so far from the sea." Mycalessus compromises itself by inattention to its walls and its gates, due not so much to carelessness as to a misplaced trust in human rationality. Remote and insubstantial, it is neither prize nor threat. Moreover, while the Athenians are amazing for engaging "a city [Syracuse] that was by itself not inferior to Athens," the enemy in Mycalessus comprises women, children, and even animals. The complete vulnerability of Mycalessus and the pathetic helplessness of the victims make their destruction a matter for shame, not boasting.[16]

Athens is connected with the slaughter in ways beyond the complicity of a single commander, involving those aspects of Athens' political-cultural identity that have prompted widespread amazement.

The Thracian incursion into Boeotia happens because Athens is fighting two wars at once and more fundamentally because it is driven by relentless love of victory and honor. Pericles says that this exercise of power and daring is the basis for Athens's "schooling" the rest of Hellas. Thus, what both links and separates Athens and Mycalessus most dramatically is education;[17] the only collective action of the Mycalessians expressly mentioned is the education of its boys. Since the form of its education seems more culturally organized than that of the Athenians, Mycalessus's activities are more conventionally Hellenic.[18] This education is not expressible as power; indeed, it seems rather to be closely tied to quietness or moderation, for the city is more concerned for its schools than for its walls. The eventual fate of Mycalessian education is obliteration by a violence caused by the expressions of power that Pericles believes distinguish the Athenian regime as unique.

Within the narrative of Mycalessus, then, Thucydides offsets both the cultural valorization of Greekness over barbarianism and the Periclean encomium to Athenian distinctiveness with a disclosure that what seems to be perfected culture and the "most bloodthirsty barbarians" have together collaborated in the destruction of a decent community. It is not simply that Athens's impressive cultural identity fails to prevent its involvement with barbarian bloodthirstiness; certain aspects of that identity exacerbate Athens's responsibility. The result of this close association of Athens with its seeming other is not the deconstruction of Athens's self-understanding, but a warning, expressed in the strongest narrative and rhetorical terms, about the need to be attentive to the darkness that may lurk within even the seemingly most enlightened culture and therefore to be cautious about culture's potential for eliminating forms of darkness. As part of his boast over Athens's reputation in his last speech, Pericles claims that "hatred does not persist for long" its prompting causes are forgotten and its intensity of feeling is diminished with passing time. It will be replaced by an enduring fascination with the "brilliance of the instant and glory thereafter [remaining] in eternal memory." The story of Mycalessus offers a reminder of what can be hateful about Athens, not to reinforce "bitterness among the enemies of the Athenians" (Gomme, Andrewes, and Dover 1970, 410), but to elicit critical self-examination.

Erotic Otherness in Plato's *Symposium*

At first blush, the recollected speeches on love in the *Symposium* have little to do with the exposure of mass murder at Mycalessus. Yet there are intriguing and unsettling connections. The dramatic structure of the

Symposium frustrates any precise sense of time; a series of narratives continue the memory of a conversation held years before. Still, both the symposium and its narrations seem to take place during the war. The symposium celebrates Agathon's winning the prize at the Dionysia for his first tragedy (in 416 BCE) (Lamb 1967, 78). The finale dramatizes the flamboyant and assertive behavior of Alcibiades, who is apparently at the height of his conspicuous controversy in Athens, and who is still alive at the time of the narrations.[19] The pragmatics of the *Symposium* are thus tied intimately to the activities of Alcibiades, the architect of both the invasion of Sicily (Thucydides 6.16–18) and the fortification of Deceleia (6.91), the events that frame the destruction of Mycalessus.

There are thematic parallels between the works as well. The *Symposium*, too, discloses things that might otherwise be hidden or forgotten. Both works pragmatically pose the question of how memory intersects with privileged symbol systems. Pericles wants the Hellenes to remember Athens's brilliance and to forget the things that might cause her to be hated.[20] In the *Symposium*, Apollodorus and Aristodemus frame their stories by what they believe was most worth remembering. If Thucydides wishes to reconstruct symbol systems for the purpose of education, he needs to preserve the memory of Mycalessus.[21] To the degree that Socrates affects how the symposium will be remembered, he must also have influenced Apollodorus's and Aristodemus's criteria of assigning worth, though this influence is meaningful in ways that are not altogether consistent with Socrates' intentions.[22]

The dialogue itself thematizes the question of otherness at a variety of levels. Most striking are the parallel alterities of Socrates and *erōs*, signaled by Socrates' claim that the sole area in which he is expert is erotics (*Symposium* 177d–e). The strangeness of Socrates' identity is repeatedly underscored, culminating in Alcibiades' praise of him as someone "who is in no respect like other human beings" (221c). More broadly, the uncertain identity of *erōs* is the focus of the symposium's range of speeches. In this context, *erōs* emerges as the human passion for satisfaction or completion that threatens to challenge, if not to overthrow, the stabilizing meanings and practices that constitute culture. In parallel, Socrates emerges as one whom Connolly would call a carrier of critique and destabilization. The city responds by condemning him for not believing in the city's gods and for corrupting the youth (*Apology* 24b–c), drawing upon a broader suspicion against philosophy, which is in many ways construed as the hostile other to politics. For Socrates' principal accuser, Anytus, philosophy undermines the respected meanings and exemplars that hold a society together and is corrupting (*Apology* 29c) or countercivilizational (*Meno* 94e) at its core.

However, the *Symposium* also suggests that Socrates' (and philosophy's) otherness to politics is more than the outcome of cultural contestation. As Socrates offers his own speech on love, recounting a conversation with the mysterious Diotima, he reveals a human potential rooted in the love of the beautiful itself that is the source of the philosopher's continued attempts to move beyond appearances toward reality. This impulse carries critique and destabilization by discovering possibilities lying beyond any limited cultural experience. Like the Mycalessus episode, the *Symposium* reveals an activity that both belongs to our humanness and is also problematically other to so much of it. While the otherness displayed at Mycalessus sinks brutally below stabilizing cultural practices, the otherness revealed in the *Symposium* rises serenely above them.

In different ways, all of the speeches that precede Socrates' treatment of love engage the question of how culture can accommodate an *erōs* that is to some degree its other. The first three speeches are individually rich and complex. Yet there are formal parallels that relatively brief assessments can highlight. Each of the speeches envisages a community built on one view of *erōs*. While these conceptions of love seem to set standards for evaluating culture, each privileges a particular cultural template that is used to regulate eroticism. All three are fundamentalist in Connolly's sense, for they treat partial and contestable views as universalist and conclusive; each thus creates its own suspect other. Yet each proposal dissolves due to the vulnerabilities of fundamentalism, creating conditions that are simultaneously oppressive and unstable, precisely those characteristics to which critical pluralism responds. These are followed by two more comprehensive representations of *erōs*, offered by the poets Aristophanes and Agathon, respectively. Aristophanes' speech offers a view of *erōs* that is less controlling and more pluralized, yet ultimately tenuous and disordered. In response, Agathon sketches an erotic community that replaces exclusionary and fragile forms of culture with one that is more cosmopolitan and stable. Yet this cosmopolitanism is compromised by its drive toward a regulative culture, and its stability is challenged by erotic expressions that it is unable to control. In a sense, Aristophanes and Agathon would appear to sketch two opposing cultural strategies for coping with erotic otherness. Yet together they end by displaying the illusions besetting projects of cosmopolitan pluralization. Inevitably, such projects fall victim either to disintegration or to the reassertion of some form of controlling power. The succeeding speeches of Socrates and Alcibiades do not provide a view of a culture that can somehow avoid these hazards. Instead, they offer a more fruitful glimpse of the dangers of and resources within communities that are always problematically pluralized.

Phaedrus first praises *erōs* as the source of the great and noble deeds (*megala kai kala erga*), performed most perfectly in war, that are most deserving of renown. Love is thus the basis of both individual greatness and civic virtue. Cities and armies composed exclusively of lovers would be victorious over the whole of humankind owing to the lovers' passions to distinguish themselves in each other's sight (178c–d). Yet this encomium also raises the possibility of tensions between erotic honor and cultural stability. The proposal for solidifying cities and armies on the basis of erotic attachments obscures the fact that each pair of lovers is a dyad whose joint interests may not always cohere with those of the wider community. Phaedrus's example of the noblest beloved is Achilles, the man whose love and anger converge to disrupt the Hellenes (180b).[23] Moreover, the praise of love as the condition for honor fails to consider the possibility of an *erōs* for honor itself that is not dependent on any particular attachment and that would thus stand as an outsider to any particular culture.

While Phaedrus praises the heroic young beloved, Pausanias esteems the urbane, mature lover. He distinguishes the elder, nobler, and heavenly (*ouranian*) brand of love from the younger, baser, and popular (*pandēmon*) sort (180d–e). Each has clear parallels within contemporary erotic practice. The baser performs its work opportunistically (*tychē*), loving boys or women indiscriminately and focusing on the body in disregard of intelligence or the soul. The nobler is expressed through an elder man's passion for a thoughtful boy on the brink of maturity (181b). He instructs his beloved in virtue in return for pleasurable gratification. In support of noble love, Pausanias praises those cultures or laws that permit noble and forbid base eroticisms (182b–c). In so doing, he seems to apply a divinely ordered standard to forms of love and their appropriate cultures. Yet he strives to establish rather than simply to reveal meanings, for these erotic/cultural proposals can be assailed for using instruction in the supposed virtues (which simply seem to be the valued practices of the gentleman class) as instrumental to erotic gratification. A more skeptical interpretation of Pausanias's speech sees him presenting the needs and priorities of a certain subculture as if they were signs of the divine and employing an invented version of heavenly love as a weapon within cultural conflicts over *erōs*.[24]

The physician Eryximachus follows by substituting science for culture and nature for divinity. His speech maps the distinction between heavenly and popular love onto all of nature and redefines the two forms as healthy or diseased relationships among natural things (186b). Experts, such as physicians, are able to foster healthy love and cure diseased attractions (186d). They can, therefore, manage the effects of popular love to allow the enjoyment of pleasure without harm (186e). From this perspective, conflicts between culture and *erōs* over the validation of sexual practices could be eliminated through the intervention of the skilled expert. Whereas Pausanias had claimed that the manner in which various things are done determines their nobility or baseness (181a), Eryximachus implies that the enjoyment of pleasure is only base if it is followed by the curable otherness of disease. If particular cultures designate some erotic pleasures as "sick" because of the manner of their enjoyment, they foolishly or cruelly align themselves against nature. Correcting misguided cultural judgments would seem to be one of the expert's most important contributions. Yet this correction is not so much an appreciation of love's plurality as a demand that all forms of love be measured according to the expert's single scale. Nonetheless, Eryximachus's speech, which is less a praise of love than an encomium to *technē*, inevitably reveals the limitation of science's power over its erotic objects. As applied to natural attractions, Eryximachus's science traces the course of things across the seasons, where fertility gives way to drought (188a–b). Though technical knowledge may explain and approximately predict natural changes, it does not seem able to control them. In arranging pleasure without disease, art is subordinate to pleasure. Expertise eventually gives way to divination, the art in which human beings assume the roles of subordinates and supplicants, not of supervisors and agents (188c–d).

Each of the first three speeches constructs a view of love based on the priority of an accessible cultural template—noble bravery, gentlemanly eroticism, or technical knowledge—that should guide the reconstruction of a healthy society; yet each fails because the power of love escapes cultural or scientific control. Aristophanes follows by offering an account of the precultural origin and function of love that accommodates a more pluralistic series of erotic practices. Its pluralistic content and mythic form make his speech seem less fundamentalist. Yet his vision of eroticism sees culture as fragile and contentious, held together not by fundamentalist dogma but by coercion born of necessity.

Aristophanes wishes to correct a nearly universal ignorance of love's power. This power is in truth philanthropic, for love allows each human being to search for, to discover, and to enjoy the presence of his or her own proper beloved. However, this benefit originated in arrogance and violence, uncovered in Aristophanes' narrative of the nature or development (*physis*) of human beings and their proper or "very own" affections (*ta pathēmata autēs*). This is a story of dramatic anthropological change, for "our ancient nature was not the same as now, but other" (189e). Humans were originally a race of circle beings, endowed with two faces, four limbs, two sets of genitals, and so on. Individuals could be of three sexes—some male, others female, and others androgynous (190a–b). They were endowed with an awesome *(deinos)* degree of strength and consequently conceived "big ideas" *(phronēmata megala)* about displacing the gods (190b–c). To this point, Aristophanes says nothing about forms of *erōs* among the circle beings, but we might infer that their strongest drive was for self-assertion or power. The rebellion ended when Zeus split each of the circle beings in half. Humbled and incomplete, each half longed desperately for its other. Those who failed pressed on until they died; those satisfied had no ambition for anything else (191a–b). Faced with the disappearance of the race, Zeus reengineered the halves to make sexual intercourse possible, thus implanting *erōs* in human beings (191d). This origin thus explains inclinations toward different types of erotic gratification, for all pursue the completion cognate to their circle ancestors (191d–e). Instead of threatening humanity, then, erotic satisfactions have substantial benefits. Heterosexual intercourse continues the species. Homoerotic *erōs* gratifies its partners so that they can turn themselves toward deeds *(erga)* and the care of the other things of life, particularly political distinction (192a). Far from being an enemy of culture, then, *erōs* enables its construction. Unlike the cultural proposals implied by the first three speeches, Aristophanes' seems to accept the legitimacy of a plurality of erotic expressions traceable to different origins among the circle beings. Yet this pluralized erotic community can only be stabilized by continuous coercion. The gifted homoerotic males charged with directing the community's affairs must be "compelled by the laws" to have children for the city's sake (192b). More generally, all human beings must be threatened into piety lest Zeus punish them again (193c). Plurality's giving way to coercion may be a part of what Rosen (1987, 134) calls the comic poet's tragic view of love. Yet the seeds of coercion are embedded in the very view of *erōs* that Aristophanes offers. Each descendent of the severed circle beings searches for its own completion out of necessity. There seems no place (as there is in Socrates' second speech on love in the *Phaedrus* [252c ff.]) for discursive explorations into the goods of erotic partnerships and the development of the self into a worthy partner.[25] The elimination of choice and reflective development is paralleled by the absence of reciprocal respect and nurture. In Aristophanes' tale, relations among erotic partners are either instrumental (the gratification that allows the best males to go on to politics) or transformative (those fortunate enough to find their other halves and become as one).[26] A view of natural *erōs* that excludes choice, reflection, and mutuality implies that culture is held together not by discursive reflectiveness and self-criticism but by threats and fear.

For all of their power, however, none of these attempts at coercion prevent the erotic search for individual completion that can destabilize the erotic community. Aristophanes maintains that those blessed enough to find those loved as their other halves will wish for nothing more than to continue together throughout life, "though they could not say (*oud . . . eipein*)what they would wish to come from their being together" (192c). If such lovers could have their deepest wish granted, it would be that they be rejoined, sharing a common life and death. *Erōs* thus wishes for a condition that would render both *erōs* and culture unnecessary, and in seeking completeness it recognizes the pain of its own longing, which it strives to overcome permanently. A full appreciation of the most complete form of *erōs* thus inevitably casts a shadow over the experiences and activities of most ordinary loves. The education of children and the ordering of cities seem attractive only to those heterosexual or homoerotic couples who are mismatched with respect to their own proper halves. Successful cultural functions therefore require the frustration of the most perfect *erōs*. Aristophanes does not indicate what, if any, *erga* fully completed lovers would practice, but we should remember that the circle beings sought to storm heaven and replace the gods. Human piety is enforced by an appreciation of the gods' power, but envy of that power can render such piety useless as it dares further mutilation.

One way of reading Agathon's subsequent praise of love is as an attempt to eliminate these tensions through the creation of a form of cultural life permeated with an *erōs* that supplants violence and longing (195c, 196c, 197b). In a sense, Agathon's proposal attempts to combine the benefits of pluralization and stability within a certain kind of erotic paradise. His encomium concludes (197d–e) with a simultaneous praise of love and of the peace love brings:

> [Love] casts otherness out and draws closeness in; he brings us together in all friendly gatherings as [our own] at this time; at feasts and dances and oblations, he becomes leader; gentleness creating, violence expelling; giving kindness, withholding enmity; gracious, benign; a wonder to the wise, a delight to the gods; coveted by those deprived, treasured by those possessing; father of luxury, tenderness, elegance, delights, yearning and longing; caring for the good, dismissive of the bad; in labor and in fear, in drink and in speech, our best helmsman, boatswain, champion and savior; ornament of the world of gods and human beings; leader most beautiful and best, whom all should nobly follow, sharing abundantly in the song that enchants the thought of all gods and humans.

Like Pericles' vision of Athens in the funeral speech, Agathon's vision of erotic cosmopolitanism harmonizes qualities or practices that seem mutually exclusive. However, whereas Pericles' cosmopolitanism requires conformity with the most-demanding Athenian priorities (Periclean philosophy must be practiced "without softness"—*aneu malakias*—and Periclean education is hostile to inactivity and privateness [2.40]), Agathon relies precisely on the capacity of love's softness (*malakia*) and pliability (*hygrotēs*) to render potential opponents harmonious and receptive. Love draws together the contentious gods who, prior to love's birth, committed multiple outrages against one another (195c). Love also provides the basis for a unity among the virtues, for love, properly understood, perfectly exemplifies not simply heroic nobility, as Phaedrus had claimed, but justice, courage, moderation, and wisdom (196b–d). Finally, love enables the association of the useful arts within a beneficial community, for Eryximachus apparently was wrong when he gave the arts power over love. Rather, all individual arts or makings have their origins in an *erōs* that is now seen as essentially poetic. Consequently, Agathon's poetry challenges Pericles' marginalization and overcomes Aristophanes' deference. Whereas Pericles had said that Athens needed no Homer to sing her praises, Agathon maintains that love needs a poet such as Homer to show (*epideixai*) love's "divine delicacy" (195c–d). Love's effectiveness in shaping a humane society thus depends upon the mediation of poets, first Homer and now Agathon. Yet the poets are not simply those who join with Aristophanes in appreciating love's power; they embody love's presence among humans, and the best poet comes closest to representing the presence of love itself (196e–97a).

However, no less than Pericles' harder form of cosmopolitanism, Agathon's proposal for a community softened and enriched by love only succeeds by excluding everything foreign. Love's eternal (*aei*) youth requires a continued flight from old age, "hating (*misein*) it by nature and refusing to approach it" (195b). Love exercises its humane dominion only if its other is despised and excluded. Thus, love's (and the poets') education of humanity demonizes not simply the old but eventually the ugly and the hard. In this respect, Agathon's proposals for cultural education seem more exclusionary than Pericles', for the funeral speech presented the spectacular achievements of the modern Athenians as being continuous with, though undeniably superior to, the modest progress of the ancients (2.36).[27] Agathon's worship of love's youth is more consistent with Alcibiades' attitude in the speech pressing for the Sicilian invasion. In ridiculing Nicias's fear of youthful folly, Alcibiades insists (6.18) that the city can only retain its identity through continuous energy and that this common project requires the old to emulate the practices of the young. Likewise, Agathon's praise of love's virtues demands a radical reconception of the content of the various *aretai*. Love's *sōphrosynē* is exhibited as being the strongest of all pleasures, so that *sōphrosynē* engages the desires not through education, but through control (*kratein*) (196c). Love's courage is imaged by Aphrodite's ability to ensnare the war god Ares through erotic temptation (196d). Agathon's conception of erotic virtue thus rejects a *sōphrosynē* that improves the desires or a courage that fights against the attractions of the pleasures as imposters, for both would be suspicious of love's power and would, as such, be subversive of love's hegemony. As the contours of Agathon's soft and inclusive community become more specific, its rigidity and exclusions become clearer. Agathonian *erōs* is compatible with culture only because it assumes the most aggressive and encompassing of cultural functions.

Consequently, Agathon's erotic culture is beset by a series of deep contradictions. Love's identity can only be secured if love is guided by a certain kind of hate; the peaceful god declares total war on age, ugliness, and hardness. At one level, these difficulties simply clarify that no cultural identity can be established without excluding, by force if necessary, those conditions or practices that threaten its integrity. Yet these exclusions also call Agathon's characterization of love's nature into serious question, for it is difficult to see how the resolute enemy of age and hardness can be defined as the essence of amity and peace. To the extent that Agathon's experience is a useful guide to those attempting to argue for a cosmopolitan community based on an ethos of pluralization, it may serve as a reminder that what Connolly calls the borders of pluralization may need to be very tightly and rigidly patrolled. Not surprisingly, this fundamentalism encounters Socrates as a carrier of critique.

Philosophy as Other

Socrates responds to Agathon's speech by comparing its finale to an oration of Gorgias. Though Agathon may be flattered, the implications are deeply critical. Like Gorgias's orations, Agathon's encomium is unable to respond to interrogation (cf. *Gorgias* 457e–58a), for Socrates quickly unsettles his confident praise of love by asking a series of perplexing questions. Agathon must admit that if love always searches for the beautiful (to kalon) and the good (to agathon), it cannot simply possess either (*Symposium* 201c). Consequently, love itself may have a much different identity than the one Agathon has confidently proclaimed. Within Agathon's own practice, the inability to deal with Socrates' questions reflects the absence of self-knowledge. Within the vision of a community permeated by *erōs*, Socrates' questioning reveals the deficiencies of a culture devoid of resources for self-criticism. The illusional cosmopolitanism of Agathon's erotic community renders it vulnerable to disclosures of incompleteness. Socrates' immediate response appears, in a way, pluralizing, both because its form relies on interactions that respect only the adequacy of the argument (198c–d) and because its implied conclusion is that Agathon's uniform community needs to take its problematizing other more seriously. Assuming the symposium's dramatic date as 416, Socrates is well into middle age. He can also reasonably be described as hard (*Symposium* 219e–20a), and he is without question ugly (*Theaetetus* 143e–44a).

Socrates' rejoinder involves more than destabilization, however. He offers his own substantive praise of love, rooted in a vision of the deepest longings of human beings. He recalls his earlier conversation with Diotima,[28] whose identity as a woman from Peloponnesian Mantineia makes her strikingly other to the masculine Athenian culture that surrounds the symposium. Her vision of love unsettles competing cultural images, for she portrays love as an affective condition analogous to philosophy, the cognitive state between wisdom and ignorance (*Symposium* 202a, 204b). Since love is neither beautiful nor ugly, soft nor hard, Agathon's complete community is at variance with love's essential incompleteness. Prompted by Socrates, Diotima says that love's usefulness to human beings is found in its desire to make good things its own forever (206a). This pursuit of the good must be continuous (as in "tireless"), for no human good is guaranteed once and for all. In its concern for making the human good accessible, love's urge overlaps one of culture's central functions. Yet this love's insistence that one's own be truly good stands against the cultural proclivity to esteem simply what is embedded in its own horizon (cf. 205b). Love's need to be continuously active in exploring and pursuing the good suggests that attempts to establish permanent cultural agreements about the good only work by disregarding the existential conditions that make love necessary and possible. Agathon's completed erotic community would be perfectly unerotic.

Yet Diotima's *erōs* seems as disregarding of human plurality as Agathon's. She describes the lover's ascent from an active involvement with beautiful things (ranging from the begetting of children to the creation of laws or cultures) to a more contemplative engagement with the beautiful itself. What drives this ascent is a desire for immortality that cannot be fully satisfied apart from communion with the beauty that transcends all particulars (206e–7a). In the course of the ascent, the philosophic lover comes to dismiss differences among bodies, souls, or cultures, seeing only the beauty within each and treating that beauty not as something to be appreciated and questioned in itself but as a stage in the progression toward "an amazing sight, beautiful by its very nature" (210e).

However, if Diotima's project seems transcendent in its ambitions, Socrates' representation of her vision brings it closer to cultural contingencies. First, there is a pointed dissimilarity between Diotima's philosophic lover and the philosophic practices of Socrates. For all of his social oddities, Socrates is heavily invested in concrete cultural situations because of his more particular eroticisms, including his love of discourse.[29] Socrates does not treat beautiful bodies and souls as undifferentiated stages within the progression toward the beautiful itself; in the final portion of the *Symposium* he clearly appreciates the substantial differences between the beautiful Alcibiades and the beautiful Agathon. Likewise, Socrates' partial ascent up the ladder of love intensifies rather than diminishes conflict with cultural conceptions of the good. The progress of Diotima's philosophic lover eventually causes him to disregard cultural differences not only between Athens and Sparta, but also between Greeks and barbarians (209d–e). Because the philosophic lover is no prisoner of culture, he apparently sees no reason to challenge the influences of cultural stereotypes on those not blessed or gifted enough to be his equal. By contrast, Socrates is sufficiently driven by his own eroticisms to interrogate the content and influence of the cultural forces that impact his discourse partners. He begins by questioning Agathon about his practical relationship to his adoring Athenian audience (194b–d). Finally, though Diotima's explicit treatment of culture is serenely synoptic, Socrates' representation of her speech is culturally destabilizing. She transforms personally driven desires for genealogical or reputational immortality into the longing for an experience in which personal identity is all but lost. In the middle of an intercultural conflict that is extraordinarily intense, she implies that taking cultural differences too seriously is a mark of arrested development.

Yet we should not for this reason presume that Diotima's representation of *erōs* simply contrasts with the culturally embedded nature of Socrates' own eroticisms, for Socrates manifests his own disconnection from culture in the mysterious trances that fascinate Agathon and Alcibiades (174d–75a, 220c–d). While Socrates' philosophizing may not be as permanently transcendent as Diotima's, it includes a distancing from as well as an embeddedness in the pragmatics of democratic culture. Socrates' philosophy is daimonic as well as dialogic and, thus, is always somehow other to political life even as it is active within it.[30] The importance of this philosophic distancing from politics emerges with the entrance of a very different other into the *Symposium*'s conversations.

Alcibiades arrives to praise Agathon but ends by offering his own intoxicated and sarcastic encomium to Socrates. In so doing, he reveals the varying ways in which both he and Socrates are cultural outsiders and displays why an ethos of pluralization cannot fully respond to the realities of human otherness. While Alcibiades says he resents erotic rejection, his real complaints go deeper. He sought Socrates' assistance in an attempt to make himself into "the best" (218d). This does not mean practicing the conventional virtues of the gentleman (à la Pausanias), for Alcibiades is attracted precisely because Socrates is "completely unlike other human beings" (221c). His uniqueness is expressed in his way of speaking—not in his exterior speeches, which seem trivial, but in his deeper *logoi* (216d, 216e), which can exert enormous power. Socrates is the only person able to make Alcibiades ashamed for neglecting himself while "doing the things of the Athenians" (216a). Because he sees no difficulty in extending Socrates' interior speeches to a public context, Alcibiades believes that they would have the ability to astound and entrance others even if articulated by a poor speaker (215d). What makes Socrates different, then, is not so much his speech as his influence. Alcibiades illustrates Socrates' distinctiveness by comparing him with ancient and modern exemplars of the powerful. Though Pericles, the most famous Athenian, and Brasidas, the most notable Spartan, each have cognates among the Homeric heroes, Socrates has no parallel (221c–d). While this assessment of the basis of Socrates' uniqueness may be mistaken, it clarifies Alcibiades' proposal to make himself into the best man possible. Socrates' assistance is indispensable if Alcibiades is to exceed Pericles and Brasidas in power and reputation. If Socrates' diagnosis in the first *Alcibiades* dialogue is accurate, Alcibiades is not content to become simply the most distinguished Hellene, for he sees only Cyrus and Xerxes as worthy competitors for the distinctiveness he seeks: that of extending "his name and his power over, so to speak, all of humankind" (*Alcibiades* 105a–c).

Within the flow of speeches in the *Symposium*, Alcibiades' presence both emerges from and challenges Agathon's comprehensive community. The priorities of Agathon and Alcibiades converge in their obsession with youth, though they differ dramatically in their conceptions of its content and their strategies for its pursuit. For Agathon, the erotic community and its members can remain forever young through continuous participation in poetry. Alcibiades claims that the youthfulness of a community can be preserved tangibly as its name or reputation is enhanced by permanent political competitions (Thucydides 6.18). For Agathon to remain forever young, he and his poetry need to be as memorable as the names and the accomplishments of Pericles and Brasidas. Whereas

Agathon had sought to poeticize the virtues and the arts, Alciabiades would insist on the need to energize Agathon's poetry, just as he envisaged the politicization of Socrates' interior speeches. For Agathon, youth means continued involvement with the softest poetry. Alcibiades affirms competition among aggressively powerful males. His aged other is Nicias, whose speeches of inactivity turn the Athenians away from glorious achievement (6.18). Age is not maturation, but weakness and decay. And youth is not reckless inexperience (as it is for Nicias), but energy. Agathon's commitment to youthfulness can only be preserved if he replaces softness with brilliant energy.[31] Otherwise, he will be as irrelevant to Alcibiades as Homer was to Pericles.

In Thucydides' narrative, Alcibiades confronts substantial political opposition, particularly the suspicion that he aims at creating a tyranny, democratic Athens's own persistent other (6.15). While Pericles affirmed distinction within a rhetoric of democratic equality (2.37), Alcibiades defiantly proclaims his own superior abilities (6.16). If the democracy and Alcibiades are to be reconciled, it must be through the city's committing itself to projects of brilliant daring. The Sicilian expedition shows Alcibiades' partial success in this regard, but the panic over the statues and the mysteries (6.27-28), resulting in Alcibiades' subsequent flight and condemnation (6.61), reveals both personal rivalry and civic mistrust. As a fugitive in Sparta, Alcibiades attempts to mitigate Spartan suspicions (6.89) and to encourage Spartan proactivity in both Sicily and Attica. In response, the Spartans send symbolic help to Syracuse and fortify Deceleia (6.93).[32] Alcibiades' distinctive energy is expressed in his orchestrating the framing events of Mycalessus. If Thucydides works backward to reveal the human and cultural roots of that atrocity, the *Symposium* anticipates the devastating consequences of Alcibiades' striving to be the best. Were Socrates able to redirect this striving, he would contribute both to the well-being of Alcibiades and to the civility of political life.

Any proposal to redirect Alcibiades' energies must respond to his aspirations for uniqueness. All cultural resources seem either dangerous (the competition with the Persian Great Kings) or inadequate (the contempt for Nicias and the traditional moderation he represents). Socrates thus draws upon his own otherness as an alternative. The representation of Diotima offers a distinction that extends beyond, rather than clashes with, the political culture of any community. This vision would invite Alcibiades to revise his earlier view of Socrates' interior speeches by hearing them not as strategies for influence, but as activities that both elevate and edify. Socrates' uniqueness lies not in his potential to outshine Pericles and Brasidas according to a conventional scale of distinctiveness, but in his receptivity to an experience of a radically distinctive type.[33]

Yet Socrates eventually reconnects this form of otherness with cultural practice. He has not used Alcibiades as a means toward the beautiful itself, but has proposed that they deliberate on the courses of action that would be best for them both (219a–b). Philosophy is not transcendence but conversation. This proposal fails because Alcibiades is unwilling to give up his pursuit of renown to experience something more sublime, and Socrates' invitation seems insulting (222a–b). Yet this attempt provides an image of how a set of possibilities that are other to a political culture can be employed within a critical discourse that examines what it would really mean to improve oneself or one's society. If Mycalessus is otherness as severe pathology, Socratic philosophy is otherness as deepest therapy.

Classical Political Philosophy and Postmodernism

The view of the relation of politics to the other that emerges from these interpretations is significantly different and, I believe, more expansive and substantial than what is offered by even the deepest and most nuanced statements of postmodernism. In different ways, these latter statements envisage a form of politics in which the problem of the other can in principle be solved, where the other either sheds its reputation for evil and achieves the character of difference or stands necessarily and permanently excluded as the dark. These solutions rely on the continued presence of a political-cultural field whose boundaries are internally fluid yet externally fixed. Consequently, conceptions of permanent characteristics that define the human are excluded from postmodern political theory. On the one hand, they limit the dynamic fluidity of democratic culture; on the other, they stand as problematic reminders of the impermanent boundaries between democracy and the dark. By contrast, the classical perspective that emerges here provides a richer vision of politics, particularly democratic politics as the realm in which the problem of the other is continually engaged and therefore as the context in which the problems of the human are especially challenging and compelling. One of the most important functions of this classical focus on the human lies in its capacities to challenge rather than to validate the political and moral categories of one's own cultural home. How the treatment of the other within these texts both intersects with and challenges the central contentions of postmodernism can be sketched by reading the classical position against the statements of Jacques Derrida and Judith Butler.

Derrida's treatment of the political other in *The Politics of Friendship* works toward a new and emerging form of democracy that has the status only of the *perhaps*, a transformative possibility that is identified through deconstructing the androcentric and aggressive forms of social identity that have to date dominated the tradition of Western political philosophy (Derrida 1997, 28, 199, 232, 236, 263, 278, 306). For Derrida, the democracy that is *perhaps* to come preserves alterity in a realm of freedom and equality where otherness does not reinforce the closed borders of the insider, but enriches an openness held together by the absence of exclusion (37, 42, 163, 245, 250, 306). Yet this vision of a transformed democracy is also one that inevitably courts paradox. The precise characteristics that mark this democracy as transformed, the openness to those who might be seen as enemies reconceived as potential friends, would also seem to depoliticize it. Derrida asks whether a radically transformed democracy would be a politics at all (43, 277, 294, 305).

He responds by finding a politics of paradox to be particularly at home in a democracy, for democracy itself depends on two requirements that work fundamentally against each other: that its members be seen as heterogeneous individuals while at the same instant as identical by virtue of equal citizenship (22). In this respect, one of the cohering conditions of democracy is, paradoxically, a deep form of incoherence, understood as a practical project that involves continued interactions and dynamic engagements aiming to keep together political characteristics that threaten to fly apart. Consequently, democracy and the textual and cultural interrogations that constitute the project of deconstruction coalesce. Unlike authoritarian or hierarchical forms of politics, democracy can withstand the challenges of deconstruction, because its unifying framework is enrichingly unstable. In democracies "one keeps this indefinite right to question, to criticism, to deconstruction..." (105; cf. 1997, 38–39, 42–43, 103–4, 199, 214, 216).

Yet for all of this prospective democracy's transformative possibilities, it does not seem to avoid at least one paradoxical condition that does threaten to call its basic character into question. The democracy that is perhaps to come must still stand in a relation of hostility to a certain form of otherness as criminality—namely, "the crime of stopping to examine politics... reducing it to something else and preventing it from being what it should be" (ix; cf. 1997, 237, 273, 275). In this respect, the criminality that is other to politics could be seen as a refusal to interrogate critically the conception of politics that has been dogmatically accepted throughout the Western tradition (28, 218, 263). Dogma is thus other to democracy just as fundamentalism is other to critical pluralism. Like Agathon's community held together by *erōs*, Derrida's democracy requires a certain kind of enmity toward some other, absent which that projected democracy would be overwhelmed (38, 179, 219).

Derrida's reverence for an alterity that informs the relationship among the free and equal may thus obscure the extent to which certain forms of otherness must be regarded as legitimately threatening and demonic. In both Agathon's and Derrida's formulations, the absence of a hostile response toward demonic otherness is affirmed but illusory and is, for that reason, resistant to critical scrutiny. Agathon's vision of love must include forms of hatred. If the democracy that is perhaps to come is envisaged as being beyond certain determinations of law but not beyond law in general (cf. 237), aiming at a justice beyond justice (278) and providing an environment within which the problem of the other can be resolved, perhaps that same democracy is also incapable of seeing its own aggression and *perhaps* its own injustice. Consequently, it retains the problematic character of any politics while distancing itself from a remedy that might originate politically (216).

Derrida sees the hostile rejections of alterity that have constituted so much of the Western tradition as rooted in harsh androcentric visions of the other that are condensed in Carl Schmitt's treatment of the concept of the political. Schmitt's politics presupposes the continuing presence of other as enemy as a fundamental condition for politicality itself (cf. Derrida 1997, 77, 80–85, 88–89, 124); the essential activity of such a politics is captured in the fight to the death between hostile political communities (88–89, 123–24). One of Derrida's central projects in *The Politics of Friendship* is therefore to deconstruct what he construes as Schmitt's unavoidably unstable efforts to articulate the bases of political stability (32–33, 100, 114, 116, 152, 244–49). Yet Derrida is mistaken to read all political hostilities toward the other as variations on Schmitt's androcentrism. Thucydides, to be sure, sees politics as being constructed on the bases of oppositional dynamics. A significant theme throughout the *History*, pointedly illustrated in the Mycalessus narrative, is the diagnosis of how that dynamic turns on politics itself. Consequently, a full appreciation of the politics of opposition also opens on to the critical need for a vigilance against and a rejection of those forms of otherness that are particular hazards within one's own political culture—in the Thucydidean case, the daring and energy that end in slaughter. In this respect, the oppositional character of politics is reflected not in a fight to the death among communities, but in an intellectual and moral aggressiveness directed against what is worst in oneself. Thucydides does not construct an other that is the condition for one's own, but discovers that one's own has fostered a proximate, dangerous other.

Butler's understanding of the place of the other in politics is far less connected to a radical transformation that is perhaps to come. Her focus is not on texts but on speeches and on the political contexts that are both supportive of and constructed by speech-acts. Butler's concerns are also decidedly critical, in both immediate and extended senses. Her entry into conflicts that arise out of current efforts to regulate political space opens on to deeper tracings of the power dynamics though which institutions and subjectivities intersect. What emerges is an account of the movements that make political criticism possible. Institutions exercise political control by articulating or authorizing forms of speech that create marginalized or demonized categories of practice. Yet while such categories are intended to constrain or exclude, they also empower and extend subjectivities by creating discursive fields in which contestations and counteraffirmations become possible (cf. Butler 1997a, 157–58; 1997b, 12–13). Even political censorship can elicit new sites that challenge the boundaries of social memberships and political spaces (1997a, 161).

Butler's insights are particularly helpful for interpreting the classical texts that have been the focus of this chapter. The empowering reversal of denigrating speech is reflected in Thucydides' Mycalessian narrative, where the trope "barbarian" is redeployed within a critique of Athenian daring. And we can detect the varying dynamics of subject formation in the very different ways that Alcibiades and Socrates resist and transform hegemonic political-cultural discourses. Yet the ways in which Thucydides and Plato redirect political templates and challenge political-cultural power go beyond reflections on how forms of subjectivity are constructed and empowered; Thucydides and Plato go on to offer considerations of how empowerment is to be both practiced and suspected within a broader horizon of political and human possibilities.

Thucydides' use of the trope "barbarian" does not speak more affirmatively in the name of the demonized other. Indeed, it reinforces the sense that what is called the "barbarian" is to be legitimately rejected in a civilized culture. Yet this cultural demonization serves to inform Thucydides' readers that the depths of barbarism are frighteningly close to the practices that a seemingly civilized culture valorizes as noble. In this respect, Thucydides' redeployment of a term of demonization falls far short of the contributions that Butler sees emerging from the political movements of what she calls excitable speech. Yet in another sense, Thucydides goes much further than Butler by problematizing the Athenian or Hellenic use of the trope "barbarian" to engage deeper questions about the character and the direction of the Athenian praise of political energy. That the Athenians give neither themselves nor others any peace is now seen in its darkest human manifestation. In responding to demonization not with affirmative resistance but with a deeper form of problematization, Thucydides goes beyond the binary possibilities of domination and resistance to prompt a fuller appreciation of political dynamics and a deeper form of political critique.

In parallel fashion, the intersecting and conflicting Alcibiadean and Socratic responses to the dominant forms of Athenian political discourse both reinforce and go beyond Butler's insights. In a sense, Alcibiades' subjectivity can be seen as emerging out of a series of resistances, first against the egalitarian ethos of Athens's democratic political culture, then against Pericles' valorization of daring in the service of the city, and finally against Socrates' shaming interrogations of Alcibiades' own way of life. Against the ethos of democracy, Alcibiades affirms his own uniqueness (Thucydides 6.16.1); against Pericles' *erōs* for the city, he conflates the city's well-being with his own victories in endless competitions (6.16.1–3); against Socrates' powerful and shaming speeches, he attempts to make the capacity to speak Socratically his own and to transfer Socratic uniqueness from the internal speeches of philosophy to the external speech-acts of politics (*Symposium* 221e–22a). All of these resistances condense within Alcibiades' drive to affirm his name and power over the known world. Yet none of these affirmations born of resistance take seriously the need for a deeper reexamination of the quality, rather than the distinctiveness or power, of one's own identity, the project to which Socrates invites Alcibiades without success.

In both content and form, Socrates' own resistance to dominant cultural and subcultural valorizations challenges the completeness of Butler's framework. In insisting on the importance of examining one's life, Socrates offers a view of the psychic life of reflexive subjectivity that goes beyond the psychic life of power. What is central to identity is not power understood as the capacity for self-assertion, but activity, understood as the practices that construct a human life as a certain kind of existence. In inviting Alcibiades to engage in a discursive project that requires mutuality, Socrates points to a form of intersection different from the collision of institutional and psychological forces. To a considerable degree, of course, the Socratic response to the Athenian valorization of nobility and power is clearly political in that it inevitably engages Socrates in power contests with dominant political cultural voices. Yet this form of political engagement also goes further than that traced by Butler in that it challenges the valorization of power itself. In politicizing the conflict between the city and what he calls philosophy, Socrates draws upon the realities of politics in general and democratic politics in particular for the purpose of gesturing beyond them. From this perspective, the political value of otherness lies not simply in its ability to challenge power relations, but in its capacity to elicit the serious reflection that politics requires.

What inferences emerge from these readings of two classical texts about conditions for self-criticism in a pluralized democratic society? First, they suggest that postmodernism's attempt to separate democratic politics from what is truly other is both impossible and undesirable. Thucydides' treatment of Mycalessus implies that any confidence that one's culture permanently excludes barbarism must be suspect. That our cultural practices may intersect with our worst potentials means that even the most civilized society requires a critical rationality that interrogates the grounds, contents, and consequences of proposed collective action. Socrates' practices point to the positive contributions that forms of cultural otherness can make to democratic critical rationality. He cannot exert the constructive influence he envisages without speaking from a perspective that is to a degree confrontationally other to culture.[34]

Second, these readings imply that democratic self-criticism must reflect on the full range of human possibilities, rather than simply encourage pragmatic experiments within the boundaries of a pluralized culture. This reflection enables more critical appreciations of the human content and significance of cultural practices. Within our own political debates, defenders of the dignity of women's bodies and opponents of capital punishment would surely claim that reducing their arguments to socially constructed political acts creates serious misunderstanding and underestimation. In the absence of a series of essential human concerns (Do persons deserve equal social regard simply by virtue of their being human? Is the taking of human life as punishment ever justifiable?), critical judgment runs the risk of being relegated to strategic calculations or absorbed within cultural self-definitions.

Yet while both the Thucydidean and Socratic treatments of political culture include references to the nature of the human, neither exhibits the fundamentalism that Connolly assails. For Thucydides, the human is not reducible to a rigidly configured set of drives that make sense of our apparently turbulent condition. It is, rather, a range of puzzling expressions (the civil war at Corcyra and the slaughter at Mycalessus versus the nobility of individual Athenians during the plague and the sparing of the Mytilene democrats) that need to be sorted out. For Socrates, this range of human possibilities demands the activity of an examined life. The absence of what Connolly calls fundamentalism is reinforced by Thucydides' and Plato's own practices. Thucydides doubts that humans can be educated, but his project implies that improvement is somehow possible. In presenting the sublime vision of Diotima within his practical dialogues, Socrates stimulates reflection upon the meaning of philosophy. Here performative contradictions enrich rather than indict the practices in question.

The reconstructed classical position does not, however, soften fundamentalist claims simply to redefine them as critical pluralism, for the classical view is distinct in two basic ways. First, while critical pluralism treats the problem of otherness as something to be solved for democratic politics to be possible, the classical reconstruction implies that the hazards and benefits of others are problems with which even the best democratic politics must continually cope. Second, while critical pluralism's view of the self as socially constructed eliminates references to conceptions of essential humanness, the classical reconstruction sees such conceptions as necessary for self-critical political discourse.[35] These differences remind us that both critical pluralism and fundamentalism believe that they have achieved forms of closure. Through reading Plato and Thucydides, we may doubt that such closures are possible. What seems more promising is a style of political theory that assists thoughtful citizens to cope with the political dilemmas that arise out of the continued and intersecting presence of what is both strikingly other and intimately familiar. What this style of politics might look like within contemporary political conversations is provisionally suggested in the conclusion.

6

Conclusion:
Extending the Limits of Democracy

Lacunae in Democratic Theory

This book has been organized around two central claims. The first is that contemporary forms of democratic theory focus principally on characterizing and evaluating the space within which democratic politics can take place. Beyond attempting to ensure the continued democratic character of that space, these formulations generally avoid commentary on the specific outcomes that democratic politics should generate. In examining four influential theoretical frameworks, I have tried to suggest why this focus is insufficient. Some of my objections are theoretical. Though all of these perspectives restrict the sorts of questions that can be asked about political outcomes, none are as agnostic about ends as they pretend. Consequently, each provokes serious questions about internal consistency and all have a tendency to speak effectively only to those already convinced of their validity. These concerns do not end with theory, however. Democratic regimes are not unchallenged politically across the world, and one cannot effectively respond to such challenges simply by appealing to the commitments that democrats accept. Furthermore, when democracy's moral confidence is accompanied—as it is in the established Western democracies, at least—by a highly effective capacity to develop and exercise economic and military power, critical conversations about political purposes are particularly necessary. When contemporary forms of democratic political theory are compromised in their ability to contribute to such scrutiny, they undercut their own prospects as resources for democratic citizens.

My suggestion has been that these limitations are connected with broader theoretical restrictions on the sorts of things that can legitimately be spoken about within democratic political contexts. For many of the representative voices that this book has examined, the limitations that democratic theory imposes on itself are appropriate and desirable. How can democratic theory provide resources for assessing and criticizing the substantive content or outcomes of political practice without supplanting politics or democracy? For most current forms of democratic theory, the answer is that it cannot. No matter how the precise mission of democratic theory is understood, its practitioners agree that its deepest adversaries are those who treat questions of ends or goods as being capable of theoretical resolution. Though these alleged opponents to democracy are characterized in different ways (metaphysicians for Habermas, fundamentalists for Connolly, foundationalists for Warren), their common hallmarks are endorsements of single purposes as best for human beings (rejecting the democratic social condition of plurality) that are justified by appeals to authorities that should not be challenged (declaring war on the democratic processes of discursive exchange and political engagement). For such critics, Leo Strauss confirms the antidemocratic credentials of much of the premodern Western political philosophical tradition when he characterizes its project in chapter 2 of *Natural Right and History*: "The whole galaxy of political philosophers from Plato to Hegel, and certainly, all adherents of natural right assumed that the fundamental political problem is susceptible of a final solution" (1953, 35–36). Any suggestion that these final solutions are intelligible seems to position itself indisputably among the enemies of democratic politics, reinforcing Warren's (1994, 153) diagnosis of war between foundationalism and democracy.

Yet the collection of thinkers whom Strauss identifies as "the whole galaxy of political philosophers" offer a range of various and conflicting final answers to "the fundamental political problem" and, indeed, characterize the problem itself in significantly different ways. In response, Strauss's paradigmatic philosopher is not Weber, who sees the selection of practical ends as "a series of ultimate decisions in which the soul . . . chooses its own fate" (Weber 1949, 18), but Socrates, the gadfly or midwife who, while insisting that questions about the good are the most important ones we face (*Republic* 505e–6a), also remains continually dissatisfied with every final answer offered, including his own (cf. *Republic* 533a; *Gorgias* 527a–b).[1] Though Strauss is sometimes regarded as a signature figure of antidemocratic dogmatism, the complexities of his statement suggest that contemporary democratic theory's characterization of all serious attempts to provide substantive answers to questions concerning the ends of politics as metaphysical or foundational and, therefore, as antidemocratic is erroneous.[2]

My second claim has been that we can find resources for extending the limits of acceptable democratic conversations through reconstructive readings of the texts of Thucydides and Plato. What the Platonic Socrates and Thucydides have in common are the sense that questions about political goods are both unavoidable and elusive. While both attempt to provide substantive guidance about how those questions might be answered, neither does so in a way that is rigid or dogmatic. This nonfundamentalist concern with fundamental questions is reinforced by the literary character of their texts, fostering critical reflectiveness, engagement, and multivocality. On the basis of their examples, it seems inaccurate to dismiss all attempts to discover intellectually compelling conclusions about the ends or goods of political life as products of epistemological imperialism or pseudoreligious fundamentalism. Suitably practiced, such attempts can serve as resources for the activities of citizens within democratic political spaces. They do so most of all when they suggest that the basic templates governing democratic political discourse are incomplete or problematic.

Democracy's Problematics Revisited

I began by suggesting that liberal democratic political theory encounters at least three broad quandaries emerging out of its basic commitments. These raised questions about rights, governance, and ways of life. What kinds of contributions can classical political theory make to understanding the complexities and problematics of these commitments? How do these contributions stretch the limits of what should be spoken about within democracies? And what benefits follow from stretching these limits in these particular ways?

Rights and the Human

I suggested that the problematic character of liberal democracy's conception of rights becomes apparent when the universal bases of those rights encounter their more confined institutional establishment within constitutional democracies (cf. Narayan 1999, 49; Benhabib 2004, 2–4, 43–48). The liberal democratic case for rights thus encounters two distinct challenges. The first argues that restricting the benefits or the protections of human rights to citizens of liberal communities is morally untenable.

If such commitments are traceable to an understanding of the rights that should be accorded to all human beings, on what moral basis are they denied to those who stand outside the bounds of our own civic community? Yet attempts to establish congruencies between the political rights of democratic citizens and universal human rights introduce a second set of challenges. Since progress in protecting human rights in the developed West is historically associated with the spread of Enlightenment institutions, there is considerable pressure to treat Western forms of democratization as the normative standard measuring social and moral advancement. This raises vexing questions about how liberal democratic communities should relate to cultures or subcultures that do not share liberal democracy's rights commitments. Should such communities be influenced (through the application of hard or soft power) to adopt liberal democratic priorities? Furthermore, construing the rights currently accorded to citizens of liberal democracies as the political establishment of human rights may prematurely terminate conversations about the scope and content of those rights. Critics of the partiality or incompleteness of liberal democratic rights (on the basis of what might be seen as their excessive deference to radical individualism, secularism, or private property)[3] are left with nowhere to stand; the terrain of the human has been appropriated by the alleged foundations of liberalism.[4]

In spite of these difficulties, relying exclusively on historically determined political cultural justifications for rights is self-defeating. Those who insist on grounding rights only in the constructions of localized political cultures have limited resources for determining when local processes go awry (Ignatieff 2001, 76). While the relativization of liberal democracy's ethical templates may soften the moral force behind liberal crusades, it also eliminates one of the most important bases for intersocietal responsibility. Very often, those who wish to argue that the liberal democratic conception of rights is local and partial confront the task of criticizing one form of localism while denying the intelligibility of the vantage point most equipped to challenge purely localized claims.[5] Indeed, a rejection of the intelligibility of human rights impedes access to resources that are often essential even within particularly wrenching local debates.[6]

Of course, Thucydides and Plato are not human rights theorists. Neither provides a systematic statement that articulates or secretes particular conceptions of human rights. And neither endorses the priority of the concept of rights. Nonetheless, their common focus on the importance of characteristics belonging to human beings as such preserves the validity of the context in which human rights can be talked about intelligibly. For both authors, this context emerges as they investigate the relation between nature and culture. Both recognize that culture plays an essential role in enhancing or debasing human possibilities. Yet both also insist on the need to become clearer on the content and significance of the human or species characteristics that extend beyond the outcomes of cultural membership. As I interpret the classical framework, it continues to insist on the importance of questions about human nature without pretending that this awareness ends with a definitive and authoritative account of the human good. In different ways, Thucydides and Plato simply insist that questions about the basic capacities and inclinations of human beings are essential to serious investigations into political cultural practices of whatever sort. What Seyla Benhabib calls (2002) the claims of culture arise within rather than emerge as alternatives to investigations into human nature.

However, important perspectives in contemporary political theory conclude that it is necessary to frame human rights discourses in ways that do not depend on problematic assumptions about human nature. Rejecting such assumptions as "metaphysical," Benhabib offers discourse ethics as an alternative (2004, 130–32; cf. 2002, 11–12). From this perspective, the most basic human rights are those conditions that make it possible for affected parties to participate in argumentative discourses on an equal level, the rights to express one's voice and to have that voice heard (Benhabib 2004, 133). On this basis, more-specified human rights are those resources or conditions that affected parties engaging in open and free argumentation would refuse to see compromised. Michael Ignatieff attempts to move even further away from controversial philosophical involvements by appealing to what the experiences of history tell us about the kinds of damage that occur if human beings "lack a basic measure of free agency" (2001, 54). Human rights are identified on the basis of our responses to historical experiences of damage; our most central commitments are indexed by our degrees of horror and outrage.

In spite of these serious and intelligent efforts, however, it is not clear that attempts to move beyond substantive consideration of what it means to be a human being can succeed. Benhabib's insistence on the need to think postmetaphysically is based on a rejection of the reductive and dogmatic understandings of human nature that seem to underlie Enlightenment social contract theories (2004, 129–30), in which human nature becomes a foundation for explanation rather than a context for investigation and questioning. Yet while these criticisms plausibly apply to some texts within Enlightenment political theory, particularly classical liberalism and its ancestors, it is less clear that they indict treatments of the human in classical political theory, where the relation of the natural and the cultural and the content of the human are matters of unresolved but persistent concern.

Moreover, it remains dubious just how successful Benhabib and Ignatieff are in dispensing with implicit understandings of the human within their own formulations. Benhabib's reliance on discourse ethics presumes the involvement of human beings capable of taking the structuring conditions of discursive engagement seriously.[7] And Ignatieff acknowledges the need for some sort of foundational equivalent to foundationalism even as he distinguishes metaphysical groundings of human rights from more pragmatic assessments of what human rights can do for human beings (2001, 54). For we cannot articulate a clear conception of the functional value of human rights without identifying those human functions that are valuable and central enough to justify such protections, considerations that rational discourse partners must take seriously.[8] A focus on the dignity of the individual is based on a substantive and hardly noncontroversial conception of individuation.[9] In relying on what history can tell us, Ignatieff presumes a particular membership in that "us" and a particular content for those lessons.[10] This bespeaks the need to move beyond an appeal to historical experience to a reliance on a human judgment that is responsive to historical events in light of identifiable and privileged human priorities.

The unavoidable need to pay attention to basic human needs as a framing context for human rights claims both enriches and complicates how we assess connections between the historical rights specified by liberal democracies and the more encompassing but less definite horizon of human rights. Liberal democracies may well be particularly effective in doing good things for human beings by establishing and protecting liberal democratic rights. Yet this does not mean that such rights are grounded exclusively in the will formations or cultural templates of democratic societies. We can also affirm those outcomes according to requirements discovered by a more cosmopolitan reflection on human experience, on the implications and responsibilities of our common species membership. Inevitably, this reflection validates rights on the basis of a privileged schedule of needs. Yet the project of identifying such privileged needs and rights is a continuous challenge that cannot be completed either through the discovery of a universally valid metaphysics or through the establishment of a politically cosmopolitan system of governance (cf. Benhabib 2004, 104–5). Liberal democratic cultures cannot in principle claim to provide a completely adequate home for the articulation and protection of human rights.[11] For similar reasons, even the most well-intentioned attempts to support liberal democratic rights in resistant cultural contexts need to be cautiously scrutinized. This is not because all cultural standards are relative and politicized, with no intelligible or innocent conception of humanness available, and still less because liberal democracy is an imperial wolf in a moralizing sheep's clothing, but because no political culture is guaranteed to be comprehensive enough to encourage the development of fully human beings or mature enough to understand completely the limitations and damages of even the most progressive political cultural agendas.

While the first complication introduced by Thucydides and Plato suggests that there may be more to human rights than the priorities embraced by even the most humane or comprehensive society, the second suggests that there is more to humanness than rights. Contemporary concerns to ensure the widespread recognition of and respect for human rights stem not simply from historical outrage at brutal violations of human dignity that have been all too common. They are traceable more fundamentally to a philosophical commitment to the centrality of autonomy.[12] When Thucydides and Plato engage the nature of humanness, however, neither valorizes what a later moral philosophical tradition theorized as autonomy. However, while affirmations of something like Kantian autonomy fall outside of the classical purview, broader concerns for the value of human rationality do not. Critics such as Habermas object that the forms of rationality endorsed by the classical perspective are either embedded in premodern cultural forms or transported to some elevated metaphysical vantage point (1993, 5–7, 10, 116–17, 125). Yet, as I have suggested, applying these assessments to Thucydides and Plato is complicated by the literary form chosen by both authors. While Thucydides' *logos* draws on cultural templates, it also challenges them. Plato's metaphysics are provisional and enabling, not dogmatic and transcendent (cf. *Republic* 532d–33a).

The classical perspective does depart from the moral case for democracy by implicitly challenging the priority—or, at least, the completeness—of autonomy, contending that moves to establish the right prior to the good are themselves dependent on a prior understanding of the good.[13] From the perspective of the Platonic Socrates in the *Republic*, the most important project for rationality is not to assure the self-directed character of our individual and collective practices but to contribute to the quality of our self-direction by examining the merits and deficiencies of competing individual and collective ways of life, so that we may both do well and be happy (cf. *Republic* 621d). A fulfilled human life is achieved not simply through the protection and practice of autonomy, but through a much more complicated practical reflection that considers how different activities and choices might create shares in the good or bad prospects that the human psyche and human cultures make available. Rationality is central not because there is one right way of living that we are somehow called to discover and follow, but because there are so many possibilities for enhancing or debasing our humanity that need to be sorted out and assessed (cf. *Republic* 618b–19b). The most important practical task for rationality, then, is not to establish its own realm of autonomy, but to cope with the risk (*kindunos*) associated with the appealing and frightening life prospects that human beings must continuously confront (*Republic* 618b).[14]

Here Thucydides' narrative seems to challenge Plato's by underscoring ways in which powerful aspects of our humanness are sources of disintegration and disruption. His most pointed authorial statement comes, of course, in his commentary on the significance of the *stasis* in Corcyra. "And there fell upon the cities many hardships on account of *stasis*, events that take place and will recur always as long as human beings have the same nature, worse or gentler in their types (looks), depending on the changes presenting themselves in each instance. In times of peace and goodness, cities and individuals are better disposed because they are not overthrown by the constraints of necessity. But war, depriving [human beings] of daily resources, is a violent teacher, making the dispositions of most like that [harsh] condition" (3.82.2). Plausible readings of Thucydides conclude that this portrait of human beings discourages any confidence in rationality by revealing the destructive actions of which humans seem endlessly capable.[15] Yet Thucydides' diagnosis of the causes and consequences of political disintegration is less a basis for condemnation and disgust than an argument for forgiveness and extenuation. This is seen most clearly in Diodotus's speech on Mytilene. In commenting on the significance of Diodotus's speech, Orwin offers the striking formulation that "Diodotus announces a more terrible truth than that human beings are evil; namely, that they are not" (1994, 203). This certainly gets at a significant part of the truth. Diodotus says that human damages stem less from injustice (*adikia*) than from error (*hamartia*) (3.45.3). For this reason, political condemnations of allegedly evil populations are misguided and destructive. These very designations emerge from and reinforce the passions (anger, fear, greed, ambition) that make political rationality so difficult (cf. 3.42.1).

Yet to say that human beings are not evil implies a truth that is far from terrible. To the extent that Diodotus urges his audience to acknowledge that hideous things emerge not from evil but from error, he also appeals to the human capacity for understanding and responding appropriately to error, not with slaughter but with prudence and moderation. More broadly, to the degree that Thucydides speaks through Diodotus's speech-act, he does not altogether despair of possibilities for identifying a human rationality that might, as one of its many tasks, discover and justify conceptions of human rights. At the same time, Diodotus's exploration of the darker sides of our most fundamental human needs and vulnerabilities also makes clear that what we have come to call human rights are threatened not only by predatory state practices or social pathologies but also by characteristics and urges that are as human as those that ideas of human rights are intended to enhance.

From the perspective of classical political philosophy, then, neither the political institutions of democratic culture nor the moral framework of democratic autonomy provides a completely adequate context for understanding the complexities of human rights. This is not because "modern" defenses of human rights need to be absorbed within a stronger and more encompassing moral community or transformed into a thicker practice of the virtues. Rather, the Thucydidean and Platonic focus on the importance of cultures suggests that no culture can ensure an altogether reliable context for the development and protection of the capacities that serve as the conditions for human rights. And the narrow conception of human choice that lies at the heart of democratic autonomy, as in Habermas's identifying the capacities that allow human beings to engage in the discursive process of reaching understanding or Rawls's continued insistence on the presence of the reasonable in politics,[16] pays too little attention to the more complicating human purposes that human rights support and fails often to acknowledge that, precisely with respect to the protection of its members' rights, the human species can be its own worst enemy.[17]

Governance and Democratic Power

The second broad area in which the functions of liberal democracy were problematized concerned how liberal societies preserve conditions for democratic governance. For rational choice theory, the answer is straightforward. Since governance coordinates individual pursuits of advantage (Downs 1957, 9), political cooperation is self-reinforcing. However, the other forms of democratic theory considered here—deliberative democratic theory, the interpretation of democratic culture, and postmodernism—treat such conditions less derivatively. Rather than emerging from the self-interested strategies of individuals, the institutions and culture of democracy are generated by collective will formation (Habermas), historical constructions of cultural meanings (Rawls), or political conflicts (Butler, Connolly, Honig). Far from being the outcomes of prepolitical forms of rationality, the right institutions or cultural templates make democratic rationality possible.

There are important differences between the democratic theories that focus on the various roles of institutions and culture, but there is general agreement that the enabling conditions of democracy are those that allow democratic political processes to function most effectively. Healthy democratic ecologies (Warren's term at Warren 2001, 207) make democracy more democratic (cf. Warren 2001, 226).

The perspective on democratic governance implicit within the classical view emphasizes the need to see democratic governance as fragile in two distinct ways. First, the classical view is sensitive to how the conditions for democracy's political functioning might be compromised or dissolved by tendencies that are themselves fostered within democratic societies. Both Thucydides and Plato would agree with critics of the rational choice position who reject the facile notion that democratic norms are reinforced by the sensible decisions of utility maximizers. Yet the constitutive importance of political-cultural priorities does not mean that an authentically democratic culture is free from its own disorders. Democratic governance cannot be guaranteed through an artificially closed political sociology (as in Rawls 2005, 193, 398). And suggestions that democratic institutions function well when communicative contexts are protected from the corruption of power and money (cf. Warren 2001, 109–12) may need to be extended to investigate how authentically democratic influences can also work against important political goods.[18] Why should we be so confident that democratic deliberation will not be polluted by the political rhetoric that democratic culture in some respects supports? (Ironically, this is suggested by Cleon, of all people, when he complains that the deliberations of the democratic assembly have come to resemble entertainment venues [3.38.4–7].)[19] The political resources and capacities that are most pronounced within democratic societies can surely be turned in a wide variety of directions.[20]

Underlying much of democratic theory is the assumption that enhancing prospects for rational interaction or constructive political engagement is inextricably linked to the expansion and deepening of democracy. Influences that strengthen communicative rationality or energize participatory politics are democratic. Those that distort communication or debase political engagement are non- or antidemocratic, foreign invaders that weaken or pathologize an otherwise healthy organism (cf. Warren 2001, 60–61). The classical view suspects that this division is too simple. A consistent theme is that sources of democratic corruption reside not only within non- or counterdemocratic societal features (the incursions of markets into nonmarket spheres or the abuses of technological power by bureaucracies insulated from democratic accountability), but also within societal possibilities tied more closely to the characteristics of democracy itself (the abuse of certain forms of free speech, the recklessness or injustices of certain majorities, or excesses of individualism).[21]

Thus, when Socrates talks of the democratic culture as a "bazaar of regimes" in book 8 of the *Republic* (557d–e), he also points toward internal disputes about both the identity and the goods of democracy. According to the "bazaar" image, democracy encloses and encourages sources that contribute not only to its own enhancement and flourishing but also to its own distortion or corruption (cf. *Republic* 562b–c). There are similar prospects for contention over healthy and damaging democratic potentials in Thucydides. The stirring possibilities for democratic action that Pericles identifies within Athenian political culture in the funeral speech are part of a politicized statement used to overcome those (denigrated as the uselessly inactive) who oppose the Periclean vision of political well-being. Consequently, the funeral speech endorses a conception of democratic achievement that undermines the democratic commitment to political equality.[22]

From the classical perspective, democratic institutions are also fragile in a second sense, concerning not simply coherence but direction. The question of how democratic governance can be enhanced is different from the question of how strengthened forms of democratic governance could be employed. In this respect, I have suggested that the concerns of Thucydides and Plato are not principally to assail the exercise of political power by democracies but rather to remind their readers of the dangers of political power more generally—dangers to which democracies are not immune. This theme links the speech of Diodotus (*hybris* continually overreaches and *erōs* leads hope toward destruction [cf. Thucydides 3.45.4–6]) with the closing myths of both the *Gorgias* (most of those deemed incurable in their viciousness by the judges in the afterlife have come from the ranks of the powerful [525d–26a]) and the *Republic* (Socrates' character Er reports that the soul of Odysseus has been cured by his former labors of the love of honor and chooses the life of a private man who minds his own business [620c–d]).

For the classical view, enhancing the quality of democratic politics requires not simply the further empowerment of democratic institutions but also the presence of a thoughtful rationality supportive of moderation. Perhaps contemporary democratic theory is too sanguine when it suggests that the remedy for potential abuses of democratic power is to be found simply in more or stronger democracy.[23] Perhaps theories of democratic citizenship are too limited when they interpret their primary responsibilities to democratic citizens as articulating just conditions for membership. Such postures bespeak not simply a confidence in the merits of democratic regimes as compared with all other plausible alternatives but also an unexamined confidence in the capacity of this particular political arrangement to exercise power without creating its own possibilities for injustice, a prospect that even the rule of the philosopher-kings is eventually unable to avoid (cf. *Republic* 540e–41a). According to this view, the standards we use to compare democratic polities need to be extended beyond strength and scope to include considerations of better and worse. And contributions made to the health of democratic citizenship need to go beyond scrutinizing membership arrangements to providing resources enabling the exercise of citizenship's substantive responsibilities.

There is a sense, then, in which critics are right to say that the classical perspective opposes a certain kind of virtue to democracy. This is not because the classical perspective condemns democracy as a vulgar and ordinary political arrangement, but because it emphasizes the vital importance of virtues beyond, and perhaps even skeptical of, those needed for the effective functioning of democratic power. The virtuous dispositions shaped and required by the priorities and functions of democratic practices may be too embedded and confident to offer necessary criticisms of the political directions that democratic regimes may, qua democracies, follow.[24] In this respect, conceptions of the virtues espoused by cultural, deliberative, and postmodern democrats may be surprisingly close in form to those supported by communitarian and civic republican traditions that are often criticized as being excessively supportive of political cultural templates that hold vigorous societies together.[25] In this light, the most important political virtues within democracies would be precisely those enabling critical judgment to scrutinize the exercise of democratic power, those that stretch the limits of democratic discourse and practice in challenging and unsettling ways. One of these challenges insists on the political relevance of conceptions of human flourishing.

Democratic Politics and the Quality of Life

The third area in which the functions of democratic society were problematized concerned the impacts of liberal-democratic political culture on the encouragement or frustration of certain ways of life. For all of the contemporary positions that I have examined, democratic political theory's ability to comment on ways or qualities of life is constrained at the outset by the categories of social analysis that are selected. Because rational choice theory disaggregates ways of life into a series of preferences and decisions, its framework discourages any conception of human practices as intelligible wholes. "Ways of life" become abstractions for regular or predictable behaviors.[26] The interpretation of democratic culture treats the flourishing or withering of certain forms of practice as the predictable outcome of the influence of societal templates (Rawls's commonsense fact of political sociology [2005, 193]). Deliberative democratic theory understands conceptions of and justifications for ways of life as constructed outcomes of the dialogic processes belonging to the appropriate form of practical communication.[27] Postmodernism redescribes ways of life as the fluid outcomes of interaction between social influences and individual moves of self-creation (cf. Butler 1997b, 13–18, 29–30).

While each of these contemporary approaches to democratic theory relies on different conceptual and analytic resources, they are linked by a recognition of the priority of some understanding of human freedom, the right to form preferences, the crafting and recrafting of symbol systems, the dignity supported by autonomy, or the self-creativity expressed in pragmatic experiments. The overlapping concern with freedom explains why all of these perspectives believe that classical political philosophy's more pronounced attention to conceptions of virtue can be sustained only under the supervision of essentializing metaphysics and coercive authority (cf. Habermas 1993, 125; Rawls 2005, 379; Connolly 1995, 106–9; Warren 1994, 153; Honig 1993, 3). Consequently, when Amartya Sen introduces his capabilities approach for assessing the functions and dynamics of economic systems, he distances that perspective from the closely associated neo-Aristotelianism of Martha Nussbaum because Aristotelianism limits human freedom through a "tremendously overspecified" conception of human nature (Sen and Nussbaum 1993, 47). Sen substitutes a conception of capabilities that includes the valuation of freedom as a good in itself (Sen and Nussbaum 1993, 43; Sen 1999, 285–86).

Concerns about the threats that conceptions of virtue or flourishing pose for agency underlie two important objections to any move linking substantive conceptions of human well-being to politics. The first is that such politics inevitably privilege one way of life or limited sets of lives over others and reinforce that privileging through applications of power—for example, the denial of marriage opportunities to same-sex couples on the basis of a restricted understanding of the family. The second is that a politics that takes a critical stance toward alternative ways of life often responds to social damages by blaming the victims, reducing political and economic "systems to the aggregate effects of individual character" (Warren 2001, 20). According to this criticism, the friends of virtue not only misread the dynamics of social causality out of moral ideological fervor, but also intensify this distortion by assigning culpability precisely to those most lacking the agency that assessments of culpability assume.

A number of the voices speaking in the name of "virtue" often say the things that their critics accuse them of saying.[28] Yet these are inadequate grounds for excluding critical judgments on ways of life from constructive conversations about democracy. As noted, all of the forms of contemporary democratic theory treated here take their own decisive positions on the value of particular ways of living. For Habermas and Warren, an autonomous existence is better than a dependent one. For Butler, Connolly, and Honig, lives informed by self-creative energy and experimentation are preferable to those held back by the delusions and compulsions of fundamentalism. In such cases, healthy politics enhances prospects for autonomy or expands the possibilities for self-creation. Read against this backdrop, when the classical view connects questions about the appropriate structuring of political communities to questions concerning the goods or deficiencies of particular ways of life, it contends only that examining the quality or content of the influence of politics on ways of life is as important as scrutiny of its extent or degree.[29] Resting on Rawls's commonsense political-sociological claim that such influences simply happen just won't do.

Moreover, serious questions about the value of different ways of life are so inextricable from contemporary political experiences that excising attention to those questions would distort and diminish the ability to cope with the experiences themselves. Defenses of same-sex marriage may often begin with and employ rights claims, but most do not end there. Instead, the focus turns to the personal and societal goods that are intrinsic to the marital relationship, concluding that giving same-sex couples access to the institution will enhance desirable qualities of life, in ways that legalizing other proscribed sexual relations would not.[30] In such discourses, establishing same-sex marriage as a right is a consequence of and not a foundation for arguments discussing its goods. Such assessments can be challenged, of course, but the very turn toward arguments of this sort suggests that conceptions of valuable or damaging ways of life are integral parts of our political-cultural conversations.

Discoveries of social pathologies may also be intensified rather than muted by an attention to the resulting quality of life. It would be mistaken and cruel to trace harsh social conditions to the moral character of those entrapped. Yet an appreciation of the impacts of such conditions on quality of life, not only for those immediately involved but also for society, is one of the most powerful indictments of those conditions. Do we adequately characterize the situations of those locked within impoverishing or oppressive social structures by pointing to lack of agency?[31] What are the impacts of institutionalized poverty or racism, grossly inequitable pathways to education and health care, and widespread violence against women, children, or animals on the quality of societal life as a whole? When such questions are excluded from theoretical democratic discourse, theory fails to connect with the experiences and the problems of the political communities it engages.

Finally, there are clearly cases where the presence of certain moral ways of life is essential to positive political action. For example, debates over the ways in which representative politics can be made more accommodating to marginalized social groups presuppose not only institutional reforms but also a more widely dispersed and deeply ingrained sense of justice.[32] Possibilities for the success of effective institutional responses to poverty through the tax system depend eventually on voter acceptance and therefore on more highly developed commitments to generosity and responsibility.[33]

The reconstructed classical position reinforces the importance of each of these areas of problematization for the healthy functioning of democracies. By placing the classical position in conversation with contemporary forms of democratic theory, we find that the conceptual boundaries that these formulations impose often prevent those questions from being adequately engaged. In response, the style of political theory represented by the classical position envisages a more extended conversation within and about democratic regimes. In extending questions that begin with the problematic relation between rights belonging to human beings as members of the species and rights created for citizens as members of democratic political communities, the classical perspective suggests that both the templates of democratic culture and the priority of democratic autonomy fail to capture everything about our humanness that is politically or civically important. In extending questions that begin with problematics of how democratic governance can be strengthened, the classical perspective doubts that the exercise of power in democracies can be managed simply by making power more democratic. Finally, in extending questions that begin with the tension between a democratic politics grounded in freedom and equality and its own critical scrutiny of ways of life, the classical view reasserts the importance of a strong and substantive ethical discourse for the appropriate tasks of democratic political theory. The freedom (Sen) and equality (Young) that form the bases of democratic political theory must be understood in light of broader and deeper conceptions of worthwhile freedom and an equality of desirable things.

Thucydides and Plato as Contributors to Democratic Conversations

In arguing for the importance of extending the conversational limits of democracy, I have drawn on the texts of Thucydides and Plato. These authors are important not only because their themes complicate and enrich the frameworks informing contemporary democratic theory, but also because their styles of presentation demand the involvement of their readers. The literary character of these texts also reflects their presence as speech-acts within political cultural conversations. Because both are produced within an Athenian regime that is strongly, though controversially, democratic, their immediate audiences are comprised of both supporters and critics of the regime and its directions. Against this backdrop, interpretations dismissing these authors as irrelevant for democratic political choice seem mistaken. I close by sketching the more general contributions that each makes to democratic conversational frameworks and by suggesting the ways in which these contributions both intersect with and diverge from each other.

Thucydides and the Risks of Politics

One reason for skepticism about Thucydides' contribution to practical life is that his vision of the nature of politics seems unremittingly bleak, diagnosing the inevitability of political disintegration and despairing of the possibility of remedy. That this assessment is validated in a great deal of the *History* goes without saying. However, the readings I have offered in the previous chapters cautiously suggest that Thucydides' reflections on politics can be read in ways that contribute more positively to political thought. They do so by offering glimpses into the functioning of various political dynamics, making both the vulnerabilities and the resources of political life clearer.[34] In this respect, war is the focus of Thucydides' attention because of the insights that it discloses and not, as for Pericles (2.64), because of the achievements it enables.

Hannah Arendt (1968) has located politics as occurring in the space "between past and future." Thucydides' treatments of politics also include a variety of narrative possibilities as to how political practices can deal with the future and the past. Though these are generally tales of disintegration, Thucydides' narratives also invite his readers to think seriously about the conditions that can contribute to political health. Two approaches to politics as a space between past and future emerge powerfully within the *History*: one treats the future as a field for manipulative and self-interested strategic power moves; the other treats the past as a stable pattern calling for continuous repetition. Thucydides' renditions of these approaches display their political damages in a way that facilitates reflection on better alternatives.

The first of these approaches emerges from the pairing of the Corcyrean speech at Athens (Thucydides 1.32–36) with Euphemus's speech at Camarina (6.82–87) that I have provided in chapter 2. As I have suggested, both speakers offer their audiences prospects for benefits received in return for cooperation. They offer bargains that rely heavily on certain kinds of promises. Corcyra will be "eternally" (*aiei*) grateful for Athenian support, and the Camarineans can rely on the predictability of Athens's interests as a guarantee of its trustworthiness. In parallel, both speeches also argue that barriers to cooperation emerging from past commitments or obligations should be forgotten. Athens should overcome its anxiety about the tottering truce, and Camarina should ignore evidence of Athenian hypocrisy. Yet the very forms of forgetting that are treated as conditions for political action also turn back on possibilities for promising in ways that undercut prospects for constructive political action.[35] Corcyra points not to new political possibilities created by promises and reaffirmed by memory, but to the abandonment of stable political possibilities altogether. Its eventual self-destruction as a political community reveals the absence of both stabilizing memory (oaths and sacred spaces facilitate destruction) and trustworthy promises (the political principles articulated by oligarchs and democrats are smoke screens for power grabs) (3.81.5). Euphemus replaces promises with predictions in a way that serves rather than limits exercises of power; Athens can be predicted to do whatever is necessary for advancing its interests. Consequently, his statement reveals the antipolitical tendencies of empire that leave no room for binding and reliable kinds of promising and remembering that can establish more associational political forms or for a political agency that requires freedom from imperial control (1.94.2, 1.96.1–2, 2.37.1). Neither Corcyra nor Euphemus acknowledges the need to reexamine conceptions of political self-interest, and neither identifies grounds for failing to keep promises beyond the fact that they have become strategic liabilities.

A second set of distortions, the reliance on permanent remembrance as a guarantor of political civility, is revealed within the speech of the Corinthians at Athens (1.37–43) and in the broader practices of Spartan political culture. In different ways, both regimes treat memory as an acknowledgment of place within a settled moral order. Yet though both regimes valorize memory as a stable resource, their practices show that it is always a work in progress, connected inevitably with contests over power. Corinth uses the tropes of duty or obligation (Corcyra as Corinth's colony and Athens as its partner in a sworn truce) to reinforce its own power position. Sparta all too often behaves in the ways claimed by the Athenians on Melos; it treats interest as justice and advantage as nobility. Remembrance as institutionalized through the laws of Spartan order do not encourage any vision of the future that accommodates more creative forms of political agency. Indeed, the recognition of set places within hierarchies (the older over the younger, the sworn to over the swearing) rejects attempts to foster agency as destabilizing and dangerous. What passes for promising is a reconfirmation of expectations already implicit within familiar interactive patterns (cf. 5.104), the reassuring yet restraining reminder of what is, not the critical consideration of what is or the constructive imagination of what might be. Spartan memory and the political culture with which it intersects are thus sustained through a series of compelled repetitions. Consequently, Sparta's moral identity both emerges from and reinforces deep-seated political cultural fears (of the Helots, of the gods) that often compromise its efforts at civic education (the destabilizing examples of Pausanias and Brasidas [1.95.7, 1.128–38, 4.108.7]) and distort its response to political change (suggested by Spartan reaction to the defeat at Pylos [5.34.2, 7.18.2–3]). In this respect, Thucydides' verdict on a political culture held together by the ties of deep remembrance may be harsher than Crane (1998, 15–19, 252–53) suggests. A politics supported by reified memory is not only vulnerable to the external challenges posed by more innovative regimes (1.70.3), but also deficient in its efforts to create its own internal well-being.[36]

In different ways, the Corcyrean manipulation of the future and the Spartan reverence for the past reflect political constructions that frustrate political agency. The Corcyrean plan for the future is an unstable sequence of strategic aggressions; the Spartan vision of the past is a rigid set of imperatives that forbid innovation. These politics are also characterized by a diminution of the possibilities of *logos*. For Corcyra, *logos* is the crafty representation of political prospects aiming at strategic success. For Sparta, it is a patterned acknowledgment of stable forms that resists critique. In neither case is *logos* the capacity to examine political power critically or to envisage new political possibilities.

The deficiencies of these politics are particularly pronounced when set against Pericles' vision of politics, expressed in different ways in all three of his direct speeches. The Periclean view valorizes the possibilities of an agency that is all the more vital because it connects speech (*logos*) with action (*ergon*). As I have suggested, these commitments to agency and *logos* are embedded within a controversial and contested project of creating an Athens worthy of memory.[37] When Pericles urges commitment to creating a political image that lives eternally in memory, he asks that the Athenians submit themselves to a remembrance that extends political vision from the immediacy of the Corcyreans into eternity. Yet this vision of eternity is not that of the permanently balanced order in which the Corinthians (1.38.1–3) and the Spartans (7.18.2–3) believe, for Pericles underscores that this eternally memorialized image is itself an Athenian creation. In the funeral speech, one of the marks of Athens's power is that it has "established everlasting (*aidia*) memorials (*mnēmeia*) of harm and good everywhere" (2.41.4–5). Since this power (*dynamis*) is also proof of Athens's being an "education to Greece" (2.41.1–2), the city's ability to create such memorials implies an authorial rather than a deferential stance toward limits on political activities in the future. In envisaging that Athens's energy will create a memorial drawing eternal respect, Pericles implies that no innovative political energy will eclipse Athens's brilliance, even though, as is recognized in the last speech, "it is in the nature of all things to be diminished."[38]

Pericles' success in establishing the memory of Athens's greatest name thus requires an equally energetic project of forgetting. Unlike the strategic forgetting urged by Corcyra, Periclean forgetting supports a more indefinite range of active agency. Pericles' speeches thus call for the forgetting of the kinds of reverence and attachment that could serve as impediments to innovation. While the early (1.72–78) speech of the unnamed Athenians at Sparta proudly points back to the heroic Athenian defeat of the Persians, Pericles' funeral oration quickly passes over the achievements of the early Athenians and noticeably avoids the symbol of Athens's Persian victories won at such risk and cost. Instead, the deeds of prior generations are praised only to the extent that they are the conditions for remarkable civic achievements in the present.[39]

Pericles' overarching concern with establishing foundations for Athens's eternal remembrance thus embeds both *logos* and democracy within a project of daring achievement. In the funeral oration, he connects Athens's unique ability to meld speech with action to its equally unique identity as a democracy (2.37.1, 2.40.1–3). Yet this speech is valorized to the degree that it is subordinated to the power of Athens's deeds (*erga*) (2.41.1–3). The anticipated response to memory as Periclean project is a wonder or amazement (cf. 7.28.3) that dispenses with the contributions of the poets or culture (2.41.4). Though this praise of Athens's *erga* depends on the prior success of Pericles' *logos*, without which the *ergon* of power would remain hidden, this *logos* itself is offered as a powerful *ergon* whose accomplishments are measured by the creation of a strong community among the Athenians as assembled citizens.[40] Similarly, the recognition of the democratic culture as demanding equality before the law is quickly replaced by an image of democracy as a regime giving individual excellence free play (2.37.2). Thucydides' own conclusion that Periclean Athens was democratic only in name (2.65.9–10) is anticipated by the rhetoric of Pericles' speeches.[41]

From this perspective, the meaning of Pericles' commitment to establishing Athens's memory within the *History* is less clear. Within a turbulent and ultimately evanescent world where political cultures arise and disappear, such a project may well appear as the most noble aspiration.[42] Yet Thucydides' own efforts to ensure that the experience of the war is retained as a possession forever (1.22.4) can be interpreted as a challenge to this way of remembering the war, as in his two different explanations for why he chose to "write about" the war. The first (1.1) focuses on the energy expended and the scope of those involved; the second (1.23) focuses on the widespread sufferings and bloodshed that it occasioned. One consequence of controlling the memory of the war as greatest motion is an inattention to or forgetting of this greatest suffering.[43] The greatest motion is no less spectacular, but remembering its brilliance cannot mean forgetting its parallel darkness. Thus, Thucydides' narrative also encloses an important alternative to Periclean politics that relies upon different conceptions of memory and agency embedded within a different and, indeed, potentially more democratic political vision.

As I have suggested throughout the book, the most complex practice of political *logos* in the *History* is found in Diodotus's speech on Mytilene. Cleon's preceding speech combines the most damaging aspects of the Corcyrean and Spartan positions. He embraces a Corcyrean view of interest (successful cities should amass wealth and power [3.39.7–8]) supported by the binding character of what he calls *nomos* (3.37.3–4). Yet this vision of interest is directed by the passions of anger and fear (3.40.7–8). And *nomos* is simply the assembly's prior decision to destroy Mytilene made under the influence of his own rhetoric (3.37.3–4).[44] Memories recall harm inflicted, and the future is a continued struggle for material security and political preeminence.

Diodotus's more complicated political *logos* encourages ways of engaging the past and the future that may question and improve rather than validate and serve exercises of power. Thus interpreted, Diodotus's proposal embeds the activities of remembering and forgetting within a certain kind of political judgment that looks more positively toward the future. Yet while the speech itself envisages an alternative politics to those of Corcyra, Sparta, and Pericles, its surrounding context and eventual implications reveal the fragile and risk-laden character of that alternative.

What Diodotus encourages his democratic audience to remember is neither their rage at the Mytilenes' defection nor the binding character of previously established *nomoi*, but the human passions and vulnerabilities that should soften outrage and reveal the limits of extreme punishments (3.45.1–7). To this extent, political memory involves a different form of practice than simply honoring prior agreements or acknowledging factual realities.[45] The memory that Diodotus encourages requires an active appreciation of the significance of what is remembered in a way that shapes how alternatives for action are understood. Remembering the loves and hopes that inspire overreaching exposes the failure of capital punishment and requires us to rethink how we respond to the disorders that overreaching causes. This form of memory goes beyond an intellectual grasp of the direction and power of human motives, for it requires considerable strength to forget those influences (the anger and fear that Mytilene's rebellion elicits) that urge us to employ political memory in more damaging ways.

Such a damaging usage of memory appears within Thucydides' account of how the story of the achievements of the tyrannicides affects the city's response to the mutilation of the statues of Hermes that occurs on the eve of the Sicilian expedition. Early in the narrative (1.20), Thucydides criticizes the Athenian memory that valorized the liberating sacrifice of Harmodius and Aristogeiton. They mistakenly believe that the tyrannicides killed the tyrant, Hippias, rather than his brother Hipparchus, and they erroneously associate the killing with the end of Peisistratid rule. Here memory failed in what Paul Ricoeur (2004, 88) calls its truthful function. Yet in the later reflection on how the tyrannicide legend influenced responses to the mutilation (6.53–60), Thucydides contends that the Athenians knew that the tyranny was removed not by themselves and Harmodius but by the Spartans.[46] This correct memory does not, however, ensure appropriate practice. Here memory fails in Ricoeur's pragmatic function, for a more or less accurate recall of the facts surrounding the tyranny's overthrow leads the Athenians to reenact a politics of suspicion and fear. Knowing that the tyranny had become harsh in the end, the Athenians nonetheless fail to understand the causes and character of that harshness. In some respects, the severity of the tyranny can be traced to the thoughtless daring (*alogiston tolma*) of the tyrannicides themselves (6.59.1), for Hippias's rule became truly violent only after the killing of Hipparchus. Responding to the mutilation in an atmosphere haunted by a sense of vulnerability and a fear of new subversions, the city behaves in a way that parallels the intensified harshness of the last Peisistratid. Owing to failures of pragmatic memory, the democrats, too, kill out of fear.

By contrast, Diodotus's case for moderation toward the Mytilene democrats relies on more positive and reconstructive sources within

Athens's historical political commitments. This reliance is implicit in the connections between Diodotus's speech and the tropes of justice and equality within Athenian political discourse. Though Diodotus rejects arguments explicitly centered around justice, he convinces the Athenians to be moderate toward the Mytilene democrats and therefore to be more just than their material power requires. In so doing, his practice reflects seriously what the Athenians at Sparta affirm rhetorically: that Athens's rule exhibits a kind of justice by allowing more equality to the subject cities than measures of power would demand (1.72.2–3). In this respect, both the justice and moderation implicit in Diodotus's speech respect the priorities of a democratic culture that measures equality on terms other than power. It is, indeed, the institutions of democracy itself that make conversations about the meaning and importance of political priorities such as equality possible. Consequently, the speech of Diodotus might be read as fostering the democratic political good of equality through a deception made regrettably necessary by the distortions that democratic practices themselves foster, simultaneously acknowledging the strengths and deficiencies of democracy.

Building upon this sense of Athens's past, Diodotus' engagement with the future envisages alternative possibilities for political practice.[47] When he says that Athens should respond to the restiveness of the subject cities by guarding against them (3.46.5–6), he potentially invites reconsideration of the nature and benefits of the empire.[48] Though Pericles' remark in his last speech that the empire may have been unjust to take up but is now dangerous to put down (2.63.2–3) suggests that it is generally not possible for complex and powerful regimes with long histories of commitments and resentments simply to start over, Diodotus's comments recognize some possibility for new beginnings. While Diodotus does not envisage Athens surrendering its rule, he invites reconsideration of what ruling requires, implying that examining alternative forms of political identity is the most important function of *logos*. This understanding of political agency offers more substantial reasons for refusing to keep promises, namely when doing so would conflict with more carefully chosen political goals. According to this view, for example, the promise of an opportunistic alliance with Corcyra could be broken not when Athens gets a better offer, but when the vision of the city's good that informed that promise is rejected in the face of more considered political judgment and criticism.[49]

Yet any appreciation of Diodotus's subtle contributions to saving the Mytilene democrats must be tempered by the flow of the broader narrative in the *History*. I have suggested throughout that Diodotus's complex rhetoric turns back on itself[50] at least twice, first, when his claim to be

Conclusion 249

speaking solely with a view to Athens's interests is problematized by his admission that all proposals before the assembly require deception in order to succeed; and, second, when his reliance on deception is justified by its contribution to the democratic good of critical *logos*. A third, and grimmer, turn is signaled by the realization that his calculated appeal to interests can foster disregard of both justice and *logos*. The Athenian participants in the Melian dialogue reveal debts to a variety of previous Athenian speakers, including Diodotus. Their insistence that all parties interact exclusively with eyes turned toward interests rests on an explicit dismissal of a justice that is now characterized only as mutual deference in the face of equal coercive capacities (5.89.1). The so-called dialogue that follows is a collision between two forms of *logos* that replicate the Corcyrean and Spartan distortions, a calculative Athenian argument that submission is the only rational alternative for Melos, and a Melian repetition of hopes for rescue within an ordered cosmos structured by kinship and just gods.

This linkage with the Athenians on Melos is misread if it indicts Diodotus.[51] What it reveals instead is the impossibility of assuring how political actions undertaken under one set of circumstances will influence political outcomes in another. This tempers Saxonhouse's assessment of Diodotus's speech as one that positively accommodates political change.[52] While Diodotus may encourage one reexamination of the empire, the Athenian speech on Melos signals a different reconception of the empire's condition, one that combines the ambition behind the invasion of Sicily with fear of a reputation for weakness. Diodotus's speech can no more control this longer prospect than it can prevent the more immediate prospect of the execution of the Mytilene oligarchs under the influence of the relentless Cleon. For all of their prospective advantages over the Corcyrean, Spartan, and Periclean templates, Diodotus's engagements with past and future cannot eliminate the unpredictability and risk of the politics they foster.[53]

In several respects, Thucydides' wider narrative parallels and generalizes his representation of Diodotus's political speech.[54] Like Diodotus, he positions himself between past and future not to perform feats that stimulate longings for renown but to offer guidance that prompts moderation. This is not the moderation imposed by a disciplinary culture or an anxious piety, as for the Spartans, but one resting on a careful reflection on the human condition. This conclusion sheds a somewhat different light on Thucydides' contention that his *logos* will be valuable as a resource forever (*aiei*), as long as human nature is the same.[55] This sense of *aiei* is fundamentally different from its meanings in the rhetorical ploys of the Corcyreans, the ironic naming of the father (Aieimnestos) of the spokesman for the doomed Plataeans, or the anticipatory oration of Pericles. Here *aiei* signals an endless encounter with the dangerous attractions and obsessive motivations that accompany the construction and functioning of political cultures. Thucydides' time horizon is neither a determinate focus set by pragmatic or strategic interests, nor an imagined trajectory into an infinite future where criteria for praise remain strangely permanent. It is, instead, coterminous with the experiences of human beings whose cultural constructions (Hellenism, the barbarians) and political capabilities (the Athenian imperial infrastructure, the Spartan culture of discipline) may change, but whose essential characteristics and dilemmas remain. Consequently, Thucydides' claim about the value of his own *logos* offers neither a bargain nor a doctrine, but an invitation.

For this reason, the value of Thucydides' insights are contingent on their being employed well, a prospect that Thucydides as author can in no way guarantee. The work can only fulfill its promise if the events narrated are remembered in ways the text tries to influence. As any review of Thucydidean interpretations will show, it has been more common to read him as the frank expositor of realism, the first systematic diagnostician of power, or the starkest representative of pessimism.[56] Like Diodotus's speech, Thucydides' text invites an appreciative reflection on its message only by accepting possibilities that its own most fundamental insights will be misapplied.[57] In this respect, Thucydides' *History*, understood as both narrative and practice, engages and reflects the most permanent and inescapable qualities of political life.

Yet if Thucydides' *History* can be read as a source for a certain kind of political activity, what kind? I began these concluding observations on Thucydides' value by recalling a claim about politics made by Hannah Arendt. The prospective character of the political agency to which Thucydides contributes can be sketched by a necessarily brief comparison of his approach with Arendt's. In her treatment of politics in *The Human Condition* she interprets the political realm as that in which human beings discover possibilities for bringing something altogether new into the world (1958, 176–77, 247, 325). Unlike *poiēsis* (making), which relies on rules and produces replications, *praxis* (acting) grows out of creativity and engenders innovation. The internal conditions for this *praxis* are a plurality of agents who reveal their identities through interactive display and a reliable space that makes such interaction possible (220). To construct a stable space that nonetheless encourages innovation, Arendt relies on practices embedded within politics itself: forgiveness and promising (244). Without forgiveness, "our capacity to act would ... be confined to one single deed from which we could never recover; we would remain the victims of its consequences forever."[58] Absent promising, political action would be undercut by "the basic unreliability of men who can never guarantee today what they will be tomorrow, and ... the impossibility of foretelling the consequences of an act within a community of equals where everyone has the same capacity to act" (244). Thus understood, promising and forgiveness enable an agency through which political actors reveal who they really are and a form of speech that plays an essential role in such revelations (186–88).

In suggesting that politics depends on a public space that allows for civic agency, Arendt's perspective opposes both the Corcyrean obsession with strategic competition, because it erodes any possibility for stable public space, and the Spartan reverence for memory, because it frustrates creative agency. Her work intersects more sympathetically with the practices of Pericles. While Diodotus may be the Thucydidean character who mostly closely exhibits the Arendtian courage "to [leave] one's private hiding place and [show] who he is, in displaying and exposing one's self" (186), and while Arendt's political theory is far more than a simple restatement of the Periclean linkage of display with recognition,[59] her allegiances clearly lie with a vision of politics that "teaches man how to bring forth what is great and radiant" (206). In his own complex treatment of Pericles, Thucydides acknowledges the attractions of that vision. Yet his narrative also suggests the need for and possibility of an alternative to a politics of performance that can emerge within political practice itself, particularly within a democratic politics that allows a variety of political speeches and projects. Consequently, Thucydides' treatment of Diodotus's politics both intersects with and challenges the Arendtian perspective. At least five areas of difference stand out.

First, the principal condition for Diodotean politics is not simply plurality among political agents but the pragmatic encounter with wrenching dilemmas. As impressive as Diodotus's appearance as a distinctive political agent may be, the significant question within the narrative concerns how Athens as a political community responds to the Mytilene revolt.[60] Second, the outcome of engaging such dilemmas is not display but appropriate choice. What is at issue in the Mytilene debate is not only the fate of the city's democrats, but also the character of the Athenian regime itself.[61] Thucydides' Diodotus makes clear that the principal political concern lies with what is done and not with the energies and disclosures revealed in the doing.[62] Third, Diodotus values speech not because of its role in self-revelation (cf. Arendt 1958, 175–81), but because of its ability to provide critical distance from more passionate attachments and resentments. Political speech is a critical resource allowing reconsideration of seemingly settled courses of action and a constructive resource allowing the articulation of new political possibilities. Fourth, while Diodotus is in no sense a natural philosopher, his proposals insist that even the most immediately compelling political dilemmas require an attempt to grapple with the realities of human nature. Mytilene's offenses are to be forgotten in light of the more pressing need to remember the flawed character of all human projects and the extenuations that should temper responses to all human injuries. Though Arendt finds human nature inaccessible (1958, 181), Diodotus insists that situations of regime stress, in particular, should draw us to reflections on the basic human characteristics that are shared by all members of the species. Finally, Diodotus's resulting attitude toward the possibilities and risks of politics is not exhilaration at the prospect of "bring[ing] forth what is great and radiant" but the far more modest project of coping with problems that are striking by virtue of their sheer persistence and inevitable reappearance. Though much more clearly needs to be said, these differences suggest that the speech-acts of Diodotus and Thucydides, while less venturesome than the performative displays envisaged by Pericles and Arendt, may also in the end be truer to the character of politics.

Socrates and the Resources for Political Criticism

For all of his range and depth, however, Thucydides does not offer anything close to a positive program for political reform. Plato, in contrast, eagerly proposes sweeping political changes, most notably through Socrates' assertion in the *Republic* that only philosophic kingship will effect a cessation of evils both for the cities and for humankind (473c–e). Yet the overall impression created by such proposals might seem to be the same pessimism that follows Thucydides' dismal assessment of educability. Short of philosophic kingship or other equally radical reforms, evils for cities and humankind will persist.

However, it needs to be remembered that all of Plato's institutional proposals, including those offered by the Eleatic and Athenian strangers in the *Statesman* and the *Laws*, are introduced within particular dramatic contexts and are addressed to particular individuals, suggesting that the pragmatic outcomes of such offerings are conversations about them, not attempts to make them real. Ultimately, the philosophically ruled city in speech in the *Republic* becomes an example or paradigm for creating a city in the soul (592b). By far the majority of the conversations that comprise the Platonic dialogues are less ambitious in envisaging dramatic political change. These involve interactions between Socrates and other named characters, many of whom are known to us from other classical sources (including Thucydides) and most of whom are Athenians.[63] Since so many

Conclusion 253

of these encounters occur within cloistered environments and involve a limited number of participants, we might accept at face value Socrates' contention in the *Apology* (31c–d) that his activities are not political; they address the choices made by individuals, not broad alternative directions for societies. However, many of these conversations also occur against the backdrop or draw upon images of the war and its bracketing political events, the intimidating Athenian empire and the subversion of the democracy by the Thirty. The political cultural circumstances inscribed within the dialogues as well as the political roles and ambitions of so many of the speakers imply that Socrates' reluctance to speak in the assembly or the law courts does not signify disconnection from politics. Socrates' alternative political contributions are more indirect, as he tries to influence the speeches and actions of his interlocutors.

Some have read these influences as antidemocratic, pointing to the activities of interlocutors such as Alcibiades and Critias.[64] However, Socrates' conversations are more often supportive of a political morality compatible with democratic conventions (as in the concluding statements of the *Crito* [54b–e], the *Gorgias* [527c–e], and the *Republic* [621c–d]).[65] And his political advice to his interlocutors is not uniform. He encourages a certain kind of involvement in democratic politics on the part of people such as Adeimantus or Menexenus, while trying, usually without success, to constrain the political activities of dangerous men such as Critias and Callicles. Far from being reactionary, Socrates' speech-acts throughout the dialogues exemplify and call for the thoughtful and critical civic involvement that would challenge both imperial ambitions and authoritarian domestic subversions.

Recently, Dana Villa has gone further and detected in those dialogues that he sees as genuinely Socratic[66] a specific political posture of dissent. This is not what Ober reads as aristocratic dissent challenging democratic power; it is individual moral dissent rooted in the philosophical imperative to avoid injustice (Villa 2001, 24, 58). Focused on the need to protect the soul's integrity, Socratic politics avoids proposals for political structural reform. Indeed, in terms of political structures and actions, Socratic citizenship is almost entirely skeptical and resistant (2001, 58). Insofar as Socratic dissent has a positive purpose or outcome, it lies in encouraging his fellow citizens to consult their individual consciences. (2001, 56).

Villa's portrait of Socratic citizenship reminds us that political philosophy can be something besides offering proposals for radically reformed institutions. Still, there are two ways in which the Platonic position as I have interpreted it would see Villa's Socratic citizenship as problematically incomplete.[67] First, without a more active form of civic involvement, this form of Socratic citizenship may come perilously close to the self-absorbed soul's exclusive concern with its own integrity (cf. Villa 2001, 55). Finding the benefits of Socratic citizenship in the dissemination of a skeptical rationality across a broader spectrum of citizens seems inadequate when decisions need to be made and actions initiated. Thus, even among Socratic apologists, *some* more active citizens must become involved if Socrates' dissenting rationality is to be politically salutary. Villa notes the two examples that Socrates gives in the *Apology* of how he avoided injustice through political resistance: his refusal to be implicated in the judicial murder of Leon of Salamis under the rule of the Thirty and his declining to bring the unconstitutional indictment of the Arginusae generals before the assembly. However, since Socrates' resistance to the Thirty is simply passive, it hardly benefits Leon of Salamis, and within Xenophon's narration (*Hellenica* 1.7) of the Arginusae trial it is left to the more active citizen Euryptolemus to speak assertively (though unsuccessfully) in support of Athens's own democratic procedures. Could this sort of Socratic citizenship play any constructive role in the Mytilene debate?

A simply dissenting Socrates may also obscure the resources and trajectories of critical rationality. Absent some sense of a human good that can be damaged by political assertiveness, the dissidence of the critical citizen seems more agonistic than philosophical. Conversely, the dissident citizen's explaining why certain widely shared views court injustice may lead him or her to more positive discoveries about what it means for a human being to be just and good. This need not be a quest for the essentialist and oppressive foundations that postmodernists fear; it may simply reflect the need to explore more fully the bases and implications of one's critical judgments.

I have tried to argue throughout this book that both of these limitations seem to be acknowledged and countered within a more expanded reading of the Platonic dialogues. Villa is reluctant to draw more general political conclusions from Socrates' critical citizenship because the available alternatives within the dialogues seem to be either the more directive politics of the virtue "expert" or the even more dogmatic rule of the philosopher-king (Villa 2001, 27, 260). Yet once one focuses on the dialogues as interactive dramas, a more diverse range of possibilities emerges. Consequently, I believe it is misleading to see Socrates' activities in (any of) the dialogues as aiming at the simple reproduction of his own skepticism among the Athenians he interrogates. Many of his conversations with influential Athenians would have substantial indirect consequences for the quality of Athens's politics were they to be taken seriously. And his insistence that conversations about justice be framed by an awareness of the importance of the question of the good reflects a sense that political conversations cannot in the end be isolated from broader and deeper human questions. Perhaps one could read the dialogues as revealing the nature of politics, by underscoring both its need for and its resistances to the contributions of critical rationality.

One example arises within Socrates' conversation with Polemarchus in book 1 of the *Republic*. Polemarchus offers what can be seen as a political definition of justice: helping friends and harming enemies (332a–b). Socrates challenges this position on a number of grounds, eventually concluding that it is not proper for the just person to harm anyone (335b). Within this rebuttal, Socrates does not go as far as Diodotus, who seems to resist the urge to call human beings simply good or evil. For Socrates, while we may not know who our friends and enemies are because it is so difficult to sort out the identities of the good and the evil (334c–35a), it is never suggested that goodness and evil do not exist. In fact, by characterizing just human beings as those who harm no one, Socrates offers a clear basis on which the evil may be identified: they are those doing harm. Of course, this Socratic characterization of justice is still subject to considerable unclarity owing to confusions about what helping and harming might mean (cf. *Gorgias* 466b ff.). Yet the most striking implication of Socrates' claim is that it depoliticizes Polemarchus's conception of justice. Insisting on the political establishment of Socrates' understanding of justice as a refusal to harm would make a political community of just people completely vulnerable to the predatory actions of the unjust and render any distinction between just and unjust political harm impossible. While injustice or evil may call philosophically for a thoughtful admonition, it calls politically for hard resolve. The harming of the unjust, through the punishment of criminals or the defeat of aggressors, may be at one level morally suspect but the infliction of harm in such cases is not any the less necessary. In this respect, at least, the conclusion of Socrates' interaction with Polemarchus and the end of Diodotus's speech on Mytilene intersect. For though Diodotus's speech undercuts the bases for calling populations good and evil, it leaves room for acknowledging friends and enemies. That enemies are not evil does not make them into friends. Even though Socrates has insisted that the just must do no harm, he also insists that he and Polemarchus must join together to do battle (*machoumetha*) against, and therefore to harm, those who slander justice (335e).[68] One inference is that while Diodotus warns against the excesses that follow from demonizing others as evil, Socrates reminds us of the problems of eliminating the evil as both a moral and a political category. The need to defend justice reintroduces a harm whose necessity can never be transcended, but whose exercise must therefore be sharply interrogated.[69]

Thucydides and Plato, War and Peace

Thucydides' and Plato's general agreement about the need for and barriers against political rationality occurs against the backdrop of differences whose continued significance reinforces the conclusion that the classical view does not speak with a unified voice about the problems that democratic political communities face. Instead, these works reveal the most important contextualizing questions that extended democratic conversations need to recognize. These concern the promises and ambiguities of human nature, of practical rationality, and of democracy itself. Ultimately, these differences converge on the even more fundamental question of whether the human condition is best understood within the context of war or peace, motion or rest.[70] Political reflections on all of these questions are often discouraged by the forms of modern political theory considered here. The questions themselves seem to imply an epistemically suspect essentialism, the most important answers seem settled, or the lines of inquiry seem to invite comprehensive and potentially domineering discourses that threaten democratic politics. That an interactive reading of Thucydides and Plato can refocus their audiences on the continued importance of these questions identifies a final way in which such readings can beneficially stretch the limits of democracy.

The first difference between Thucydides and Plato concerns the content and function of what both authors call "nature." I have argued that Thucydides has a very different view of nature than that offered by his characters who claim that nature mandates the control of the weaker by the stronger. Yet Thucydides does not offer the contrasting view that nature is an ordering of things for the best. The appropriate framework or metaphor for Thucydidean nature is neither a physics of power nor a teleology of flourishing. Instead, Thucydidean nature is turbulence and disorder where notions of strength and weakness have no stable meanings and where the best conditions are often those that are most quickly overwhelmed (cf. 3.83.3–4, 2.51.5–6). Nature thus sets no positive standard for politics or culture. The depressingly rare successes of convention occur when politics is able to exclude or diminish natural intrusions.

Plato, however, continually insists on the importance of understanding nature as a guide for assessing the merits and deficiencies of political and cultural arrangements (cf. *Republic* 453b; *Gorgias* 489a–b; *Phaedo* 98a–b). Numerous commentators have of course suggested that he can only reach this vantage point by denying or surpassing the experienced world, where horrors and cruelties abound (cf. de Romilly 1963, 362, 365; Crane 1998, 324–25). Yet such Platonic movement beyond the empirical world is always conditioned and bounded by experiences within that world. The ideas are introduced in books 6 and 7 of the *Republic* not to move beyond the world, but to enable partial and provisional attempts to clarify it (533a). Socrates' positing the idea of the good as the primary cause of both knowability and knowledge grows out of a human need to become clearer about the pragmatic good and a consequent dissatisfaction with the guidance supplied by preference or convention. "And if we don't know [the idea of the good], without it, even if we should have the most knowledge of the rest, there is no profit to us, just as there would be none in possessing something without the good" (505a). That reflections on nature, understood most broadly as the horizon that surrounds and limits human beings, are essential to political thought is reaffirmed, though how access to nature is to be gained and the precise benefits that such access can provide are matters for continued inquiry.

Consequently, Thucydides' and Plato's differences over nature seem consistent with their more pragmatic differences over the practice of *logos*. Thucydides partners his own assessment of nature with the observation that war, the most violent teacher, reveals something fundamental about human beings, tendencies that peaceful circumstances may dangerously obscure. Thucydides' contention thus seems to be that the human condition is clearest under the harshest stress. What this harshness reveals are the destructive influences of the love of gain and honor. In the face of these influences, *logos* loses much of its capacity to serve as a constructive resource for human practice and is instead always in danger of being instrumentalized within contests over power. Plato, in contrast, discovers something more promising in the human capacity for *logos* itself. Indeed, the ideas, generally, and the idea of the good, particularly, seem to be conditions inferred from the need to enable meaningful discourse. In declining to provide Glaucon with an exact account of the power, forms, and ways of a dialectic that can articulate the precise structure of the knowable, Socrates comments, "Whether it really is so or not can no longer be affirmed confidently. But that there is some such thing to see must be affirmed" (533a).

Since the richest political contextualization for the human capacity for *logos* is democracy, these differences between Thucydides and Plato also connect with different assessments of and engagements with democratic regimes.[71] These differences are imaged by the relations that the dramatic voices closest to their own, Diodotus and Socrates, bear to the Athenian political culture. While Socrates is generally the destabilizing gadfly, he is positively connected to the discursive opinions of the culture in a way that Diodotus is not (cf. *Phaedrus* 230d–e). While Diodotus is perhaps too frank about the ways in which democratic institutions obstruct possibilities for the discursiveness that is so desperately needed, he is himself generally silent about the ways in which democratic culture might contribute resources for rationality's development and influence. Does Thucydides see these insights as gifts from Zeus as well? Or might we imagine a conversation between the citizens Socrates and Diodotus that would provide a resource, both more philosophical and more democratic, for the Mytilene debate?[72]

At first blush, these differences over nature, rationality, and democracy might seem to cohere around the more basic conclusion as to whether war or peace is more definitive of the human condition. The turbulence of nature, the futility of rationality, and the pathologies of democracy are crystal clear to those instructed by the most violent of teachers (cf. 3.82.2). Conversely, nature's serving as a standard for practice, rationality's promise to make life more intelligible and more decent, and democracy's educational possibilities can be illuminated in an environment of greater leisure and civility. Must we, after all, endorse Nietzsche's interpretation in *Twilight of the Idols* that Thucydides and Plato diverge fundamentally because of their different postures toward the violent or peaceful character of the relevant lifeworld?

Throughout this book I have suggested that this broadly Nietzschean interpretation is wrong. Of course Thucydides finds this greatest war as the deed most worthy of being spoken about. And this focus on war may indeed distort as well as enable many of Thucydides' discoveries. But here, too, his indefinite time horizon complicates things. His narrative makes the truths revealed by war accessible to those who may be at war, at peace, or somewhere in between.[73] Where those truths are seen by those at peace or in between, Thucydides completes a picture of the human condition that requires an awareness of war without necessarily requiring the direct experience of war. To this extent, Thucydides' narrative may bridge war and peace in way that attempts to overcome the distortions of each, appealing, a bit like Diodotus's *logos*, to pity and a love of speeches in a way that hopes for reasonableness. In this respect, Thucydides writes, at least at times, not in the mode of Derrida's *perhaps*, but *as if* something more stable were possible, even as he recognizes the overwhelming forces that make such hopefulness suspect.[74] Read this way, his concerns intersect more closely with those Platonic dialogues that inscribe the events of war within their drama even as the dramas themselves revolve around the activity of discourse. Within representations of a human experience that is both violent and thoughtful, Plato discovers possibilities that Thucydides acknowledges but does not fully explore, while continuing to confirm the reality of the world that Thucydides knows only too well. As Socrates will tell a future casualty of another future war, "You are beautiful and not . . . ugly, Theaetetus, for one who speaks beautifully (*kalōs*) is beautiful and good" (*Theaetetus* 185e).

To this extent, Thucydides and Plato, read separately, but more intriguingly together, challenge the simplicity of the still powerful oppositional perspectives of Hobbes and Nietzsche, two of Thucydides' greatest admirers and two of Plato's most important opponents in modernity and beyond. Hobbes's dominant metaphor is condensed in his first law of nature—to seek peace and follow it (*Leviathan* 14.4)— a conclusion supported by both the theorems of moral science and the urgings of our deepest inclinations. His consequent political theory envisages an institutional environment supportive of peace, "designed to live as long as mankind, or as the laws of nature, or as justice itself" (29.1).[75] Nietzsche's dominant metaphor is war, applicable at least as much to turbulence within oneself as to any conflict between nations or across political cultural classes (Nietzsche 1966, 204). His politics is inevitably a politics of unending contention between coercion and overcoming.[76] For Thucydides and Plato, both metaphors are partial, and the political consequences of each are misleading. Peace is never complete, and wars are not constant. In a world positioned always between motion and rest, the conversations of those who acknowledge the continued and fluctuating presence of both conditions, albeit with differing degrees of emphasis, must be ongoing. In this light, providing resources for citizens who find themselves so positioned is a project of greater usefulness and nobility than confidently crafting permanent institutional arrangements or courageously accepting ceaseless contestation.

Notes

Chapter One: Political Space and Political Purpose in Contemporary Democratic Theory

1. See, for example, Caldeira 2000, 51–52; Bermeo 2003, 252–56; Putnam 1993, 182–83.

2. See, for example, arguments that substantial improvements within global political relations require creating political forms that enable democratic decision-making on a more cosmopolitan or denationalized scale (Benhabib 2004, 213–21; Gould 2004, chap. 7; Held 2004 chap. 6; Honig 2001, 102–3).

3. As Shapiro (2003, 1) comments, "The democratic idea is close to non-negotiable in today's world."

4. Habermas is inclined to take seriously only those social analyses cognizant of the differentiated structure of modern societies (1996, 106–7) and only those epistemological perspectives that reflect what he calls a postmetaphysical mode of thought (1996, 443–44; 1979, 201). See also Warren 2001, 5–7; and Benhabib 2004, 129–30.

5. An assessment made by both friendly and critical commentators. As an example of the former, see Strauss 1964, 238; and 1989, 97. As an example of the latter, see Wood and Wood 1978, 64, 111, 121–28; and Ober 1998, 9–10. For interpretations more sympathetic to Thucydides' and Plato's democratic involvements, see, for example, Euben 1990, 198–201, 236–37; Euben 1997, 78–90; Mara 1997, 258–59; Mara 2001, 821–45; Mara 2003, 739–58; Saxonhouse 1996, 78–79, 113–14; and Saxonhouse 2006, chaps. 7 and 8.

6. Reconstructed readings develop a text's implications for questions that may not have been part of the author's original concerns. Yet these readings still need to conform to standards regarding the use of evidence and the construction of arguments. In this respect, reconstructive readings can also be guides to deeper discoveries about the texts. This is what makes them reconstructive rather than creative. For a general discussion of reconstructive interpretations, see Habermas 1990, 21–42.

7. On the undermining and overriding of normative political arguments, see Taylor 1967, 38–39.

8. As reaffirmed recently by Mark Warren (2001, 91).

9. Cf. Cohen and Arato 1992, 385–86; Gould 2004, 128–29; Habermas 1996, 133–34; Kymlicka 1995, 163–70; Wallach 2004, 132.

10. For example, Gould 2004, 124–25; and Sanjek 1998, 368–69.

11. Cf. Jean Cohen 1999, 228–39. Warren addresses this by drawing on the sociological distinction between manifest and latent functions (2001, 37). A church's or religion's manifest function may be to establish its own moral authority over its members, but it may also include latent functions (teaching organizational or verbals skills or introducing moral issues into public discourse) more conducive to strong democracy. Yet determining the relevant weight to be given to manifest versus latent functions—or, indeed, identifying latent functions themselves—presupposes a prior perspective on the strengths and vulnerabilities of democratic society. By declining to see the effective functioning of democratic procedures as a sufficient guarantee of the rightness of decision, religious discourse may have the additional latent function of encouraging a critical posture toward some outcomes of democratic deliberation.

12. The foundational statements of the postmaterialist thesis have been provided by Ronald Inglehart. His earlier (1977, 12–18) confidence that the development of identifiable postmaterialist values (less concern with accumulation and more with self-development and effective political agency) is a predictable outcome of long periods of material security and political peace has given way to less-definite hypotheses about what exactly is valued postmaterially (1990, 5–7, 152–53; 1997, 33–39).

13. See Sen and Nussbaum 1993, 1–2, 30–32, 40–42.

14. I take this to be one of Warren's (2001, 52) central claims as well.

15. As noted by Cohen and Arato 1992, 8–10; Habermas 1996, 99–111; Richardson 2001, 8–12; Rosenblum 1998, 36–46; and Warren 2001, 21–29.

16. Though for good illustrations of the dialectical connections see Habermas 1996, 333–41; Shapiro 2003, 21–22; and Warren 1999, 335–36.

17. Recognizing that there are at least as many differences as similarities between deliberative democratic theory and communitarianism. See (e.g.) Warren's criticisms (2001, 22–24) of Michael Walzer and Michael Sandel, as well as his general distinction between associations and communities (2001, 43–48).

18. Particularly with respect to the social construction of the self and the centrality of power relations within both social and epistemic forms. Cf. Foucault 1979, 29–30; 1984b, 83–85.

19. Salkever 1990, 57–60. On the dialogic aspects of Aristotle's mode of discourse, see Mara 1995, 280–303; Mara 1998, 301–29; and Tessitore 1996, 9–23.

20. For example, the reconstructive treatments of democratic regimes in *Politics* 4.4 and 6.1–8 have no obvious parallels in either Plato or Thucydides.

21. A caution reinforced by Williams's point that a good bit of the "modern world was European creation presided over by the Greek past" (1993, 3).

22. On the parallel functions of focus and exclusion within social theory, see Taylor 1967.

23. The most sustained and sophisticated statement of this case has probably been made by Salkever 1990. See also Williams 1993, 7–8.

24. Cf. Mara 1997, 102–3.

25. Even historically, this endorsement can also be read as more provocative than conclusive. On the basis of remarks by Thucydides (8.89.2–3, 8.92.11, 8.93.1–2, 8.97.1–3) and Aristotle (*Ath Pol* 41.2–3), it appears that this regime existed only for a brief period.

26. For example, Rawls's conception of primary goods (those things we want regardless of what else we want) are not as noncontroversial as they first appear (1971, 62–63, 440–41). Habermas and the deliberative democrats, generally, begin from the ethical privileging of a life of individual autonomy (Habermas 1996, 42–43; and Warren 2001, 62–63). And Connolly (1990, 82–83) favors a politics that allows for a continued challenging of settled meanings on the basis of an express thesis about the good life ("one in which creative tension is generated between the claims of individuality and commonality").

27. Cf. *Nicomachean Ethics* 1.9.

28. Compare Rawls 1971, 325–32 with *Nicomachean Ethics* 2.6 and *Republic* 618b–19b. Rawls sees Aristotle softening Nietzsche's severe perfectionism by recognizing competing goods to be balanced by intuition. For Aristotle, though, what is the extreme from the point of view of excellence and the good is the mean for us, as individuals.

29. The Aristotelian and Platonic understandings of virtue often seem far more definite in what they oppose than in what they affirm. In a striking number of cases they oppose the moral valorizations of the Athenian or Hellenic elites.

30. As suggested by (for example) Morrison 2006, 175–79 and Yunis 2003, 189–212.

31. This both reflects and extends Butler's (1997a, 157–63) understanding of how performance enables action by breaking with surrounding contexts. Here performance redeems the possibility of action not by contradicting attempts to establish linguistic hegemony (through "subversive resignification"), but by redeeming prospects that are explicitly denied (restorative resignification).

32. At one level, Thucydides' book must be read as a history. Yet his concerns are not fully captured if we evaluate him according to the criteria of the modern discipline of history, as Kagan (1969, 373–74) does. Beyond providing a narrative and explanatory account of the events, Thucydides also offers guidance on how human beings might respond to events such as these should they recur. We might well agree with Williams (2002, 161–71) that Thucydides discovered historical time and yet contend that what he says about the events that occurred within that time goes beyond what we now expect from historians and that, *pace* Kagan, these additional intellectual activities are strengths, not weaknesses. In Greek, *historia* is simply investigation.

33. Paralleling the assessment recently offered by Morrison (2006, 4).

34. Cf. Strauss 1964, 228; Orwin 1994, 205; and Yunis 2003, 211.

35. Hobbes 1975, 25.

36. For some critics, Strauss's interpretation tells us more about Strauss than it does about Plato. Holmes (1993) assails Strauss's alleged elitism as one of the cornerstones of antiliberal thought. While Shadia Drury (1988, 194–95) sees Strauss's separation of the philosophic from the vulgar as an elitism that is compatible with a certain kind of democracy, she indicts Strauss for what she

sees as his exempting philosophers from normal requirements of political decency (Drury 1988, 194–97). My concern is not to assess the merits of these judgments about Strauss (a project executed thoroughly and convincingly by Zuckert and Zuckert 2006), but to determine whether an acceptance of Strauss's approach to reading Plato requires an endorsement of Strauss's substantive conclusions, whatever they may be.

37. See also Wood and Wood 1978, 64, 111, 121–28; Crane 1996, 256–58; and Crane 1998, 324–25.

38. In this respect, Craig's assessment of Plato's sensitivity to multiple audiences is perhaps more nuanced than Strauss's: "[I]n saying the same thing to one and all [Socratic irony] implicitly acknowledges their common humanity, allowing everyone without personal prejudice an equal opportunity to make of the words what they will" (1994, xxxii).

39. For particulars, see Benardete 1991, 7–8.

40. As Wallach also notes, the Platonic dialogues "[transcend] the conventional boundaries between text and context" (2001, 42). For Wallach, too, the dialogues respond to the particular problems that Plato saw afflicting democratic Athens in part by inscribing and transforming the history within the texts (2001, 39, 49, 81).

41. Thus, I would go further than Wallach in employing this inscribed history within interpretations of the texts. Critias's and Charmides' directive roles within the Thirty suggest that the "political representation of sōphrosynē in the *Charmides*" may in fact be consistent with "a radically restructured society" (Wallach 2001, 138). For assessments closer to mine, see Brann 2004 and Hyland 1981, 22–23, 147.

42. This reading may also qualify Wallach's critical assessment of the supposedly nonpolitical interpretation of the *Republic* offered by Strauss and some of his students (Wallach 2001, 31).

43. Understanding *erga* may not be the same as controlling them. At times, Parry (1981, 182–83) suggests that Thucydides treats these purposes as identical. While this may be true for the Thucydidean Pericles, it may be less accurate as an account of Thucydides' own view. Williams's allusive but undeveloped suggestion (1993, 161) seems closer to my interpretation.

44. Parry's (1981) systematic effort to trace the pattern of the *logos* and *ergon* distinction in Thucydides reinforces the sense that the categories are not easily susceptible to clear differentiation. Price's questions (2001, 74–75) about Thucydides' reasons for adopting different methodologies for the two spheres are, if anything, intensified by these ambiguities. For a reading that treats the categories *logos* and *ergon* as more stable, see Hunter 1973, 180.

45. As in Forde 1989, 119–21. The speech of the oligarchic conspirator Peisandros urges a kind of moderation on the city (Forde 1989, 119, 141). Ober might interpret this as an indication of the incompatibility of moderation with democratic speech. Yet one also needs to read this speech remembering that "moderate aristocracy" is said (Thucydides 3.82.8) to be a slogan used by oligarchies in the pursuit of power. Virtually every word Peisandros says is a

lie. Groundwork for the speech has been laid by assassination (8.65.2) and the circulation of a rumor that misrepresents oligarchic ambitions (8.65.3). Success is followed by a reign of violence and suspicion reinforced by the silence of political criticism (8.66.3–5). For Forde (1989, 140–41), subsequent events represent a degeneration of the oligarchy. For Connor (1984, 225–26) the eventual conduct of the oligarchs reveals the corruption infecting oligarchy from the beginning. I am inclined to agree more with Connor. See also Saxonhouse 2006, 45.

46. At the same time, Thucydides uses this occasion to comment on Alcibiades' singular service to Athens, thus setting this against Alciabiades' other, more spectacular achievements. In this case, Alcibiades is praised as a peacemaker, and the grounds of praise are refigured.

47. Cf. Debnar 2001, 1. Butler (1997a, 44), following Austin, distinguishes between perlocutionary and illocutionary speech-acts, where the former are separable from the action done, while the latter are themselves the acts or accomplish action in transitive ways (as enactments) rather than in instrumental ways (as means). As she indicates, the distinction is not always stable. Thucydides' narrative reinforces the complexities and instabilities of these categories.

48. Even here there are differences and complexities. In Butler's terms, the pragmatics of Diodotus's speech are instrumental, while the speech of the Melians is much more enactment. Yet Diodotus's speech also enacts the complex kind of speech that is needed, given the condition of Athenian democratic institutions at this particular point in its political history. And the Melians' deficiency may lie in part in the failure to see the consequences of defiance. In this respect, the way we interpret speech-acts may be extended to include disclosures of the complex and often contradictory characteristics of individuals and cultures.

49. As in Crane 1996, 75.

50. In this respect, I disagree with the views of (for example) Parry (1981, 180–81) and numerous others (Edmunds 1975, 52–53; Euben 1990, 191; Farrar 1988, 158–59; Ober 1998, 94; Price 2001, 237–29; Wohl 2002, 70–72; and Yunis 1996, 67) who construe Thucydides' *logos* as a higher-order affirmation of Periclean leadership.

51. This parallels and, I think, reinforces Saxonhouse's provocative contention (2004, 64–66; 2006, 149) that Thucydides' historical treatment of the facts (that come to his attention only through ambiguous and conflicting speeches) mirrors practices in the democratic assembly.

52. Contra Crane 1996, 22–23. Wohl (2002, 39) focuses as well on "the [funeral] speech's hegemonic dynamic . . . that allows no retort." I depart from Wohl's view in two respects. First, I suggest that the excluded voices are not only those of class and gender but also those (potentially undifferentiated by external markers) that offer different articulations of Athens's good. Second, I disagree that Pericles' dramatic voice is identical to Thucydides' authorial voice.

53. Thus, I agree with Strauss's assessment (1964, 231) that "Diodotus' speech reveals more of Thucydides himself than any other speech." See also Orwin 1994, 204–6; and Saxonhouse 2006, 214. My view of exactly what is revealed is closest to Saxonhouse's.

Chapter Two: The Borders of Rational Choice

1. Cf. Rawls 1971, 11–17.

2. The rational choice framework encloses two broad projects. Within the first, rationality is represented by axioms that are said to follow from stipulated motivational and situational premises. In this respect, rationality is a positive construction that generates hypotheses that can be tested empirically, as in Downs (1957, 295–300), Riker (1962, 4, 23), or Waltz (1979, 13–17). The second direction interprets empirical political events to discover how they can be explained by reconstructions of the rational choices of political agents (as in Hardin 1995, 11, 16–17; Chong 1991, 1–3; and Chong 2000, chap. 5). I do not draw a systematic distinction between these two projects in this chapter, in part because their shared premises seem at least as important as their different realms of application. There is also work such as Chong's (1991, 2000) that encompasses both.

3. Thus, Riker (1980a, 432) chooses to characterize practical ends as values, opinions, or tastes. This makes it easier to analyze practical ends solely in terms of utility functions.

4. In Riker's (1962, 21–22) view, winning rather than losing; in Brams's (1980, 5), better rather than worse outcomes.

5. Cf. Downs 1957, 296–300; Riker 1962, 47; Ordeshook 1980, 449; and Chong 1996, 44. For a pointed emphasis on the need for empirical confirmation, see Chong 2000, 64–65.

6. In later work, Riker (1980a, 443) despairs of the possibility of prediction in the social sciences absent the identification of political equilibria. He softens this claim in his response to critics (1980b, 457) by expressing skepticism about equilibria of outcomes while retaining cautious confidence in equilibria of processes.

7. For Downs, equilibrium emerges from the tendencies of policy proposals to overlap in two-party systems (1957, 297). For Riker, equilibrium is reached through the creation of the smallest possible winning coalition (1962, 33). For Putnam, the social contexts for cooperation in northern Italy and for mistrust in the southern area constitute two stable social equilibria that are reinforced by predictable behaviors of dramatically different kinds (1993, 177).

8. Chong's careful and interesting defense of the rational choice model is nonetheless flawed by its casual reduction of rationality to the instrumental calculation of economic agents (2000, 4, 175, 184, 231). Riker (1980a) comes close to equating rationality with predictability, the alternatives to which are "tricks and accidents" (443). See also Ordeshook 1980, 447. For skepticism regarding the equation of rational choice's explanatory power with its predictive capabilities, see Friedman 1996, 18.

9. A critique made, for example, by Sen 1999, 265–69.

10. By contrast, Riker's understanding of rationality as the desire to win suggests that the most rational political agent or leader is the opportunist (1962, 208).

11. Cf. Axelrod 1997, 5: "The real advantage of the rational choice assumption is that it often allows deduction." What is often deduced are substantive and

therefore normally controversial conclusions about human goods. Riker 1962, 22: "Politically rational man is the man who would rather win than lose regardless of the particular stakes." Downs 1957, 296: "Party members have as their chief motivation the desire to obtain the intrinsic rewards of holding office; therefore they formulate policies as means to holding office rather than seeking office in order to carry out preconceived policies."

12. As in Riker's "size principle": "In social situations similar to n-person, zero-sum games with side payments, participants create coalitions just as large as they believe will ensure winning and no larger" (1962, 32). In political environments not informed by Riker's transactional assumptions, a rational strategy for coalition formation would look very different.

13. Only partially captured in Hardin's observation that "our sunk costs are us" (1995, 15–17) See also Chong 2000, 52–53.

14. Chong's model presumes an initial neutrality (2000, 78) with respect to dispositions (enduring personal characteristics "that often guide choices" [2000, 46]). At one level, this parallels Geertz's contention that human behavior is "extremely plastic" (1973, 216). But neutrality and plasticity are not the same, for neutrality presumes a stable if uncommitted identity ready to be extended in determinate directions as instrumental calculation speaks, whereas plasticity presumes a much greater degree of malleability in the constitution of rationality itself.

15. In Axelrod's more recent work, he therefore separates rational agents from adaptive agents (1997, 153), implying that rational choice theory cannot accommodate the endogeneity or dynamics of needs and interests. Perhaps this is due to the destabilization that dynamic interests would introduce into the theory's deductive power (1997, 4). Axelrod's replacement of rationality with adaptation illustrates how the rejection of rational choice theory in favor of some sort of attention to culture (1997, 151) can create a framework dismissive of the importance of examining how rationality intersects with politics. Adaptive agents follow "simple rules about giving and receiving influence." Since they do not necessarily engage in rational calculation, these agents "simply adapt to their environment" (1997, 155). See also Axelrod 1997, 146–47.

16. A case that could be strengthened at least rhetorically by Hardin's (1995, 177–78) and Chong's (2000, 230–31) endorsement of rational choice on the basis of what the manipulation of incentives can accomplish.

17. This forms part of the basis of McCarthy's critique (1990, 445) of Foucault.

18. Illustrated also by Green and Shapiro's offering explanations based on "normative, cultural, psychological and institutional" phenomena as alternatives to explanations based on rationality (1994, 184). Chong, likewise, sees appeals to symbolic politics as denials of the role of rationality. Chong insists that an effective political science will need "to reserve a central place for rational action" (1996, 37) or "rational lives." In light of this imperative, rational choice's incapacity to deal fully with rationality becomes more, not less, problematic.

19. Or lamenting political science's inability to do so, as in Riker 1980a, 444: "In the earlier tradition of studying constitutions it was customary to look

for the centers of power in a constitutional structure.... That is, of course, an interesting practical question for the world, because it concerns the distribution of 'power.' But while such distributions are a fascinating subject for ideologues and inside dopesters, they are not of much scientific interest because the idea of power is itself an inexact and probably meaningless notion."

20. Axelrod's more recent work goes, if anything, further in this direction as he moves from game theory to computer simulation (1997, 3).

21. On the significance of *gnōmē* as used by Thucydides, see (for example) Parry 1981, 13; Farrar 1988, 155–56, 158–69; and Price 2001, 24–25. I endorse Price's observation that the word's significance is not simply cognitive; it embraces "thought, judgment, purpose" and so designates not simply a way of thinking or speaking, but also a way of being. Its "other" is a way of being informed by *orgē*, not simply anger, but passion, turbulence, and eroticism (as in Farrar 1988, 156; and Allen 2000, 138–40).

22. For the challenges of verifying rational choice explanations via observation, along with a confidence that such challenges can be met, see Chong 2000, 27–30; 64–65. For a critique of the possibility of verifying rational choice explanations through the observation of behavior, see Ross 1993, 48.

23. Thucydides distinguishes (1.23.6) between the "truest causes" of the war, Athenian greatness and Spartan fear, and those most openly spoken about. This is not to suggest that those most openly spoken about are pretexts. Rather, the causes most openly spoken about are only fully intelligible in light of the influence of the truest causes.

24. E.g., Price 2001, 83; and Orwin 1994, 38–39.

25. So, the first condition for trust is having common enemies (Thucydides 1.35.5).

26. Cf. Orwin 1994, 39; and Crane 1998, 107.

27. Cf. Price 2001, 65; and Balot 2001, 138.

28. In this respect, Euphemus's speech can be said to focus on the motives or forces of fear and interest. What is notably absent is the concern for honor, central to the speech given (in book 1) by the unnamed Athenians in Sparta (1.75.3, 1.76.2) and constitutive of Pericles' conception of Athens's good (1.144.3, 2.43.2–4, 2.64.5–6).

29. For an illuminating, though very different, interpretation of Euphemus's speech, see Forde 1989, 61–66.

30. Orwin suggests that this sense of power reveals a parallel Athenian weakness (1994, 129). In this respect, Euphemus's speech has affinities with the claims made by the ambassadors to Melos.

31. Cf. Lattimore 1998, 346, note to 6.81–87.

32. See Price 2001, 143.

33. This sense of necessity bears some resemblance to what Williams (1993, 103) characterizes as an internal necessity, though the implications I draw are somewhat different.

34. Though both Mytilene and Scione were subject cities, while Melos was not. Perhaps for this reason, the Athenians justify their aggression against the Melians in terms of the need to maintain the reputation for their capacity

to coerce among the increasingly restive "allies." In this respect, the empire is treated as something that is in principle boundless and yet continuously vulnerable.

35. Noted as well by Morrison 2006, 83.

36. Clearly, the best outcome for the Athenians (securing Melos's submission without even having to insist) is the worst for the Melians (submission without even being threatened) and vice versa. In this respect, the game is one of total conflict (cf. Brams 1980, 17), yet it is not strictly speaking zero-sum, since what either winner wins is not identical to what each loser loses. However, the outcome that is actually reached (the Athenians attempting to impose dominion by force and the Melians resisting) is in the end rational according to the templates of rational choice. Given their preference ordering, it is in Melos's perceived interest to resist becoming part of Athens's empire, whether Athens moves to impose itself forcibly or not. In this respect, nonsubmission is a dominant strategy for Melos, while the Athenian strategy (attempt to impose dominion or not) depends on their anticipation of Melos's actions. If the Melians are expected to respond to Athenian deference by voluntarily requesting to become one of the subject cities, this is Athens's best outcome. Yet once the Athenians recognize that the Melians will not submit regardless of what Athens does, they will, as rational actors, choose to demand submission, since this decision results in the more preferred Athenian outcome. Together, "impose" and "resist" are the rational outcomes.

37. In a sense, the Melians attempt to initiate a new game in which they have the first move; they hope to force the Athenians to reconsider their preference ordering in light of Melian resistance. This is also an attempt to change the game from one of total conflict to one of partial cooperation, where the two sides can converse about how the benefits of cooperation can be distributed. The Athenians refuse this offer and insist on a repeat playing of the first game.

38. Cf. Morrison, 2006, 92.

39. In game-theoretic terms, the Melians see themselves as playing parallel two-person games with the gods and the Spartans. Because the Melians believe that it would be rational for one or both of these sources to provide assistance (otherwise the gods' influence is undercut and the Spartans' reputation as liberators is compromised) as long as Melos continues to play its ascribed role within that morally ordered universe, continued resistance to the Athenians is rational.

40. Cf. Ross 1993, 26.

41. Compare with Pouncey (1980, 143) on the influence of individuals.

42. The Athenians thus counter with their own parallel game between them and the subject cities. The Athenians anticipate that the subject cities will follow a contingent strategy of continuing to defer to Athenian domination or venturing defections, depending on Athens's apparent strength or weakness. To this extent, the Athenian decision to subjugate Melos is contingent on Athens's expectations regarding the strategies of the subject cities. Since Athens expects that either acceptance of Melian neutrality or withdrawal in the face of Melian resistance will be seen by the subject cities as weakness, harshness is the rational choice.

43. See Wohl's observation that Athenian "freedom breeds its own necessity" (2002, 184).

44. "The Athenian arguments on Melos are thus just as ideological as the Spartans' claims to virtue" (Crane 1998, 291). One can extend this to a broader conception of political imagination. The Athenians imply that the sense of fear is connected with the regime's imperial identity. The same point is underscored in Alcibiades' speech on Sicily at 6.18.6–7.

45. See Palmer's comment (1992, 70): "What the Athenians believe they know about men determines what they believe about the gods."

46. This chapter has been identified by numerous commentators as spurious (see Smith 1962–88, 3:150–51 n. 1; and Lattimore 1998, 171 nn. 3–84). Connor (1984, 102 n. 60) sees this as a surviving portion of an earlier draft and considers it—rightly, I think—to be quintessentially Thucydidean in spirit. It is hardly in tension with the remarks on human nature in 3.82.

47. Cf. Price 2001, 27.

48. Lattimore (1998, 301, note to 5.116) sees the name and patronym of the commanding general as a coincidence that Thucydides emphasizes for its political-cultural significance. This may also be an instance of Thucydides constructing characters for his own authorial purposes. There is apparently no historical information on Philocrates' identity (Gomme, Andrewes, and Dover 1970, 189).

49. As several commentators (Strauss 1964, 184 n. 53; Palmer 1992, 73; Orwin 1994, 112–13) note, there is no necessary connection between what is done and what is said. Yet if Thucydides' naming of the Athenian commander is thematically significant, he may suggest that the speeches and the deeds on Melos are more intimately integrated with Athens's political cultural identity.

50. Cf. Orwin 1994, 109–11 on the ambiguities involved in linking the two disasters.

51. Paralleled in Thucydides' own comments reflecting on the hasty enthusiasm for defection among the subject cities after Brasidas's successes in the north. He notes that human beings are all too eager to reject inconvenient facts at the direction of *logismō autokratoi*. Though not strictly literal, Crawley's ([1910] 1993, 232) translation, "sovereign reason," communicates the irony wonderfully. Here reason is anything but sovereign.

52. Rational choice theory's use of terms such as "values," "tastes," and "preferences" (Riker 1980a, 432) both reinforces and legitimates this resistance.

53. The contradictory character of Cleon's speech is highlighted (for example) by Wohl 2002, 97. My explanation for how his rhetoric is crafted to avoid contradiction is different, as is my assessment of the democratic character of Cleon's speech.

54. To this extent, Cleon's "[u]nwillingness to consider rational factors as motivating human action" (Price 2001, 93) is rooted in a deeper acceptance of certain irrational imperatives.

55. Cleon thus assumes the role of a democratic orator by reversing the valuational tropes that normally function to privilege the few over the many. Nicely noted as well by Wohl 2002, 118.

56. In this respect, Cleon employs the strategy traced by Ober (1989, 93), both taming and employing qualities of distinction by placing them in the service of the *dēmos*. Yet Cleon's ultimate purpose is to silence democratic speech. In this respect, I disagree with Wohl's (very interesting) interpretation that reads (2002, 95) Cleon's appeal as an attempt to foster active listening among the audience. Any activity that is elicited is to be subordinated to Cleon's own immediate purposes.

57. Kagan 1974, 157–58; Farrar 1988, 169–70; Ober 1998, 96; Orwin 1994, 20–22; Palmer 1992, 61; and Pouncey 1980, 100–2.

58. Suggested, for example, by Crane 1996, 232–33; Johnson 1993, 102–3; and Orwin 1994, 144.

59. Cf. Saxonhouse 2006, 155.

60. Cf. Orwin 1984, 315.

61. A connection noted also by Price 2001, 94.

62. See also Zumbrunnen 2002, 567–69.

63. Thus, Johnson (1993, 104–7); and White (1984, 75–76).

64. Consequently, I see more room for justice in Diodotus's account than do Ober (1998, 102–3), Price (2001, 99), or White (1984, 75–76). I also question whether Diodotus's explicit argument from interest and the potential argument from justice necessarily diverge as in Johnson's (1993, 108–9) reading. Views much closer to my own are those of Strauss (1964, 233), Orwin (1994, 152–53); and Saxonhouse (2006, 160–61).

65. Morrison (2006, 112–13, 130) approaches this conclusion when he points to Thucydides' strategy of analogizing cities and individuals as providing a framework for interpolis relations that depends on interactions not characterized by force. But he does not go further to consider whether his model of individual interaction might hold only within certain kinds of communities.

66. This goes further than Orwin 1994, 157–58, but it is in the same spirit. Zumbrunnen's (2002, 579) and Saxonhouse's (2006, 161) views are perhaps closer to mine.

67. See also Euben 1997, 233.

68. Perhaps a particular illustration of the broader methodological observations of Balot (2001, 179–80).

69. Cf. Mara 1997, 99–102. Again, differing from Wallach 2001, 138. For a view much closer to my own, see Brann 2004, 66–87.

70. For interpretations that this is in fact the (early) Platonic position, see Nussbaum (2001, 110–11, 117) and Irwin (1977, 106–7). For views that are less certain, consider Coby 1987, 157; Euben 1997, 258–60; Mara 1997, 65–74; Mara 1988, 486–87; Weingartner 1973, 121, and Wolz 1981, 154–56.

71. The importance of education as a general theme in the dialogue is suggested by (among others) Bartlett, 2004, 87–89; Coby 1987, 172–75; Euben 1997, chap. 9; Weingartner 1973, 45–47; and Wolz 1981, chap. 5.

72. Perhaps because he is aware of the Sophists' shady reputations but perhaps also because the Sophists are insufficiently active. For a fuller treatment of the implications of Hippocrates' blushing at the prospects of becoming a Sophist himself, see Saxonhouse 2006, 183–84.

73. Suggested in different ways by Bartlett 2004, 67–68; Coby 1987, 23–24; Weingartner 1973, 46; and Mara 1997, 41, 43.

74. A goal that Nussbaum (2001, 103) ascribes to Protagoras.

75. See Mara 1997, 103–6.

76. Noted as well by Weiss 2006, 38–41.

77. Whose presence and significance is noted as well by Euben 1997, 242. Wolfsdorf (1998, 127–30) provides a comprehensive treatment of the historical identities of the named members of the dialogue's immediate audience of gentlemen, arguing convincingly that appreciating the identities and reputations of these people is crucial for interpreting the dialogue. I owe my acquaintance with this source to Richard Avramenko.

78. As Weiss comments, in "the *Protagoras* Socrates deliberately contorts and impoverishes the human personality" (2006, 67).

79. See also Euben 1997, 258–59.

80. Nicely formulated by Wolz (1981, 157): "The satisfaction from having done his duty, the pride felt at having acted like a man—these might be called pleasures, but they are no longer the sense pleasures associated with the hedonistic theory of morality."

81. Quantitative commensurability implies the possibility of clear preference orderings, at least from the perspective of the individual. However, identifying a single preference ordering would presuppose a basic commensurability among the larger, the more, and the greater, on the one hand, and the smaller, the fewer, and the less, on the other. For Aristotle (*Nicomachean Ethics* 1169a16–25), the lover of the noble prefers one great and distinctive enjoyment over many small and ordinary ones. The great succeeds by eclipsing the ordinary rather than by outscoring it.

82. And a single agent understood in a way that paradoxically eliminates many of the characteristics that we might see as conferring individuation. By insisting that pleasures not be distinguished in terms of their proximity or remoteness (*Protagoras* 356a–b), Socrates seems to deny the relevance of changeable individual experiences in the calculations that come to comprise hedonics.

83. This provides a slightly different basis for Euben's (1997, 239) contention that the dialogue reveals the incapacity of the science of measurement to serve as the science that would save us.

84. On the different senses of how teaching in the *Protagoras* might be understood, see Bartlett 2004, 87–88; Coby 1987, 173–75; Weingartner 1973, 132–33; and Mara 2001, 832–33.

85. In this respect, I differ from Euben (1997, 263–65), who reads the conclusion of the dialogue as a Platonic critique of Socrates.

86. Saxonhouse (2006, 200–5) explores the same kind of tension in her examination of how the *Protagoras* images the conflicting imperatives of *parrhēsia* and *aidōs* in democracies.

87. In a way, this describes the irony of Richard Rorty (1989, 80–81). This kind of irony is thus unsuited to play any role in public or political education (1989, 87–88).

88. See chapter 1, pp. 24–25.

89. This is the suggestion of Strauss (1964, 240–41), though I have a different view of what the condition of not being at war might mean. See the conclusion, pp. 258–59.

90. In this respect, I do not share Koziak's (2000, 64–65) assessment that Platonic political theory disregards the importance of affect.

91. See also Xenophon *Memorabilia* 3.10.1–5; and Keuls 1978, 102–3.

92. On Charmides' genealogy, see Davies 1971, 329–33.

93. On possible connections between the Spartans and the Thirty, see Krentz 1982, 63–68; and Wolpert 2002, 124–25.

94. On the deficiencies of Socrates' arguments, see Hyland (1981, 58–59); Bruell (1977, 153–55); and West and West (1986, 26 n. 28). Like all of these commentators I read these deficiencies as deliberate and not as indicating a philosophical naïveté on Plato's part (cf. Bruell 1977, 159–60; and Hyland 1981, 70–71).

95. On the difficulties ensnaring Critias in his attempts to separate makings from doings see Hyland 1981, 84.

96. Cf. Hyland 1981, 95; 113–14; 124. The significance of the epistemic error can only be fully appreciated in light of Critias' pragmatics. To this extent the dialogue is political in its dynamics as well as in its implications. My reading focuses on the pragmatic dimensions of Socrates' philosophic alternative to Critias' science, whereas Hyland emphasizes the deep and subtle eroticism of Socratic philosophy. I see these readings as complementary rather than competitive and Hyland's book remains the most persuasive extended treatment of the *Charmides* that I have read.

97. As nicely forumated by Hyland 1981, 98–99.

98. For a dicussion of how this second version of the common good might intersect with an erotic view of the self, see Hyland 1981, 101–3.

99. Cf. Bruell 1977, 174–75; on Critias's inattention to the soul, see Hyland 1981, 119–20; and West and West 1986, 41–41 n. 51.

100. See Brann's nice observations (2004, 86–70) and the provocative reference to "Lysander's list" in Wolpert 2002, 112.

Chapter Three: Deliberating Democracy

1. Cf. Habermas 1990, 103: "It would be utterly pointless to engage in a practical discourse without a horizon provided by the life world of a specific social group and without real conflicts in a concrete situation in which the actors consider it incumbent upon them to reach a consensual means of regulating some controversial social matter."

2. This feature of deliberative democratic theory is more characteristic of Habermas than of Rawls. Though both attempt to deal with controversies among those who hold different comprehensive conceptions of the good, Habermas proceeds by attempting to outline the procedures by which those partisans could participate in public deliberations, while Rawls precludes the examination of certain kinds of questions from occurring in the public sphere altogether. Habermas calls these "gag rules" (1996, 309). Rawls justifies the restriction by

appealing (2005, 145) to the constitutive features of a pluralist culture. Rawls's understanding of deliberative democracy is more substantive, while Habermas's is more procedural. (For an insistence, well-taken, that Habermas cannot avoid substantive commitments, see Rawls 2005, 431–32). For this reason, Habermas is a principal discourse partner in this chapter. A fuller treatment of Rawls is deferred until chapter 4.

3. The sharp disagreements among liberals, communitarians, deliberative democrats, and postmodernists certainly involve disputes over the goods that democracy does and can make available. In all cases, understandings of democratic institutions and processes are informed by understandings of democracy's normative potentials. Shapiro's recent (2003, 148) minimalist vision of democracy's good as the management of power relations so as to minimize domination stipulates that there is no overarching good that is more important.

4. For Habermas (1996, 418), "the idea of a just society is connected with the promise of emancipation and human dignity.... The normative key is autonomy, not well-being." One could plausibly argue that autonomy can just as easily be seen as an alternative conception of well-being. For a discussion of similar teleological commitments in the earlier Habermas, see Mara 1985, 1051–52.

5. Well put by Salkever 2002, 358: "The deliberative model ... both presupposes and conceals, and so transmits without the opportunity for reflection, an animating drama of the emancipation of humanity from the mechanical nature that frames and severely limits our understanding of the relationship between emotion and reason."

6. Against the communitarian criticism that a reliance on procedures bespeaks a problematic neutrality with regard to purposes, Warren contends that establishing the validity of procedure over power and money as a means of social organization is far from neutral (2001, 53). However, it is not clear that acknowledging this characteristic of proceduralism eliminates all of the difficulties embedded in an exclusive reliance on democratic procedure. There are objections to proceduralism beyond those offered by communitarians.

7. See the parallel assessment of Markovits, forthcoming.

8. Habermas's (1996, 355; cf. 1993, 108–11) illustrative list of the public interest positions (environmental protection, consumer product safety, animal welfare) that an enhanced deliberative process would empower is hardly neutral with regard to content. Yet from a strictly procedural perspective, there is no reason to presume that these outcomes are any more integral to deliberative democracy than are empowering those who favor an expanded use of natural resources, freeing enterprise from the constraints of governmental regulations, and the instrumental use of animal species for human well-being. For Habermas, apparently one of the principal values of deliberative procedures is that they empower voices deserving empowerment.

9. Cf. Habermas 1996, 414: "Discourse theory explains the legitimacy of law by means of procedures and communicative presuppositions that, once they are legally institutionalized, ground the supposition that the processes of making and applying law lead to rational outcomes."

10. The term "postpositivism" is deliberately vague. At a minimum, postpositivist social science includes studies of public institutions and practices framed by an orientation toward problem solving rather than by a commitment to the development of rigorous and parsimonious theories with broad explanatory and predictive reaches (as in Gurr 1970, 357). Postpositivism also rejects the ethical neutrality of positivist social science (Gurr 1970, x), either because attempts at neutrality disconnect social science from attempts to structure good government (Putnam 1993, 63) or because supposedly neutral analyses mask normative agendas.

11. Thus Warren 2001, 53: "[D]emocratic procedure alone makes effective the normative question of What shall we do?—a point rightly emphasized by Benjamin Barber when he characterizes democracy as 'the most political of theories.' "

12. A similar perspective informs Galston's (1991, 280) distinction between intrinsic and functional traditionalism.

13. Chapter 2, pp. 55–56.

14. For a range of interpretations beyond those discussed here, see Cogan 1981, 55–65; Connor 1984, 79–91; Johnson 1993, 104–10; Palmer 1992, 62–63; Strauss 1964, 231–36; White 1984, 72–76; and Yunis 1996, 92–101.

15. This is, for example, the conclusion of Ober (1998, 104).

16. Cf. chapter 2, pp. 58–59. Palmer (1992, 63) also sees a connection between Diodotus's speech and that of the Athenians at Sparta, though the connection is presented in terms of gentleness of rule, rather than a regard for equality. The kinds of justice consistent with these commitments could conceivably be very different.

17. In a sense, Diodotus's appeal to the possibility of an enhanced rationality and an enhanced sense of horizontal trust is implicitly recognized by Orwin (1984, 324) when he comments that Diodotus's speech is an appeal to the Athenians' better selves.

18. To this extent, Diodotus does not anticipate any political environment that can deal with conflicts over the good in a way that is completely adequate. For deliberative democrats such as Habermas, it is possible to settle questions about process, even though the substantive conclusions of politics cannot in principle be anticipated.

19. See Farrar (1988, 77–98), Nussbaum (2001, 103–5), and Schiappa (1991, 181–87).

20. Sharing the assessment of Saxonhouse 2006, 63–64.

21. Implications of this statement are also noted by Saxonhouse 2006, 188; and Weiss 2006, 37.

22. See, for example, Farrar 1988, 79–80; Coby 1987, 51; and Bartlett 2004, 74.

23. In this respect, Socrates' statements about the assembly are compatible with the views of more committed democrats. This may be another instance of what Sara Monoson (2000) sees as a Platonic use of the resources of democracy within his own complex criticism of democracy.

24. The contributions and problematics of *aidōs* and *dikē* as the bases for political-cultural identity are expertly explored by Saxonhouse 2006, chap. 3.

25. As in Weiss 2006, 38–41; Bartlett 2004, 88.

26. Remembering that both are present for this conversation.

27. Chapter 2, pp. 70–71.

28. The most unsettling example of the noble reduced to the pleasant in Thucydides occurs during the plague (2.52.2–4, 2.53.1–4) where the enjoyment of the grossest physical pleasures occurs amid putrefaction and decomposition. Yet the ability to secure the most pleasant enjoyments for oneself becomes the basis of a perverted standard of nobility. The continued need to identify *to kalon* indicates the simultaneous presence of increasing social fragmentation and a persisting need to stay within some sort of community of ethical naming.

29. Near the end of the funeral speech, Pericles exhorts the members of the audience to "pay regard to the power of the city every day and become her lovers (*erastai*)" (Thucydides 2.43.1). Shortly, those memorialized are said to have been overcome by "unfelt" (*anaisthētos*) death (2.43.6). In a striking juxtaposition with the plague episode, individual physical experiences are redescribed in the context of a cultural project that Pericles attempts to construct.

30. Monoson (1994, 253–76; and 2000, chap. 3) makes a strong case that Pericles' call for the audience of the funeral speech to become Athens's lovers (*erastai*) aims at establishing reciprocity, not subservience, between citizens and regime. However, the sort of reciprocity at which Pericles aims requires individual citizens to reconceive their own good as cultural recognition, rather than as personal security or even personal survival. Pericles' rhetoric may also misrepresent the degree to which reciprocity between lover and beloved can be reproduced in the relationship between citizen and regime. In a way, this parallels the illusion that Periclean Athens was democratic in fact and not merely in name.

31. An instructive contemporary illustration of how the absence of warranted trust can be treated teleologically in this sense is provided by Constable and Valenzuela's analysis (1991) of the unraveling of the fabric of civic trust in Chile under the dictatorship of Pinochet.

32. This teleological understanding of trust both expands upon and falls short of Jane Mansbridge's (1999b, 290–309) altruistic trust, where one trusts more than the available evidence would warrant "as a gift, for both the good of others and the community" (1999b, 290). It expands upon this view by indicating that political trust, understood teleologically, can be connected with other intrinsic goods of political communities. It falls short by not recommending a trust that is more generous than evidence would warrant. If the pragmatic context of political trust is a disagreement about the good within an environment characterized by power competitions, the wisdom of altruistic trust is less clear. Mansbridge may move too easily from a description of moral interpersonal trust to politics.

33. In a way, this assessment of philosophical mistrust underscores the tensions between philosophy and even the most open democratic regime. See Saxonhouse 2006, 204–5 for a statement that focuses on their compatibility.

34. This signals intriguing connections between the *Protagoras* and the *Laws*. The nocturnal synod practices its philosophical investigations in ways

that recognize the need to keep them relevant for politics, yet separate from it (*Laws* 951d–52a). What prompts this sort of philosophy is the vexing relationship between the whole and the parts of virtue (965c–e).

35. For the differences between discursive philosophy and politics, see Deneen (2000, 427).

36. As in Rawls 2005, 36–37; and Rosenblum 1998, 26.

37. The historical origins of this conception of democracy can be traced to the political forms of the ancient Greek city-states or the Italian republics of the Renaissance. Yet a number of modern social theorists such as Robert Bellah and Michael Sandel see civic republican possibilities extending beyond their historical points of origin and identify traces of the tradition in aspects of the American experience. See Bellah 1985, 38–39; and Sandel 1996, 124–33. For Barry Shain (1994, 38–41) the historical alternative to individualism in American political culture is found not in civic republicanism but in the institutions of American Protestantism.

38. Dahl 1989, 298. In his historical examination of the public rhetoric employed by Whigs and Democrats during the Jacksonian era, John Patrick Diggins notes that appeals to public conceptions of virtue often masked partisan attachments to the political and economic policies favorable to more-divisive social interests (1984, 111).

39. Cf. Machiavelli, *Discourses* 3.49; Rousseau 1964, 43; and Rousseau 1979, 40.

40. For those who read Thucydides as critical of Pericles, see the different presentations of Monoson and Loriaux 1998, 285–97; Orwin 1994, 25–28; Strauss 1964, 193–94; and Balot 2001, 148–49.

41. On the continuities among the three speeches, see (e.g.) Parry 1981, 150; Price 2001, 172; and Yunis 1996, 77. Note Pericles' own comment at 2.61:"I am the same (*autos*) and am not changed. . . . It is you [the *dēmos*] who have altered."

42. Price (2001, 238–39, 260) therefore also goes too far in seeing Pericles' political practice as reflecting a more selfless form of civic devotion.

43. For numerous commentators this is essentially the basis of the behavior of Alcibiades. See Forde 1989, 195–202; Orwin 1984, 124–25; and Palmer 1992, chap. 3. Forde's analysis is especially sophisticated and points to the differences as well as to the similarities between Alcibiades and Pericles (1989, 91–92).

44. Parry comments, "Hence it is that while in the Funeral Speech Pericles steps back in his own person, out of reverence to those who gave their lives, and in awe at the present glory of the city, in the Last Speech he asserts himself strongly, making it clear that the heroic decision is his creation" (1981, 173). I am less inclined than Parry to see fundamental differences in Pericles' presence in the two speeches or to interpret this heroic creation as an unambiguously positive feature of Pericles' leadership.

45. For a different reading of the call to become the city's lovers, see Monoson 2000, chap. 3. While Monoson emphasizes reciprocity, I suggest that the erotic relation between citizen and city would require a radical redefinition of the citizen's own identity. This reading is closer to Wohl's (2002, 57–61), though I disagree with Wohl's contention (31) that the Periclean and Thucydidean views are the same.

46. Wohl (2002, 200) sees the plague narrative as exposing the hollowness of the funeral speech. This and similar assessments make it difficult to accept her contention that the funeral speech is Thucydides' own statement of Athenian ideals.

47. Pericles' own vision of his political gifts (judgment, the ability to speak, and love of the city) is thus a condition for Thucydides' own assessment, just as the speech of the Athenians at Sparta is an enabling condition for the Pentecontaetia.

48. For example, Pouncey 1980, 79–80; Farrar 1988, 165–69; and Ober 1998, 92–93.

49. Suggested in a slightly different context by Saxonhouse 1996, 65.

50. See Morrison's (2006, 148–49) illuminating insights on Thucydides' choice of the term *archē* to designate Pericles' rule.

51. This must qualify Parry's assessment that Thucydides' representation of Pericles' last speech, which anticipates the disappearance of Athenian culture, gives "Pericles a prophetic grandeur which is serenely unhistorical" (1981, 180). In some respects, Pericles' capacity for prophecy is inferior to the darker intimations of the Spartans Archidamus (Thucydides 1.81.6) and Melissipus (2.12.3–4).

52. For different and more appreciative views see Balot 2001, 161–62, 184; Saxonhouse 1996, 82; and Saxonhouse 2004, 80–82.

53. A point also noted by Saxonhouse 2006, 177.

54. Reinforced by Orwin 1994, 186.

55. Cf. Saxonhouse 2006, 173: "Thucydides had emphasized the role of eros, a desire for adventure and for wealth (6.24.3) in the decision to set sail for Sicily. Hermocrates, the rational one, with the emphasis on *gnōmē*, accepts this point; Athenagoras, the fiery orator, focuses on what is irrational."

56. Wohl's interpretation of the *Gorgias* (2002, 97) is representative: "The mob doesn't know what's good for it; seduced by flattery and pleasure, looking only to its gratification and not to its edification, it is weak, infantile and sick."

57. *Gorgias* 500c, 521d. This possibility is left out in the pairing at 459a–b.

58. Barber 2003, 175. For a discussion that connects this capacity for listening with democratic practice, see Goldhill 1999, 5–9.

59. Eric Havelock thus discovers within the teachings of Sophists or orators like Protagoras and Gorgias commitments to develop the public competence of citizens so as to make them more effective political participants (1957, 169ff.). Brian Vickers (1988, 139) rejects Plato's alternative to rhetorical politics as an intellectual and practical authoritarianism.

60. For an extended discussion of Socrates' use of irony in the *Gorgias*, see Markovits, forthcoming, chap. 3.

61. Callicles' historical identity, assuming his historical existence, is a mystery, however. Is it significant or merely accidental that he is one of the few Athenian interlocutors of Socrates about whom we have no historical information? Cf. Benardete 1991, 7. For views that see Callicles as a historical figure, see Dodds, 1959, 12–13; and Balot 2001, 5, 200. See also Nails's interesting treatment (2002, 75–76).

62. This is nicely captured by Beiner's "sympathy and detachment" (1983, chap. 6).

63. Though Callicles' speeches clearly offer an express contempt of the many and a praise of the young lions whose flourishing is stunted by convention, his speech-acts, particularly at the end of the dialogue, suggest that his tendency to move to and fro with the many's shifting humors is due at least as much to fear as to manipulation. Thus, in my view, the associations of Callicles with a kind of Nietzscheanism by Dodds (1959, 387–91) and Roochnik (1990, 50) are mistaken.

64. Cf. Thucydides 2.36–41. For this reason, I am not persuaded that the Pericles criticized by Socrates is solely or simply the Pericles who is seen through the eyes of Polus or Callicles. While many of Socrates' criticisms of the notable Athenian leaders of the past are clearly inadequate (the Athenians turn on Socrates at least as intensely as they turn on Pericles), the divisions between Socratic and Periclean statesmanship seem decisive. This is indicated very clearly in the striking differences between their two funeral speeches. See Salkever 1993.

65. As in Gilligan, 1982, chap. 3. On moral particularism, see Hooker and Liitle 2000.

66. Cf. Beiner 1983, 144–45; and Salkever 1990, 122–29.

67. Cf. Habermas 1973; 18, 1990, 58–59, 86–94.

68. This distinguishes politically immediate forms of enabling from what Narayan calls the social preconditions (quality education, access to child care) for active citizenship.

69. A dated though still relevant image of the respect for and perversion of the jury system from the point of view of deliberative rationality is Sidney Lumet's 1957 film, *Twelve Angry Men*.

70. Compare with Warren 2001, 70. The developmental effects of democracy on individuals are assessed in terms of their potential for cultivating individual autonomy.

71. In this respect, the differences that Price (2001, 267–68) notes between Thucydides and the *Menexenus* over the duration of the war go beyond differing historical interpretations.

72. For interpretations that connect portions of the *Republic* with Aristophanic comedy, see Strauss 1964, 61–62; Bloom 1968, 380–82; Saxonhouse 1978, 888–901; and Lombardini, forthcoming.

73. A general possibility noted by Nightingale's (1995, 180–81) discussion of philosophy and comedy as intersecting genres.

74. See the criticisms of the new generation of Athenian politicians at *Acharnaeans* 676–91.

75. Indeed, Callicles encourages Socrates to practice the activities of the "lowly Mysians" (*Gorgias* 521b) if such would be necessary for survival. In the *Acharnaeans*, the protagonist Dicaeopolis (the just city) uses the wretched clothing of the Mysian Telephos (429–39) as a disguise to help in the dangerous enterprise of convincing the warlike Acharnaean chorus of the justice of a peace with Sparta. In this instance, Dicaeopolis's speech is prompted by the Acharnaeans'

outrage at his having made his own separate peace (280–92). Thus, the concerns with personal security and civic benefit intersect.

76. Images connecting rhetoric to food or cookery occur frequently in the *Knights*. See 212–18, 640–62, 671–82, 715–18, 777–78, 814–16, 1162–82, 1204–5. For a more extensive comparison of the *Gorgias* and the *Knights*, see the fine discussion in Lombardini, forthcoming.

77. For speculations on Plato's historical knowledge of Cinesias and Meles, see Dodds 1959, 323–24.

78. On Aristophanes' valorization of manliness, see Rademaker 2003, 121–22, though this treatment sees Aristophanes as more conventional than I do.

79. Intersecting provocatively with the dialogue's refiguration of Euripides' tragedy *Antiope*, persuasively interpreted by Nightingale 1995, chap. 2. While Nightingale contends that "there is very little humor in the *Gorgias*" (1995, 187), she notes (1995, 90–91) that Plato's rewriting of the *Antiope* casts Callicles as a ridiculous figure and not as a tragic one.

80. Allen (2000, 250–51) notes Callicles' recognition of the comedic character of this reversal as he asks if Socrates is playing (*paizei*) in his conclusions about the relation among rhetoric, injustice, and punishment. If he is serious (*spoudazei*), he would turn the whole world upside down. While Callicles may see a comic representation of rhetoric as pointless, Socrates and Plato, as author, may also see a more serious purpose behind playing. Turning the world upside down may be "*but* a matter of comedy" (Allen 2000, 251, my emphasis) only for Callicles.

81. Cf. Halperin 1990, chap. 5. On the sexual images in the *Knights*, especially connected with the sausage seller, see Rademaker 2003, 119–20; Wohl 2002, 83–92; and Lombardini, forthcoming.

82. The comedic aspects are reinforced by Nightingale's noting (1995, 82 n. 57) that Socrates' move to monologue is introduced by a reference (505e) to a comedy by Epicharmus. The prospects of a dialogue turned monologue is, however, enthusiastically anticipated by Rawls 1971, 141–42. On the eventual outcome of decisions made by the partners to the original position, he says "[O]nce knowledge is excluded [under the proviso of the veil of ignorance] the requirement of unanimity is not out of place and the fact that it can be satisfied is of great importance. It enables us to say of the preferred conception of justice that it represents a genuine reconciliation of interests."

83. On the parallels between Thersites and Callicles, see Benardete 1991, 100–1. For the significance of Thersites as a democratic figure, see Saxonhouse 2006, 1–10, 207–13.

84. This is not to deny that Socratic irony can also be capable of insulting the reader, as in Nehamas 1998, 43–45. I thank John Lombardini for this observation.

85. Cf. Lombardini, forthcoming.

86. For a discussion of the characteristics of the comic and tragic audiences, see MacDowell, 1995, chap. 2.

87. Consider *Philebus* 50b–c.

88. In the context of the *Symposium* this would suggest the superiority of Agathon to Aristophanes. What challenges this inference is Aristophanes'

speech on love in the dialogue, which contains at least as many tragic as comic elements. This can be set against Agathon's speech, which turns out to be comically inadequate under the withering interrogation of Socrates. Perhaps the real implication of this statement is that the categories of tragedy and comedy are not so easily distinguished (cf. *Philebus* 50b).

89. Treating this incident as comic also images Socrates' distance from and confrontation with the city. Ober's (1998, 197) sense that Socrates' characterization of the reaction of the assembly may be historically accurate seems premature. A much more likely response would have been intense anger.

90. The limits of the kind of justice that Socrates endorses in the face of Callicles' attacks are perhaps underappreciated by Weiss 2006, chap. 3.

91. Thus, the restored Demos of the *Knights* embraces the manly rather than the thoughtful practices of citizenship (*Knights* 1375–82). Wohl's criticisms (2002, 119–21) go even deeper, reading the reconstructed Demos as an image of elitism. Yet if comedy respects the audience in ways that pandering rhetoric does not, then the performance of comedy may also work against its elitist content. In this respect, the alternative interpretations that the comedy is either "the gift of a *kaloskagathos* suitor or the come-on of a whore" (120) may not be the only ones available, and it may not be "so difficult to differentiate the pleasure of the text from the pleasure [Aristophanes] so reviles in Cleon." For a different reading of the ending of the *Knights*, see Lombardini, forthcoming.

92. Since so much of Socrates' rhetoric in favor of order and moderation is prompted by Callicles' own passionate praise of disorder (cf. Weiss 2006, 107–8), geometry may be a vision of wisdom through the lens of order. This form of wisdom (whose currency is proof and whose affect is serenity) is very different from Socrates' conversational and erotic philosophy (481d–e). This affirmation of an ordered cosmos also stands in sharp contrast to the persistent references to the overwhelmingly disordering war.

93. In this respect, I would go beyond Nightingale's (1995, 191) contrast between Plato's philosopher as an "outsider... disembedded from the social and political economy of the city" and the comic poet who speaks as a "citizen before citizens." Socrates' conversations are destabilizing (*Gorgias* 481c), but one reason is the possibility of communication (481c–d), which implies a degree of embeddedness. Socrates thus stands between philosopher and citizen and in so doing is both and neither.

94. Directions taken in Euben's (1990, 180–82), Ober's (1998, 102–3), and Orwin's (1994, 158–59) readings of Diodotus's speech and in Yunis's (1996, 122–25) and Ober's (1998, 206–13) readings of the *Gorgias*.

Chapter Four: Culture's Justice

1. See Rawls on the Enlightenment project (2005, xvii).
2. For Geertz (1973, 5) and Taylor (1971, 3–5) societies are interpreted as symbol systems or text analogues. For Winch (1961, 21–24), they should be

seen as epistemological fields, implying that social science and philosophy are parallel enterprises.

3. This is the basis of Connolly's (1990, 66) and Rorty's (1989, 57–58) insistence that Rawls's position must be honestly extended to a much more radical appreciation of historicism and contingency. For a denial that this direction is implicit in Rawls's cultural turn, see Habermas 1996, 62–63.

4. While Winch (1961, 107–11) draws this conclusion from his assessment of the formal properties of linguistic communities, Rorty (1989, 16) bases a similar assessment on the contingent nature of language itself.

5. As in Winch's (1961, 95–103) critique of Pareto's treatment of magic, in particular, and of evolutionary anthropology's attitude toward so-called primitive societies, in general.

6. Cf. Rorty 1982, 163–64; Taylor 1967, 56–57; and Taylor 1985, 98–104. Unlike Rorty, Taylor retains the possibility of identifying better and worse forms of coping.

7. Cf. Foucault 1979, 305; 1984b, 83.

8. Cf. Connolly 1990, 72; 1995, 106.

9. Most of all, perhaps, in Foucault (1979, 307–8; 1994, xxiv), but similar impulses clearly inform the positions of political theorists such as Connolly (1990, 77) and critical anthropologists such as Borneman (1992, 285) and Daniel and Peck (1996, 2).

10. Cf. Habermas 1996, xli: There "is neither a higher nor a deeper reality to which we could appeal [lying beyond or beneath] our linguistically structured form of life." This understanding of metaphysics as the affirmation of such a remote or removed reality is far too narrow. The categories, metaphysical and postmetaphysical, must also be interrogated in light of the rhetorical purposes that often guide their deployment. The need to consider questions connected with first philosophy is not disposed of by the claim that we inhabit a postmetaphysical age.

11. Though Pangle (1989, xxxii) is right to say that this comparison of Thucydides and Plato (contained in a lecture posthumously published in 1989, but delivered much earlier, probably in the 1950s) is substantially revised in Strauss's *The City and Man* (published in 1964), this aspect of the comparison seems constant. In *City*, "Thucydides does not rise to the heights of classical political philosophy because he is more concerned than is classical political philosophy with what is 'first for us' as distinguished from what is 'first by nature'" (Strauss 1964, 239).

12. The ability to release from bonds anyone one wants is one of the activities that Glaucon says characterizes the powerful enemy of convention (*Republic* 360c).

13. Sahlins (2004, 3, 16, 118–20, 123) concludes the opposite and finds Thucydides' voice to be resolutely anti-cultural, seeing through cultural varieties "to discount... conventional differences in culture in favor of... essential similarities in nature—human nature" (16). In this respect, Sahlins accepts the culture/nature binary that Thucydides can be read as challenging. Sahlins goes on (46–49) to fault Thucydides not so much for ignoring culture as for essential-

izing it into differences of national character. Both charges are serious complaints, but they are not identical. Sahlins detects solid reasons for taking the role of culture seriously in Thucydides own narrative, but does not go further to wonder whether the narrative is as reductive as he says it is.

14. Price (2001, 142) connects these self-deceptions to the effects of *stasis*.

15. Departing (largely) from Crane 1998, 67–68, who sees the intensified focus on individuals in book 8 as a decline whose significance Thucydides himself fails to appreciate. In this respect, Crane treats cities and individuals as alternative rather than intersecting units of analysis.

16. Luginbill's (1999) statement is the most categorical. For that very reason, he tends to read Thucydides' narrative far too simply, as a reinforcement of the basic differences between Athenian and Spartan regimes (cf. Sahlins 2004, 46). For deeper treatments, see Jansson (1997) and Zumbrunnen (2002).

17. On the focus of a psychocultural analysis, see Ross 1993, 53–57. Ross's primary focus is on the impacts of society on child-training practices, but there is no reason to limit the influence of the culture on psychological development to the early years.

18. Cf. Loraux 1986, 123.

19. As, for example, Connor 1984, 215; Crane 1998, 68; and Rood 1998, 252–53.

20. The logic of the constructed categories of self and other is given its most noted rendition by Said, 1994, 3. See also Kristeva 1991, 2–3. For particular applications to Greek culture, see Hall 1989, chap. 1; Kristeva 1991, chap. 2; and Loraux, 1986, 165–69.

21. As in Said 1994, 3, 46, 104, 280.

22. In recognizing that the continuous connection between culture and nature also generates a series of problematics, Plato and Thucydides differ from Midgley (1995, 273–305), whose insightful statements may underplay the tensions between culture and nature.

23. As in Mara 1997, 154–65; and Euben 1990, chap. 8.

24. All of these are voiced by Adeimantus or Polemarchus. Adeimatus as critic of culture is also the one most attuned to the importance of convention. Their concerns differ dramatically from those of Glaucon (*Republic* 471e), who wants to be told how the city in speech can be made real.

25. Other commentators who have read Thucydides as accepting the validity of claims that the rule of the strong reflects a certain kind of natural standard or order include Ostwald (1988, 38, 55) and Pouncey (1980, 104). Crane (1998, 324–25) sees Thucydides arguing for the directive influence of power on human practice, but ultimately revealing (against his own intentions) power's inadequacy. I agree that Thucydides reveals "the limits of political realism," but am less convinced than Crane that this revelation departs from Thucydides' authorial intent.

26. I agree with Price (2001, 197) that "[w]hen the Athenians refer to a law of nature whereby men and perhaps even the gods rule when they have the advantage of strength ... they pronounce no permanent truth endorsed by the historian but rather reveal how their present circumstances influence the way they see the world and themselves."

27. In this respect, my account differs from Price's (2001, 29), which sees normal forms of sociability replaced by distorted cultural forms in Corcyra, but disappearing entirely under the stresses of the plague.

28. As Orwin (1994, 60) comments, "At Athens this charge sinks without a ripple."

29. Among the numerous commentators who have pointed this out are Orwin (1994, 197–98) and Strauss (1964, 209). For a somewhat different view see Edmunds 1975, 112–15.

30. See, for example, Keuls 1985, 385–91; and Wolpert 2002, 65–67.

31. A point made also by Crane (1996, 197–98). I do question Crane's general claim (1996, 206–8) that Thucydides dismisses the social and political consequences of religious beliefs and practices.

32. On the importance of Thucydides' observations on Corcyra for determining his own views on nature, see especially Price 2001, 11.

33. In this respect, Athens may be significantly different from Corcyra. Cf. 8.94, which seems to describe a parallel situation to that initiating the sustained Corcyrean bloodletting, but where the outcome at Athens is very different. My view on the Athens/Corcyra parallel differs significantly from Ober's in Ober 1998, 120–21.

34. See also Price 2001, 47, 57.

35. In notable parallel to Nietzsche's treatment in Nietzsche 1966, 15.

36. Price also notes Thucydides' reluctance to base evaluative judgments on any stable interpretation of nature (2001, 27). This is not due to Thucydides' avoiding the question of the kind of condition that nature is.

37. Differing from Johnson 1993, 44.

38. Foucault 1979, 27–28. On Thucydidean similarities with Foucault, see Crane 1998, 316.

39. Literally "uneducated anger." The spirit of the passage is Thucydidean (cf. Connor 1984, 102, n. 60), even though there are numerous reservations about assigning this chapter a definitive place in the final text (cf. Lattimore 1998, 171, n. 3.84). Speculatively (to be sure), the extreme statement offered in 3.84 may provide a narrative parallel to the thematic point that nature is best seen in its extremities.

40. Cf. Foucault 1979, 308; 1984b, 83.

41. Callicles' apparent admiration and envy of Pericles emerges at *Gorgias* 503c. And a good bit of Socrates' attack on the politics that Callicles admires is a not altogether fair attack on Pericles (cf. *Gorgias* 515d–16d).

42. Among them, Connor 1984, 63–64; Orwin 1994, 174; and Strauss 1964, 153.

43. And the plague's devastation is not simply natural (Thucydides 2.52.1–2).

44. In this connection, justice is not simply harming enemies (*Republic* 332b), for it presupposes some prior harm to oneself or one's friends at the enemies' hands. In a sense, it is not simply that one harms enemies but that one makes enemies through the infliction of harm within an endlessly reinforcing pattern.

45. As in the speech of Euphemus (6.83.3–85.1–2).

46. Cf. Orwin 1994, 55; and Palmer 1992, 63. One of the outcomes of this claim is that even the boast that Athens treats the subject cities as sometime equals reinforces the reality of inequality. So, I am not altogether convinced by Debnar's claim (2001, 57) that the Athenian praise of those who act more moderately than necessity requires softens the harsher implications of their power.

47. Thucydides 1.76.2. This broad "Athenian thesis" is interpreted extensively by Orwin 1994, 44–56.

48. For interpretations that see the Melian dialogue as evidence of a dramatic Athenian decline, see, for example, Ober 1998, 104; Johnson 1993, 130; and Pouncey 1980, 15. Cogan 1981, 126–28 sees the Melian episode as marking a third, and final, turning point in the war's conduct. On the corruption of Athens during the war, see Euben 1990, chap. 6; and Farrar 1988, 150–52, 176–77. Crane (1998, 250) reads the dialogue as an episode narrated so as to reinforce Thucydides' general claims about how the influence of power displaces ancient simplicity. Those who see more continuity include Connor 1984, 150–53; Palmer 1992, 64; and White 1984, 76–77. Palmer wishes to counter interpretations that the dialogue reflects Athens's degeneration into brutality and, therefore, emphasizes Athenian candor rather than Athenian cynicism. I am inclined to see more continuity than change, yet this continuity is surely complex, since the Athenian speeches bear traces not only of the Athenian speech at Sparta, but also of speeches given by Pericles, Cleon, and Diodotus.

49. A connection emphasized most recently by Price 2001, 197.

50. As in Crane 1998, 105.

51. Chapter 2, pp. 50–52.

52. Sahlins (2004, 48–49) notes that the image of Sparta's long-standing political stability conceals the relatively recent origins of Sparta's political forms. What is perhaps more important in this context is the way in which Sparta represents the stability of its traditions.

53. Crane (1998, 206) may focus too much on Sparta's development of a certain kind of autonomy.

54. Cf. Debnar 2001, 35–36.

55. In this respect, my interpretation of this speech of Archidamus is far less generous than Debnar's (2001, 101).

56. Saxonhouse (2006, 190) contends that Spartan culture is "the extreme expression of a society governed by Protagorean *aidōs* in the cohesion expressed by their reverence for the past and their concern for what others see." On shame as an ethical emotion, see Williams 1993, chap. 4.

57. On the broad significance and functions of *aidōs* and *aischynē* in classical Greek culture, see Cairns 1993, particularly chap. 6. Within this generally informative study, there is less discussion of Archidamus's speech than one might wish.

58. This harshness or shaming is consistent with the observations in Xenophon's extensive account of Spartan education in the *Lacedaemonian Constitution*. This education proceeds through social practices that mark and dishonor those seen as cowards (*Lac Pol* 9.3–5) and is reinforced by a general culture of publicity (10.4–6). In some respects, this set of practices seems an ancient version of

Foucault's modern disciplined and normalizing society, held together by forms of surveillance and punishment applied by the widely dispersed agents of social power (Foucault 1979, 29–30). The psychocultural basis of this form of education is also elaborated by Aristotle as he describes political courage or the courage of the citizen in *Nicomachean Ethics* 3.8.

59. As in Williams 1993, 67, where the fear of shame is to "anticipate how you will feel if someone sees you [commit a disgraceful act]."

60. Thus, I come to a different conclusion than Debnar (2001, 68), who interprets Archidamus's speech as enlisting emotion in support of reason.

61. The increasingly despotic conduct of the general Pausanias is traced to his being "corrupted away from home" (Thucydides 1.95.7). The separation of Brasidas and his largely Helot army from the Lacedaemonians provides considerable space for his pursuit of individual distinction (4.97.1–2; 5.16.1). See also Debnar 2001, 3.

62. The sentence in which Thucydides narrates Sparta's desire to recognize Brasidas for his extraordinary courage is full of linguistic challenges to the stable and homogenous culture fostered by Archidamus's harsh education. "[O]n account of this act of daring, [Brasidas] was the first of those commended in the war at Sparta" (Thucydides 2.25.2–3). Being first (*prōtos*) and being notably commended (*epēnethē*) work against the deference (*aischynē*) fostered by Spartan education. Brasidas's courage thus takes the form of daring (*tolma*) rather than modesty (*aidōs*). The sentence also anticipates Thucydides' later contention that Brasidas opposed the peace because of "the success and honor derived from the war" (5.16).

63. Cf. Saxonhouse 2006, 152–53.

64. In this respect, I do not agree completely with Price that "the Athenians' understanding of justice remains remarkably consistent throughout their internal debates" (2001, 91).

65. See chapter 3, 98–101.

66. On reconsideration as a mark of democratic decision-making, see Saxonhouse 2004, 65.

67. See Orwin's (1994, 146) comments on the extent to which Diodotus's speech draws on Cleon's.

68. Though Debnar is highly critical of the "rhetorical incompetence" of the Thebans, the real point seems to be adamance (cf. Crane 1996, 226). Price (2001, 125) comments, "[T]he Spartan reaction to both speeches ... show[s] that the two long speeches would as well not have been given."

69. Nietzsche 1954, 558–59.

70. Bloom (1968, 440 n. 3) speculates 411 BCE, the year in which the democracy was subverted and effectively replaced by the rule of the Four Hundred.

71. Polemarchus (Lysias *Against Eratosthenes* 17–25) and Niceratus (Xenophon *Hellenica* 2.3.39–40) are victims of the Thirty, and Lysias (*Against Eratosthenes* 17–18; *Hellenica* 2.41) is a resister. Critias is a central figure in the dialogues *Timaeus* and *Critias*, which seem to be sequels to the *Republic*. For more on the characters, see Bloom 1968, 440 n. 3; and Craig 1994, 341 n. 1.

72. Cf. *Timaeus*, 19b–20c and the comments of Strauss 1964, 140–41.

73. For excellent treatments of the importance of the image of war within the *Republic*, see Craig 1994, chap. 1; Derrida 1997, 89–93; Frank 2007; and Kochin

1999, 403–23. Baracchi (2002) suggests that war informs the dialogue as a whole as a metaphor for fundamental aspects of the human condition. None of these commentators brings Thucydides into the conversation in any sustained way.

74. As does Critias in the *Timaeus* 26c–d.

75. While Socrates' introduction of philosophy in the *Republic* is preceded by moderating the ways in which this city would make war, the focus on this city at war in the *Timaeus* is preceded by a summary of the *Republic* that ignores philosophy. For an interesting discussion of the two dialogues' parallel treatment of motion and rest, see Baracchi (2002, 139–45).

76. Read very critically by Frank 2007.

77. Kochin's fine discussion of the educational framework surrounding this treatment of war in the *Republic* may underemphasize the ways in which this education is penetrated by severity.

78. Price discusses (2001, 69) this portion of the *Republic*, but mainly for the purpose of downplaying its connection to Thucydides. Price is particularly skeptical of attempts to argue that Plato embraced a Panhellenic ideal. While I agree with this assessment, I see other potential connections (beyond the question of Panhellenicism) between this part of the *Republic* and Thucydides' narrative. For example, Socrates seems to see *stasis* as more remediable than Thucydides. Cf. Price 2001, 14–15.

79. Cf. Derrida 1997, 90.

80. Both Benardete (1989) and Craig (1994) may go too far in opposite directions. For Benardete, "Socrates philosophizes in wartime Athens as if it were at peace" (1989, 120). The frequent references to war and the intersections with Thucydides are authorial reminders of the general and particular contextualization of the conversation by war. Craig's assessment (1994, 194) that "from the moment the warriors make their first appearance, to the final discussion of selecting rulers for the regime, philosophy and war are conjoined" downplays the extent to which images of war are also offset and tempered by a conversation that is essentially civil.

81. Cf. Kochin 1999, 404–5.

82. Benardete argues (1989, 121) that images of war in *Republic*, bk. 5 overturn every principle for which Socrates has thus far argued. Perhaps one of the dramatic features of the dialogue is that it points to the distortions of both a philosophizing that ignores hazards such as war and a consciousness of war that ignores philosophy.

83. As well as those of Nussbaum (2001, chap. 5) and Reeve (1988, 206), who are more focused directly on Plato.

84. On Glaucon's revisions of the Gyges story, see Nichols 1987, 61–62.

85. Statue imagery returns at *Republic* 340c to describe Socrates' vision of the just rulers.

86. For an interesting and very different view, see Williams 1993, 99.

87. Most clearly reflected in Thrasymachus's contention that rules of justice are crafted to support the interests of the rulers. This implicates debates over justice in power contests.

88. In this respect, the relation between city and soul is pragmatic, a connection that perhaps represents a third alternative to the causal and metaphorical

relations that Ferrari considers (2005, 52–53). The pragmatic relation is bidirectional. The city presumes a certain kind of justice among the citizens as a very condition of civic identity (otherwise, there might be the desperate self-internment of mutual predators as in the mythos of Protagoras or the Corcyra of Thucydides, bk. 3). This would not, therefore, be a simple revision of Bernard Williams's Rule One ("A city is F if and only if its people are F") that Ferrari (2005, 42–46) disputes. Here the dependent condition is not a city's being F but a city's being a city. Conversely, the city exerts a substantial and not altogether consistent influence on the views of justice that inform citizen practices.

89. Agreeing with Ferrari's (2005, 42–50) response to Williams, though for different reasons.

90. Ferrari (2005, 73–82) considers the positive outcomes of applying each side of the analogy to an understanding of the other. The abuses of the analogy in a way represent the internalization and externalization moves that Ferrari criticizes (2005, 50–53) in Jonathan Lear's formulation.

91. Ferrari (2005, 82) sees this as the framework for tyranny: "The externalization rule does not apply to the city-soul analogy, it applies to the tyrannical character who becomes an actual tyrant."

92. Though in acting as a founder of a regime that is entirely new and in insisting that Socrates show how this regime can be made real, Glaucon acts as an immoderate architect of moderation.

93. For an interesting reading that outlines the first possibility, see Lear 2006, 25–43.

94. Thus differing from Ferrari (2005, 100–2).

95. Noted by Benardete, who comments that the soul in question does not appear to be exclusively human (1989, 55). The discussion is nonetheless framed by controversies about what being human involves.

96. For Ferrari, this initial attention to the soul is a departure from the general pattern that considers the city first (cf. 2005, 38, 91–93). It is, nonetheless, a particularly striking departure because of the importance of *sōphrosynē* for this city's success as a community.

97. Those would be what Reeve (1988, 135) characterizes as good independent desires and what Penner and Rowe (2005) identify as irrational executive desires. For (very different) arguments that this radical separation of desire from implicit conceptions of the good is untenable, see Penner and Rowe 2005, 227–28; and Mara 1997, 87–91. Under conditions of horrible physical duress, we may not desire good drink (Thucydides' narrations of the power of thirst during the plague [2.49], or in the midst of the slaughter of Nicias's soldiers at the Assinarus River in Sicily [7.84], are good examples). Yet in our capacity as desiring human beings, we may always desire at some level drink *as good*. When Reeve, for example, divorces desire from beliefs about the good, his example focuses on the thirsty flies. Perhaps creatures responding to desires that are completely good-independent are really less than human.

98. The best sustained analysis of the Leontius story is Allen's (2000, 245–73).

99. These sanctions extend to the public exposure of the corpses of the condemned, a practice that signals both the wrongdoer's exclusion from the social community and the body's complete vulnerability to humiliation and shaming. Consequently, gazing at the corpses without the psychic turbulence that Socrates describes would bespeak an acceptance of Athenian norms of punishment and of the Athenian template for citizenship (cf. Allen 2000, 245–46; Parker 1983, 46).

100. Allen (2000, 266) reads Socrates' telling of the Leontius story as an attempt to replace an Athenian symbolic order, in which the sight of dead criminals gratifies the anger (*orgē*) of the citizen, with a Socratic symbolic order, in which the sight is experienced as shameful and *orgē* is replaced by *thymos*, which cooperates with rationality. It is important to remember that Socrates' resignification (cf. Allen 2000, 267) of Athenian political practices draws on other cultural resources that could serve as sources of challenge. Thus, Benardete: "The desire to see [the corpses] could arise from the satisfaction of seeing justice done, and the repulsion from the shamefulness of vicarious revenge" (1989, 99).

101. In this respect, Allen (2000, 252) may see the Athenian punitive context that Socrates challenges in the Leontius story as a bit more cohesive than Plato does.

102. The guardians' skill is directed toward the good of the city as a whole (428c), the politically courageous guardians have been previously persuaded by the laws (4309a), and moderation, which stretches through the entire city, can only be understood as the rule of the better over the worse.

103. Deveoped more fully in Mara 1997, 220–26.

104. Recall the different contributions of Craig 1994, Kochin 1999, Baracchi 2002, and Frank 2007.

105. Thus, the antifundamentalist message that Lear (2006, 33) identifies in the noble lie depends to a degree on the context in which these stories are read. The lie itself strives explicitly, though unsuccessfully (a point that Lear's interesting discussion probably needs to consider more fully), to affect that context. Interestingly, one additional inference emerging from this antifundamentalist view is that in providing stories whose credibility cannot be sustained (cf. *Republic* 538c–39a), fundamentalism easily prompts cynicism.

106. Responding to a very helpful question raised by one of the manuscript's anonymous reviewers.

107. Cf. Kochin 1999, 412–13.

108. Baracchi's comment is instructive: "Socrates, besides reframing the question of identity in terms that exceed the horizon of the 'just' *polis*, that is, in terms that exceed an understanding of the political narrowly based on this city, also mitigates the distinction between the proper and the other" (2002, 167). For somewhat different accounts of the Greek-barbarian distinction in this portion of the dialogue, see Craig (1994, 12–13), Derrida (1997, 90–92), and Kochin (1999, 422).

109. Cf. Bloom 1968, 419; Mara 1997, 140; and Strauss 1964, 130–32. In attributing these variations to human nature, Ferrari (2005, 67, 73, 80) may underplay the influence of a democratic political culture.

110. See Mara 1997, 139–41.

111. For a critical assessment, see Deneen 2000, 427–28.

112. See on the other hand, Xenophon's *Apology of Socrates*, in which Anytus's hatred of Socrates is represented as a much more personal dispute over the education of Anytus's son.

113. For a connection between Socrates' culture war and our own, see Euben 1997.

114. For a more extended treatment of Socrates' final interactions with Glaucon in the *Republic*, see Mara 1997, 74–82.

115. Cf. Mara, 1997, 142–44.

116. In this respect, my account differs from Wallach's (2001, 221), which sees Socrates' *logos* in the *Republic* successfully solving the problem of political justice. Craig's account (1994, 166–67) is closer to mine.

Chapter Five: Proximate Others

1. Cf. Said 1994, 3–8; and Kristeva 1991, 183–84.

2. This is one implication of Honig's critique (2001, 63–64) of Kristeva.

3. Recently, Honig urges us to stop thinking of foreignness as a problem and to reflect instead on the problems that foreignness helps democracies solve (2001, 4). While this is a valuable and stimulating treatment of the political puzzles of foreignness, Honig's eventual endorsement of democratic cosmopolitanism also ends by envisaging a condition in which the political problematics of otherness are overcome (2001, 122). Like other postmodernists, Honig conceptualizes questions of otherness exclusively in terms of a pacifiable enmity between "us" and "them." One could argue that the same difficulty besets Jacques Derrida's vision of a democracy that is *perhaps* to come (1997, 306) of which more is said later in the chapter.

4. See Nussbaum 1996, 21, no. 5. In making this sort of argument, Nussbaum need not be asserting some dogmatically authoritative claim; she may instead be indicating that there are particularly compelling reasons for objecting to the practice at issue. Defending these practices in the face of such arguments would require responses that take the particular force of these objections seriously. Appeals to human nature would thus play particularly strong roles in what might be called the grammar of criticism and justification.

5. Connolly 1995, 194. Honig (2001, 119–20) also sees democratic cosmopolitanism fostered when "passion, involvement, and identification are daily called into action on behalf of many extra- and subnational affiliations and memberships and causes."

6. In a way, this is the eventual direction of Foucault's (1979, 92, 101) exploration of the role of power in constructing modes of social practice and social thought.

7. It can, of course, be argued that postmodernism offers its own perspective on the appropriate content of democratic decisions, concerning issues ranging from the regulation of sexuality through environmental policy (Butler 1997b, 106–8; Connolly 1990, 76; Honig 1993, 186–92; and Mouffe 2000, 111). In

so doing, it goes well beyond clearing space for politics to make some strong suggestions about how that space should be used. In failing to acknowledge its own substantive commitments, postmodernism may execute a displacement of politics of its own. More likely, this reinforces the claim that distinctions between political theory and politics are continuous ones.

8. See also Crane 1998, 88, 147.

9. See especially Price 2001, 188.

10. The widespread rhetorical practice opposing Greeks and barbarians, especially over the course of the fifth and fourth centuries BCE, is well documented (Hall 1989, chap. 1; Long 1986, 129–34; and Loraux 1986, 165–69). The terms of this opposition were not simply descriptive, separating those who spoke Greek from those who did not, but also ethical (Long 1986, 132). Hall explains this opposition by contending (1989, 1) that "Greek writing about barbarians is usually an exercise in self-definition, for the barbarian is often portrayed as the opposite of the ideal Greek." Primary evidence ranging from Herodotus's *Histories* (4.64–72, 84, 94, 103; 7.107, 114; 8.116, 118–19; 9.109–13, 119) to Euripides' tragedies (*Iphigenia in Aulis* 1400–1401; *Orestes* 485, 1508, 1522) suggests that these contrasting ethical images were imposing presences within Athens's cultural discourses. Plato (*Republic* 470b–c) and Aristotle (*Politics* 1252b8) seem to presuppose their audiences' broad acceptance of the validity of these contrasts. One could argue that Plato and Aristotle also challenge this image. I discuss Aristotle's position as it arises within the debate over slavery (Mara 1995, 281–87).

11. Thucydides 1.3, 5, 6, 23, 24, 28, 47, 50, 82; 2.7, 36, 68, 80, 82, 97; 3.34, 112; 4.25, 109, 124–28; 6.1, 2, 6, 11, 17, 18, 20, 33, 90; 7.42, 57, 58, 60, 80.

12. Thucydides 1.14, 18, 69, 73–75, 89, 90, 96, 97, 118, 131, 132, 144; 3.56, 62; 8.16, 25, 46.

13. The representation of the Ambraciots' attitude toward the Amphilocians in Thucydides 3.112 and Brasidas's direct speech at 4.126 also employ stereotypical images of the barbarian, but neither has the condemnatory tone of the characterization of the Thracians at 7.29. And neither juxtaposes the image "barbarian" with those connected with Athenian daring and achievement.

14. If Thucydides is writing at least partially in the voice of the amazed, this may help to explain the mistakes that Orwin (1994, 133 n. 28) identifies in the final sentence of the quoted passage. Thucydides' narrative strategy of sometimes representing events through the eyes of their witnesses is noted by Connor (1984, 118) and Rood (1998, 20–21).

15. For an assessment of the relation between *logos* and *ergon* in the funeral speech that is closer to my own, see Loraux 1986, 233–36.

16. These considerations link David Grene's suggestion (1965, 75) that Thucydides is drawn to the incident at Mycalessus by the gratuitousness of the violence with Orwin's (1994, 135) observation that "[w]hat is shocking is the complicity of Athens." See also Price 2001, 215–16.

17. Orwin notes (1994, 135–36) that Athens and Mycalessus are also simultaneously linked and separated by Mycalessus's resemblance to the old, rural Athens and utter difference from "fortress Athens." My suggestion is that Mycalessus is paradoxically linked to Periclean Athens as well.

18. Though this should not be interpreted as eliminating all cultural connections between the two cities. As Loraux (1986, 144–45) notes, "[A]lthough it did not organize education, [Athens] was not unconcerned about the functioning of schools or about the behavior of adults, who were permanently formed by a generalized education."

19. Rosen (1987, 7) intriguingly speculates that the symposium occurs very close to the night the Hermae are mutilated just prior to the launching of the Sicilian invasion. Nussbaum (2001, 168–71) dates the narrative around the time of the Thirty.

20. Cf. Loraux 1986, 191–92. Nietzsche comments astutely at Nietzsche 1969, 39–43.

21. Where memory might be understood as including both of Paul Ricoeur's (2004, 88) truthful and pragmatic functions. A more thematic treatment of Thucydides' treatment of memory appears in the conclusion, pp. 243–48.

22. As in Apollodorus's raging (*agriainein*) rejection of what he takes to be the nonphilosophic practices of his fellow citizens (173d).

23. Thus, Achilles' reconciliation with Priam at the conclusion of the *Iliad* occurs within a human community and not within any particular political culture. See, for example, Euben 1990, 223–24.

24. Cf. Foucault 1984a, 199–201, 221–25.

25. I discuss this aspect of Socrates' treatment of what I call the goods of *erōs* more fully in Mara 1997, 209–17.

26. For an interpretation that sees Aristophanes' vision as being more compatible with a certain kind of mutuality, see D. Anderson (1993, 44).

27. Cf. Loraux 1986, 122.

28. I agree with commentators who conclude that Diotima is a creation of Socrates. Scholars differ over the significance of Diotima's femininity, but its destabilizing influence in the masculine context of the symposium cannot be denied. For different views, see Saxonhouse 1984, 5–27, and Halperin 1990, 150.

29. Cf. Mara 1997, 205–9.

30. Philosophy's grounding in a certain form of *erōs* is one explanation for the courage in the absence of wisdom that Socrates exhibits at the end of the *Protagoras*. Yet philosophy as represented in the *Protagoras* occurs not daimonically but conversationally. The *Symposium* is connected with the *Protagoras* in a number of provocative ways reflecting both similarities (the dramatic contexts are both gatherings in private houses; there are a number of common participants) and differences (the *Protagoras* is exactly datable, whereas the *Symposium* pointedly avoids exactitude as to when the conversation has taken place; Alcibiades is Socrates' ally in the *Protagoras*, his deepest critic in the *Symposium*). One thematic link may be the implication that philosophy is neither the calculation of the consequences of action choices, nor the self-forgetting of daimonic transcendence.

31. On Nicias's and Alcibiades' different uses of youthfulness and age in the Sicilian debate, see also Saxonhouse 2006, 168–69.

32. Price (2001, 258) may, however, exaggerate the degree of Alcibiades' influence.

33. So, I question whether Alcibiades' exposure to Socratic philosophy is seen as a way of redirecting Athens's politics (cf. Wohl 2002, 159–61). Socrates' political goals for Athens may be more modest. The "dream of a philosophical city" achieved through a converted Alcibiades makes Socrates' vision of philosophy sound a bit too much like Agathon's vision of love.

34. A closer Platonic parallel to Honig's foreign-founder (cf. 2001, 38–40) is not Socrates, but Alcibiades, loved and mistrusted (*Frogs* 1425), exalted and exiled (Thucydides 6.15). And unlike Rousseau's legislator, Freud's Moses, or the Old Testament's Ruth, the ancestor of David, Socrates establishes no new orders. Instead, he envisages endless (cf. *Apology* 41a–c) critiques of all forms of order, political and psychological. In this respect, Socrates offers a vision of the foreigner that is much less prone to Honig's democratic resolution.

35. Thus, when Yael Tamir (1996, 21, no. 3) objects to the rhetorical purposes behind many contemporary criticisms of clitoridectomy, she does not do so in the name of cultural relativism, but for the purpose of arguing for a more adequate conception of the dignity of women.

Conclusion

1. Reading Strauss in a different way from Behnegar 2003, 67. The ambiguities are intensified when we consider the philosophers whom Strauss identifies as bracketing final solutions to political problems: Plato and Hegel. Hegel has understood his philosophy as going beyond, while still preserving, all previous philosophies (certainly including Plato's). Yet Hegel's failure to offer any real resolution is signaled by the rise of historicism, the intellectual posture that undercuts the Hegelian project with its own historical framework. That Plato has offered any final solution has to be questioned on Strauss's own grounds, since in the Platonic dialogues "we hear Plato never" (Strauss 1964, 50). Instead we hear his voice through the often conflicting voices of his characters, the principal one of whom is Socrates, who realizes "we are ignorant of the most important things" (Strauss 1953, 36) and who "is notorious for his irony" (Strauss 1964, 50–51). For evidence supporting this reading of Strauss's position, see Strauss 2000, 196.

2. Attacks on Strauss have become more virulent and politicized in light of the alleged involvement of some of his "students" or those who claim to be "Straussians" in orchestrating the 2003 Iraq War (cf. Norton 2004). How much of this is really connected with serious attempts to understand Strauss's ideas (not made any easier by Strauss's style, to be sure) is more questionable. See, for example, the older but still relevant essay by Tarcov (1983, 5–29) and the more recent work by Zuckert (1996) and Zuckert and Zuckert (2006). It is undeniable that Strauss's Thucydides and Plato are less democratic than those authors as interpreted here. This does not mean that Strauss's interpretations of these authors and his assessments of democracy, generally, are reactionary. In this context, my principal difference with Strauss concerns the sharp distinction he draws

between philosophers and nonphilosophers (as in Strauss 1953, 142–43). This has significant implications for reading these texts, for assessing the origins, degrees, and political relevance of natural differences found among human beings, and for the general relationship between philosophy and democracy.

3. Cf. Ignatieff 2001, 9–10.

4. A difficulty identified, for example, by Habermas (1993, 14–15): "[B]ehind a facade of categorical validity may lurk a hidden, entrenched interest that is susceptible of only being pushed through. This facade can be erected all the more easily because of the rightness of moral commands.... Liberating ourselves from the merely presumptive generality of selectively employed universalistic principles applied in a context-insensitive manner has always required, and today still requires, social movements and political struggles; we have to learn from the painful experiences and the irreparable suffering of those who have been humiliated, insulted, injured, and brutalized that nobody may be excluded in the name of moral universalism."

5. This is dilemma that besets various forms of postmodernism, as suggested by the critical appraisal of Derrida's project offered by Zuckert and Zuckert (2006, 113–14). Postmodern responses have been various, though it is generally agreed that this dilemma must be addressed politically and that means democratically. For Honig, this engagement is nourished by the ambivalence with which democratic citizens should regard their own institutions and culture. Democratic citizens should therefore interpret their communities in the way that one reads Gothic romances, realizing "that we may passionately support certain heroes (or principles or institutions) in political life while also knowing that we ought not take our eyes off them" (Honig 2001, 120). The project of discovering truths about human beings, including truths about their human rights, is replaced by a suspicion of localized closures of whatever sort. One of the principal contributions of this perspective has been to insist that the problem of the simultaneously open and exclusionary character of democratic citizenship is ongoing, setting at least one of the continuous tasks for democratic politics. (See Honig 2001, 13, 121–22.) But this perspective nonetheless presupposes that democracy is the best way and not simply "our" way of handling such dilemmas. This requires an argument that considers the merits of different forms of governance generally, not, *pace* Honig (121), simply an acknowledgment of "passionate ambivalences."

6. This difficulty must influence the way in which we interpret the idea that human rights can be globalized through localisms. See Ignatieff 2001, 133–36; and Laqueur 2001, 162–64.

7. Benhabib (2004, 133) wishes to avoid "specifying what cognitive, psychological or other attributes we must attribute to persons in order to consider them capable of discursive justification." Yet she also contends that "universality refers to what would be valid for all human beings considered as beings equally entitled to respect and concern." Seeing humans as beings entitled to respect and concern frames descriptions of their cognitive and psychological characteristics in nontrivial ways, and recourse to the activity of discursive justification performatively acknowledges the presence of discourse partners who take that vision of human beings seriously.

8. I take this to be the major point made by both Midgley (1995) and Salkever (1990).

9. Cf. Ignatieff 2001, 165–67.

10. As Sen (1999, 56–58) notes, perspectives on social justice vary in their relevant informational bases and in what is taken to be relevant and irrelevant for purposes of institutional evaluation. These differences do seem to be cued by what is seen as being most important to human life.

11. Cf. Wallach 2004, 114.

12. For the centrality of autonomy in political theory, see Benhabib 2004, 132–33; Cohen and Arato 1992, 397–98, 404: Habermas 1993, 130–31; Rawls 2005, 455–56; Richardson 2002, 17–18; and Warren 2001, 62–69. Though all acknowledge their intellectual debts to Kant, his argument for grounding rights in autonomy is seen as being fundamentally different. Kant establishes rights on the basis of the status of human beings as free rational creatures. Those writing within a "postmetaphysical" framework (cf. Habermas 1992, 34–39; Benhabib 2004, 129–32; and Cohen and Arato 1992, 369) see rights as designating those protections or endowments that no rational person would agree to have violated or identify autonomy as a specifically political requirement within conflictual environments (Warren 2001, 62). However, the difference between the comprehensive Kantian position and that taken by the postmetaphysicians may not be as great as the latter suggest, largely because they do not really avoid privileging a particular view of the person. Cf. Habermas 1993, 28–29; and Rawls 2005, 424–26. And characterizing autonomy as a particular good is only possible on the basis of a deeper understanding of the person that gives autonomy pride of place (over, say, practicing the virtues characteristic of a flourishing human being or displaying one's own particular virtuosity in situations characterized by conflict). In this respect, autonomy comes to play a constitutive role in what Rawls characterizes as a comprehensive understanding of the good.

13. The signature modern statement for the priority of right is Rawls's (1971, 24–27; 2005, 173–211). Accepting this formulation as compelling presumes conceptions of the right as an imperative disconnected from interest, and the good as a goal disconnected from the moral. These presumptions are hardly noncontroversial. Both Plato's *Republic* and Aristotle's *Nicomachean Ethics* presume an understanding of morality consistent with human interests and an understanding of the good connected with the practice of justice.

14. Habermas identifies this project as belonging to ethical practical reason, which he distinguishes (1993, 1–17) from both the pragmatic (which concerns how stipulated outcomes can be effectively achieved) and the moral (which concerns obligations toward others). See also Cohen and Arato 1992, 359–60. It does seem questionable how clear the boundaries among these three forms of practical reasoning can be from the perspective of political philosophy, since their practices are all embedded within networks of social relations (Habermas 1993, 16) or within a somewhat broader pragmatic focus generally, as in the Socratic connection linking happiness, choice, and justice in the *Republic*'s concluding myth.

15. Most recently, Price 2001, 55.

16. Cf. Habermas 1993, 54–57; Rawls 2005, 462–66; and Rawls 1999, 27–30. In distancing itself from a wide range of human emotions, the perspective endorsing communicative rationality may also misrepresent the goods and processes of practical rationality. See Salkever 2002.

17. In this respect, Thucydides may be one voice within the so-called canon that does offer some basis for comprehending the horrors of the twentieth century (cf. Kateb 2002, 482–505). His emphasis on the obsessive and potentially destructive character of political imagination (chapter 2) provides some basis for explaining the unprecedented bloodshed and dislocation of his "greatest war." More speculatively, both Thucydides and Plato seem to articulate strong warnings against the moral blindness that accompanies an inactive imagination (Kateb 2002, 487). Where both go beyond Kateb is in the recognition that no response to moral blindness can avoid courting a "hyperactive imagination" that may spawn further abuses.

18. Thus, I suggest we may need to subject democracy to the same sort of critical analysis that Warren (2004, 1, 16–18) applies to notions of social capital.

19. My appreciation of these issues has been greatly improved by conversations with Elizabeth Markovits. For an extended treatment of the complexities of democratic rhetoric, see Markovits, forthcoming.

20. This is a particular point of emphasis in the various treatments of how a vibrant associational life can strengthen democracies. Putnam's (1993, 171–76) positing a strong connection between the two has elicited a critical literature that identifies the damage that some strong associations can do to democratic possibilities. Warren (2001) addresses this in his sophisticated investigation of the democratic and nondemocratic effects of various associational forms.

21. On the potential abuses of the mass media in new democracies, see Bermeo 2003, 254 n. 107. Note that Bermeo is concerned with impacts on the *quality* of democracy.

22. Cf. Thucydides 2.37. Radicalized in the complete endorsement of an ideology of distinction in the speech of Alcibiades in 6.16–18.

23. As in Connolly 1995, 89–93; Habermas 1996, 359; Honig 2001, 118–19; and Warren 2001, 226.

24. For liberals and participatory democrats, the politically relevant virtues are those that enable citizens to function effectively within the boundaries of democratic institutions and purposes. For good statements see Rawls 2005, 205–6; and Warren 2001, 73–74.

25. Thus, in Habermas's terms confusing the moral with the ethical. Cf. Habermas 1996, 180–81; Rawls 2005, 420–21; and Warren 2001, 22–23.

26. As in Bentham, *The Principles of Morals and Legislation*, chap. 7, sec 18.

27. For Habermas, critical assessments of ethical choices belong to the clinical therapist or analogous discourse partners (1993, 11). In keeping with the principled focus on self-realization, the therapist must remain content with the conception of self-affirmation achieved on the part of the subject after suitable clarification processes have been followed. An interesting comparative focus

would be with Socrates, for whom a fully clarified conception of self-realization may nonetheless be fundamentally flawed.

28. Assessing this literature is complicated by the politicized rhetoric that often distorts arguments on all sides. The title of James Q. Wilson's essay (1985, 3–17), which identifies private character as a cause of public policy problems, initially reinforces Warren's theoretical critique of those who trace systemic disorders to the "aggregate effects of individual character" (2001, 20). Yet the substance of the essay works against the title, for in focusing on social influences on character, Wilson acknowledges that the formation of character is not simply private. Similarly, even though Bennett, Dilulio, and Walters (1996) identify "moral poverty" as the root cause of social crime, their real focus is on the ways in which moral poverty is socially created. To this extent neither Wilson nor Bennett et al. are liable to Warren's precise criticism. By escaping this critique, however, they also show the inadequacy of assessments that stop with influences of (rather than influences on) character. The language of character has often been aggressively used (against targets real and fabricated) by those supporting conservative political goals; consequently, that language becomes even more suspect for those with a different vision of the country's problems and future.

29. In this respect, what Habermas calls the ethical employment of practical reason (1993, 6) cannot be separated from political philosophy.

30. Thus, John Borneman's scholarly assessment (cf. 1992, 285, 303) of the attempts of East German and West German bureaucracies to place institutional limits on the recognition of different marriage forms reflects a goods-based argument. The creation and recognition of a variety of marriage forms make enhanced forms of self-realization and human development possible.

31. Sen's (1999, 36–41) answer seems to be yes. At the same time, once he acknowledges the necessity of focusing not simply on "means of good living [but on] the *actual living* that people manage to achieve," his understanding of capabilities expands well beyond freedom or agency.

32. See, for example, Dovi 2007, chap. 3; Guinier 1994, 1–7; Mansbridge 1999a, 628–57; Phillips 1998, 224–40; Pogge 2002, 26–54; Weldon 2002, 1153–74; and Young 1990, 91–95. In one respect or another all are concerned with the question of how minority or marginalized groups or voices are to be represented fairly. Implementing any of the proposals emerging from their reflections presumes the presence of a serious sense of justice among a significant portion of citizens who are ready to make their own voices heard in this cause.

33. Cf. Dilulio 1992–93, 17; and Koziak, 2000, 163.

34. As noted also by Zumbrunnen 2002, 567–69.

35. On forgetting as a condition for political action, see Loraux 1998, 286; and Wolpert 2002, 119. On the pragmatics of promise, memory, and forgetting, see Loraux 1986, 121–23; Loraux 1998, 85–88, 101–2; Ricoeur 2004, 82–85, 93–94, 107, 119–24, 442, 502; and Wolpert 2002, 87–90. The originary treatment is still Nietzsche's, as in Nietzsche 1980, 19–22 and Nietzsche 1989, 57–58.

36. For these reasons, I do not agree with Orwin (1994, 183, 204) that Thucydides sees a better chance for sustaining moderation through Spartan piety

than through Athenian rationalism. There are variations within Athenian rationalism, and Thucydides' own *logos* may be critical of Athenian politics without endorsing the Spartan alternative as preferable. It is questionable how highly Thucydides values what is described by the Spartans as moderation.

37. Thus, I am not in agreement with the view of Monoson and Loriaux 1998, 286, that Pericles is in this respect a follower.

38. An irony also noted by Palmer 1992, 36–37.

39. Cf. Loraux 1986, 122.

40. Cf. Ricoeur 2004, 82–83; Loraux 1986, 123; and Wohl 2002, 32–41. Whereas Ricoeur treats this as manipulation, Loraux sees it as a form of political practice.

41. Loraux (1986, 180–93) sees Pericles' aristocratic direction as being set in part by the *epitaphios* (funeral oratory) tradition, rather than as a controversial political statement of Pericles himself. In this respect, I differ a bit from Balot (2001, 148–49), who reads Thucydides as criticizing Pericles for pursuing overly democratic ideals. The ideal to which Pericles appeals maps his own vision of human excellence onto Athens's practices. My reading of Pericles is closer to Wohl's (2002, 61–61), though my assessment of Thucydides' differences from Pericles is not.

42. Cf. Loraux 1986, 191–92; Parry 1981, 173; and de Romilly 1963, 357–58.

43. For Wohl (2002, 200) such considerations reveal the hollowness of the Periclean ideal, a conclusion that I believe goes too far. Orwin notes (1994, 4) the replacement of greatness with calamity in Thucydides 1.23, though he draws no conclusions here about the implications of this shift for the standing of the Periclean ethic.

44. Recalling Orwin 1984, 315.

45. The first is the memory of rational choice theorists, as in Axelrod 1984, 59–60; the second is that of Arendt 1968, 227–64.

46. See Wohl's (2002, 7–9) provocative discussion of why Thucydides mentions only Harmodius.

47. See Nietzsche's treatment in *Genealogy*, second essay, where the forward-looking act of promising is connected with positing a new identity.

48. Both Orwin 1994, 157–58 and Zumbrunnen 2002, 580 suggest that Diodotus's speech is also about the problematic choice among political goods.

49. This reason for the failure to keep promises intersects with and differs from Butler's positing the influence of historical accidents on the meaning of a sign, resulting in augmentation "in excess of its originating intentions." (Butler 1997b, 72).

50. In a way, this understanding of a turning resembles Butler's interpretation of how the turning back of consciousness works to create the subject (1997b, 3–4). What the turning of Diodotus's rhetoric produces is not a stable outcome but a field characterized by fluidity and unpredictability, more the turning of Foucault than of Hegel.

51. As, for example, in Johnson 1993, 135.

52. Cf. Saxonhouse 1996, 76; 2006, 160–63.

53. In this particular respect, my reading differs from that of Hunter (1973, 180–84), who interprets Thucydides as revealing the predictable cycles and patterns of historical change.

54. Differing from Loraux 1986, 289–91 and agreeing with Strauss 1964, 231 and Orwin 1994, 104–6, though I offer a different interpretation of what these parallels imply. A view closer to mine is that of Saxonhouse 2006, 214.

55. On the significance of this passage for understanding the character of political memory, see also Ricoeur 2004, 417.

56. See, for example, Crane 1996, 208; Crane 1998, 99–100; de Romilly 1963, 336–37, 357; and Price 2001, 11–22. There are of course important exceptions.See especially, Euben 1990, Saxonhouse 1996, and several commentaries (Forde 1989, Orwin 1994, Palmer 1992) informed by the interpretations of Strauss 1964, but they have been exceptions.

57. This sense of the indeterminacy of political speech goes in a different direction from that traced by Butler (1997a), who sees forms of *damaging* speech as creating the conditions for their own contestation.

58. For a general critique of Arendt's treatment of political forgiveness, see Ricoeur 2004, 417.

59. Cf. Tsao 2002, 97–123.

60. Compare with Arendt 1958, 41.

61. See also Zumbrunnen 2002, 579–80. My suggestion is that this debate addresses both "who the Athenians are [and] what shall be done with their captives" (Zumbrunnen 2002, 579).

62. The comparison with Thucydides underscores the exaggerated character of Arendt's emphasis on the performative aspect of politics. This emphasis is in part traceable to Arendt's constructing her understanding of politics and action on the basis of a questionable interpretation of the Western tradition of political philosophy as a continuous attempt to convert political practice into some form of making. For a deep and appreciative account of Arendt's project see Villa 1996.

63. Cf. Nails 2002.

64. Cf. Wood and Wood 1978, 55–82.

65. Cf. Mara 1997, 43–46.

66. That is, those dialogues that reveal the commitments of Socrates, prior to the overlay of Platonic philosophy (Villa 2001, 28–29). Villa's conclusions are reinforced by a methodological acceptance of the division between the early "Socratic" (aporetic) dialogues and the later "Platonic" (dogmatic) ones (2). Despite the long-standing and well-respected scholarly tradition behind this framework, however, its validity is far from obvious. See, for example, Mara 1997, 9–13.

67. Here I expand upon points sketched in Mara 2002, 815–16.

68. See also Baracchi 2002, 158–60.

69. Perhaps reflected in the problematic case of anger. Does either Socrates or Diodotus recognize the legitimacy of anger? The continued influence of anger may be another reason why politics needs rationality even as it works against it. And the distances of both Socrates and Diodotus from anger may be another reason why neither belongs simply to the city.

70. In Strauss's (1964, 140–41) terms.

71. In this respect, both Thucydides and Plato could be read as speaking within the horizons of the city, but as raising questions about what that horizon encompasses. Together, they appear to elide the distinction between the philosophical understanding of the city and the understanding that is "first for us" (cf. Strauss, 1964, 241).

72. One might, therefore, be able to construct a useful reply to Vlastos and Euben (cf. Euben 1997, 221). Villa (2001, 37–38) distinguishes Socrates' concern for morality from Diodotus's concern for interests. I wonder if this gap is quite so wide. In this respect, also note Benardete's (1991, 7 n. 1) provocative linkage of Gorgias with Cleon.

73. This condition between war and peace would be different from the condition that Strauss (1964, 240) opposes to the city's being at war; it would be a time of peace where "the city's inhabitants are of kindlier thoughts than they are when at war." It should be noted that being "not immediately exposed to that violent teacher war" is not quite the same as being "at peace." The characteristic civic activity of this time of "not war" may therefore be something other than "the admiration of the ancient, of the ancestral." In this light, Thucydides would be a more important resource for the present than the *Hymn to Apollo*, though Thucydides' resource would include his own narrative uses of the *Hymn*.

74. For Morrison (2006, 197–98), then, "[t]here is a seed of optimism in Thucydides' work."

75. The connection between Hobbesian political theory and optimism about the consequences of institutional reform is suggested, for example, by Hardin 1995, 143–45.

76. On Nietzsche as a resource for agonistic democracy see, for example, Connolly 1990, 74.

References

Ahrensdorf, Peter. 1997. "Thucydides' Realistic Critique of Realism." *Polity* 30, no. 2: 231–65.
Allen, Danielle. 2000. *The World of Prometheus*. Princeton, NJ: Princeton University Press.
Almond, Gabriel, and Sidney Verba. 1989. *The Civic Culture Revisited*. Newbury Park, CA: Sage Publications.
Anderson, Benedict. 1991. *Imagined Communities*. Rev. ed. London. Verso.
Anderson, Daniel. 1993. *The Masks of Dionysos: A Commentary on Plato's "Symposium."* Albany: State University of New York Press.
Arendt, Hannah. 1958. *The Human Condition*. Chicago: University of Chicago Press.
———. 1968. *Between Past and Future*. New York: Vintage.
Axelrod, Robert. 1984. *The Evolution of Cooperation*. New York: Basic Books.
———. 1997. *The Complexity of Cooperation*. Princeton, NJ: Princeton University Press.
Balot, Ryan. 2001. *Greed and Injustice in Classical Athens*. Princeton, NJ: Princeton University Press.
Baracchi, Claudia. 2002. *Of Myth, Life and War in Plato's "Republic."* Bloomington: Indiana University Press.
Barber, Benjamin. 2003. *Strong Democracy*. Berkeley and Los Angeles: University of California Press.
Bartlett, Robert C., trans. 2004. *Plato: "Protagoras" and "Meno."* With notes and interpretive essays. Ithaca, NY: Cornell University Press.
Becker, Gary. 1996. "The Economic Way of Looking at Behavior." The Nobel Lecture. Stanford, CA: Hoover Institution.
Behnegar, Nasser. 2003. *Leo Strauss, Max Weber and the Scientific Study of Politics*. Chicago: University of Chicago Press.
Beiner, Ronald. 1983. *Political Judgment*. Chicago: University of Chicago Press.
Bellah, Robert, and Richard Madsen, William M. Sullivan, Ann Swidler, and Steven M. Tipton. 1985. *Habits of the Heart*. Berkeley and Los Angeles: University of California Press.
Benardete, Seth. 1989. *Socrates' Second Sailing*. Chicago: University of Chicago Press.

———. 1991. *The Rhetoric of Morality and Philosophy*. Chicago: University of Chicago Press.
Benhabib, Seyla. 1992. *Situating the Self: Gender, Community and Postmodernism in Contemporary Ethics*. New York: Routledge.
———. 2002. *The Claims of Culture*. Princeton, NJ: Princeton University Press.
———. 2004. *The Rights of Others*. New York: Cambridge University Press.
Bennett, William, John Dilulio, and John P. Walters. 1996. *Body Count: Moral Poverty . . . and How to Win America's War on Crime and Drugs*. New York: Simon and Schuster.
Bercovitch, Sacvan. 1998. "The Function of the Literary in a Time of Cultural Studies." In *"Culture" and the Problem of the Disciplines*, ed. John Carlos Rowe. New York: Columbia University Press.
Berelson, Bernard, Paul F. Lazarsfeld, and William McPhee. 1954. *Voting: A Study of Opinion Formation in a Presidential Campaign*. Chicago: University of Chicago Press.
Berkowitz, Peter. 1999. *Virtue and the Making of Modern Liberalism*. Princeton, NJ: Princeton University Press.
Bermeo, Nancy. 2003. *Ordinary People in Extraordinary Times*. Princeton, NJ: Princeton University Press.
Berns, Walter. 1962. "Voting Studies." In *Essays on the Scientific Study of Politics*, ed. Herbert J. Storing. New York: Holt, Rinehart and Winston.
Bloom, Allan, trans. 1968. *The Republic of Platio*. New York: Basic Books.
Borneman, John. 1992. *Belonging in the Two Berlins*. New York: Cambridge University Press.
Brams, Steven. 1980. *Biblical Games*. Cambridge, MA: MIT Press.
Brann, Eva. 1978. "The Offense of Socrates." *Interpretation* 7, no. 2:1–21.
———. 2004. *The Music of the Republic*. Philadelphia: Paul Dry Books.
Bruell, Christopher. 1977. "Socratic Politics and Self Knowledge: An Interpretation of Plato's *Charmides*," *Interpretation* 6, no. 3:141–203.
Buchanan, James, and Gordon Tullock. 1965. *The Calculus of Consent*. Ann Arbor: University of Michigan Press.
Butler, Judith. 1997a. *Excitable Speech*. New York: Routledge.
———. 1997b. *The Psychic Life of Power*. Stanford, CA: Stanford University Press.
Cairns, Douglas. 1993. *Aidōs*. Oxford: Clarendon Press.
Caldeira, Teresa. 2000. *City of Walls*. Berkeley and Los Angeles: University of California Press.
Carter, L. B. 1986. *The Quiet Athenian*. Oxford: Clarendon Press.
Carter, Stephen. 1993. *The Culture of Disbelief: How American Law and Politics Trivialize Religious Devotion*. New York: Basic Books.
Chong, Dennis. 1991. *Collective Action and the Civil Rights Movement*. Chicago: University of Chicago Press.
———. 1996. "Rational Choice Theory's Mysterious Rivals." In *The Rational Choice Controversy*, ed. Jeffrey Friedman. New Haven, CT: Yale University Press.
———. 2000. *Rational Lives*. Chicago: University of Chicago Press.

Coby, Patrick. 1987. *Socrates and the Sophistic Enlightenment*. Lewisburg, PA: Bucknell University Press.
Cogan, Marc. 1981. *The Human Thing: The Speeches and Principles of Thucydides' History*. Chicago: Chicago University Press.
Cohen, Jean. 1999. "Trust, Voluntary Association and Workable Democracy: The Contemporary American Discourse of Civil Society." In *Democracy and Trust*, ed. Mark Warren. New York: Cambridge University Press.
Cohen, Jean, and Andrew Arato. 1992. *Civil Society and Political Theory*. Cambridge, MA: MIT Press.
Cohen, Joshua. 1997. "Deliberation and Democratic Legitimacy." In *Deliberative Democracy*, ed. James Bohman and William Rehg. Cambridge, MA: MIT Press.
Connolly, William. 1990. "Identity and Difference in Liberalism." In *Liberalism and the Good*, ed. R. Bruce Douglass, Gerald Mara, and Henry Richardson. New York: Routledge.
———. 1993. *The Augustinian Imperative*. Newbury Park, CA: Sage Publications.
———. 1995. *The Ethos of Pluralization*. Minneapolis: University of Minnesota Press.
Connor, Robert. 1984. *Thucydides*. Princeton, NJ: Princeton University Press.
Constable, Pamela, and Arturo Valenzuela. 1991. *A Nation of Enemies: Chile under Pinochet*. New York: Norton.
Craig, Leon H. 1994. *The War Lover: A Study of Plato's "Republic."* Toronto: University of Toronto Press.
Crane, Gregory. 1996. *The Blinded Eye*. Lanham, MD: Rowman and Littlefield.
———. 1998. *Thucydides and the Ancient Simplicity*. Berkeley and Los Angeles: University of California Press.
Crawley, Richard, trans. [1910] 1993. *History of the Peloponnesian War*. Ed. W. Robert Connor. London: Dent.
Dahl, Robert. 1956. *A Preface to Democratic Theory*. Chicago: University of Chicago Press.
———. 1971. *Polyarchy: Participation and Opposition*. New Haven, CT: Yale University Press.
———. 1989. *Democracy and Its Critics*. New Haven, CT: Yale University Press.
Daniel, E. Valentine, and Jeffrey Peck. 1996. "Culture/Contexture: An Introduction." In *Culture/Contexture: Explorations in Anthropology and Literary Studies*, ed. E. Valentine Daniel and Jeffrey Peck. Berkeley and Los Angeles: University of California Press.
Davies, J. K. 1971. *Athenian Propertied Families*. Oxford: Clarendon Press.
Debnar, Paula. 2001. *Speaking the Same Language*. Ann Arbor: University of Michigan Press.
Deneen, Patrick. 2000."Chasing Plato." *Political Theory* 28, no. 3:421–39.
Derrida, Jacques. 1997. *Politics of Friendship*. Trans. George Collins. London: Verso.
———. 2005. *Rogues*. Trans. Pascale-Anne Brault and Michael Naas. Stanford, CA: Stanford University Press.

de Romilly, Jacqueline. 1963. *Thucydides and Athenian Imperialism*. Trans. Philip Thody. Oxford: Blackwell.
Diggins, John Patrick. 1984. *The Lost Soul of American Politics*. New York: Basic Books.
Dilulio, John. 1992–93. "Inner City Crime: What the Federal Government Should Do." *Responsive Community*. 3, no. 1 (Winter).
Dodds, E. R. 1959. *Plato: "Gorgias"; A Revised Text and Commentary*. Oxford. Clarendon Press.
Dovi, Suzanne. 2007. *The Good Representative*. Malden, MA and Oxford, UK: Blackwell.
Downs Anthony. 1957. *An Economic Theory of Democracy*. New York: Harper and Row.
Drury, Shadia. 1988. *The Political Ideas of Leo Strauss*. Basingstoke, UK: Macmillan.
———. 1997. *Leo Strauss and the American Right*. New York: St. Martin's Press.
Edmunds, Lowell. 1975. *Chance and Intelligence in Thucydides*. Cambridge, MA: Harvard University Press.
Elshtain, Jean Bethke. 2001. "Faith of Our Fathers and Mothers: Religious Belief and American Democracy." In *Religion in American Public Life*. New York: American Assembly.
Elshtain, Jean Bethke, et al. 1998. *A Call to Civil Society*. New York: Institute for American Values.
Elster, Jon. 1989. *The Cement of Society*. New York: Cambridge University Press.
———. 1997. "The Market and the Forum: Three Varieties of Political Theory." In *Deliberative Democracy*, ed. James Bohman and William Rehg. Cambridge, MA: MIT Press.
Estlund, David. 1997. "Beyond Fairness and Deliberation: The Epistemic Dimension of Democratic Authority." In *Deliberative Democracy*, ed. James Bohman and William Rehg. Cambridge, MA: MIT Press.
Euben, J. Peter. 1990.*The Tragedy of Political Theory*. Princeton, NJ: Princeton University Press.
———. 1997. *Corrupting Youth*. Princeton, NJ: Princeton University Press.
Farrar, Cynthia. 1988. *The Origins of Democratic Thinking*. Cambridge: Cambridge University Press.
Ferrari, Giovanni. 2005. *City and Soul in Plato's* Republic. Chicago: University of Chicago Press.
Forde, Steven. 1989. *The Ambition to Rule*. Ithaca. Cornell University Press.
———. 1995. "International Realism and the Science of Politics: Thucydides, Machiavelli and Neorealism." *International Studies Quarterly* 39:141–60.
Foucault, Michel. 1978. *The History of Sexuality. Vol. 1, An Introduction*. Trans. Robert Hurley. New York: Vintage.
———. 1979. *Discipline and Punish*. Trans. Alan Sheridan. New York: Vintage.
———. 1984a. *The History of Sexuality. Vol. 2, The Use of Pleasure*. Trans. Robert Hurley. New York: Vintage.
———. 1984b. "Nietzsche, Genealogy, History." In *The Foucault Reader*, ed. Paul Rabinow. New York: Pantheon.

———. 1994. *The Order of Things*. New York: Vintage.
Frank, Jill. 2005. *A Democracy of Distinction*. Chicago: University of Chicago Press.
———. 2007. "Wages of War: Judgment in Plato's Republic," *Political Theory* 35, no. 4:443–67.
Friedman, Jeffrey. 1996. "Economic Approaches to Politics." In *The Rational Choice Controversy*, ed. Jeffrey Friedman. New Haven, CT: Yale University Press.
Fukuyama, Francis. 1995. *Trust: The Social Virtues and the Creation of Prosperity*. New York: Free Press.
Galston, William. 1991. *Liberal Purposes*. New York: Cambridge University Press.
Geertz, Clifford. 1968. *Islam Observed*. New Haven, CT: Yale University Press.
———. 1973. *The Interpretation of Cultures*. New York: Basic Books.
———. 1983. *Local Knowledge*. New York: Basic Books.
———. 2000. *Available Light*. Princeton, NJ: Princeton University Press.
Gilligan, Carol. 1982. *In a Different Voice: Psychological Theory and Women's Development*. Cambridge, MA: Harvard University Press.
Goldhill, Simon. 1999. "Programme Notes." In *Performance Culture and Athenian Democracy*, ed. Simon Goldhill and Robin Osborne. Cambridge: Cambridge University Press.
Gomme, A. W., A. Andrewes, and K. J. Dover. 1970. *A Historical Commentary on Thucydides*. Vol. 4. Oxford: Clarendon Press.
Gould, Carol. 2004. *Globalizing Democracy and Human Rights*. New York: Cambridge University Press.
Gray, John. 1989. *Liberalisms: Essays in Political Philosophy*. New York: Routledge.
———. 1993. "Can We Agree to Disagree?" *New York Times Book Review*, May 16.
Green, Donald P., and Ian Shapiro. 1994. *The Pathologies of Rational Choice Theory*. New Haven, CT: Yale University Press.
Grene, David. 1965. *Greek Political Theory: The Image of Man in Thucydides and Plato*. Chicago: University of Chicago Press.
Gurr, Ted Robert. 1970. *Why Men Rebel*. Princeton, NJ: Princeton University Press.
Guinier, Lani. 1994. *The Tyranny of the Majority*. New York: Free Press.
Habermas, Jürgen. 1973. *Theory and Practice*. Trans. John Viertel. Boston: Beacon Press.
———. 1975. *Legitimation Crisis*. Trans. Thomas McCarthy. Boston: Beacon Press.
———. 1979. *Communication and the Evolution of Society*. Trans. Thomas McCarthy. Boston: Beacon Press.
———. 1984. *The Theory of Communicative Action*. Trans. Thomas McCarthy. Vol. 1. Cambridge, MA: MIT Press.
———. 1992. *Postmetaphysical Thinking*. Trans. William Mark Hohengarten. Cambridge, MA: MIT Press.
———. 1993. *Justification and Application*. Trans. Ciaran Cronin. Cambridge, MA: MIT Press.

———. 1996. *Between Facts and Norms*. Trans. William Rehg. Cambridge, MA: MIT Press.

———. 2001. *The Liberating Power of Symbols*. Trans. Peter Dews. Cambridge, MA: MIT Press.

Hall, Edith. 1989. *Inventing the Barbarian: Greek Self Definition through Tragedy*. Oxford: Clarendon Press.

Halperin, David. 1990. *One Hundred Years of Homosexuality*. New York: Routledge.

Hanson, Victor Davis. 1995. Introduction to *The Landmark Thucydides*, ed. Robert Strassler. New York: Free Press.

Hardin, Russell. 1995. *One for All*. Princeton, NJ: Princeton University Press.

———. 1999. "Do We Want Trust in Government?" In *Democracy and Trust*, ed. Mark Warren. New York: Cambridge University Press.

Havelock, Eric. 1957. *The Liberal Temper in Greek Politics*. New Haven, CT: Yale University Press.

Heilke, Thomas. 2004. "Realism, Narrative and Happenstance: Thucydides' Tale of Brasidas."*American Political Science Review* 98, no. 1:121–38.

Held, David. 2004. *Global Covenant: The Social Democratic Alternative to the Washington Consensus*. New York: Polity Press.

Holmes, Stephen. 1993. *The Anatomy of Anti-Liberalism*. Cambridge, MA: Harvard University Press.

Honig, Bonnie. 1993. *Political Theory and the Displacement of Politics*. Ithaca, NY: Cornell University Press.

———. 2001. *Democracy and the Foreigner*. Princeton, NJ: Princeton University Press.

Hooker, Brad, and Margaret Little, eds. 2000. *Moral Particularism*. Oxford: Clarendon Press.

Hunter, Virginia. 1973. *Thucydides The Artful Reporter*. Toronto: Hakkert.

Hyland, Drew. 1981. *The Virtue of Philosophy: An Interpretation of Plato's "Charmides."* Athens: Ohio University Press.

Ignatieff, Michael. 2001. *Human Rights as Politics and Idolatry*. Ed. Amy Gutmann. Princeton, NJ: Princeton University Press.

Inglehart, Ronald. 1977. *The Silent Revolution*. Princeton, NJ: Princeton University Press.

———. 1990. *Culture Shift in Advanced Industrial Society*. Princeton, NJ: Princeton University Press.

———. 1997. *Modernization and Postmodernization*. Princeton. Princeton UniversityPress.

Irwin, Terence. 1977. *Plato's Moral Theory*. New York: Oxford University Press.

Jansson, Per. 1997. "Identity-Defining Practices in Thucydides' *History of the Peloponnesian War*," *European Journal of International Relations* 3, no. 2:147–65.

Johnson, Laurie. 1993. *Thucydides, Hobbes and the Interpretation of Realism*. DeKalb, IL: Northern Illinois University Press.

Kagan, Donald. 1969. *The Outbreak of the Peloponnesian War*. Ithaca, NY: Cornell University Press.

———. 1974. *The Archidamian War*. Ithaca, NY: Cornell University Press.
Kateb, George. 2002. "The Adequacy of the Canon." *Political Theory* 30, no. 4: 482–505.
Keuls, Eva. 1978. *Plato and Greek Painting*. Leiden: Brill.
———. 1985. *The Reign of the Phallus: Sexual Politics in Ancient Athens*. New York: Harper and Row.
Knight, Jack, and James Johnson. 1997. "What Sort of Equality Does Deliberative Democracy Require?" In *Deliberative Democracy*, ed. James Bohman and William Rehg. Cambridge, MA: MIT Press.
Kochin, Michael. 1999. "War, Class and Justice in Plato's Republic." *Review of Metaphysics* 53:403–23.
Koziak, Barbara. 2000. *Retrieving Political Emotion*. University Park: Pennsylvania State University Press.
Krentz, Peter. 1982. *The Thirty at Athens*. Ithaca, NY: Cornell University Press.
Kristeva, Julia. 1991. *Strangers to Ourselves*. Trans. Leon S. Roudiez. New York: Columbia University Press.
Kymlicka, Will. 1995. *Multicultural Citizenship*. Oxford: Clarendon Press.
Lamb, W. R. M., trans. 1967. *Lysis, Symposium, Gorgias*. Cambridge, MA: Harvard University Press.
Laqueur, Thomas. 2001. "The Moral Imagination and Human Rights." In *Human Rights as Politics and Idolatry*, by Michael Ignatieff. Ed. Amy Gutmann. Princeton, NJ: Princeton University Press.
Lattimore, Steven, trans. 1998. *Thucydides: The Peloponnesian War*. Indianapolis: Hackett.
Lear, Jonathan. 2006. "Allegory and Myth in Plato's Republic." In *The Blackwell Guide to Plato's Republic*, ed. Gerasimos Santas. Malden, MA: Blackwell Publishing.
Lebow, Richard Ned. 1996. "Play It Again Pericles: Agents, Structures and the Peloponnesian War." *European Journal of International Relations* 2, no. 2: 231–58.
———. 2003. *The Tragic Vision of Politics*. Cambridge: Cambridge University Press.
Lombardini, John T. Forthcoming. The Comedy of Political Theory, PhD diss., Princeton University.
Long, Timothy. 1986. *Barbarians in Greek Comedy*. Carbondale: Southern Illinois University Press.
Loraux, Nicole. 1986. *The Invention of Athens: The Funeral Oration in the Classical City*. Trans. Alan Sheridan. Cambridge, MA: Harvard University Press.
———. 1998. *Mothers in Mourning*. Trans. Corinne Pache. Ithaca, NY: Cornell University Press.
Luginbill, Robert D. 1999. *Thucydides on War and National Character*. Boulder, CO: Westview Press.
Luhmann, Niklas. 1979. *Trust and Power*. Ed. Tom Burns and Gianfranco Poggi. Trans. Howard Davis, John Raffan, and Kathryn Rooney. London: John Wiley and Sons.
MacDowell, Douglas. 1995. *Aristophanes and Athens*. Oxford: Oxford University Press.

Mansbridge, Jane. 1999a. "Should Blacks Represent Blacks and Women Represent Women? A Contingent 'Yes.'" *Journal of Politics* 61, no. 3:628–57.

———. 1999b. "Trust as an Altruistic Move." In *Democracy and Trust*, ed. Mark Warren. New York: Cambridge University Press.

Mara, Gerald. 1985. "After Virtue: Autonomy: Jürgen Habermas and Greek Political Theory." *Journal of Politics* 47, no. 4:1036–61.

———. 1988. "Socrates and Liberal Toleration." *Political Theory* 16, no. 3:468–95.

———. 1993. "Cries, Eloquence and Judgment: Interpreting Political Voice in Democratic Regimes." *Polity* 26, no. 2:155–87.

———. 1995. "The Near Made Far Away: The Role of Cultural Criticism in Aristotle's Political Theory." *Political Theory* 23, no. 2:280–303.

———. 1997. *Socrates' Discursive Democracy*. Albany: State University of New York Press.

———. 1998. "Interrogating the Identities of Excellence: Liberal Education and Democratic Culture in Aristotle's *Nicomachean Ethics*." *Polity* 31, no. 2:301–29.

———. 2001. "Plato and Thucydides on Democracy and Trust." *Journal of Politics* 63, no. 3:820–45.

———. 2002. Review of *Socratic Citizenship*, by Dana Villa. *American Political Science Review* 96, no. 4:815–16.

———. 2003. "Democratic Self-Criticism and the Other in Classical Political Theory." *Journal of Politics* 65, no. 3:739–58.

Markovits, Elizabeth. Forthcoming. *The Trouble with Being Earnest*. State College: Pennsylvania State University Press.

Matthews, Donald. 1973. *U.S. Senators and Their World*. New York: Norton.

McCarthy, Thomas. 1990. "The Critique of Impure Reason." *Political Theory* 18, no. 3:437–69.

Midgley, Mary. 1995. *Beast and Man*. Rev. ed. New York: Routledge.

Monoson, Sara. 1994. "Citizens as *Erastes*: Erotic Imagery and the Idea of Reciprocity in the Periclean Funeral Oration." *Political Theory* 22, no. 2:253–76.

———. 2000. *Plato's Democratic Entanglements*. Princeton, NJ: Princeton University Press.

Monoson, Sara, and Michael Loriaux. 1998. "The Illusion of Power and the Disruption of Moral Norms: Thucydides' Critique of Periclean Policy." *American Political Science Review* 92, no. 2:285–97.

Morrison, James. 2006. *Reading Thucydides*. Columbus: Ohio State University Press.

Mouffe, Chantal. 2000. *The Democratic Paradox*. London: Verso.

Nails, Debra. 2002. *The People of Plato*. Indianapolis: Hackett.

Narayan, Uma. 1999. "Towards a Feminist Vision of Citizenship: Rethinking the Implications of Dignity, Political Participation and Nationality." In *Reconstructing Political Theory: Feminist Perspectives*, ed. Mary Lyndon Shanley and Uma Narayan. Cambridge: Polity Press.

Nehamas, Alexander. 1998. *The Art of Living: Socratic Relections from Plato to Foucault*. Berkeley and Los Angeles: University of California Press.

Nichols, Mary. 1987. *Socrates and the Political Community*. Albany: State University of New York Press.
Nietzsche, Friedrich. 1954. *Twilight of the Idols*. In *The Portable Nietzsche*, trans. Walter Kaufmann. New York: Viking Press.
———. 1966. *Beyond Good and Evil*. Trans. Walter Kaufmann. New York: Vintage.
———. 1969. *"On the Genealogy of Morals" and "Ecce Homo."* Trans. Walter Kaufmann. New York: Vintage.
———. 1980. *On the Advantage and Disadvantage of History for Life*. Trans. Peter Preuss. Indianapolis: Hackett.
Nightingale, Andrea Wilson. 1995. *Genres in Dialogue: Plato and the Construct of Philosophy*. Cambridge: Cambridge University Press.
Norton, Anne. 2004. *Leo Strauss and the Politics of the American Empire*. New Haven, CT: Yale University Press.
Nussbaum, Martha. 1988. "Non-Relative Virtues; An Aristotelian Approach." *Midwest Studies in Philosophy* 13:32–53.
———. 1990. "Aristotelian Social Democracy." In *Liberalism and The Good*, ed. R. Bruce Douglass, Gerald Mara, and Henry Richardson. New York: Routledge.
———. 1996. "Double Moral Standards?" *Boston Review* 21, no. 5.
———. 2001. *The Fragility of Goodness*. Rev. ed. New York: Cambridge University Press.
Ober, Josiah. 1989. *Mass and Elite in Democratic Athens*.Princeton, NJ: Princeton University Press.
———. 1998. *Political Dissent in Democratic Athens*. Princeton, NJ: Princeton University Press.
O'Connor, David. 2002. "Leo Strauss's Aristotle and Martin Heidegger's Politics." In *Aristotle and Modern Politics*, ed. Aristide Tessitore. Notre Dame, IN: Notre Dame University Press.
Offe, Claus. 1999. "How Can We Trust Our Fellow Citizens?" In *Democracy and Trust*, ed. Mark Warren. New York: Cambridge University Press.
Ordeshook, Peter. 1980. "Political Disequilibrium and Scientific Inquiry." *American Political Science Review* 74, no. 2:447–50.
Orwin, Clifford. 1984. "Democracy and Distrust." *American Scholar* 53 (Summer): 313–25.
———. 1994. *The Humanity of Thucydides*. Princeton, NJ: Princeton University Press.
Ostwald, Martin. 1988. Ananke *in Thucydides*. Atlanta: Scholars Press.
Palmer, Michael. 1992. *Love of Glory and the Common Good*. Lanham MD: Rowman and Littlefield.
Pangle, Thomas. 1989. Introduction to *The Rebirth of Classical Political Rationalism*, by Leo Strauss. Chicago: University of Chicago Press.
Parker, Robert. 1983. *Miasma: Pollution and Purification in Early Greek Religion*. Oxford: Clarendon Press
Parry, Adam. 1981. Logos *and* Ergon *in Thucydides*. New York: Arno Press.
Penner, Terry, and Christopher Rowe. 2005. *Plato's "Lysis."* Cambridge: Cambridge University Press.

Phillips, Anne. 1998. "Democracy and Representation: Or, Why It Should Matter Who Our Representatives Are." In *Feminism and Politics*, ed. Anne Phillips. New York: Oxford University Press.
Pogge, Thomas. 2002. "Self-Constituting Constituencies to Enhance Freedom, Equality and Participation in Democratic Procedures." *Theoria*, June, 26–54.
Pouncey, Peter. 1980. *The Necessities of War*. New York: Columbia University Press.
Price, Jonathan. 2001. *Thucydides and Internal War*. Cambridge: Cambridge University Press.
Putnam, Robert. 1993. *Making Democracy Work*. Princeton, NJ: Princeton University Press.
———. 1995. "Tuning In, Tuning Out: The Strange Disappearance of Social Capital in America." *PS: Political Science and Politics* 28, no. 4:664–83.
———. 2000. *Bowling Alone*. New York: Simon and Schuster.
Rademaker, Adriaan. 2003. "Most Citizens Are *Europroktoi* Now: (Un)manliness in Aristophanes." In *Andreia: Studies in Manliness and Courage in Classical Antiquity*, ed. Ralph Rosen and Ineke Sluiter. Leiden: Brill.
Rawls, John. 1971. *A Theory of Justice*. Cambridge, MA: Harvard University Press.
———. 1999. *The Law of Peoples*. Cambridge, MA: Harvard University Press.
———. 2005. *Political Liberalism*. New York: Columbia University Press.
Reeve, C. D. C. 1988. *Philosopher Kings*. Princeton, NJ: Princeton University Press.
Richardson, Henry. 2002. *Democratic Autonomy*. Oxford: Oxford University Press.
Ricoeur, Paul. 2004. *Memory, History, Forgetting*. Trans. Kathleen Blamey and David Pellauer. Chicago: University of Chicago Press.
Riker, William. 1962. *The Theory of Political Coalitions*. New Haven, CT: Yale University Press.
———. 1980a. "Implications from the Disequilibrium of Majority Rule for the Study of Institutions." *American Political Science Review* 74, no. 2:432–46.
———. 1980b. "A Reply to Ordeshook and Rae." *American Political Science Review* 74, no. 2:456–58.
Roochnik, David. 1990. *The Tragedy of Reason*. New York: Routledge.
Rood, Tim. 1998. *Thucydides: Narrative and Explanation*. Oxford: Oxford University Press.
Rorty, Richard. 1979. *Philosophy and the Mirror of Nature*. Princeton, NJ: Princeton University Press.
———. 1982. "Pragmatism, Relativism, Irrationalism." In *Consequences of Pragmatism: Essays (1972–1980)*. Minneapolis: University of Minnesota Press.
———. 1989. *Contingency, Irony and Solidarity*. New York: Cambridge University Press.
Rosen, Stanley. 1987. *Plato's Symposium*. 2nd ed. New Haven, CT: Yale University Press.
Rosenblum, Nancy. 1998. *The Morals of Membership*. Princeton, NJ: Princeton University Press.

Ross, Marc Howard. 1993. *The Culture of Conflict.* New Haven, CT: Yale University Press.
Rousseau, Jean-Jacques. 1964. *The First and Second Discourses.* Trans. Roger D. and Judith Masters. New York: St. Martin's Press.
———. 1979. *Emile.* Trans. Allan Bloom. New York: Basic Books.
Sahlins, Marshall. 2004. *Apologies to Thucydides.* Chicago: University of Chicago Press.
Said, Edward. 1994. *Orientalism.* New York: Vintage.
Salkever, Stephen. 1990. *Finding the Mean: Theory and Practice in Aristotelian Political Philosophy.* Princeton, NJ: Princeton University Press.
———. 1993. "Socrates' Aspasian Oration: The Play of Philosophy and Politics in Plato's *Menexenus.*" *American Political Science Review* 87:133–43.
———. 2002. "The Deliberative Model of Democracy and Aristotle's Ethics of Natural Questions," In *Aristotle and Modern Politics,* ed. Aristide Tessitore. Notre Dame, IN: Notre Dame University Press.
Sandel, Michael. 1996. *Democracy's Discontent: America in Search of a Public Philosophy.* Cambridge, MA: Belknap Press of Harvard University Press.
Sanjek, Roger. 1998. *The Future of Us All.* Ithaca, NY: Cornell University Press.
Saxonhouse, Arlene. 1978, "Comedy in Callipolis." *American Political Science Review* 72, no. 3:888–901.
———. 1984. "Eros and the Female in Greek Political Thought." *Political Theory* 12, no. 1:5–27.
———. 1996. *Athenian Democracy: Modern Mythmakers and Ancient Theorists.* Notre Dame, IN: University of Notre Dame Press.
———. 1998. "Democracy, Equality and *Eide*: A Radical View from Book 8 of Plato's *Republic.*" *American Political Science Review* 92, no. 2:273–83.
———. 2004. "Democratic Deliberation and the Historian's Trade." In *Talking Democracy: Historical Perspectives on Rhetoric and Democracy,* ed. Benedetto Fontana, Cary J. Nederman, and Gary Remer. University Park: Pennsylvania State University Press.
——— 2006. *Free Speech and Democracy in Ancient Athens.* Cambridge: Cambridge University Press
Schattschneider, E. E. 1960. *The Semi-Sovereign People.* New York: Holt, Rinehart and Winston.
Schiappa, Edward. 1991. *Protagoras and Logos.* Columbia: University of South Carolina Press.
Schlatter, Richard, trans. 1975. *Hobbes's Thucydides.* Ed. Richard Schlatter. New Brunswick, NJ: Rutgers University Press.
Sen, Amartya. 1999. *Development as Freedom.* New York: Knopf.
Sen, Amartya, and Martha Nussbaum. 1993. *The Quality of Life.* New York: Oxford University Press.
Shain, Barry. 1994. *The Myth of Individualism: The Protestant Origins of American Political Thought.* Princeton, NJ: Princeton University Press.
Shapiro, Ian. 2003. *The State of Democratic Theory.* Princeton, NJ: Princeton University Press.

Smith, Charles Forster, trans. 1962–88. *Thucydides*. 4 vols. Cambridge, MA: Harvard University Press.
Strauss, Leo. 1953. *Natural Right and History*. Chicago: University of Chicago Press.
———. 1964. *The City and Man*. Chicago: Rand McNally.
———. 1983. *Studies in Platonic Political Philosophy*. Chicago: University of Chicago Press.
———. 1989. *The Rebirth of Classical Political Rationalism*. Chicago: University of Chicago Press.
———. 2000. *On Tyranny*. Ed. Victor Gourevitch and Michael Roth. Chicago: University of Chicago Press.
Tamir, Yael. 1996. "Hands Off Clitoridectomy." *Boston Review* 21, no. 3.
Tarcov, Nathan. 1983. "Philosophy and History: Tradition and Interpretation in the Work of Leo Strauss." *Polity* 16, no. 1:5–29.
Taylor, Charles. 1967. "Neutrality in Political Science." In *Philosophy Politics and Society, Third Series*, ed. Peter Lazlett and W. G. Runciman. Oxford: Blackwell.
———. 1971. "Interpretation and the Sciences of Man." *Review of Metaphysics* 25, no. 1:3–51.
———. 1985. *Philosophy and the Human Sciences*. New York: Cambridge University Press.
———. 1994. "The Politics of Recognition." In *Multiculturalism*, ed. Amy Gutmann. Princeton, NJ: Princeton University Press.
Templer, Rachel. 2007. "The Most Distinctive Tomb: Love, Empire and Democratic Citizenship in Thucydides." (Unpublished.)
Tessitore, Aristide. 1996. *Reading Aristotle's "Ethics."* Albany: State University of New York Press.
Tocqueville, Alexis de. 1988. *Democracy in America*. Trans. George Lawrence. Ed. J. P. Mayer. New York: Perennial Press.
Tsao, Roy. 2002. "Arendt against Athens." *Political Theory* 30, no. 1:97–123.
Vickers, Brian. 1988. *In Defense of Rhetoric*. New York: Oxford University Press.
Villa, Dana. 1996. *Arendt and Heidegger: The Fate of the Political*. Princeton, NJ: Princeton University Press.
———. 2001. *Socratic Citizenship*. Princeton, NJ: Princeton University Press.
von Reden, Sitta, and Simon Goldhill. 1999. "Plato and the Performance of Dialogue." In *Performance Culture and Athenian Democracy*, ed. Simon Goldhill and Robin Osborne. Cambridge: Cambridge University Press.
Wallach, John. 2001. *The Platonic Political Art*. University Park: Pennsylvania State University Press.
———. 2004. "Human Rights as an Ethics of Power." In *Human Rights in the "War on Terror,"* ed. Richard Ashby Wilson. New York: Cambridge University Press.
Waltz, Kenneth. 1979. *Theory of International Politics*. New York: McGraw-Hill.
Walzer, Michael. 1977. *Just and Unjust Wars*. New York: Basic Books.
Warren, Mark. 1992. "Democratic Theory and Self-Transformation." *American Political Science Review* 86, no. 1:8–23.

———. 1994. "Non-Foundationalism and Democratic Judgment." *Current Perspectives in Social Theory* 14:151–82.

———. 1999. "Democratic Theory and Trust." In *Democracy and Trust*, ed. Mark Warren. New York: Cambridge University Press.

———. 2001. *Democracy and Association*. Princeton, NJ: Princeton University Press.

———. 2004. "Social Capital & Corruption." *Democracy & Society* no. 1:1.

Weber, Max. 1949. *The Methodology of the Social Sciences*. Trans. Edward Shils and Henry Finch. New York: Free Press.

Weingartner, Rudolph. 1973. *The Unity of the Platonic Dialogue*. Indianapolis: Hackett.

Weiss, Roslyn. 2006. *The Socratic Paradox and Its Enemies*. Chicago: University of Chicago Press.

Weldon, S. Laurel. 2002. "Beyond Bodies: Institutional Sources of Representations for Women in Democratic Policymaking." *Journal of Politics* 64, no. 4:1153–74.

West, Thomas G., and Grace Starry West, trans. 1986. *Plato: Charmides*. Indianapolis: Hackett.

White, James Boyd. 1984. *When Words Lose Their Meaning*. Chicago: University of Chicago Press.

Williams, Bernard. 1993. *Shame and Necessity*. Berkeley and Los Angeles: University of California Press.

———. 2002. *Truth and Truthfulness*. Princeton, NJ: Princeton University Press.

Wilson, James Q. 1985. "The Rediscovery of Character: Private Virtue and Public Policy." *Public Interest* 81 (Fall): 3–16.

Winch, Peter. 1961. *The Idea of a Social Science*. London: Routledge and Kegan Paul.

Wohl, Victoria. 2002. *Love among the Ruins: The Erotics of Democracy in Classical Athens*. Princeton, NJ: Princeton University Press.

Wolff, Robert Paul. 1965. "Beyond Tolerance." In *A Critique of Pure Tolerance*. By Robert Paul Wolff, Barrington Moore, Jr., and Herbert Marcuse. Boston: Beacon Pess.

Wolfsdorf, David. 1998. "The Historical Reader of Plato's *Protagoras*." *Classical Quarterly*. 48, no. 1:126–33.

Wolin, Sheldon. 2004. *Politics and Vision*. Expanded ed. Princeton, NJ: Princeton University Press.

Wolpert, Andrew. 2002. *Remembering Defeat*. Baltimore: Johns Hopkins University Press.

Wolz, Henry. 1981. *Plato and Heidegger*. Lewisburg, PA: Bucknell University Press.

Wood, Ellen Mieksnins, and Neal Wood. 1978. *Class Ideology and Ancient Political Theory*. Oxford: Blackwell.

Yack, Bernard. 1997. *The Fetishism of Modernities*. Notre Dame, IN: Notre Dame University Press.

Young, Iris Marion. 1990. *Justice and the Politics of Difference*. Princeton, NJ: Princeton University Press.

———. 1997. "Difference as a Resource for Democratic Communication." In *Deliberative Democracy*, ed. James Bohman and William Rehg. Cambridge, MA: MIT Press.

Yunis, Harvey. 1996. *Taming Democracy*. Ithaca, NY: Cornell University Press.

———. 2003. "Writing for Reading: Thucydides, Plato and the Emergence of the Critical Reader." In *Written Text and the Rise of Literate Culture in Ancient Greece*, ed. Harvey Yunis. Cambridge: Cambridge University Press.

Zuckert, Catherine. 1996. *Postmodern Platos*. Chicago: University of Chicago Press.

Zuckert, Catherine, and Michael Zuckert. 2006. *The Truth about Leo Strauss*. Chicago: University of Chicago Press.

Zumbrunnen, John. 2002. "Democratic Politics and the 'Character' of the City in Thucydides." *History of Political Thought* 23, no. 4:565–89.

Index

Acharnae/Acharnaeans, 135, 279–80n75
Achilles, 210, 292n23
Adeimantus, 22, 134, 173, 176–79, 182, 189, 253, 283n4
Aecus, 136
Aeschylus, 136–37
Against Eratosthenes. *See* Lysias
Agathon, 137, 208–9, 213–19, 221–22, 280–81n88, 293n33
Agoracritus, 137
Ahrensdorf, Peter, 49
Aieimnestos, 249
Alcibiades, 23, 67, 106–7, 110, 121, 136, 151, 155, 193, 208, 214, 217–20, 223–24, 253, 265n46, 270n44, 292nn 30–31, 293nn33–34, 296n22; and Pericles, 277n43
Allen, Danielle, 186–87, 268n21, 280n80, 288n98, 289nn99–101
Almond, Gabriel, 111
Ambraciots, 291n13
Amphilocians, 291n13
Anderson, Benedict, 112
Anderson, Daniel, 292n26
Andrewes, A., 207, 270n48
Anytus, 191, 208, 290n112
Aphrodite, 215
Apollodorus, 208, 292n22
Arato, Andrew, 9, 87–88, 92, 112, 262n9, 295 n12, 295n14
Archidamus, 151, 166–68, 173, 278n51, 285n55, 285n57, 286n60, 286n62

Arendt, Hannah, 112, 242, 250–52, 298n45, 299n58, 299n60, 299n62; and Pericles 251–52
Ares, 215
Arginusae, 131, 135–36, 139, 254
Argives, 165
Aristides, 129
Aristodemus, 208
Aristogeiton, 247
Aristophanes, 134–37, 139, 279n72, 280n78, 281n91; of the *Symposium*, 209, 211–14, 280–81n88, 292n26; works of: *Acharnaeans*, 135, 138, 279n74, 279–80n75; *Assembly of Women*, 137; *Birds*, 137; *Clouds*, 135, 137–38; *Festival of Women*, 137; *Frogs*, 136–38, 293n34; *Knights*, 136–37, 276n76, 276n81, 281n91; *Wasps*, 57, 136
Aristoteles (of the Thirty), 21
Aristotle, 14–16, 158, 263nn28–29; works of: *Athenian Constitution*, 263n25, 291n10; *Nicomachean Ethics*, 16, 263nn27–28, 272n81, 285–86n58, 295n13; *Politics*, 16, 120, 166–67, 175, 183, 262n20
Aspasia, 133
assembly: Athenian, 19, 26, 131; in Corcyra-Corinth debate, 40; democratic, 23, 116–17; in Mytilene debate, 54, 56–57, 99–101; in *Protagoras*, 103–4; and rhetoric, 124

315

Index

Athenagoras: and Cleon, 120–21; on democracy, 120–21; deficiencies of, 121–23, 278n55; identity of, 123; speech at Syracuse, 116, 118–23
Athenian Stranger, 252
Athens/Athenian/Athenians: 201, 217, 252, 254, 265n48, 265n50, 268n23, 268–69n34, 270n43,if 283n16, 283n26, 297–98n36; citizens at Sparta, 59, 154, 160–64, 169, 268n28, 275n16, 278n47, 285n46, 285n48; and Corcyra, 284n33; culture of, 134, 137, 150, 158–59, 160, 168–71, 176–78, 202–7, 214, 258, 291n10, 292n18; as daring regime, 23, 128, 204–7, 219, 223–24, 291n13, 291n17; as democracy, 123, 126, 242; envoys on Melos, 46–54, 56, 154–55, 160–64, 166, 244, 268n30; imperial identity of, 39, 50–54, 104, 135, 154, 158, 161–63, 173, 195, 204, 243, 250, 253, 299n61, 270n44, 270n49; and justice, 160–64, 248, 255, 286n64, 289nn99–101; religion in, 155–56, 284n28; subversion of the democracy (in 411), 23, 62, 123, 286n70
Attica, 44, 205, 219
Austin, John, 265n47
autonomy, 6, 233–34, 239–40
Avramenko, Richard, 272n77
Axelrod, Robert, 8, 27, 31, 33–36, 38, 43, 72, 266–67n10, 267n15, 268n20, 298n45

Balot, Ryan, 23, 113, 268n27, 271n68, 277n40, 278n52, 278n61, 298n41
Baracchi, Claudia, 287n73, 287n75, 289n104, 289n108, 299n68
barbarians, 24
Barber, Benjamin, 6, 112, 124, 275n11, 278n58
Bartlett, Robert, 271n71, 272n73, 275n22, 276n25
Becker, Gary, 31
Behnegar, Nasser, 243n1

Beiner, Ronald, 130, 279n62, 279n66
Bellah, Robert, 6, 93, 277n37
Benardete, Seth, 135, 264n39, 278n61, 287n80, 287n82, 288n95, 289n100, 300n72
Benhabib, Seyla, 5, 9, 12–13, 86–88, 130, 229, 231–32, 261n2, 261n4, 294n7, 295n12
Bennett, William, 297n28
Bentham, Jeremy, 296n26
Bercovitch, Sacvan, 16–18
Berelson, Bernard, 111
Bermeo, Nancy, 261n1, 296n21
Berns, Walter, 111, 132
Bloom, Allan, 190, 279n72, 286nn70–71, 289n109
Boeotia/Boeotian/Boeotians, 201, 207
Borneman, John, 282n9, 297n30
Brams, Steven, 32, 266n4, 269n36
Brann, Eva, 191, 264n41, 271n69, 273n100
Brasidas, 39, 49, 107, 151, 168, 218–19, 244, 270n51, 286nn61–62, 291n13
Bruell, Christopher, 273n94, 273n99
Buchanan, James, 32–34, 72
Butler, Judith, 10, 28, 197–98, 220, 222–24, 235, 239–40, 263n31, 265nn47–48, 290–91n7, 298nn49–50, 299n57

Cairns, Douglas, 285n7
Caldeira, Teresa, 261n1
Callias, 102
Callicles, 110, 125–27, 131, 134–39, 142, 157, 159, 253, 278n61, 279nn63–64, 279–80n75, 280nn79–80, 280n83, 281n90, 281n92, 284n41
Camarina/Camarinean/Camarineans, 43–45, 243
Carter, L.B., 76
Carter, Stephen, 6
Cephalus, 152
Chaerephon, 73, 75, 125
Chalchidike/Chalcidean/Chalchideans, 44, 47
character: and politics, 132–33, 297n28

Index

Charmides, 21, 62, 73–78, 80–81, 264n41, 273n92
Chong, Dennis, 8, 27, 31–32, 266n2, 266n5, 266n8, 267n14, 267n16, 267n18, 268n22
Cinesias, 137, 280n77
City and Man, The. See Strauss, Leo
city/soul analogy, 179–87
civic republicanism, 90, 93, 112, 238
civil society: and democracy, 6
classical political philosophy: mistrusted by democratic theory, 2, 13–16; and social theory, 13–15
Cleon, 151, 281n91, 285n48, 300n72; on Athenian empire, 56, 59, 97, 141, 163; on democracy, 55, 97, 99, 236; on human interests, 56–57, 97, 107–8, 127; in Mytilene debate, 40, 54–61, 97–99, 116–18, 122, 160, 169–70, 246, 249, 270nn53–55, 271n56, 286n67; on trust and mistrust, 97–98, 109, 120–21
Coby, Patrick, 271nn70–71, 272n73, 272n84, 275n22
Cogan, Marc, 275n14, 285,n48
Cohen, Jean, 9, 87–88, 92, 112, 262n9, 262n11, 262n15, 295n12, 295n14
comedy, 134–39
communitarianism: on political voice, 112; on trust, 93–95; and virtue, 238
compulsion (*anankē*), 41; Athenian power as a source of, 45, 51–54; for control in the Charmides, 73, 84; ranges of meaning in Thucydides, 45–46
Connolly, William, 10–12, 201, 208–9, 215, 225, 228, 235, 239–40, 263n26, 282n3, 282nn8–9, 290n5, 290–91n7, 300n76
Connor, W. Robert, 41, 47, 53, 120, 123, 168, 171, 265n45, 275n14, 283n19, 284n39, 284n42, 285n48, 291n14
Constable, Pamela, 276n31
Corcyra/Corcyrean/Corcyreans, 39–43, 150, 158, 160, 164, 243–46, 248–49, 251, 284n27, 288n88; *stasis* within, 18, 43, 52, 156–57, 173, 189, 225, 234, 284nn32–33
Corinth/Corinthian/Corinthians, 62, 73, 160, 163–66, 243, 245
courage, 68–71, 106–8, 167, 185–86
Craig, Leon, 264n38, 286n71, 286–87n73, 287n80, 289n84, 289n108, 290n116
Crane, Gregory, 17–18, 21, 52, 150–51, 172, 176, 244, 257, 264n37, 265n49, 265n52, 268n26, 270n44, 271n58, 283n15, 283n19, 283n25, 284n31, 284n38, 285n48, 285n50, 285n53, 286n68, 291n8, 299n56
Crawley, Malcolm, 270n51
Critias, 21, 62–63, 67, 72–74, 76–84, 86, 106, 253, 264n41, 273nn95–96, 273n99, 286n71, 287n74
culture: and meaning, 36, 52, 145–46; and nature, 149–60, 180–82, 185, 194–95. *See also* democratic culture
Cyrus, 218

Dahl, Robert, 8, 35, 111, 132, 277n38
Daniel, E. Valentine, 282n9
David, 293n34
Davies, J.K., 273n92
de Romilly, Jacqueline, 18, 21, 46, 49, 52, 154, 156, 172, 176, 257, 298n42, 299n56
Debnar, Paula, 168, 265n47, 285nn54–55, 286nn60–61, 286n68
Deceleia, 205–6, 208, 219
deconstruction, 221–22
Delian League, 161
deliberative democratic theory, 2, 86–93, 235; and autonomy, 10, 88, 90, 131, 241; criticism of by Thucydides and Plato, 89–93, 96, 141–42; and fairness, 9; and institutions, 87, 110, 118; and judgment, 111–13; and Kantian rationality, 9; and procedure, 12, 27, 88, 90–92, 95–96, 113, 141–42; and rational choice, 8, 87, 89; and self transformation, 89, 94,

deliberative democratic theory *(continued)*
  101; and teleology, 88–90, 94–95, 109, 113, 129, 141; and virtue, 90–91, 95, 238
Delium, 23
Delphic oracle, 79
Demeas, 53
democracy: governance in, 4–5, 7, 235–38; and oligarchy, 23. *See also* Athens/Athenian/Athenians; democratic culture; democratic theory; *dēmos*
democratic culture: and complexity, 189–91; and discourse, 28, 217; and humanness, 10; and reading of texts, 20; theories based upon, 2, 9, 143–48, 235–36, 239, 241; and ways of life, 239
democratic theory: consistency within, 2–3; contemporary forms of, 2, 27–29, 227–41; democratic elitism, 6, 111–12; and democratic purposes, 2, 7–8, 10, 12, 227–28; and democratic space, 11, 27, 227, 229; and democratic transformations, 1; and human nature, 11, 225–26, 233–35; and the other, 10, 28; as paradigm in political theory, 1; as resource for citizens, 12; suspicion of classical political theory, 2; and ways of life, 6–7, 238–40
dēmos, 53–55, 99, 114, 131, 190, 192
Demos (of the *Knights*), 135–37, 281n91
Demos (son of Pyrilampes), 131, 136
Deneen, Patrick, 277n35, 290n111
Derrida, Jacques, 220–22, 258, 286–87n73, 287n79, 289n108, 290n5, 294n5
Descartes, Rene, 17
Dewey, John, 147
Dicaeopolis, 279–80n75
Dietrephes, 201
Diggins, John Patrick, 277n38
Diiulio, John, 297n28, 297n33

Diodotus, 18–19, 285n48; on Athenian empire, 58–59; and deliberative democracy, 99–101, 116–17, 142; on democratic institutions, 54, 59–60, 98–101; and forgiveness (*epieikeia*), 57–59; identity of, 123, 171; on interest and justice, 58–59, 99, 122, 160–61, 271n64; on *logos*, 58, 61, 99–101, 275n17; and Melian dialogue, 248–49; in Mytilene debate, 23, 26, 40, 54, 57–61, 74, 98–101, 160, 169–70, 237, 246–48, 251–52, 265n48, 275n16, 281n94, 286n67, 298n48, 298n50; on politics, 251–52, 275n18; and Socrates, 104–5, 108, 123–24, 138, 255–58, 299n69, 300n72; and Thucydides, 26, 171, 234, 249–52, 258
Dionysius, 136
Diotima, 209, 216–17, 219, 225, 292n28
discourse ethics, 87–89, 91–92, 94–95, 110, 129, 141, 232
Dodds, E.R., 278n61, 279n63, 280n77
Dover, K.J., 207, 270n48
Dovi, Suzanne, 297n32
Downs, Anthony, 8, 32–36, 40, 64, 266n2, 266n5, 266n7, 266–67n11
Drury, Shadia, 263–64n36
Dworkin, Ronald, 199

Edmunds, Lowell, 21, 23, 113, 171, 265n50, 284n29
education: as theme in the *Protagoras*, 101–2, 105–6
Egypt, 181
Eleatic Stranger, 252
Elshtain, Jean Bethke, 6, 93–94
Elster, Jon, 32, 89, 92
Epicharmus, 280n82
Epidamnus, 41, 164
equality, 100, 219, 224, 237, 241; and justice, 58–59, 100, 161–64, 169–71, 248
equilibrium: as contested concept in Thucydides, 40–42; in Melian dia-

logue, 50; in Mytilene debate, 58; in rational choice theory, 33–34, 64
Er, myth of, 192, 194, 237
ēros: and philosophy, 215–17, 219–20; in *Symposium*, 208–20
Eryximachus, 210–11, 214
Estlund, David, 87, 95–96, 109
Euben, Peter, 98–100, 176, 191, 261n5, 265n50, 271n67, 271nn70–71, 272n77, 272n79, 272n83, 272n85, 281n94, 283n23, 285n48, 290n113, 292n23, 299n56, 300n72
Euboia, 44
Euphemus, 43–45, 56, 154, 170, 193, 243, 268nn28–30, 284n45
Euripides, 136–37; works of: *Antiope*, 280n70; *Iphigenia in Aulis*, 291n10; *Orestes*, 291n10
Euryptolemus, 254
Euthyphro, 254

Farrar, Cynthia, 113–14, 116, 265n50, 268n21, 271n57, 275n19, 275n22, 278n48, 285n48
Ferrari, Giovanni, 179, 288nn88–91, 288n94, 288n96, 289n109
Five Thousand: in Thucydides, 15, 116
Forde, Steven, 123, 264–65n45, 268n29, 277n43, 279n56
Foucault, Michel, 10, 37, 147–48, 157–58, 195, 262n18, 267n17, 282n7, 282n9, 284n38, 284n40, 285–86n58, 290n6, 292n24, 298n50
Frank, Jill, 3, 286–87n73, 287n76, 289n104
freedom, 192, 239–41; as power, 133
Freud, Sigmund, 293n34
Friedman, Jeffrey, 33
Fukuyama, Francis, 93
fundamentalism, 198–201, 209, 211, 215, 221, 225–26, 228, 240

Galston, William, 6, 275n12
Geertz, Clifford, 9, 10, 13, 29, 36, 145–47, 180, 188, 267n14, 281–82n2

Gilligan, Carol, 130, 279n65
Glaucon, 18, 22, 78, 157, 173–74, 176–79, 182, 184, 187–88, 191–92, 257, 282n12, 283n24, 287n84, 288n92, 290n114
gods, 49, 53, 59, 155, 164–65, 178–79, 185, 208, 212–13, 244
Goldhill, Simon, 278n58
Gomme, A.W., 207, 270n48
Gorgias, 124–28, 133, 135, 138–39, 142, 215, 278n58, 300n72
Gould, Carol, 261n2, 262n10
Green, Donald, 34, 267n18
Grene, David, 291n16
Guinier, Lani, 297n32
Gurr, Ted Robert, 275n10
Gyges, ring of, 176, 287n84
Gylippus, 160

Habermas, Jürgen, 2, 9, 11–13, 27, 47, 86–92, 94–95, 99, 101–2, 112, 116–17, 131, 143–44, 228, 233, 235, 239–40, 261n4, 261n6, 262n9, 262nn15–16, 263n26, 273n1, 273–74n2, 274n4, 274nn8–9, 275n18, 279n67, 282n3, 282n10, 294n4, 295n12, 295n14, 296n16, 296n23, 296n25, 296n27, 297n29
Hall, Edith, 202, 283n20, 291n10
Halperin, David, 280n81, 292n28
Hardin, Russell, 8, 27, 31–33, 40, 93–94, 112, 266n2, 267n13, 300n75
Harmodius, 247, 298n96
Havelock, Eric, 278n58
Hegel, G.W.F., 228, 293n1, 298n50
Held, David, 261n2
Hellas (Greece)/Hellenes (Greeks), 24, 44, 49, 64, 114, 158, 200, 208, 210, 218; and barbarians, 140, 174–75, 189, 201–7, 217, 223, 250
Helots, 151, 156, 165, 244, 286n61
hermeneutic social science, 144–46
Hermes, 105, 247
Hermocrates, 154; speech at Camarina, 43–44; speech at Syracuse, 116, 118–19, 121–22, 278n55

Herodotus, 176, 291n10
Hesiod, 78
Hipparchus, 247
Hippias, 247
Hippocrates, 64–65, 101–3, 271n72
historicism, 149
Hobbes, Thomas, 22, 176, 259, 263n35, 300n75
Holmes, Stephen, 263n76
Homer, 24, 77, 138, 185, 214, 218–19; works of: *Hymn to Apollo*, 300n73; *Iliad*, 138, 194, 292n23; *Odyssey*, 77, 194
Honig, Bonnie, 2, 10, 12, 28, 197–98, 200, 235, 239–40, 261n2, 290nn2–3, 290n5, 290–91n7, 293n34, 294n4, 296n23
Hooker, Brad, 279n65
Human Condition, The. *See* Arendt, Hannah
human rights: and cultural constructions, 147–48, 230–33; in democratic societies, 4–5, 7, 229–30; and rationality, 235
Hunter, Virginia, 264n44, 299n53
Hyland, Drew, 73, 79, 82, 264n41, 273nn94–99

Ignatieff, Michael, 5, 230, 232, 294n3, 294n6, 295n9
imagination, political: and *logos*, 59, 62, 80; in Melian dialogue, 49–54; Syracusan, 118
Inglehart, Ronald, 262n12
Ionians, 161
Irwin, Terence, 271n70
Isocrates, 15
Ithaca, 77

Jackson, Jesse, 199
James, William, 147
Jansson, Per, 283n16
Johnson, James, 2, 88, 90
Johnson, Laurie, 271n58, 271nn63–64, 275n14, 284n37, 285n48, 298n51

judgment: in democracies, 28, 111–13, 125–32; and institutions, 131–33; and teleology, 127
justice: for Corcyra, 41; for Corinth, 42; and equality, 58–59, 100, 161–64, 169–71, 248; in Melian dialogue, 47, 49–50, 53; in Mytilene debate, 56, 58–59, 160–61; and power, 148, 162–63; in *Republic*, 77, 172–94; in Thucydides, 160–72; comparing Thucydides and Plato, 194–95. *See also* Athens/Athenian/Athenians, and justice

Kagan, Donald, 45, 263n32, 271n57
Kant, Immanuel, 10, 131, 295n12
Kateb, George, 296n17
Keuls, Eva, 273n91, 284n30
Khomeini, Ayatollah, 199
Knight, Jack, 2, 88, 90
Kochin, Michael, 286–87n73, 287n77, 287n81, 289n104, 289nn107–8
Koziak, Barbara, 273n90, 297n33
Krentz, Peter, 273n93
Kristeva, Julia, 283n20, 290nn1–2
Kymlicka, Will, 9, 262n9

Lamb, W.R.M., 208
Laqueur, Thomas, 294n6
Lattimore, Steven, 14, 268n31, 270n46, 270n48, 284n39
law (*nomos*), 164, 166, 177, 210, 212
Lazarsfeld, Paul, 111
Lear, Jonathan, 288n90, 288n93, 289n105
Leon of Salamis, 84, 254
Leontini, 44
Leontius (son of Aglaion), 186, 288n98, 289nn100–1
Lesbos, 54
Leviathan. *See* Hobbes, Thomas
liberal democracy: benefits of, 4, 233; criticisms of 2. *See also* prolematization
liberalism: classical, 231; debates with communitarians, 8; on political

trust, 90, 93–94. *See also* social contract theories
lifeworld, 143
Little, Margaret, 279n65
Locke, John, 111
Lombardini, John, 279n72, 280n76, 280n81, 280nn84–85
Long, Timothy, 291n10
Loraux, Nicole, 283n18, 283n20, 290n10, 290n15, 292n18, 292n20, 292n27, 297n35, 298nn39–42, 299n54
Loriaux, Michael, 277n40, 297n37
Luginbill, Robert, 283n16
Luhmann, Niklas, 93
Lumet, Sidney (dir: *Twelve Angry Men*), 279n69
Lysander, 273n100
Lysias, 22, 172, 286n71

MacDowell, Douglas, 280n86
Machiavelli, Niccolo, 112, 277n39
Mansbridge, Jane, 276n32, 297n32
Mantineia, 216
Markovits, Elizabeth, 110, 274n7, 278n60, 296n19
Marx, Karl, 17
Matthews, Donald, 35
McCarthy, Thomas, 158, 267n17
McPhee, William, 111
Megarian Decree, 51
Meles, 137, 280n77
Melian dialogue, 46–54, 170, 285n48; Athenian realism within, 49; as game, 47–48, 269nn36–37, 269n39, 269n42; political imagination in, 49–54. *See also* Athens/Athenian/Athenians, envoys on Melos; Diodotus, and Melian dialogue; justice, in Melian dialogue; nature, in Melian dialogue
Melissipus, 278n51
Melos/Melian/Melians, 23, 40, 47–54, 155, 162–65, 202, 265n48, 268–69n34, 270n49. *See also* Melian dialogue
memory, political, 115, 208, 218, 243–47

Menexenus, 128, 133, 141, 253
Messenia, 167
Midgley, Mary, 283n22, 295n8
Minos, 136
Monoson, Sara, 176, 191, 275n23, 276n30, 277n40, 277–78n45, 298n37
moral particularism, 129
Morrison, James, 263n30, 263n33, 269n35, 269n38, 271n65, 278n50, 300n74
Moses, 293n34
Mouffe, Chantal, 10, 28, 197–98, 290n71
Mycalessus, 201–2, 204, 206–7, 209, 219–20, 222–23, 225, 291nn16–17
Mysians, 279–80n75
Mytlilene/Mytilenes, 18, 23, 26, 39, 47, 97, 99–101, 122, 160, 162, 169–70, 225, 246–48, 268–69n34. *See also* Mytilene debate
Mytilene debate, 54–61, 96–101, 116, 254. *See also* assembly, Athenian, in Mytilene debate; Cleon, in Mytilene debate; Diodotus, in Mytilene debate; justice, in Mytilene debate; passion, and rationality in Mytilene debate

Nails, Deborah, 278n61, 299n63
Narayan, Uma, 5, 229, 279n68
Natural Right and History. *See* Strauss, Leo
nature: and culture, 149–60, 180–82, 185, 194–95; in Melian dialogue, 51–53; in Thucydides, 154–58, 256
Nehamas, Alexander, 280n84
Niceratus, 172, 286n71
Nichols, Mary, 287n84
Nicias, 23, 121, 151, 155, 201, 214, 219, 288n97, 292n31; and Melos, 47, 53
Nietzsche, Friedrich, 20–21, 172, 258–59, 263n28, 279n63, 284n35, 286n69, 292n20, 297n35, 298n47, 300n76
Nightingale, Andrea, 135–36, 279n72, 280n79, 280n82, 281n93

noble, the (*to kalon*)/nobility, 50, 69–71, 74, 77, 79, 107–8, 155, 163, 166, 177, 186, 214, 246
noble lie, 182, 185
Norton, Anne, 293n2
Nussbaum, Martha, 5, 7, 199, 239, 262n13, 271n70, 272n74, 275n19, 287n83, 290n4, 292n19

Ober, Josiah, 13, 20, 22–23, 42, 98–100, 206, 261n5, 264n45, 265n50, 271n57, 271n64, 275n14, 278n48, 281n89, 281n94, 285n48
O'Connor, John Cardinal, 199
Odysseus, 77, 138, 237
Offe, Claus, 94–95, 102
"Old Oligarch," 15
oligarchy, 192
Ordeshook, Peter, 266n5, 266n8
Orwin, Clifford, 41, 46, 51–52, 58, 98–100, 121, 149, 154, 157, 168, 171, 205, 234, 263n34, 265n53, 268n24, 268n26, 268n30, 270nn49–50, 271nn57–58, 271n60, 271n64, 271n66, 275n17, 277n40, 277n43, 278n54, 281n94, 284nn28–29, 284n42, 285nn46–47, 286n67, 291n14, 291nn16–17, 297–98n36, 298nn43–44, 298n48, 299n54, 299n56
Ostwald, Martin, 46, 49, 283n25
other, the, 28, 152, 198, 207–9, 214–15, 217, 219–22, 224–26

Paches, 54, 99
Palmer, Michael, 123, 270n45, 270n49, 271n57, 275n14, 275n16, 277n43, 285n46, 285n48, 298n38, 299n56
Pangle, Thomas, 282n11
Pareto, Vilfredo, 280n5
Parker, Robert, 289n99
Parry, Adam, 113, 264nn43–44, 265n50, 268n21, 277n41, 277n44, 278n51, 298n42
passion: and rationality in the *Charmides*, 74–76, 86; and rationality in the Mytilene debate, 55, 57, 61, 100–1, 170–71, 234, 246–47
Pausanias (Athenian), 210–11
Pausanias (Spartan), 151, 166, 168, 244, 286n61
Peace of Nicias, 47, 167
Peck, Jeffrey, 282n9
Peisandros, 264–65n45
Peisistratids, 247
Peloponnese/Peloponnesian/Peloponnesians, 40–41, 51, 59, 116, 167, 173, 205, 216
Peloponnesian War, 16, 21, 40, 62, 174
Penner, Terry, 288n97
perfectionism, 13
Pericles, 15–16, 39, 103, 107, 119, 127–28, 141, 150–51, 155, 167, 205–6, 208, 218–19, 252, 264n43, 265n52, 268n28, 277n41, 278n51, 279n64, 284n41, 285n48, 298n37; and Alcibiades, 277n43; and Athenian empire, 56, 114–15, 163; on daring achievement, 24, 43, 114, 122, 203, 205–7, 224, 242, 244–46, 250–51, 298n41, 298n43; as first man in Athens, 14–15, 26, 98, 246; funeral oration of, 23–25, 39, 57, 114–15, 127, 133–34, 151, 158–59, 162, 174, 204, 214, 237, 245–46, 276nn29–30, 277nn44–45, 298n41; political leadership of, 113–16, 173, 277n42, 277n44, 278n47, 278n50; strategies of, 42, 51; Thucydides' judgment on, 114–16, 159, 246–52, 277n40
Persia/Persian/Persians, 119, 161, 174, 204, 219
Persian wars, 203
Phaedrus, 210, 214
Phillips, Anne, 297n32
Philocrates, 53, 270n48
philosopher-kings, 15, 18, 22, 84, 183–84, 187, 252
philosophy, as discourse, 63–85
Phoenicia/Phoenician/Phoenicians, 181–82

Pinochet, Agosto, 276n31
Piraeus, 22, 186
Plataea/Plataean/Plataeans, 23, 160, 166, 170, 250
Plato, 2–3, 13–22, 27–29, 38, 61–62, 85–86, 93, 96–97, 113, 124–25, 129–30, 141–42, 148–50, 152, 168, 172, 175–76, 193–95, 200–1, 207, 223, 225–26, 228, 230–31, 233–36, 252–54, 261n5, 262n20, 263n29, 264n40, 271n70, 272n85, 273n94, 275n23, 278n59, 280n77, 280nn79–80, 281n93, 282n11, 283n22, 287n78, 287n83, 291n10, 293n34, 293n1 (Conclusion), 296n22, 299n66, 300n71; and Thucydides on war and peace, 73–74, 85–86, 256–59; *works of:* Alcibiades I, 218; *Apology*, 21, 61, 84, 129–30, 138, 191–92, 208, 253–54, 293n34; *Charmides*, 21–22, 61–64, 72–85, 175, 264n41, 273n96; *Cratylus*, 21–22; *Critias*, 486n71; *Crito*, 21, 191, 253; *Euthyphro*, 21; *Gorgias*, 17, 19, 21, 83, 85, 97, 104, 110, 124–42, 157, 159, 187, 190–91, 215, 228, 237, 253, 255, 257, 278nn56–57, 278n60, 279–80n75, 280n76, 280n79, 281n94, 284n41; *Laws*, 14, 257, 276–77n34; *Menexenus*, 127–28, 133–34, 140–41, 279n71; *Meno*, 21, 67, 85, 208; *Parmenides*, 21–22; *Phaedo*, 21, 257; *Phaedrus*, 19, 191, 212, 258; *Philebus*, 280n87, 280–81n88; *Protagoras*, 19, 21, 61–73, 83, 96, 101–11, 142, 272n78, 272n82, 272n86, 276–77n34, 292n30; *Republic*, 14, 15, 18, 77–81, 85, 125, 131, 138, 140–41, 152–53, 157, 166, 168, 172–94, 228, 233–34, 237–38, 252–53, 255, 257, 263n28, 264n42, 279n72, 280n12, 283n24, 284n44, 287n75, 287nn77–78, 287n82, 287n85, 290n114, 290n116, 291n10, 295nn13–14; *Second Letter*, 17, 20; *Seventh Letter*, 17, 62, 77; *Sophist*, 21; *Statesman*, 21, 166, 252; *Symposium*, 110, 137, 139, 201, 207–20, 224, 280–81n38, 292n30; *Theaetetus*, 21, 216, 259; *Timaeus*, 286nn71–72, 287nn74–75

pleasure: and courage, 70–71; and the good, 68, 70–71; and pain, measurement of, 69–72; and the noble, 68–70, 107–8

pluralism, 111–12, 197–98; agonistic, 10, 12; critical, 198–200, 209, 215, 221, 226; reasonable, 10, 144–47

plurality/pluralization, 209, 211–12, 216, 225

Pogge, Thomas, 297n32

Polemarchus, 22, 152, 172, 189, 255, 283n24, 286n71

Political Liberalism. See Rawls, John

political voice: in democracies (111–13)

Politics of Friendship, The. See Derrida, Jacques

Polus, 125–27, 137–38, 142, 279n64

postmaterialism, 6–7

postmodern democratic theory, 2, 10, 197–201, 238. *See also* Connolly, William; Honig, Bonnie; Mouffe, Chantal

postmodernism, 152, 220–26, 239. *See also* Butler, Judith; Derrida, Jacques; Foucault, Michel; power

Potideia/Potideian/Potideians, 27, 62, 73, 84, 204

Pouncey, Peter, 49, 52, 119, 269n41, 271n57, 278n48, 283n25, 285n48

power: and criticism, 158–59, 168–72; and culture, 147–48, 154–57, 194–95; as drive, 212; and trust, 94, 104; and postmodernism, 10, 147–48, 184, 222–25, reality of, 21; ubiquity of, 7

Priam, 292n23

Price, Jonathan, 18, 41, 113, 202, 264n44, 265n50, 268n21, 268n24, 268n27, 268n32, 270n47, 270n54,

Price, Jonathan *(continued)*
  271n61, 271n64, 277nn41–42,
  279n71, 283n14, 283n26, 284n27,
  284n32, 284n34, 284n36, 285n49,
  286n64, 286n68, 287n78, 291n9,
  291n16, 292n32, 295n15, 299n56
problematization: definition, 4; of
  democratic goods, 4–7, 28
promising, political, 243–44, 248,
  250–51
Protagoras, 64–72, 80, 101–3, 105–6,
  108–9, 122, 142, 285n56, 288n88
psychocultural phenomena: dynamics of, 151; as sources of obsession,
  53–54
Putnam, Robert, 6, 8, 32–33, 36, 72,
  92, 261n1, 266n7, 275n10, 296n20
Pylos, 167, 174, 244

Rademaker, Adriaan, 280n78, 280n81
rational choice theory, 2, 27, 31–32,
  180, 235–36, 238; borders of, 27, 34,
  54, 61–62, 72, 85–86; and classical
  liberalism, 8; and compulsions, 38;
  criticism of its blindness to culture,
  31, 36–37; criticism of its blindness
  to power, 31, 37; and equilibrium,
  34–35, 81; and explanation, 31–32;
  and institutions, 8, 10, 31, 33–34,
  235–36; and interests, 32, 34–36;
  and liberal democracy, 32–33; in
  Melian dialogue, 47–49, 53–54; and
  methodological individualism, 8,
  32; and Mytilene debate, 60–61;
  and neorealism, 33; and neutrality,
  32, 35–36; in the *Protagoras*, 64–72;
  and purposes, 32, 35–37; and rationality, 31, 34, 37–38; and strategy,
  8, 35, 37–38; and trust, 93–94; and
  ways of life, 38, 238–39
rationality (*logos*): and justice, 168–69,
  172; in Mytilene debate, 54–59; in
  Platonic dialogues, 61–85, 257; and
  political agency, 244–52; and ways
  of life, 233–34

Rawls, John, 5, 9–11, 13, 28, 92,
  143–48, 188, 193, 195, 197, 235–36,
  239–40, 263n26, 263n28, 266n1, 273–
  74n2, 277n36, 280n82, 281n1, 282n3,
  295nn12–13, 296n16, 296nn24–25
Reagan, Ronald, 126–27
Reeve, C.D.C., 287n83, 288n97
religion, 6, 50, 93, 145, 155–56
Rhadamanthus, 136
rhetoric, 55–57, 97, 124, 126, 133–34,
  137–38, 162, 236
Ricoeur, Paul, 247, 292n21, 297n35,
  298n40, 299n55, 299n58
rights: and goods, 231–32, 240; in liberal democracies, 4, 7, 229–33, 241.
  See also autonomy; discourse ethics;
  human rights
Richardson, Henry, 9, 131, 262n15,
  295n12
Riker, William, 27, 31, 33, 35–37,
  64, 266nn2–8, 266n10, 266–67n11,
  267n12, 267–68n19, 270n52
Robertson, Pat, 199
Roochnik, David, 279n63
Rood, Tim, 46, 283n19, 291n14
Rorty, Richard, 146–47, 198, 200,
  272n87, 282nn3–4, 282n6
Rosen, Stanley, 212, 292n19
Rosenblum, Nancy, 262n15, 277n36
Ross, Marc Howard, 35, 268n22,
  269n40, 283n17
Rousseau, Jean-Jacques, 112, 277n39,
  293n34
Rowe, Christopher, 288n97
Ruth, 293n34

Sahlins, Marshall, 282–83n13, 283n16,
  285n52
Said, Edward, 283nn20–21, 290n1
Salkever, Stephen, 130, 133, 262n19,
  262n23, 279n64, 279n66, 295n8,
  296n16
Samos, 23
Sandel, Michael, 112, 262n17, 277n37
Sanjek, Roger, 12, 262n10

Saxonhouse, Arlene, 23, 99, 118, 120, 123, 249, 261n5, 265n36, 265n51, 265n53, 271n59, 271n64, 271n66, 271n72, 272n86, 275nn20–21, 276n24, 276n33, 278n49, 278nn52–53, 278n55, 279n72, 280n83, 285n56, 286n63, 286n66, 292n28, 298n52, 299n54, 299n56
Schattschneider, E.E., 112, 198
Schiappa, Edward, 275n19
Schmitt, Carl, 222
science (*epistēmē*): architectonic, 80–85
Scione, 47, 202, 268–69n34
Scythians, 181
Sen, Amartya, 7, 239, 241, 262n13, 266n9, 295n10, 297n31
Shain, Barry, 277n37
shame (*aidōs*), 49–50, 69, 77, 79, 105–6; in Spartan education, 166–67, 174
Shapiro, Ian, 2, 8, 34, 90–92, 261n3, 262n16, 274n2
Shorey, Paul, 190
Sicily/Sicilian/Sicilians, 41, 44–45, 53, 116, 118–19, 155, 163, 171, 204, 208, 214, 219, 247, 249, 270n44, 288n97, 292n19
Smith, Charles Forster, 164, 270n46
social contract theories, 31, 231
Socrates, 15, 18–20, 61–86, 101–10, 124–42, 150, 152–53, 172–94, 208–20, 224–26, 229, 257–59, 272n85, 278n61, 279nn63–64, 280n80, 280n82, 281n90, 287n80, 287n85, 288n92, 289nn99–101, 289n108, 290nn112–14, 290n116, 292n25, 292n28, 292n30, 293nn33–34, 293n1 (Conclusion), 296–97n27, 299n66, 300n72; and deliberative democratic theory, 108–11; and democratic culture, 189–94, 237, 257–58, 275n23; and Diodotus, 104–5, 108, 123–24, 138, 255–58, 299n69, 300n72; discursive philosophy of, 64, 71–72, 75, 83–84, 192, 201, 217, 220, 228, 273n96, 289n92; *erōs* of, 208–9, 215–20; and examined life, 38, 61–62; execution of, 16, 21, 139; irony of, 20, 71, 110, 125, 128, 278n60, 280n84; political activity of, 20–22, 71–72, 108–11, 126, 130, 139–41, 224–25, 253–56, 281n89, 281n93; at Potideia, 62
Sophists, 64, 69, 122
sōphrosynē: in the *Charmides*, 22, 62–63, 74–84; in the *Republic*, 185–86; in Sparta, 166–67; in the *Symposium*, 215
soul (*psychē*), 65, 75–78, 81–83, 210
Sparta/Spartan/Spartans (Lacedaemon/Lacedaemonian/Lacedaemonians), 42, 45–46, 49–50, 53, 74, 76–77, 112, 150–51, 155–56, 160–68, 173, 193, 201, 203–5, 217, 219, 243, 251, 268n23, 268n28, 269n39, 273n93, 283n16, 285nn52–53, 285n56, 286nn61–62, 286n68, 297–98n36; education within 166–68, 174, 243–44, 250, 285–86n58, 286n62; justice of, 164–68, 170, 244
speech (*logos*): and action in Thucydides, 22–24, 39, 159; direct and indirect forms in Thucydides, 23. *See also* rationality
speech acts, 223; of Thucydides' characters, 23; of Thucydides and Plato, 15–20, 242
Sphacteria, 167
Sthenelaidas, 151
Strauss, Leo, 20, 41, 58, 149–50, 228, 261n5, 263n34, 263–64n36, 264n38, 264n42, 265n53, 270n48, 271n64, 273n89, 275n14, 277n40, 279n72, 282n11, 284n29, 284n42, 286n72, 289n109, 293n1, 293–94n2, 299n54, 299n56, 300nn70–71, 300n73
Strepsiades, 135, 160
Syracuse, 43–45, 116, 118–19, 121, 123, 154, 201, 204, 206

Tamir, Yael, 293n34

Tarcov, Nathan, 293n2
Tarentum, 118
Taylor, Charles, 11, 144–46, 261n7, 262n22, 281–82n2, 282n6
Telemachus, 77
teleology, 13, 15–16, 88–90, 94–96, 127, 129, 141, 256. *See also* deliberative democratic theory; virtue
Telephos, 279–80n75
Tessitore, Aristide, 262n19
Thasos, 171
Theaetetus, 259
Thebes/Theban/Thebans, 150, 170
Themistocles, 118, 151
Theory of Justice, A. See Rawls, John
Thersites, 138, 280n83
Theseus, 118
Thirty Tyrants, 21–22, 62, 73–74, 81, 84, 106, 172, 253, 273n93, 286n71, 292n19
thought (*gnōmē*), 38–39, 113, 115–16
Thrace/Thracian/Thracians, 181–82, 201–2, 204, 207, 291n13
Thrasymachus, 79, 125, 152, 287n87
Thucydides, 2–3, 13–29, 38–60, 85–86, 93, 96–98, 113–16, 121, 123, 134, 141–42, 148–52, 154–60, 171–75, 193–95, 200–7, 218–19, 222–23, 225–26, 230–31, 233–36, 242–47, 252, 256–59, 261n5, 262n20, 263n25, 263n32, 264nn43–45, 265nn46–47, 265nn50–53, 268n21, 268n23, 268n25, 270n46, 270nn48–49, 270n51, 276nn28–29, 278nn50–51, 278n55, 279n64, 279n71, 282n11, 282–83n13, 283nn15–16, 283n22, 283n25, 284nn31–32, 284n36, 284nn38–39, 284n43, 285n47, 286nn61–62, 287n73, 287n78, 288n88, 288n97, 291nn11–14, 291n16, 292n21, 293n34, 293n2 (Conclusion), 296n17, 296n22, 297–98n36, 298n41, 298n43, 298n46, 299n53, 299n62, 300n71, 300n73–74; and democratic theory, 2, 13, 27–29, 242–52; and Diodotus, 26, 171, 234, 249–52, 258; as historian, 16, 19; and Periclean ethic, 14, 24–26, 113–16, 206, 237, 277n40, 277n45, 278nn46–47; rationality in, 38–40; and the *Republic*, 172–75; and social theory, 17–18
timarchy, 192
time horizons, 43
Tocqueville, Alexis de, 12
trust: and conceptions of the good, 100–1, 108–9; in democracies, 11, 28; and judgment, 118; and power, 104–5; in the Mytilene debate, 97–101; in the *Protagoras*, 101–11; and teleology, 84–85; theories of, 93–96; and virtue, 95, 105–10
Tsao, Roy, 299n59
Tullock, Gordon, 32–34, 72
Twilight of the Idols. See Nietzsche, Friedrich
tyrannicides, 247
tyranny, 192–93

Valenzuela, Arturo, 276n31
Verba, Sidney, 111
Vickers, Brian, 278n58
Villa, Dana, 112, 253–54, 299n62, 299n66, 300n72
virtue, 62, 239–40; civic, 65, 103–7, 210; and democratic theory, 15, 238; and equality, 15–16, 104, 106, 241; and essentialism, 13, 15–16; parts of, 67, 68, 106; teachability of, 66, 71–72, 103–5, 110; and teleology, 90, 141

Wallach, John, 262n9, 264nn40–42, 271n69, 290n116, 295n11
Walters, John P., 297n28
Waltz, Kenneth, 27, 33, 35, 37, 266n2
Walzer, Michael, 5, 262n17
Warren, Mark, 9, 13, 27, 86–90, 92, 94–96, 102, 112, 117, 131, 236, 239–40, 261n4, 261n8, 262n11,

262nn14–17, 263n26, 274n6, 275n11, 279n70, 295n12, 296n18, 296n20, 296nn23–25, 297n28
ways of life: in liberal democracies, 6–7, 238–41. *See also* rational choice theory, and ways of life; rationality, and ways of life
Weber, Max, 36, 228
Weingartner, Rudolph, 271n71, 272n73, 273n84
Weiss, Roslyn, 272n76, 272n78, 275n21, 276n24, 281n90, 281n92
Weldon, S. Laurel, 297n32
West, Grace Starry, 273n94, 273n99
West, Thomas, 273n94, 273n99
White, James Boyd, 271nn63–64, 275n14, 285n48
Williams, Bernard, 262n21, 262n23, 264n43, 268n33, 285n56, 286n59, 287n86, 288nn88–89
Wilson, James Q., 297n28
Winch, Peter, 144, 146, 281–82n2, 282nn4–5
Wittgenstein, Ludwig, 146
Wohl, Victoria, 17, 265n50, 265n52, 270n43, 270n53, 270n55, 271n56, 277n45, 278n46, 278n56, 280n81, 281n91, 293n33, 298nn40–41, 298n43, 298n46
Wolff, Robert Paul, 112, 198

Wolfsdorf, David, 272n77
Wolin, Sheldon, 112
Wolpert, Andrew, 273n93, 273n100, 284n30, 297n35
Wolz, Henry, 271n71, 272n80
Wood, Ellen Meiksnins, 261n5, 264n37, 299n64
Wood, Neal, 261n5, 264n37, 299n64

Xanthias, 136
Xenophon: works of: *Apology of Socrates*, 290n112; *Constitution of the Lacedaemonians*, 285–86n58; *Hellenica*, 62, 131, 254, 286n71; *Memorabilia*, 273n91
Xerxes, 218

Yack, Bernard, 14
Young, Iris Marion, 9, 27, 86–87, 89, 94, 241, 297n32
Yunis, Harvey, 113, 263n30, 263n34, 265n50, 275n14, 277n41, 281n94

Zeus, 105–6, 123, 171, 212, 258
Zuckert, Catherine, 264n36, 293n2, 294n5
Zuckert, Michael, 264n36, 293n2, 294n5
Zumbrunnen, John, 271n62, 271n66, 283n16, 297n34, 298n48, 299n61

www.ingramcontent.com/pod-product-compliance
Lightning Source LLC
Chambersburg PA
CBHW030128240426
43672CB00005B/58